Plug-in JavaScript

100 POWER SOLUTIONS

Robin Nixon

New York Chicago San Francisco
Lisbon London Madrid Mexico City
Milan New Delhi San Juan
Seoul Singapore Sydney Toronto

The McGraw·Hill Companies

Cataloging-in-Publication Data is on file with the Library of Congress

McGraw-Hill books are available at special quantity discounts to use as premiums and sales promotions, or for use in corporate training programs. To contact a representative, please e-mail us at bulksales@mcgraw-hill.com.

Plug-in JavaScript: 100 Power Solutions

1234567890 DOC DOC 109876543210

ISBN 978-0-07-173861-3
MHID 0-07-173861-4

Sponsoring Editor
Wendy Rinaldi

Editorial Supervisor
Jody McKenzie

Project Manager
Tania Andrabi,
Glyph International

Acquisitions Coordinator
Joya Anthony

Technical Editor
Alan Solis

Copy Editor
Sally Engelfried

Proofreader
Carol Shields

Indexer
Jack Lewis

Production Supervisor
George Anderson

Composition
Glyph International

Illustration
Glyph International

Art Director, Cover
Jeff Weeks

Cover Designer
Pehrsson Design

For Julie

About the Author

Robin Nixon has worked with and written about computers since the early 1980s (his first computer was a Tandy TRS 80 Model 1 with a massive 4KB of RAM!). Since then, he has written in excess of 500 articles for many of the U.K.'s top computer magazines. *Plug-in JavaScript* is his sixth book.

Robin lives on the southeast coast of England with his wife Julie, who is a trained nurse, and five children. He also finds time to foster three disabled children and works full time from home as a technical author.

Also by Robin Nixon

The PC Companion, Sigma Press, 1993, ISBN 978-150585138

The Amstrad Advanced User Guide, Sigma Press, 1993, ISBN 978-150585152

Learning PHP, MySQL, and JavaScript, O'Reilly, 2009, ISBN 978-0596157135

Ubuntu: Up and Running, O'Reilly, 2010, ISBN 978-0596804848

Plug-in PHP, McGraw-Hill Professional, 2010, ISBN 978-0071666596

About the Technical Editor

Alan Solis has more than 30 years experience designing, writing, and maintaining software for companies ranging from small start-ups to large corporations. He currently designs and maintains websites and web applications using PHP, JavaScript, Java, and various relational databases.

In his spare time, Alan enjoys creative writing and is a published short story and poetry author. Alan lives in the San Jose, California area with his wife, Cheryl.

Contents at a Glance

Contents

Acknowledgments

I would like to thank Wendy Rinaldi for giving me the opportunity of putting together another book of handy plug-ins. I also want to thank Joya, Alan, Melinda, Tania, and everyone else who has helped create this book, without whom it would not be the same. McGraw-Hill is an exceptionally professional and friendly company to work with, and it has once again been a pleasure.

Introduction

JavaScript is the free language built into all modern browsers including Internet Explorer, Firefox, Safari, Opera, and Chrome. It is the power behind dynamic HTML and the Ajax environment used for Web 2.0 websites such as Facebook, Flickr, Gmail, and many others.

Plug-in JavaScript is aimed squarely at people who have learned basic HTML (and perhaps a little CSS and JavaScript) and are interested in doing more. For example, you may wish to create more dynamic menu systems, provide mouse hover effects, or support Ajax functionality. In this book you will be shown how to do all these things and much more using very simple JavaScript, and it is never assumed that you know anything about a solution. Instead, you are taken through each example step by step with the explanations included, so there is no need to look up anything elsewhere; every solution is complete and applicable immediately.

Where possible, the book purposefully ignores more advanced JavaScript techniques such as object oriented programming (even though they may sometimes be more powerful) to make it easy for you to understand all the plug-ins. Not using these advanced techniques doesn't mean the plug-ins are any less useful; rather, they may simply take a few extra lines of code to achieve the same result, which will generally run just as fast as more compact code.

The book can be dipped into as required because each chapter is self contained—when you have a particular problem to solve, you can refer to the relevant chapter and it will be all that you need.

About JavaScript

The JavaScript programming language is already over 15 years old and is more popular than ever. Written by Brendan Eich at Netscape and previously known by the names Mocha and LiveScript, JavaScript was first incorporated into the Netscape Navigator browser in 1995, the same time that Netscape added support for Sun's Java technology.

JavaScript is a quite different language from Java but, as part of a marketing deal made between Netscape and Sun Microsystems, it was given its name to benefit from the general buzz surrounding the Java language. To justify this naming, all Java keywords are reserved in JavaScript, its standard library follows Java's naming conventions, and its Math and Date objects are based on Java 1 classes. Also, the trademark name "JavaScript" now belongs to Oracle Corporation—but the similarities end there.

Microsoft's version, called JScript, was released a year later as a component of Internet Explorer 3 and, as you might expect, it differed in several important respects, making it less than 100 percent compatible with JavaScript. Unfortunately, that remains true to this day, as you will see in several of these plug-ins that work differently depending on which browser they find themselves running in.

Unlike other languages used for creating websites, such as Perl, PHP, and Ruby, JavaScript runs within the web browser, not on a web server. This makes it the perfect tool for creating dynamic web pages because it can modify HTML elements in real time. It is also the technology behind Web 2.0 Ajax functionality, in which data is transferred between a web server and web browser behind the scenes, without the user being aware of it.

As you will learn in Chapter 2, JavaScript's great power lies in its ability to access HTML's Document Object Model (DOM), in which every element on a web page can be individually addressed (either reading or modifying its value), and elements can also be created and deleted on the fly, as well as layered over each other and moved about. You can even go so far as to treat a web browser window as a blank canvas and build entire applications and arcade games from scratch using JavaScript and the DOM (although doing so takes some quite advanced programming skills).

Because Oracle owns the trademark to its name, JavaScript has officially been known as *ECMAScript* ever since the language was submitted to ECMA, the European Computer Manufacturers Association (a nonprofit standards organization).

JavaScript Frameworks

Even with recent steps towards standardization, different browser developers still implement JavaScript in slightly different ways, giving rise to the plethora of JavaScript frameworks now available such as JQuery, YUI, Mootools, and so on. These technologies handle all the inconsistencies for you, providing a set of functions you can call without worrying about browser differences.

The plug-ins in this book provide much of the functionality of these frameworks without actually constituting a framework. Procedural programming techniques make them easy to use and also to understand their workings. And, although the plug-ins are often interconnected and draw on each other's features, it's possible to copy just a single plug-in and its dependencies to a web page. On the other hand, with the major frameworks it's quite difficult to extract just the functions you need.

Although at only around 25Kb for the compressed file containing all the plug-ins, the additional tiny amount of bandwidth used means you probably will never want or need to extract just a few functions: you can simply drop a link to the file in any web page to have access to all the plug-ins.

What This Book Provides

This book provides 100 ready-to-go plug-ins you can draw on, usually with a simple, single call. Of course, because all projects are different, I provide only the bare bones needed and leave layout and styling to the absolute minimum. This leaves you free to insert the functions into your own programs and then tailor them to your exact requirements.

The types of plug-ins supplied offer quick and simple solutions to a very wide range of problems, allowing you to avoid having to reinvent the wheel each time you need a new feature—because the chances are that the module you need (or one very similar) can be found in this book as a plug-in. Even if it isn't, because each and every one is broken down into component parts and explained in detail, you can cherry-pick code segments from different plug-ins to build your own.

About the Plug-ins

All this book's plug-ins are ready to run and can be either typed in (if you don't have Internet access) or downloaded from *pluginjavascript.com*, where they are stored as a complete collection in a single file.

When you visit the website, you can navigate through the plug-ins chapter by chapter and view the JavaScript code highlighted in color for clarity. From there, you can copy, paste, or download the plug-ins directly to your computer.

What Is and Isn't Included

Although the first aim of this book is to provide newcomers to JavaScript with a comprehensive resource of functions and routines to draw on, it has a secondary goal, which is to help you move up to the next level and to build your own programming toolkit. Therefore, all the plug-ins are thoroughly documented and explained in detail, and advice is given on ways to improve and extend them, as well as how to adapt them to your own requirements.

While this book isn't a programming manual or a teaching guide, I do hope that by reading through the explanations, rather than just including the plug-ins in your projects, you'll pick up a number of tips and tricks that many programmers take years to discover, and by osmosis you will learn more about the JavaScript programming language.

Plug-in License

You are free to use any of the plug-ins in this book in your own projects, and you may modify them as necessary without attributing this book—although if you do give credit, it will always be appreciated.

However, you may not sell, give away, or otherwise distribute the plug-ins themselves in any manner, whether printed or in electronic format, without the written permission of the publisher.

Companion Website

A companion website (*pluginjavascript.com*) accompanies this book, where all 100 plug-ins are available to download, along with example code for you to experiment with.

The website is best used in conjunction with this book. As you read a chapter, call it up on the website, and you can view each plug-in onscreen with color-highlighted syntax. This makes it very easy to see the structure of each program.

Then, when you wish, you can click a link to copy and paste code right into your own programs. Or, if you prefer, you can download all the plug-ins to your computer and from there transfer them to your own website.

CHAPTER 1

Making the Best Use of These Plug-ins

Because JavaScript is supported by all major browsers, you might think that setting yourself up as a JavaScript programmer is as easy as having a text editor and a web browser. Well, you could get by with just those, but there's actually a lot more to it if you want to produce code efficiently, quickly, and with the minimum of bugs.

First of all, although JavaScript is available on almost all web browsers it varies slightly between them in the way it implements certain features. This means that you need to be able to test your code on all the main browsers to ensure that it works correctly in all cases. So you really need to have access to a Windows computer, because recent versions of Internet Explorer (IE) are available only for that operating system.

Downloading and Installing Web Browsers

Table 1-1 lists the five major web browsers and their Internet download locations. While all of them can be installed on a Windows PC, some of them are not available for Mac OS X or Linux. The web pages at these URLs are smart and offer up the correct version to download according to your operating system, if available.

Before proceeding with this book I recommend that you ensure you have installed as many of these browsers on your computer as you can.

If you're running any version of Windows from XP onward, then you will be able to install all of them, but on other operating systems it's not quite so easy. For example, because development of IE for the Mac was halted many years ago at IE version 5, you can install all the browsers on Mac OS X except for Microsoft Internet Explorer. And, although it's possible to install the Wine windows application interface on a Mac and run Internet Explorer using it, I have found it to be a laborious process with inconsistent results, and therefore wouldn't recommend that method. Neither would I suggest you rely on those websites that take screen shots of a web page in different browsers, because they can't tell you whether the mouse, keyboard, and other features are working well, or even at all.

Instead, your best option is to either perform a dual install of Windows alongside Mac OS X, or ensure you have access to a Windows PC. After all, unless you intend to develop only for Mac computers, people using a Windows operating system will represent by far the majority of your users.

As for Linux, not only does it not have access to Internet Explorer, there is no version of Safari either, although all the other browsers do come in Linux flavors. And, as with OS X, while various solutions exist that incorporate Wine for running Internet Explorer, they seem to work only with some distributions and not others, so it can be a bit of a minefield trying to find a bulletproof way to run Windows browsers on Linux.

Table 1-1 Web Browsers and Their Download URLs

Web Browser	Download URL
Apple Safari	*apple.com/safari*
Google Chrome	*google.com/chrome*
Microsoft Internet Explorer	*microsoft.com/ie*
Mozilla Firefox	*mozilla.com/firefox*
Opera	*opera.com/download*

What it all comes down to is that, if you will be developing on a non-Windows computer I recommend that you have access to a Windows PC or have Windows installed as a dual boot (or a virtual machine) alongside your main operating system so that you can fully test your programs before publishing them to the web at large.

Choosing a Program Editor

Long gone are the days of relying on a simple Notepad program for coding. Software for writing program code has progressed in leaps and bounds in recent years, with text editors being replaced by powerful program editors that highlight your syntax using different colors and can quickly locate things for you like matching (and missing) brackets and braces and so on.

Table 1-2 lists a number of free program editors that will do a great job of helping you to write JavaScript code quickly and efficiently.

Which one you choose is largely down to personal preference—in my case I settled on Notepad++ (see Figure 1-1).

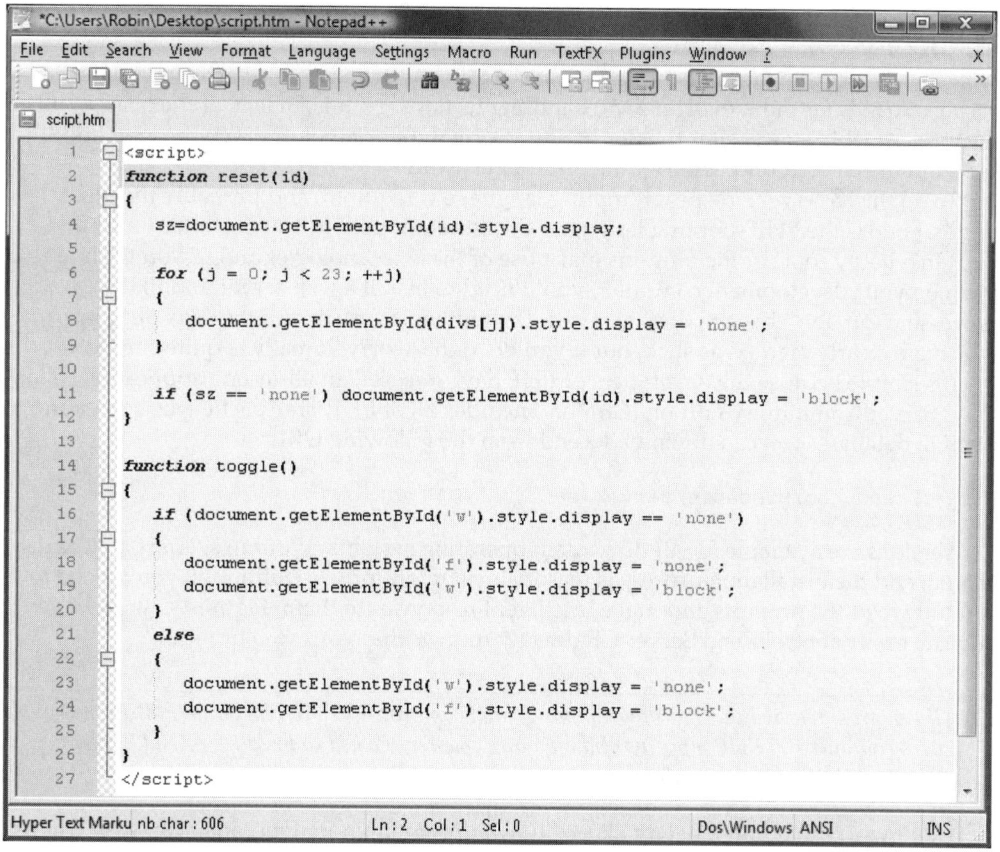
*C:\Users\Robin\Desktop\script.htm - Notepad++
File Edit Search View Format Language Settings Macro Run TextFX Plugins Window ?
script.htm
<script>
function reset(id)
{
sz=document.getElementById(id).style.display;
for (j = 0; j < 23; ++j)
{
document.getElementById(divs[j]).style.display = 'none';
}
if (sz == 'none') document.getElementById(id).style.display = 'block';
}
function toggle()
{
if (document.getElementById('w').style.display == 'none')
{
document.getElementById('f').style.display = 'none';
document.getElementById('w').style.display = 'block';
}
else
{
document.getElementById('w').style.display = 'none';
document.getElementById('f').style.display = 'block';
}
}
</script>
Hyper Text Marku nb char : 606
Ln : 2 Col : 1 Sel : 0
Dos\Windows ANSI
INS

FIGURE 1-1 The Notepad++ program editor

Program	URL	Windows	Mac	Linux
Bluefish	*bluefish.openoffice.nl*		✓	✓
Cream	*cream.sourceforge.net*	✓		✓
Editra	*editra.org*	✓	✓	✓
Free HTML Editor	*coffeecup.com/free-editor*	✓		
jEdit	*jedit.org*	✓	✓	✓
Notepad++	*notepad-plus.sourceforge.net*	✓		

Table 1-2 A Selection of Free Program Editors

In most program editors, moving the cursor to different parts of a program usually allows you to highlight sections of the code. For example, placing the cursor next to any bracket in Notepad++ automatically highlights the matching one.

Managing Ajax

Ajax stands for Asynchronous JavaScript and XML, but the name is really a misnomer because Ajax is far more than an XML handling technology. It is, in fact, at the heart of all the modern Web 2.0 websites that exchange information between the web browser and server in the background, without the user being aware.

To do this, a server side programming language is required, and probably the most popular one is the PHP scripting language. So, although this isn't a book about Ajax and PHP, inevitably some of the plug-ins make use of these technologies and, if you wish to test them on your development computer, you'll need to install a web server and PHP processor. You don't have to do this if you don't intend to use any of the Ajax plug-ins, which are clearly marked as such, but if you do, don't worry: it really is quite simple.

It's simple because the developers of PHP have released an all-in-one application called Zend Server Community Edition (CE) that includes all of PHP, an Apache web server and a MySQL database. You can download Zend from the following URL:

```
http://zend.com/products/server-ce
```

Versions are available for all three main operating systems (Windows, Mac OS X, and Linux), and the installation process is reasonably straightforward, although you'll need to carefully read the prompts and make intelligent responses to them. Figure 1-2 shows how you can easily control Zend Server CE directly from within your web browser.

Tip *If you are interested in PHP programming, my book* Plug-in PHP *(McGraw-Hill/Professional, 2010) contains 100 PHP plug-ins and an entire chapter devoted to installing Zend Server CE and other PHP solutions on different platforms.*

Don't worry that you'll need to know how to program in PHP because you won't, as the server side scripts can be typed in or downloaded from this book's companion website—all

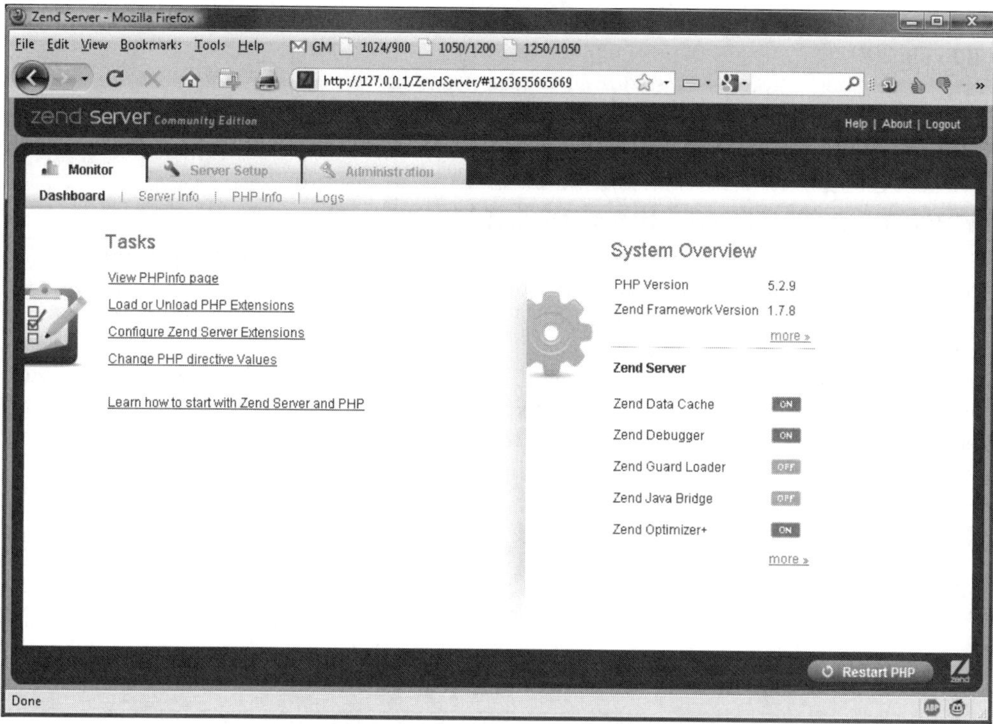

FIGURE 1-2 The Zend Server CE dashboard

you have to do is place them in the same Zend Server CE document root folder as your HTML and JavaScript files.

Table 1-3 details the default locations of document root that Zend Server CE creates on different operating systems. If you keep your various HTML, JavaScript, and PHP files in that folder (and subfolders), then they can all be served up by the Apache web server.

Unfortunately there's no room to go into much detail about Zend Server CE in this book, although there is one thing I should mention: you may find the Zend Server CE document root folder doesn't allow you to copy files into it by default. If you find this to be the case, you should change the folder permissions to grant access.

TABLE 1-3 Zend Server CE Document Root on Various Platforms

Operating System	Document Root
Windows	*C:/Program Files/Zend/Apache2/htdocs*
Mac OS X	*/usr/local/zend/apache2/htdocs*
Debian/Ubuntu Linux	*/var/www*
Fedora Linux	*/var/www/html*
Generic Linux	*/usr/local/zend/apache2/htdocs*

There is also a very good Zend Server CE online user guide, which you can access at the following URL:

```
http://files.zend.com/help/Zend-Server-Community-Edition/welcome.htm
```

Older Versions of Microsoft Internet Explorer

The latest version of Internet Explorer (IE8 at the time of writing) has made tremendous strides toward compatibility with the other major browsers, but there are still large numbers of users running IE7 and even IE6. Figure 1-3 shows the breakdown of browsers by use as of the end of 2009 according to *statcounter.com*.

As you can see, IE6 and IE7 have over 35 percent of all users between them. Because of this, and because each version of Internet Explorer works differently, you need to test your web pages in the older versions in addition to testing them in the latest versions of the

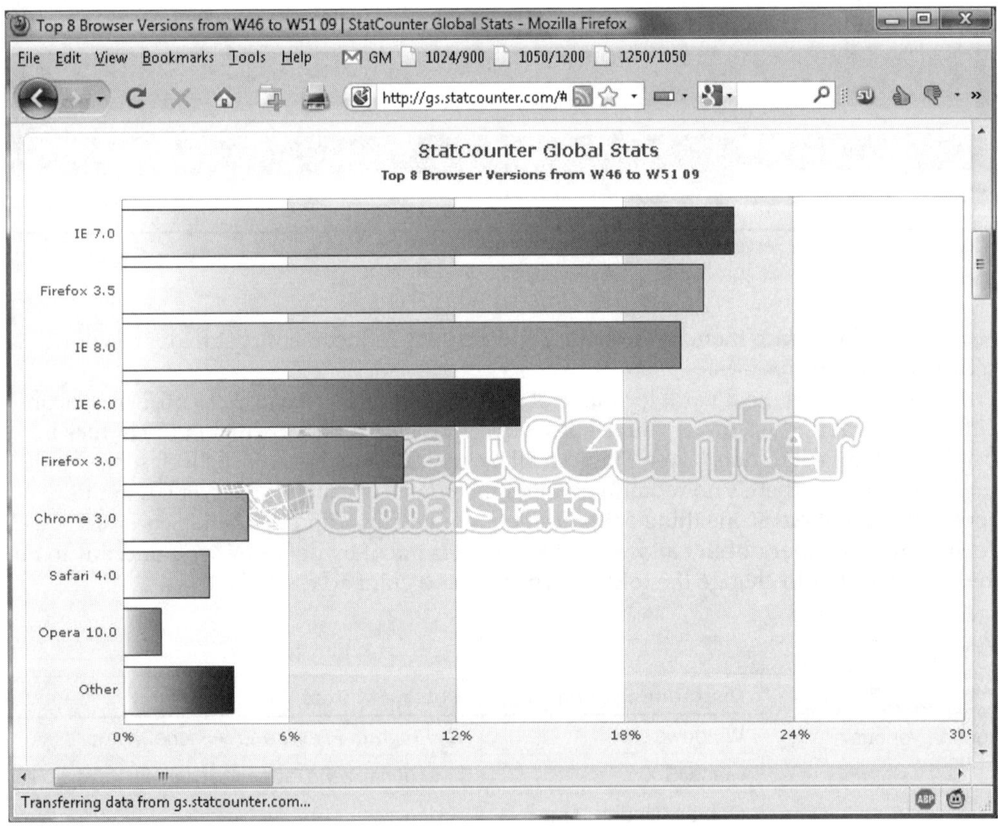

FIGURE 1-3 Browser market share as of December 2009

main browsers. I know, it's a pain, but it has to be done. Luckily, there's a trick to make this easier than it might otherwise be.

Emulating Internet Explorers 6 and 7

To aid developers who have designed websites to work specifically with older versions, the developers of Internet Explorer created a meta tab that you can add to the head of a web page to make IE think it is an earlier version of itself. Here are the two main meta tags you will use:

```
<meta http-equiv="X-UA-Compatible" content="IE=7" />
<meta http-equiv="X-UA-Compatible" content="IE=5" />
```

This is an example of how to incorporate the IE7 tag:

```
<html>
<head>
<meta http-equiv="X-UA-Compatible" content="IE=7" />
<title>My Website</title>
</head>
<body>
... Website Contents ...
```

There is no `IE=6` option (presumably because the rendering engines for IE5 and IE6 are so similar), so using the `IE=5` option makes Internet Explorer enter what is known as "quirks" mode, in which it behaves like both IE5 and IE6.

Incidentally, if you wish to force Internet Explorer into full standards mode (to be as compatible as possible with other browsers) you can use the option `IE=8`. Without the meta tag, Internet Explorer will use its proprietary and optimal settings, known as "edge" mode, which you can also select with the option `IE=edge`. Of course, once you have finished testing, you should remove or comment out these meta tags unless you wish to use one for a particular reason.

In addition to using the meta tags, you should always ensure that you have a suitable HTML doctype declaration at the start of each document. The most commonly found doctype is the following, which has been fully tested and works with all of this book's plug-ins.

```
<!DOCTYPE HTML PUBLIC "-//W3C//DTD HTML 4.01 Transitional//EN"
"http://www.w3.org/TR/html4/loose.dtd">
```

CAUTION *If you use a different doctype from the one listed, certain plug-ins may behave differently, and you may find you have to slightly modify them. I often use both the preceding "loose" doctype and the IE7 meta tag to get the most compatible results with other major browsers. Remember, if IE behaves strangely when all other browsers appear to work well with your code, the solution could be to change the doctype and or IE5/IE7 meta tags. If you are interested in the subject of browser compatibility and its various nuances, I recommend visiting the Quirks Mode website at quirksmode.org.*

The Companion Website

To save you the effort of typing all the plug-ins in this book, you can download them from this book's companion website at *pluginjavascript.com* (see Figure 1-4).

Click the "Download Plug-ins" link to download the file *plug-ins.zip*, which is an archive file (easily extractable on all operating systems) containing all the plug-ins. Once extracted, in the root of the *plug-ins.zip* archive you'll find the files *PJ.js* and *PJsmall.js*, which contain the plug-ins in a ready-to-use form. Also in the root is a file called *ReadMe.txt*, which contains the latest details about the plug-ins, including any improvements or updates that have been made since this book was published.

There are also eleven subfolders labeled from 3 to 13, corresponding to chapters in this book. Within each folder you'll find various example HTML and JavaScript files showing the use of each function that you can load into a browser to try out for yourself. Some plug-ins also make use of Ajax techniques and may include other associated files (such as those with *.php* extensions), in which case they will be documented in the associated chapter.

FIGURE 1-4 The companion website at *pluginjavascript.com*

Including All the Plug-ins

The easiest (and recommended) way for you to use these plug-ins is to load them all into a web page as a complete set, which you can do with the following command, assuming you saved the file *PJ.js* into the current folder:

```
<script type="text/javascript" src="PJ.js"></script>
```

In fact, by default all modern browsers assume that scripts will be JavaScript, so you can use the following short form, which omits the `type=` parameter:

```
<script src="PJ.js"></script>
```

Or, if you have *PJ.js* located elsewhere, such as in the root folder, you change the command slightly to include the path, like this:

```
<script src="/PJ.js"></script>
```

Alternatively, if you use a specific folder for your JavaScript files, such as *scripts*, you use this command:

```
<script src="scripts/PJ.js"></script>
```

And the compressed version of the file, *PJsmall.js*, can be included instead, like this:

```
<script src="scripts/PJsmall.js"></script>
```

Immediately following the line that includes the file, you need to add a second line as follows, which will initialize the plug-ins, ready for use:

```
<script> Initialize()</script>
```

The benefits of doing this are that you only need to add a couple of lines to your web pages to have access to all the plug-ins, and there is only one file to change when you modify any plug-ins. Also, at only around 60KB for the raw JavaScript file, it doesn't take very long to load or consume much bandwidth.

What's more, as already mentioned, you can choose to use the compressed version of the file, called *PJsmall.js*, which is under half the size and can be found in the zip file along with *PJ.js*. The only difference between the two files is that the larger one has all the functions shown in plain text where they are easy to see and edit if you wish, and the small version is tightly compressed and not easy to understand if you view it. Regardless of this difference, they both work identically to each other.

Including Single Plug-ins

All of the plug-ins included in this book are tightly integrated with each other, and as you progress through the book you'll see how the later plug-ins rely more and more on earlier ones, until you reach the point where plug-ins that would normally require dozens of lines of code only take up a handful of lines because they can draw on the wealth of features provided by other plug-ins.

Therefore, because you have the option of using the compressed JavaScript file, which takes up less space than even most small images, I don't recommend trying to copy and paste individual plug-ins into your web pages unless reduced size and bandwidth usage are essential, because you will have to follow the subfunctions and sub-subfunctions, until you have located all the dependencies required for a particular plug-in to work.

Where to Include the JavaScript

The best place to insert the plug-ins is in the head section of your web pages so the whole page will have access to them. The following example (which assumes that *PJsmall.js* is in the document root) illustrates the recommended way to insert the file (shown in bold text):

```
<html>
<head>
<script src="/PJsmall.js"></script>
script>PJ_Initialize()</script>
<title>My Website</title>
</head>
<body>
... Website Contents ...
```

Placing the code in the head section means the file of plug-ins will load in first and, therefore, your own JavaScript code can be placed anywhere you like within the rest of the web page (including the head) and when it calls one of the plug-in functions it's guaranteed to be available.

Cherry Picking Code Sections

Although the primary objective of this book is to provide you with a comprehensive toolkit of plug-in JavaScript functions to save you having to reinvent the wheel, I also hope that the full documentation of the plug-ins will make them easy for you to adapt to your own purposes. In fact, I encourage you to take what you can from this book and extend and improve it.

If that means you want to cherry pick a routine from here and a code snippet from there and build your own new plug-ins, then this book will have succeeded in its secondary goal of helping you to take your JavaScript programming skills to the next level.

Bug Fixing and Reporting

The raw JavaScript plug-ins comprise over 2500 lines of code, which has been tested over and again in as many different conditions as possible. But you should realize that this book represents a major amount of programming and it is inevitable that some unforeseen bugs will show up.

Hopefully there aren't too many of them, and those that there are will be of minimal consequence. Even so, this means that to ensure you have the latest versions, you should grab the plug-ins from the companion website at *pluginjavascript.com*. Speaking of which, if you come up with any fixes or improvements please send them to me via the website and I'll use them to update the source files and improve their capabilities for all readers—you will be credited in the source code. Please include a note to say that I have your permission to post your code online and in future editions of this book or, sadly, I will not be able to use it.

Waiting Until the Web Page Has Loaded

Quite often, and particularly on longer web pages, you will not want your JavaScript to run until all elements in a page have loaded. One reason is that the graphics you'll be using may not be ready, or the contents of objects such as divs and spans may not yet be available for manipulation.

Also, some browsers will return incorrect values when a page hasn't yet loaded. For example, if you request the width of the browser too early you may be given a value that doesn't include the vertical scroll bar, and therefore if you try to place anything in that part of the screen (thinking that it is available to you) it will be hidden by a scroll bar.

Some browsers don't even return a semi-useful value. For instance, when asked for the location of an object prior to a page loading, Internet Explorer will always return the coordinates 0,0.

Therefore, you will usually need to place all your JavaScript within the body of the following function:

```
<script>
window.onload = function()
{
   // Your code and all its functions goes here...
}
</script>
```

This makes it so that your code will not get executed until the very last item has been loaded into the web page and has been fully rendered. If you get into the habit of enclosing all your code within this function, you'll ensure that all objects accessed by it are available and avoid error messages and initially unsightly web pages.

By the way, although you could move the call to `Initialize()` here rather than in the <head> of a web page, I don't recommend it. `Initialize()` doesn't rely on any elements of the web page since it interacts only with the browser to create global variables and attach functions to some keyboard and mouse events, so you don't need to move it here. Also, placing the call to `Initialize()` right next to the command that loads in the plug-ins is sensible practice, as you can't have one without the other.

TIP *On very busy pages, a long initial delay can be quite annoying because various elements you will be using are simply loaded in and displayed where they lie within the HTML—only later reaching their final destinations and dimensions. The first solution to this is to ensure that you use a CSS (Cascading Style Sheet) (more on that in Chapter 2) that is loaded in right at the start. This will help your page layout to form itself correctly on the fly. Another trick you can use is to assign zero values to the width and height of objects that you don't want the user to see until later, using standard HTML* `width=` *and* `height=` *keywords (accepted by tables, images, and other objects). Then, once your code is called up after the page has fully loaded, you can give these objects their correct dimensions. Or you can use an element's* `style` *argument to make it invisible, like this:* `style='display:none'`*, and then change the property to* `visible` *when you are ready to display it.*

Summary

By now you should have a computer configured as a suitable development workstation and should know how you intend to include the plug-ins in your web pages. Before moving on to explaining plug-ins in detail, however, it's important to make sure you understand the DOM (Document Object Model) that is used by JavaScript for manipulating elements within a web page. We'll take a look at that next, as well as the use of CSS (Cascading Style Sheets).

CHAPTER 2

JavaScript, CSS, and the DOM

The great thing about JavaScript is that it could have been designed purely as a stand alone scripting language and it would still have been very useful. But the developers did something that would help form the future of the Web, which was to link it to the HTML Document Object Model (DOM), a way of defining an HTML document in a structured way that can then be accessed by languages such as JavaScript and Microsoft's VBScript (although I don't cover the latter in this book).

Whenever you see something dynamic happening on a web page such as an image popping up when you pass the mouse over a link, graphic images zooming out when you click them, or menus altering according to your selections, this is usually accomplished using JavaScript, which offers functionality not offered elsewhere other than by Flash or Java apps—whose scope is limited to the area in which they are embedded.

And speaking of Java, you may be forgiven for thinking that JavaScript is connected with the Java programming language when, in fact, it has little to do with it; JavaScript was purely given the name as a marketing ploy to cash in on the popularity of the Java language. Because of this, some people refer to JavaScript as ECMAScript, but since that doesn't roll off the tongue easily, I doubt it will take over as the language's most popular name.

Anyway, once you have the DOM and a language to access it, you can do almost anything with a web page, such as easily add new paragraphs; change focus and select text; replace images; play sound effects, music, and videos; and much more.

When you add Cascading Style Sheets (CSS) to the mixture you can apply style changes to a page, completely changing the way it looks, without altering the HTML. Actually, CSS has something in common with JavaScript in that certain style settings can apply dynamic effects to page elements such as changing their color and other properties when the mouse passes over them (as you'll see implemented in some of the plug-ins).

Therefore the plug-ins in this book use both CSS and JavaScript to achieve the required functionality in the simplest and easiest way possible. But in order to understand what is going on in many of the plug-ins, it's important that you first have a grounding in both the DOM and CSS.

TIP *You may already be experienced with programming in JavaScript and using CSS and the DOM. If so, you may wish to simply skim through this chapter for a quick refresher on the subject. But if you are relatively new to JavaScript I recommend you familiarize yourself with the contents of this chapter, because the plug-ins in this book are built on the principles discussed.*

The Document Object Model (DOM)

The Document Object Model (DOM) separates the different parts of an HTML document into a hierarchy of discrete objects, each one having its own properties and methods. Methods are functions that can do something with an object, while properties are attributes of an object such as the value it holds in the case of a text object, or its width and height in case of an image, and so on.

The outermost object possible is the *window* object, which is the current browser window, tab, or popped up window. Underneath this is the *document* object, of which there can be more than one (such as several documents loaded into different frames within a page). Inside a document there are other objects such as the *head* and *body* of a page.

Within the head there can be other objects such as the *title* and *meta* objects, while the body object can contain numerous other objects, including HTML tags such as *headings*, *anchors*, *forms*, and so forth.

Figure 2-1 shows the DOM of an example document, with the title "Hello" and a meta tag in the head section and three HTML elements (a link, a form, and an image) in the body section.

Of course even the simplest of web pages has more structure than outlined in this figure, but it serves to show how the DOM works; starting from the very outside of the DOM is the window, inside which there's a single document (although more are allowed), and within the document are the various elements or objects, which connect to each other.

The only one of the items in the figure that is a property is the string "Hello," which is the property of the `title` object. All the other items are objects or object argument names. If the figure were to extend further down, the property for the `meta name` might be found to be "robots" and the URL property for the `a href` could be "google.com," and so on.

Representing this as HTML code the structure of the head section looks like this:

```
<head>
   <meta name="robots" content="index, follow" />
   <title>Hello</title>
</head>
```

The meta tag in this case is one that allows search engines and other web crawlers (or robots) to index the page and follow any links found within it.

The body section of HTML looks like this:

```
<body>
   <a href="http://google.com">Visit Google</a>
   <form id="login" method="post" action="program.php">
      <input id="name" type="text" name="username" value="fred" />
      <input type="submit" />
   </form>
   <img src="/photos/vacations/cancun/photo11.jpg" />
</body>
```

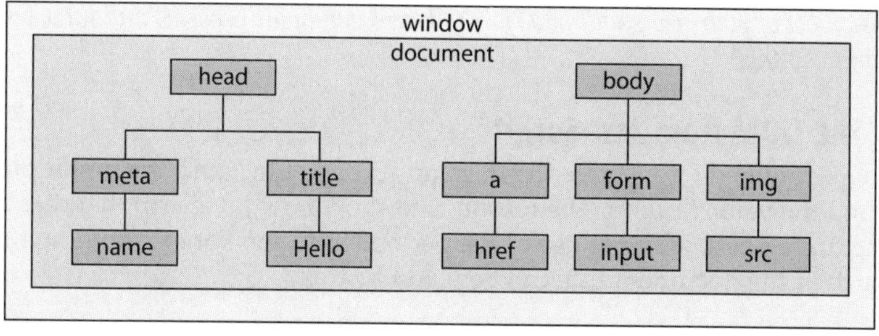

FIGURE 2-1 Example of a DOM showing head and body sections

Remembering that these two sections of HTML are part of the same document, you bring them both together inside an <html> tag, like this:

```
<html>
   <head>
      <meta name="robots" content="index, follow" />
      <title>Hello</title>
   </head>
   <body>
      <a href="http://google.com">Visit Google</a>
      <form id="login" method="post" action="program.php">
         <input id="name" type="text" name="username" value="fred" />
         <input type="submit" />
      </form>
   <img src="/photos/vacations/cancun/photo11.jpg" />
   </body>
</html>
```

Of course, a web page can look quite different from this, but it should follow the same form. Even though modern browsers are very forgiving and allow you to omit many things, such as the opening and closing tags, I don't recommend you do this, because one day you might want to convert your page to XHTML, which is a lot stricter. It's always a good idea to close every tag and make sure you do so in the right order. For example, you shouldn't close a document by issuing </html> followed by </body> because the proper nesting of tags would be broken.

For the same reason, you should also get into the habit of closing any tags that do not have a closing version, such as <img src="..." />, which does not have a matching </img> tag, and therefore requires a / character right before the final > in order to properly close it. In the same way <br> becomes <br />, and so on.

You should also remember that arguments within tags must have either single or double quotation marks to be XHTML compatible, even though nearly all browsers allow you to omit them.

NOTE *In the early days of the Web, when most users had very slow dial-up modems, it was common to see all manner of things such as quotation marks and various tags omitted from web pages. Nowadays, most of your users will have fairly decent bandwidth speeds, and there's no longer any reason to do this.*

Accessing the DOM from JavaScript

You may have wondered why I gave the form an ID of "login," and the first input tag an ID of "name" (and the value "fred"). The reason is to show how JavaScript handles all of this DOM nesting quite easily with the use of the period character. For example, some standard properties such as the document title can be read like this:

```
title = document.title
```

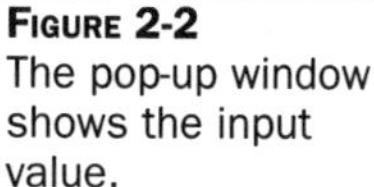
FIGURE 2-2 The pop-up window shows the input value.

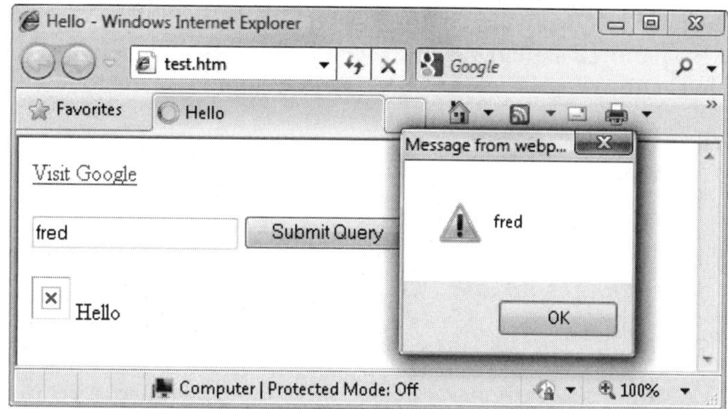

But in order to access most other object properties you need to assign an ID to the object. For example, once the name is assigned to the input field, you can find its current value (if any), in the following manner, which assigns the value to the variable `username`:

```
username = document.forms.login.name.value
```

The reason that `.value` is added after `.name` (but not after `.title` in the preceding example) is that `.title` is already a property, whereas `.name` is a form input object that itself has properties, including its value in `.value`.

The reason for prepopulating the input statement with the value "fred" also becomes apparent if you add the following four lines of code before the closing `</body>` tag, and then load the preceding example into a browser:

```
<script>
   document.write(document.title)
   alert(document.forms.login.name.value)
</script>
```

The browser will then display the value of `document.title` just after the missing graphic icon, which is there because the image *photo11.jpg* doesn't exist, and the current value of the input statement, "fred", is also displayed in a pop-up alert (shown in Figure 2-2).

Cascading Style Sheets

Using CSS, you can apply styles to your web pages to make them look exactly how you want. This works because CSS is connected to the DOM so that you can quickly and easily restyle any element. For example, if you don't like the default look of the `<h1>`, `<h2>`, and other heading tags, you can assign new styles to override the default settings for the font family and size used, or whether bold or italics should be set and many more properties, too.

The main way you add styling to a web page is similar to including JavaScript; you insert the required statements in the head of a web page between the <head> and </head> tags. To change the style of the <h1> tag you might use the following code:

```
<style>
   h1 { color:red; font-size:3em; font-family:Arial }
</style>
```

Within an HTML page this might look like the following (see Figure 2-3):

```
<html>
   <head>
      <style>
         h1 { color:red; font-size:3em; font-family:Arial }
   </style>

   </head>
   <title>Hello World</title>
   <body>
      <h1>Hello there</h1>
   </body>
</html>
```

Or you can use one of the preferred methods of including a style sheet, which is particularly useful when you wish to style a whole site, rather than a single page.

The first way you can do this is by using the CSS `@import` directive, in place of a sequence of style statements, like this:

```
<style>
   @import url("/css/styles.css");
</style>
```

This statement tells the browser to fetch a style sheet with the name *styles.css* from the */css* folder. The `@import` command is quite flexible in that you can create style sheets that themselves pull in other style sheets, and so on. Just make sure that there are no <style> or </style> tags in any of your external style sheets or they will not work.

Figure 2-3 Styling the <h1> tag, with the original style shown in the smaller window

You can also include a style sheet using the HTML `<link>` tag, as follows:

```
<link rel="stylesheet" type="text/css" href="/css/styles.css" />
```

This has the exact same effect as the `@import` directive, except that the `<link>` tag is not a valid style directive, and so it cannot be used from within one style sheet to pull in another—and it, therefore, should also not be placed within a pair of `<style>` ... `</style>` tags. Just as you can use multiple `@import` directives within your CSS to include multiple external style sheets, you can also use as many `<link>` statements as you like in your HTML.

There's also nothing stopping you from using external style sheets and then overriding certain styles for the current page by inserting style statements, either with `<style>` ... `</style>` tags or directly within HTML, like this (which results in italic blue text within the tags):

```
<div style="font-style:italic; color:blue;">Hello</div>
```

A better solution is to change the HTML by assigning a class value, as follows:

```
<div class="iblue">Hello</div>
```

Then you can use the following style setting, either in the page header or within an external style sheet for referring to the class:

```
.iblue { font-style:italic; color:blue; }
```

Of course, if you use another style inside the div, then any attributes that are the same will override those of the div styling. In the case of the `<h1>` tag that was styled earlier, the font color of red that was assigned to `<h1>` will override the `iblue` class setting of blue, but the other `.iblue` attribute of italic text will stay unaltered—resulting in the same Arial font "Hello there" text as Figure 2-3, except that it will be changed to italic.

Properly explaining CSS would easily fill a large book, so these are just the bare bones basics you need to know in order to understand what is going on in the plug-ins. If you are interested in learning more about the subjects of XHTML and CSS in depth, I recommend the book *HTML & XHTML: The Complete Reference*, by Thomas A. Powell (McGraw-Hill/Professional, 2003).

Accessing Styles in JavaScript

Using JavaScript you can also change on the fly many of the same styles you can define using CSS. This is possible because the CSS attributes are also DOM object properties. For example, here's how you use CSS to set an attribute for a particular ID:

```
#under { text-decoration:underline; }
```

Any text within the element that has an ID of `under` will now be underlined. This element can also be accessed from JavaScript, so let's change it to another decoration type with this JavaScript statement:

```
document.getElementById('under').style.textDecoration = 'line-through'
```

All text items within the `under` ID will now be changed from underlined to line-through. To help make this clearer, the following example combines these two statements into a working HTML page (see Figure 2-4):

```
<html>
   <head>
      <style>
         *#under { text-decoration:underline; }
      </style>
   </head>
   <title>Hello World</title>
   <body>
      <div id="under"><h1>How are you?</h1></div>
      <div id="under">A second line</div>
      <div id="under">And a third</div>
      <script>
         document.getElementById('under').style.textDecoration =
            'line-through'
      </script>
   </body>
</html>
```

Straight away you can see from the figure that the "How are you" text has been changed to line-through, but take a look at the two lines underneath; they are both still underlined. The reason for this is that the same ID name was used multiple times, but JavaScript acted only on the first instance.

CSS may have allowed the use of an ID as if it were a class (which applies to a group of elements, rather than just one), but JavaScript certainly doesn't; as soon as it finishes modifying the first instance it stops because it assumes that the job is done. Therefore, the two lines following are not changed by the script.

This serves to illustrate a problem a beginner to CSS may encounter: some styles you apply may seem to work, but it's only as a side effect of how the browser implements them. In this case it reminds you to always use an ID for identifying a single element and a class for multiple ones.

By the way, modifying a class attribute can be done from JavaScript but it requires stepping through the elements in a document to locate each occurrence and then changing it.

FIGURE 2-4 Using JavaScript to change an attribute from underline to line-through

If you would like to learn more about CSS, I recommend the book *Dynamic Web Programming: A Beginner's Guide*, by Marty Matthews and John Cronan (McGraw-Hill/Professional, 2009).

JavaScript and Semicolons

There are some JavaScript programmers who always place a semicolon at the end of every statement, but it isn't necessary to do so because JavaScript interpreters accept either a semicolon or a new line as the end marker for a statement.

However, if you wish to have more than one statement in a line, you *must* use a semicolon between them. In this book I try to avoid this to keep the code as readable as possible.

On the other hand, using semicolons everywhere makes your JavaScript code more easily convertible to languages such as PHP and C, which require them. But it's up to you whether or not you use them.

TIP *Some programs that work with JavaScript directly to help find bugs or optimize or reduce your code will not work unless you have placed a semicolon after every single statement. If you will be using any of these you'll save a lot of time by getting into the habit of using semicolons right away.*

Summary

If this is all new to you, you should now have a very basic picture of how JavaScript, CSS, and the DOM relate to each other. This will help you understand the plug-in documentation in the following chapters. In them, I provide all the information you need to effectively use the plug-ins on your own pages, as well as how to modify and improve them for your own purposes.

CHAPTER 3

The Core Plug-ins

In my previous book, *Plug-in PHP* (McGraw-Hill/Professional, 2010) I was able to draw upon the wealth of ready-made functions supplied with the language. However, this hasn't turned out to be the case with JavaScript, so this chapter concentrates on providing a selection of basic functions needed in order to be able to develop JavaScript programs as quickly and efficiently as possible.

This chapter contains more plug-ins than any other chapter (18 in all), as well as a collection of handy global variables that will make your life much simpler, and will make the remaining plug-ins easier to understand and modify.

Since these core plug-ins and global variables are used throughout the book I recommend you take the time to digest the contents of this chapter as fully as possible before starting to use the remaining functions. I apologize in advance for the amount of documentation on these first few plug-ins, but they are important ones, and it's essential that you are fully familiar with their use.

PLUG-IN 1

O()

The `O()` function is the most fundamental of the plug-ins provided in this book and is used by almost all the others. In its simplest form it replaces the long-winded JavaScript function name `getElementById()`, which takes the string argument supplied to it and then returns the HTML DOM (Document Object Model) object that has been assigned that ID. The letter `O` is short for the word *Object* since the main purpose of this function is to retrieve an object or to modify its properties.

About the Plug-in

This plug-in takes one required and two optional arguments as follows:

- **`id`** This can be a string containing the ID of an object, an object, or even an array containing several objects and/or object IDs. If none of the optional arguments are also provided then the function returns the object or objects represented by `id`. If there *are* optional arguments then the purpose of the function changes to assign the value in `value` to the property in `property` of the object (or objects) in `id`.
- **`property`** This optional string argument can contain the name of a property belonging to the object (or objects) in `id` that requires modifying
- **`value`** If this optional argument is set it represents the value to be assigned to the property in `property` of the object (or objects) in `id`. Both the `property` and `value` arguments must have values, otherwise `O()` will simply return the object (or objects) in `id`.

Variables, Arrays, and Functions

`tmp[]`	Array holding the result of processing the `id` array
`j`	Integer loop variable for indexing into `id`
`UNDEF`	Global string variable with the value 'undefined'
`InsVars()`	Plug-in to insert values into a string

`push()`	Function to push a value onto an array
`substr()`	Function to return a substring from a string
`eval()`	Function to evaluate a string as JavaScript code
`try()`	Function to run a function passing an any error to a matching `catch()` statement
`catch()`	Function called when a `try()` statement fails
`getElementById`	Function to return an object by its name

How It Works

This plug-in does a lot more than simply provide a shortened name for an existing function, because you can pass it either the string ID name of an object, or the object itself. For example, consider the following HTML div:

```
<div id='outerdiv'> … </div>
```

Using the `O()` plug-in you can access the div object directly with the following command:

```
mydiv = O('outerdiv')
```

This command is equivalent to the following, which sets the variable `mydiv` to represent the div object that has the ID of 'outerdiv':

```
mydiv = document.getElementById('outerdiv')
```

This means that you can, for example, use the value returned by this plug-in to change the HTML contents of the div (the text between its opening and closing tags) as follows, by modifying its `innerHTML` property:

```
mydiv.innerHTML = "<h1>A Heading</h1>"
```

Or, you can bypass assigning the object to a variable and access the object directly from the `O()` plug-in, like this:

```
O('outerdiv').innerHTML = '<h1>A Heading</h1>'
```

Passing Either Strings or Objects

The `O()` function is also very versatile in that sometimes you may have a variable containing a string name, like this:

```
myvariable = 'outerdiv'
```

On the other hand, it can represent the actual object itself, like this:

```
myvariable = O('outerdiv')
```

The former contains simply the string of characters comprising 'outerdiv', while the latter is an object. Because the job of `O()` is to return the object referred to by the string name it is passed, if you happen to pass it an object instead of a string it will simply return that object back to you. Therefore whether `myvariable` contains a string that refers to an object or the object itself, you can use just the one statement to access it, like this:

```
othervariable = O(myvariable)
```

Or like this:

```
O(myvariable).innerHTML = '<h2>A Subheading</h2>'
```

Note that there are no quotation marks around `myvariable` in this instance because a variable, not a string, is being passed.

NOTE *I have used single quotation marks in these examples but JavaScript allows you to use either single or double quotation marks. However, for the sake of standardization I usually use single quotes for strings, unless a string includes a single quotes within it. In which case I use double quotation marks to enclose the string.*

Additional Arguments

As well as accepting strings and objects, the `O()` plug-in allows you to pass it an optional pair of arguments that are then used to modify object properties. For example, the previous examples can also be rewritten like this:

```
O('outerdiv', 'innerHTML', '<h1>A Heading</h1>')
O(myvariable, 'innerHTML', '<h2>A Subheading</h2>')
```

Both of the preceding are acceptable alternative syntax for assigning a value to an object's property.

Passing Arrays

You may be wondering about the point of this alternative syntax. Well, it comes into its own when you want to access many different objects at a time. This is something that you cannot do with standard JavaScript, but you can achieve it with the `O()` plug-in, which allows you to pass an array of objects, object ID names, or a combination of both.

For example, let's say that you would like to clear the HTML contents of three objects that have the names 'Fred', 'Mary', and 'Bill'. Regular JavaScript would require three separate commands, but you can easily achieve the same result with the following code:

```
ids = Array('Fred', 'Mary', 'Bill')
O(ids, 'innerHTML', '')
```

You can even mix objects and object ID names within an array, as follows:

```
ids = Array('Fred', 'Mary', 'Bill', myobject)
```

Or, you can combine everything into one line of code in the following way, which will clear out the `innerHTML` contents of all the objects:

```
O(Array('Fred', 'Mary', 'Bill', myobject), 'innerHTML', '')
```

Figure 3-1 shows a group of three divs that have all had their innerHTML properties set to the same value, using the code in the following example web page:

```
<!DOCTYPE HTML PUBLIC "-//W3C//DTD HTML 4.01 Transitional//EN"
   "http://www.w3.org/TR/html4/loose.dtd">
<html><head><title>Plug-in JavaScript</title>

<script src="PJ.js"></script>
<script>Initialize()</script>

</head><body>

Fred: <span id='Fred'></span><br />
Mary: <span id='Mary'></span><br />
Bill: <span id='Bill'></span>

<script>
ids = Array('Fred', 'Mary', 'Bill')
O(ids, 'innerHTML', 'New contents...')
</script>

</body></html>
```

This is the first time that you have seen a complete example of using the plug-ins. It begins with the <!DOCTYPE ...> setting, then adds both the page's <title> and the two <script> lines required to include and set up the plug-ins. After that the <head> is closed and the <body> of the page is opened. Then three lines of HTML create simple <span> sections that don't contain any content.

Finally, there is another <script> section in which the contents of these spans is changed so that each displays the string 'New contents...'. This is the format that most standard web pages will follow when using the plug-ins. The result of loading this page into a browser is shown in Figure 3-1.

Now that you've seen how easy it is to use the plug-ins and where the different parts fit within a web page, throughout the rest of this book's examples I will omit everything before (and including) the <body> tag (except where a plug-in affects that particular section) and concentrate only on the relevant HTML and JavaScript required to explain the use of a plug-in.

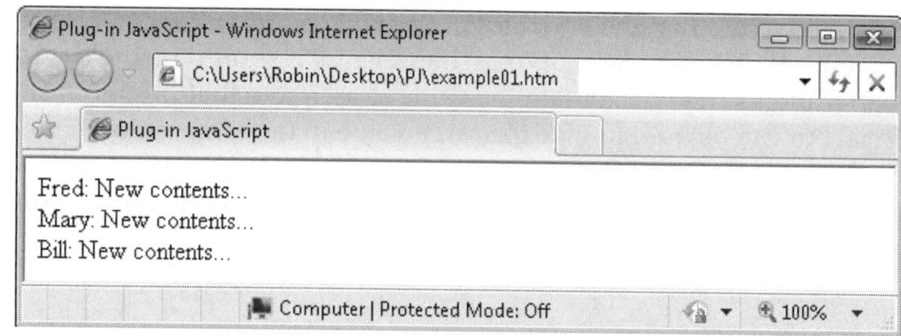

FIGURE 3-1 Changing the HTML contents of objects using O()

When an Array Is Passed

The `o()` plug-in comprises three parts. The first one tests the argument `id` to see if it is an array, which it does by using the `instanceof` operator, like this:

```
if (id instanceof Array) ...
```

If it *is* an array then more than one object has been passed to the function, so the array `tmp` is declared as a local array (that can only be accessed by this instance of this function) using the `var` keyword, like this:

```
var tmp = []
```

Then a `for()` loop iterates through the array, using the integer variable `j` as an index pointer to each individual array element.

Making Recursive Calls

Interestingly, the `O()` function is called again within each iteration, but just with the single element located at the current array index pointed to by `j`. This is known as a *recursive* function call, meaning that the function calls itself. It's a very neat way to reuse code to get a job done once you have broken it down into a more manageable chunk. The loop code looks like this:

```
for (var j = 0 ; j < id.length ; ++j)
   tmp.push(O(id[j], property, value))
```

To explain how it works in this instance, one element has been extracted from an array of elements and then that element is passed back to the same function, which will then process that element and return a value back to itself. So, for example, if an array of items is passed to `O()`, it will be iterated through in stages, each time passing one element from the array in turn to the same function, until all elements have been processed.

Looked at from the function's receiving end, when it sees that it has received a single item (and not an array), control flow drops through to the remaining code, where that item is processed and whatever value or object is calculated is returned. Upon return from the function (back to the same function), the result of the function call is placed in the next free location in the `tmp` array by using the JavaScript `push()` function and is promptly forgotten about (since it has been dealt with), and the next element of the array is then processed.

Once all elements are done with (in other words, the value of `j` equals the number of items in the array, as indicated by `id.length`), the array `tmp` is returned to the calling code.

You will notice that the variables `property` and `value` are not treated as arrays, because they aren't. If the variable `property` has a value it should be the name of an object's property, and `value` will contain the value to assign to that property. These arguments are optional but can be used to give the same value to the same properties of all objects in an array. Because the function calls itself recursively, it also has to pass `property` and `value` (whether or not they have values) along with the object to be processed, otherwise if they have values they will be lost.

TIP *If you're new to recursion and it seems somewhat complicated to you, try reading through this section a couple more times and you should soon get the hang of it. Wikipedia also has quite a good explanation of the concept at* wikipedia.org/wiki/Recursion, *and no, it doesn't just say "see Recursion"!*

Processing the Additional Arguments

In the previous section I talked about `property` and `value`, the optional arguments for modifying an object's properties. The second main section of this function is where that modification happens. The code starts by testing whether or not both `property` and `value` have a value by using the `typeof` operator, like this:

```
if (typeof property != UNDEF && (typeof value != UNDEF)
```

The variable `UNDEF` is a global variable that has been assigned the value 'undefined' by the `Initialize()` function, which is detailed a little later.

Both arguments must have a value for this `if()` statement to execute. If they *do*, it's time to make another recursive call, passing the value of `id` back to the same function. This illustrates the power of the `O()` plug-in in that you never have to worry whether the main argument you pass it is an object or the ID name of an object; either is acceptable, and so this part of the function simply passes on the value of `id`, whatever type of variable it is.

Inside this `if()` statement the `eval()` function is used to assign the value to the property, first surrounding the value with single quotation marks if it is a string (otherwise, `eval()` would try to evaluate it, rather than treat it as a string):

```
if (typeof value == 'string') value = "'" + value + "'"
return eval("O('" + id + "')." + property + " = " + value)
```

The value returned by `eval()` is then returned by the function.

At the Deepest Level

The remaining lines of the plug-in execute only when `id` is not an array and when no optional parameters have been passed. Since they come after both of the sections that can make recursive calls, they are the place where the function ultimately returns from these recursive calls.

These lines also represent the heart of the `O()` function in that they will return an object by providing its ID name. The code look like this:

```
if (typeof id == 'object') return id
else
{
   try { return document.getElementById(id) }

   catch(e) { alert('PJ - Unknown ID: ' + id) }
}
```

The first line ends function execution if `id` is an object, by simply returning it. Otherwise an attempt is made to return the object whose ID is `id`. Sometimes, though, you will accidentally pass an ID to the `O()` function that hasn't yet been assigned. If this happens, rather than having

JavaScript come to a halt (which it would do if the object doesn't exist), an error message alert is displayed to let you know this has happened.

This is achieved by using a pair of `try() ... catch()` functions. The first tries the code and passes execution to the second if there is an error.

You may wish to remove the `alert()` call in a production website so that your users won't see any errors that you might leave in your code. However, remember that trying to access a nonexistent object is a critical error that stops all program flow, and you really don't want to leave any such errors in your production code.

How To Use It

This plug-in has two distinct modes. In the first it returns an object referred to by an ID string, while in the second it updates an object's property with a new value. In either case, if the object itself is passed to the plug-in (instead of its ID name) then the object is accessed directly, since there's no need to look it up.

Furthermore, in both lookup and property setting modes you can pass an array of objects and/or ID names. If you are looking up objects, the plug-in returns an array. If you are setting properties, all the objects have the specified property set to the given value, and those values are returned.

However, the value returned by the plug-in is really only of use when looking up an object, such as in the following, which are just four of the countless ways of using the plug-in:

```
objectname = O('mydiv')
O('copyrightspan').innerHTML = '&copy; 2011')
background = O('menu').style.backgroundColor
O('menu').style.color = 'yellow'
```

When you are assigning a value to one or more properties, as in the following examples, the returned value will simply be that of the assigned value, which is not that useful to you, except perhaps when you are debugging code:

```
O(objectname, 'innerHTML', '<h1>Heading Text</h1>')
O(Array('first', 'second'), 'mouseover', 'mousehandler')
```

As you will see throughout this book, the `O()` plug-in is used in a variety of different ways, and you will soon get used to thinking of it as the main way to access individual elements in a webpage.

NOTE *Well known JavaScript frameworks, such as jQuery, Script.aculo.us Prototype, and many others, make use of a similar function to* `O()`*, but they usually call it* `$()`*. Some add even more functionality to it than there is in the* `O()` *plug-in, which makes it even more powerful, but also more complicated too. The* `$` *is a sensible choice of character for naming such functions as it's short and instantly recognizable. However I have deliberately not used the same convention precisely because other frameworks do use it. That way the plug-ins in this book should be less likely to conflict with third-party frameworks if you use them both on the same web pages.*

The Plug-in

```
function O(id, property, value)
{
   if (id instanceof Array)
   {
      var tmp = []
      for (var j = 0 ; j < id.length ; ++j)
         tmp.push(O(id[j], property, value))
      return tmp
   }

   if (typeof property !=  UNDEF && typeof value != UNDEF)
   {
      if (typeof value == 'string') value = "'" + value + "'"
      return eval("O('" + id + "')." + property + " = " + value)
   }

   if (typeof id == 'object') return id
   else
   {
      try { return document.getElementById(id) }
      catch(e) { alert('PJ - Unknown ID: ' + id) }
   }
}
```

PLUG-IN 2

S()

Probably the most common use to which JavaScript is put is modifying CSS properties in HTML documents. These include colors, dimensions, location, opacity, and much more. Generally this is done using code such as the following, which changes the foreground text color of a div:

```
document.getElement.ById('element').style.color = 'red'
```

Or, using the previous plug-in, this can be shortened to:

```
O('element').style.color = 'red'
```

This is such a common action that I have created a companion plug-in to `O()` called `S()` (for Style), which deals with handling an object's `style` subobject. Using it, the preceding commands can be reduced to the following:

```
S('element').color = 'red'
```

Figure 3-2 shows the plug-in being used to change the background colors of the three divs. Even though the figure is not in color, you can tell that by their shades that the divs are different colors.

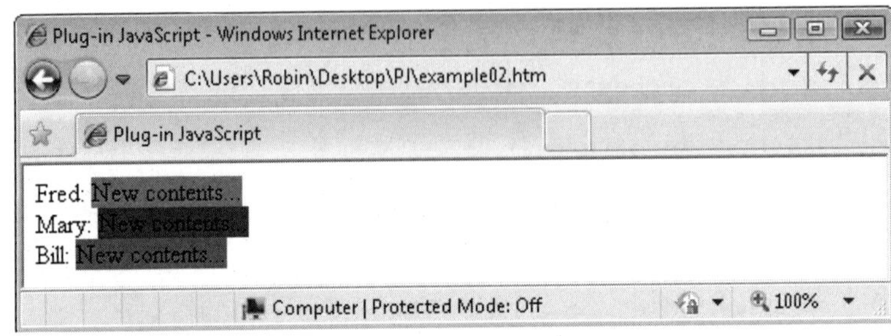

FIGURE 3-2 Using `S()` to change the background colors of some divs

About the Plug-in

The `S()` plug-in is similar to `O()` with the exception that instead of referencing an object, that object's `style` subobject is accessed. Also, since events are not used by it there is no need to check for them in this function. It accepts the following arguments:

- **`id`** This can be a string containing the ID of an object, an object, or even an array containing several objects and/or object IDs. If none of the optional arguments are also provided then the function returns the `style` subobject of the object (or objects) represented by `id`. If there *are* optional arguments, then the purpose of the function changes to assign the value in `value` to the property in `property` of the `style` subobject of the object (or objects) in `id`.
- **`property`** This optional string argument can contain the name of a property belonging to the `style` subobject of the object (or objects) in `id` that requires modifying.
- **`value`** If this optional argument is set it represents the value to be assigned to the property in `property` of the `style` subobject of the object (or objects) in `id`. Both the `property` and `value` arguments must have values, otherwise `S()` will simply return the `style` subobject of the object (or objects) in `id`.

Variables, Arrays, and Functions

`tmp[]`	Array holding the result of processing the `id` array
`j`	Integer loop variable for indexing into `id`
`style`	Style subobject
`push()`	Function to push a value onto an array
`try()`	Function to run a function passing an any error to a matching `catch()` statement
`catch()`	Function called when a `try()` statement fails
`O()`	Plug-in 1, the main "object" function. Since `O()` or `S()` are both used by almost all plug-ins, this is the last time either will be listed in a "Variables, Arrays, and Functions" section.

How It Works

Now that you understand how the O() plug-in works, you will have an idea how this one functions. Because it is so similar, I'll just outline the basics.

As with O(), this function has three main parts. The first processes id if it happens to be an array. It does this by recursively calling itself with each element within the array so as to deal with each one separately. The code that does this is as follows, with the final line returning an array of all the values returned during the process:

```
if (id instanceof Array)
{
   var tmp = []
   for (var j = 0 ; j < id.length ; ++j)
      tmp.push(S(id[j], property, value))
   return tmp
}
```

The second section handles the case when you are using the plug-in in its property assigning mode. It determines this by checking whether both the arguments property and value have values. If they do, then the property in property of the style subobject of the object represented by id is assigned the value in value.

Otherwise the object fetching mode is entered, and so the style subobject of id is returned.

However, for the reasons given in the previous section, accessing the object is embedded within try() statements so that any errors can be caught and displayed via a call to alert(), using the matching catch() statements:

```
if (typeof property != UNDEF && typeof value != UNDEF)
{
   try { return O(id).style[property] = value }
   catch(e) { alert('PJ - Unknown ID: ' + id) }
}
else if (typeof id == 'object') return id.style
else
{
   try { return O(id).style }
   catch(e) { alert('PJ - Unknown ID: ' + id) }
}
```

During development you will find this error catching very useful, as mistyping ID names or accessing them before they have been declared are common errors.

NOTE *I refer to the* style *subobject, but I could also call it the* style *property, because it is both: it's a property called* style*, which is itself an object that has properties. Therefore I tend to refer to properties that are also objects as a subobjects.*

How To Use It

You use the plug-in in much the same way as you use the O() function. With it you can either fetch the style subobject of an object, or you can modify one of the style properties of that object. Here's one way you could use the plug-in to first fetch and then use an object's style subobject:

```
var styleobject = S('mydiv')
styleobject.backgroundColor = 'cyan'
```

Or, you can access the style subobject directly, like this:

```
S('mydiv').backgroundColor = 'cyan'
```

If you wish, you can also set the value of a property from within the plug-in like this:

```
S('mydiv', 'backgroundColor', 'cyan')
```

This latter form also allows you to set style properties for several objects at once, like this:

```
ids = Array('one', 'two', 'three')
S(ids, 'backgroundColor', 'cyan')
```

In this case, all the objects in the `ids` array will have their `backgroundColor style` property set to 'cyan'. Omitting the head section and any other parts of the web page, the code used to create the output in Figure 3-2 is as follows:

```
Fred: <span id='Fred'></span><br />
Mary: <span id='Mary'></span><br />
Bill: <span id='Bill'></span>

<script>
ids = Array('Fred', 'Mary', 'Bill')
O(ids, 'innerHTML', 'New contents...')
S('Fred').backgroundColor = 'red'
S('Mary').backgroundColor = 'blue'
S('Bill').backgroundColor = 'green'
</script>
```

First, the divs are created within HTML, then a section of JavaScript follows in which the `ids` array is populated with the three ID names of the divs. After that, the `O()` plug-in is used to assign vales to the `innerHTML` properties of these divs as a group, and then each div's `backgroundColor` property is individually set using three separate calls to `S()`.

Over the coming chapters you will see the `S()` plug-in used in many different contexts, and I think you'll find that in future you'll never want to access `style` properties in any other way.

The Plug-in

```
function S(id, property, value)
{
   if (id instanceof Array)
   {
      var tmp = []
      for (var j = 0 ; j < id.length ; ++j)
```

```
         tmp.push(S(id[j], property, value))
      return tmp
   }

   if (typeof property != UNDEF && typeof value != UNDEF)
   {
      try { return O(id).style[property] = value }
      catch(e) { alert('PJ - Unknown ID: ' + id) }
   }
   else if (typeof id == 'object') return id.style
   else
   {
      try { return O(id).style }
      catch(e) { alert('PJ - Unknown ID: ' + id) }
   }
}
```

PLUG-IN 3

Initialize()

In order to set up the plug-ins ready to use, you will have to call up a small initialization plug-in at the start of your web pages. As previously mentioned, I recommend you always include the following two lines of code at the start of each one:

```
<script src="PJ.js"></script>
<script>Initialize()</script>
```

Or if you are using the compressed version of the plug-ins, *PJsmall.js*, then you would use that file in place of *PJ.js*.

This plug-in is the `Initialize()` function that is called by that code, and it prepares a wide range of functionality you can draw on, as shown in Figure 3-3, in which the browser type is detected.

About the Plug-in

This plug-in requires no arguments and doesn't return any. However, please refer to the table of variables, arrays, and functions in the next section, as some very important global variables are set up by it.

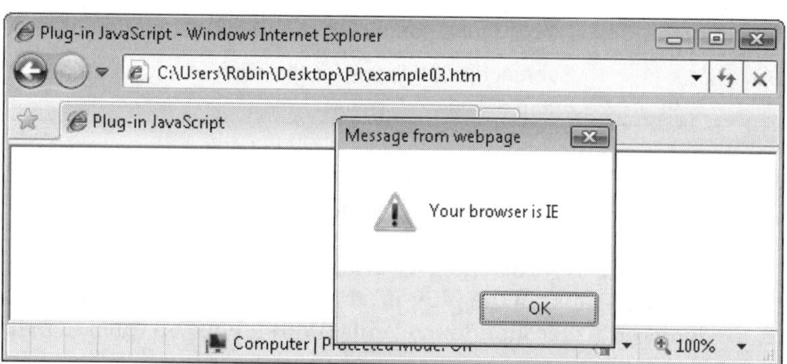

FIGURE 3-3 Displaying the variable **BROWSER** after calling this plug-in

Variables, Arrays, and Functions

`MOUSE_DOWN`	Global integer set to `true` if a mouse button is currently held down, otherwise `false`
`MOUSE_IN`	Global integer set to `true` if the mouse pointer is currently within the browser window, otherwise `false`
`MOUSE_X`	Global integer containing the current horizontal coordinate of the mouse pointer
`MOUSE_Y`	Global integer containing the current vertical coordinate of the mouse pointer
`SCROLL_X`	Global integer containing the amount the browser has been scrolled vertically, in pixels
`SCROLL_Y`	Global integer containing the amount the browser has been scrolled horizontally, in pixels
`KEY_PRESS`	Global integer containing the value of the last key pressed
`ZINDEX`	Global integer containing the maximum z-index of any object accessed via the plug-ins
`CHAIN_CALLS`	Global array containing plug-ins that have been chained together and which are yet to be executed
`INTERVAL`	Global integer containing the time in milliseconds between calls to a repeated event
`UNDEF`	Global string containing the value 'undefined'
`HID`	Global string containing the value 'hidden'
`VIS`	Global string containing the value 'visible'
`ABS`	Global string containing the value 'absolute'
`FIX`	Global string containing the value 'fixed'
`REL`	Global string containing the value 'relative'
`TP`	Global string containing the value 'top'
`BM`	Global string containing the value 'bottom'
`LT`	Global string containing the value 'left'
`RT`	Global string containing the value 'right'
`BROWSER`	Global string containing the name of the current browser
`NavCheck()`	Subfunction to check for the existence of a string in the browser User Agent string

How It Works

Let's look first at each of this plug-in's global variable definitions:

- **`MOUSE_DOWN`** This integer variable is updated by the two inline, anonymous functions (later in the plug-in) that are attached to the `document.onmouseup` and `document.onmousedown` events. With it you can quickly make a check to see whether or not a mouse button is being pressed anywhere in the browser window by simply looking at this variable, which has a value of `true` if down; otherwise it is set to `false`.

- **`MOUSE_IN`** In a similar fashion, the `document.onmouseout` and `document.onmouseover` events are captured, and this global variable is set to `true` when the mouse pointer is within the bounds of the browser window; otherwise it is set to `false`.
- **`MOUSE_X`** and **`MOUSE_Y`** This pair of global variables is constantly updated by the `CaptureMouse()` plug-in (the plug-in following this one), which is attached to the `document.onmousemove` event. Therefore, you can reference these variables at any time to determine the position of the mouse pointer.
- **`SCROLL_X`** and **`SCROLL_Y`** These global variables are also kept updated by the `CaptureMouse()` plug-in. They are continuously updated with values representing the amount by which the browser has scrolled in both vertical and horizontal directions.
- **`KEY_PRESS`** This global variable is updated by the `CaptureKeyboard()` plug-in, which captures the `document.onkeydown` and `document.onkeypress` events and sets the variable depending on the key that was pressed.
- **`ZINDEX`** This global variable starts off with a default value of 1,000. It is used by the plug-ins to determine the `zIndex` property of objects it uses. This is the depth at which it will be displayed on the screen, with lower or negative numbers being behind higher and positive numbers. For example, the `ContextMenu()` plug-in in Chapter 8, which opens a drop-down element when you right-click, uses this value to ensure that the element it displays appears in front of all other windows. Also, the `BrowserWindow()` plug-in (also in Chapter 8), which creates in-browser, moveable pop-up windows, sets windows that are clicked to the value of `ZINDEX + 1`, to ensure that they come to the front.
- **`CHAIN_CALLS`** Some of the plug-ins have the ability to be chained together so that they run consecutively, each one starting after the previous has finished. Normally, JavaScript doesn't allow such behavior and, if you call up a function that, for example, sets up an interrupt to perform an animation, that function will return immediately to the calling code without waiting for the sequence of interrupts to complete. This is exactly the behavior normally required, as it allows other things to happen at the same time. But some of these plug-ins work better when they are chained, which is achieved by placing a sequence of functions in the `CHAIN_CALLS` array so that as each function completes, the next in the chain can be called. The only reasons you might want to access this array are either to determine if (and how many) functions are queued up, or possibly to empty the array to cancel all queued up functions.
- **`INTERVAL`** After many hours of experimentation on all the major browsers across a range of computers and operating systems, I have derived a value of 30 milliseconds as being the optimal time to allow between interrupt calls, because some shorter functions complete in under 10 milliseconds, while others may take 20 or more, but none should take any longer than 30 milliseconds. Therefore, I have

set the global variable `INTERVAL` to 30. This fixed value is required for timing purposes, so that all the interrupt functions in this book can ensure that they take exactly the number of milliseconds passed to them. If JavaScript speeds creep up over the next few years, as they inevitably do, this allows you to optimize these plug-ins and drop the value of this variable to 25, 20, 15, or even fewer milliseconds, as computers get faster and JavaScript interpreters improve. This will not speed up the plug-ins, but it will allow animations to have extra steps between the first and last frame, making the transitions smoother.

Global String Variables

After these first ten global variables, a further ten global string variables are defined. These are `UNDEF`, `HID`, `VIS`, `ABS`, `FIX`, `REL`, `STA`, `INH`, `TP`, `BM`, `LT` and `RT`, and in order they stand for the strings 'undefined', 'hidden', 'visible', 'absolute', 'fixed', 'relative', 'static', 'inherit', 'top', 'bottom', 'left' and 'right'.

Although they are not essential, I have created these variables because the strings to which they refer are used frequently by the plug-ins, and this helps to keep the code more compact. It also serves to make the listings in this book narrower, so that lines that might previously have wrapped around now display on a single line. Additionally, they help to make the code more readable, as long as you refer back to this section if you forget the values of any of them.

Determining the Current Browser

Because JavaScript varies in its implementation between different developers, you sometimes need to know which browser you are dealing with. So, in conjunction with the subfunction `NavCheck()`, the next ten lines of code will set the global variable `BROWSER` to one out of the following strings, depending on the browser used: 'IE', 'Opera', 'Chrome','iPod', 'iPhone', 'iPad', 'Android', 'Safari', 'Firefox', and 'UNKNOWN'. You can then refer to this variable in the same way that some of the plug-ins do in order to offer different code to different browsers. When 'Firefox' is returned it means that a browser running on the Gecko rendering engine is in use, which includes browsers other than Firefox.

Attaching Functions to Events

Much of the functionality of these plug-ins rests on the capturing of various built-in browser events, as is done by the remaining seven lines of code. The first three attach the `CaptureMouse()` function to the `document.ommousemove` event, and the `CaptureKeyboard()` function to the `document.onkeydown` and `document.onkeypress` events. What these plug-ins do is documented in their own sections, but suffice it to say that they are called each time one of those events occurs and they keep the global variable `KEY_PRESS` updated.

The final four lines attach functions that are so small that I have created them as anonymous, inline functions. All they do is capture the `document.onmouseout`, `document.onmouseover`, `document.onmouseup` and `document.onmousedown` events, keeping the global variables `MOUSE_IN` and `MOUSE_DOWN` updated.

How To Use It

To use this plug-in you must ensure it is called prior to calling any other plug-ins, and you *must* call this plug-in in order for almost all the plug-ins to work. If you wish to check that it has been successfully called, you can try issuing the following statement from within `<script>` tags, which will display the name of the browser being used, as shown in Figure 3-3:

```
alert('Your browser is ' + BROWSER)
```

However, you will normally wish to use this and the other plug-ins only once a page has fully loaded and all its elements locations and dimensions are known and can be manipulated. Therefore, the command (and the rest of your code) is best placed within a `window.onload` anonymous function, like this:

```
window.onload = function()
{
   alert("Your browser is " + BROWSER)
}
```

The Plug-in

```
function Initialize()
{
   MOUSE_DOWN  = false
   MOUSE_IN    = true
   MOUSE_X     = 0
   MOUSE_Y     = 0
   SCROLL_X    = 0
   SCROLL_Y    = 0
   KEY_PRESS   = ''
   ZINDEX      = 1000
   CHAIN_CALLS = []
   INTERVAL    = 30

   UNDEF = 'undefined'
   HID   = 'hidden'
   VIS   = 'visible'
   ABS   = 'absolute'
   FIX   = 'fixed'
   REL   = 'relative'
   STA   = 'static'
   INH   = 'inherit'
   TP    = 'top'
   BM    = 'bottom'
   LT    = 'left'
   RT    = 'right'

   if      (document.all)        BROWSER = 'IE'
   else if (window.opera)        BROWSER = 'Opera'
```

```
    else if (NavCheck('Chrome'))  BROWSER = 'Chrome'
    else if (NavCheck('iPod')     BROWSER = 'iPod'
    else if (NavCheck('iPhone')   BROWSER = 'iPhone'
    else if (NavCheck('iPad'))    BROWSER = 'iPad'
    else if (NavCheck('Android')) BROWSER = 'Android'
    else if (NavCheck('Safari'))  BROWSER = 'Safari'
    else if (NavCheck('Gecko'))   BROWSER = 'Firefox'
    else                          BROWSER = 'UNKNOWN'

    document.onmousemove = CaptureMouse
    document.onkeydown   = CaptureKeyboard
    document.onkeypress  = CaptureKeyboard

    document.onmouseout  = function() { MOUSE_IN   = false }
    document.onmouseover = function() { MOUSE_IN   = true  }
    document.onmouseup   = function() { MOUSE_DOWN = false }
    document.onmousedown = function() { MOUSE_DOWN = true  }

    function NavCheck(check)
    {
       return navigator.userAgent.indexOf(check)  != -1
    }
}
```

PLUG-IN 4

CaptureMouse()

This plug-in is called only by the `Initialize()` function, and you should not need to call it yourself. What it does is attach to the mouse movement event, updating various global variables with details about the mouse position, as shown in Figure 3-4.

About the Plug-in

This plug-in attaches to the `document.onmousemove` event, updating the global variables `MOUSE_X`, `MOUSE_Y`, `SCROLL_X`, and `SCROLL_Y`. The event passes the value `e` to it, which is only used by browsers other than Internet Explorer. It does not require you to pass it any arguments, nor does it return any values.

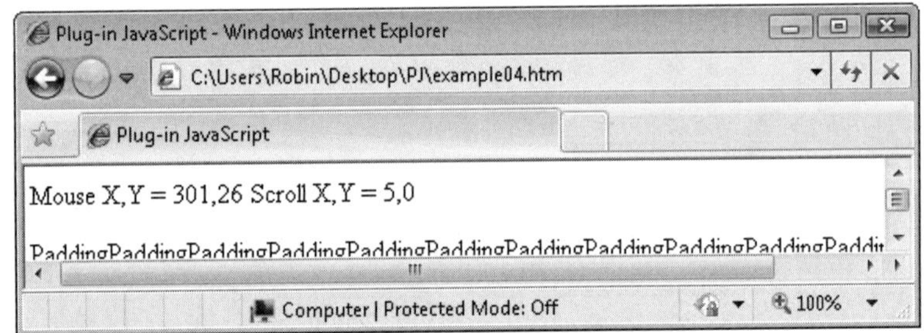

FIGURE 3-4 This plug-in lets you know where the mouse pointer is.

Variables, Arrays, and Functions

`e`	The event as passed to the function by browsers other than Internet Explorer. `e.pageX` and `e.pageY` contain the X and Y locations of the mouse pointer.
`window.event`	Internet Explorer uses the `window.event` property instead of an event passed as an argument. The `clientX` and `clientY` subproperties contain the X and Y locations of the mouse pointer.
`document.documentElement`	If the browser is Internet Explorer then the `scrollLeft` and `scrollTop` properties of this property are accessed to determine the amount of horizontal and vertical scroll.
`window`	On browsers other than Internet Explorer the `pageXOffsett` and `pageYOffset` properties of `window` are accessed to determine the amount of horizontal and vertical scroll.
`MOUSE_X`	Global integer containing the current horizontal coordinate of the mouse pointer
`MOUSE_Y`	Global integer containing the current vertical coordinate of the mouse pointer.
`SCROLL_X`	Global integer containing the amount the browser has been scrolled vertically, in pixels.
`SCROLL_X`	Global integer containing the amount the browser has been scrolled vertically, in pixels.

How It Works

This function traps the `document.onmousemove` event and accesses either the `e` value passed to it in browsers other than Internet Explorer or, in Internet Explorer, it accesses the global `window.event` property. Using these values it sets the values of the global variables `MOUSE_X` and `MOUSE_Y` to the current X and Y coordinates of the mouse pointer.

The `scrollLeft` and `scrollTop` properties of `document.documentElement` are also accessed in Internet Explorer to determine the amount of any horizontal and vertical scrolling. These values are placed in the global variables `SCROLL_X` and `SCROLL_Y`. In browsers other than Internet Explorer, `SCROLL_X` and `SCROLL_Y` are given their values based on the `pageXOffset` and `pageYOffset` properties of `window`.

The value `true` is then returned to allow the event to be acted on by the browser.

How To Use It

You will not access this function directly. Instead, by calling the `Initialize()` plug-in as recommended, the values needed to determine the X and Y locations of the mouse pointer and any horizontal or scrolling values are placed in the global variables `MOUSE_X`, `MOUSE_Y`, `SCROLL_X`, and `SCROLL_Y` and are kept constantly updated.

To illustrate how you can use these, the following code will display these values in real time:

```
<div id='output'></div><p>
PaddingPaddingPaddingPaddingPaddingPaddingPaddingPaddingPaddingPadding
```

```
<script>
window.onload = function()

{
   setInterval(simpleInterrupt, INTERVAL)

   function simpleInterrupt()
   {
      O('output').innerHTML =
         '  Mouse X,Y = ' + MOUSE_X  + ',' + MOUSE_Y +
         ' Scroll X,Y = ' + SCROLL_X + ',' + SCROLL_Y
   }
}
</script>
```

The first section is within the HTML body of a web page and is used to create a div into which the output will be inserted. Underneath the div there's a line of text made up from repeating the word *Padding*. This is used to make the text overflow (since there are no spaces in it), causing the bottom scrollbar to appear so you can move the scrollbar and see the offset value change in real time. If your browser is set very wide, you should resize it until the scrollbar appears.

In the `<script>` section there's a single main line of code that sets up a regular interrupt using the `setInterval()` function, passing it the name of the function to call (which is `simpleInterrupt`) and the frequency at which it should be called in `INTERVAL` (which is 30 by default). This means the function `simpleInterrupt()` will be called up every 30 milliseconds.

TIP *In JavaScript, whenever you wish to reference a function by its name without actually calling the function, you omit the final opening and closing brackets. In this instance, the* `setInterval()` *function knows that you are passing only the name of the function. If you used opening and closing brackets, the function would first be called and the value it returned would be passed to the* `setInterval()` *function, which is probably not what you want.*

The `simpleInterrupt()` function uses the `O()` plug-in you have already seen to select the div 'output' object by name. It then assigns the following string to that object's `innerHTML` property. This has the effect of inserting the string as if it were entered between the opening and closing div tags. The value assigned is some text and the values in the four global variables.

To try this for yourself, enter the example code (as well as entering the required initial pair of `<script>` commands to load in the *PJ.js* file and calling the `Initialize()` plug-in), or select *example04.htm* from the *plug-ins.zip* file, which you can download from the companion website at *pluginjavascript.com*.

Then resize your browser so that it is fairly small and the bottom scrollbar is visible. Move the mouse about within the browser and move the scrollbar to see the values displayed change in real time. Because of the way the scrolling event works, you will only see its values change when you release the mouse button after moving one of the scrollbars.

As you can see, with very little work you can look up important values associated with the mouse whenever you need them. You also just saw the `O()` plug-in being used in a real situation.

The Plug-in

```
function CaptureMouse(e)
{
   if (BROWSER == 'IE')
   {
      SCROLL_X = document.documentElement.scrollLeft
      SCROLL_Y = document.documentElement.scrollTop
      MOUSE_X  = window.event.clientX + SCROLL_X
      MOUSE_Y  = window.event.clientY + SCROLL_Y
   }
   else
   {
      SCROLL_X = window.pageXOffset
      SCROLL_Y = window.pageYOffset
      MOUSE_X  = e.pageX
      MOUSE_Y  = e.pageY
   }

   return true
}
```

PLUG-IN 5 CaptureKeyboard()

This plug-in makes a note of any keypresses made and stores the result in the global variable `KEY_PRESS`, as demonstrated by the example in Figure 3-5, which has detected the Alt key being pressed.

About the Plug-in

You will not need to call this plug-in yourself because it should already have been called by the `Initialize()` plug-in. It doesn't require any arguments and doesn't return any that you can use.

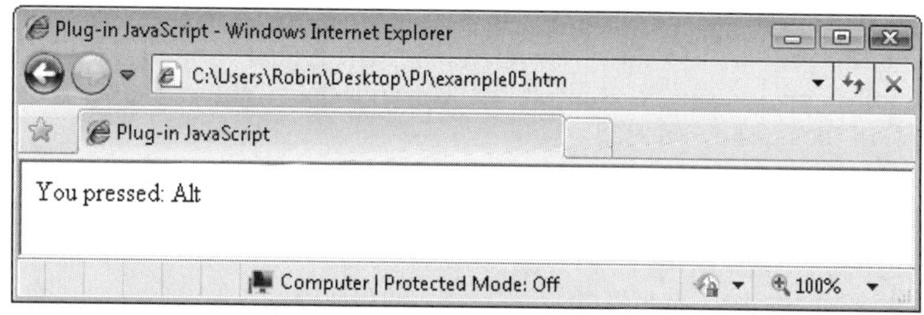

FIGURE 3-5 Determining which keys have been pressed is easy with this plug-in.

Variables, Arrays, and Functions

`e`	The event as passed to the function by browsers other than Internet Explorer. Either `e.charCode` or `e.keyCode` contains the value of the key pressed.
`window.event`	Internet Explorer uses the `window.event` property instead of an event passed as an argument. The `keyCode` contains the value of the key pressed.
`BROWSER`	Global variable used to determine the browser.
`KEY_PRESS`	Global variable to be assigned the value of the keypress.
`fromCharCode()`	JavaScript function to convert Unicode values to characters.
`FromKeyCode()`	Plug-in to return the value of a keypress or its name if it is one of many special characters such as 'Esc', 'Home', and so on.

How It Works

This function works differently depending on whether you are using Internet Explorer or not. If you are, it looks up the keypress in `window.event.keyCode` and passes it through the `FromKeyCode()` plug-in, which will assign a string if the keypress was a special one such as 'PgUp', 'Backspace', and so on. Then, if the value is still a number (that is, it hasn't been substituted for a special key name), the JavaScript `fromCharCode()` function converts it from its Unicode value to an actual key value, so that if, for example, the key `e` is pressed, then the value 'e' is returned.

On non-Internet Explorer browsers, both `e.charCode` and `e.keyCode` are checked for a value because both the events `document.onkeydown` and `document.onkeypress` are captured by this function. One function captures regular keys, while the other handles the special keys already referred to, so combining both into the same function makes sense. So, if `e.charCode` has a value, it is passed through the JavaScript `fromCharCode()` function to convert it from its Unicode value. Or, if `e.keycode` has a value, a special key was pressed, so its value is passed through the `FromKeyCode()` plug-in to look the key name up.

In either case, the result is that `KEY_PRESS` will contain a letter, number, punctuation symbol, the name of a special key, or simply a key number if it is none of the others. There is no keyboard buffering to, for example, create strings of input, as only the last key pressed is saved. However, it is quite possible to create an input function using this if you need one.

Finally, a value of `true` is returned to allow further processing of the event by the browser.

How To Use It

Using this plug-in is as simple as referencing the global variable, `KEY_PRESS`, that it maintains. The following is a simple example that continuously updates the contents of a div with the value of the last key pressed:

```
<div id='output'></div>

<script>
window.onload = function()
{
   setInterval(simpleInterrupt, INTERVAL)
```

```
    function simpleInterrupt()
    {
       O('output').innerHTML = ' You pressed: ' + KEY_PRESS
    }
}
</script>
```

Again (and I won't mention this any more), this assumes you have already included the lines to load in *PJ.js* and called the `Initialize()` function.

The interrupt is set up so that the value of the last keypress can be continuously displayed. If you prefer, you can always use a command such as the following in the loop instead:

```
alert('You pressed: ' + KEY_PRESS)
```

However, it is intrusive, and you have to click the OK button to close the alert each time it is called. What's more, it locks up the browser because the `alert()` function prevents you from doing anything else (even closing the browser) until you have clicked OK, and even then the alert will pop up again, and again, forever.

TIP *Because of the problem of* `alert()` *potentially taking over a browser if placed within a loop, this book includes an alternate function called* `Alert()` *(with an upper case A) which you may prefer to use. It does not lock the browser and has other benefits too. For further details, please refer to Chapter 13.*

The Plug-in

```
function CaptureKeyboard(e)
{
   if (BROWSER == 'IE')
   {
      KEY_PRESS = FromKeyCode(window.event.keyCode)

      if (KEY_PRESS > 0)
         KEY_PRESS = String.fromCharCode(KEY_PRESS)
   }
   else
   {
      if (e.charCode)      KEY_PRESS = String.fromCharCode(e.charCode)
      else if (e.keyCode) KEY_PRESS = FromKeyCode(e.keyCode)
   }

   return true
}
```

PLUG-IN 6

FromKeyCode()

This plug-in returns the name of the key pressed if it is a special one such as 'Ctrl' or 'Alt'; otherwise, the value passed to it is returned, as shown in Figure 3-6, in which the translations for key codes 1 through 144 are displayed.

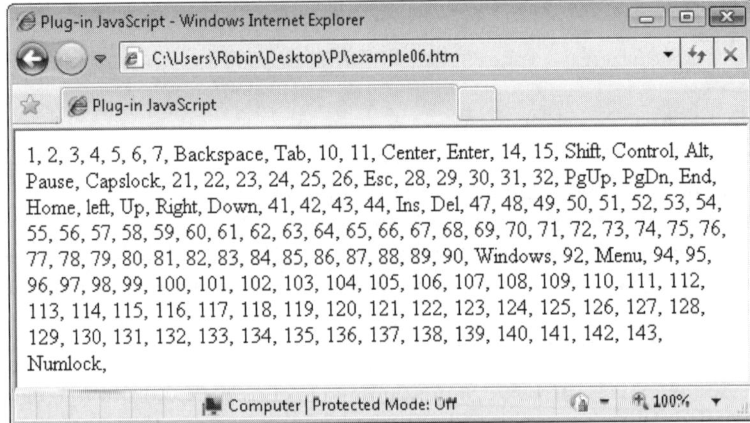

FIGURE 3-6 This plug-in returns meaningful names for key codes.

About the Plug-in

This plug in takes a key code as an argument and returns either a string representing the special key that was pressed, or the code if no such key was pressed.

Variables, Arrays, and Functions

`c`	Key code passed to the function and returned by it if it does not represent a special key

How It Works

This function uses a `switch()` statement to test the value of `c` and return various strings if it matches set values. If none of the values match, then `c` is returned.

How To Use It

Generally this plug-in will be called for you by the `CaptureKeyboard()` plug-in. However, you may have an application for which you'd rather not return the strings given, or you'd rather return different names. In these cases, feel free to modify the plug-in to your requirements.

For example, if you don't want the keypresses created by pressing the SHIFT key, you might prefer to return a value of the empty string for that value instead of the string 'SHIFT'. That way, when the user presses the SHIFT key followed by the M key, for example, you will only see the value 'M' and not 'SHIFT' followed by 'M'.

The reason I've gone to the bother of trapping these special keys is that, although there are already useful input features built into JavaScript, these plug-ins allow you to, for example, set up various special keys to move objects around the screen or perform particular functions the moment a key is pressed.

Here's a combined HTML and JavaScript example to return the translations for codes 1 through 144:

```
<div id='output'></div>

<script>
window.onload = function()
{
   for (j = 1 ; j < 145 ; ++j)
   O('output').innerHTML += FromKeyCode(j) + ', '
}
</script>
```

An interesting point to note here is the use of the += operator to keep appending to the contents of the innerHTML property of the 'output' div.

The Plug-in

```
function FromKeyCode(c)
{
   switch (c)
   {
      case   8: return 'Backspace'
      case   9: return 'Tab'
      case  12: return 'Center'
      case  13: return 'Enter'
      case  16: return 'Shift'
      case  17: return 'Control'
      case  18: return 'Alt'
      case  19: return 'Pause'
      case  20: return 'Capslock'
      case  27: return 'Esc'
      case  33: return 'PgUp'
      case  34: return 'PgDn'
      case  35: return 'End'
      case  36: return 'Home'
      case  37: return 'left'
      case  38: return 'Up'
      case  39: return 'Right'
      case  40: return 'Down'
      case  45: return 'Ins'
      case  46: return 'Del'
      case  91: return 'Windows'
      case  93: return 'Menu'
      case 144: return 'Numlock'
   }

   return c
}
```

PLUG-IN 7

GetLastKey()

This plug-in returns the value of whatever the last keypress was and then resets the stored value to the empty string to indicate that the key value has been retrieved. Figure 3-7 shows a simple input function created using this plug-in.

About the Plug-in

This plug-in doesn't take any arguments and returns the value of the most recently pressed key (if any).

Variables, Arrays, and Functions

k	Local string variable that holds the value of KEY_PRESS before resetting it and returning k

How It Works

This plug-in assigns the value in KEY_PRESS, the global variable that contains the last key pressed, to the local variable k. Then it resets KEY_PRESS to the empty string to show that the value has been read. Finally, the contents of k is returned. If there was no keypress, the empty string is returned.

How To Use It

To use this plug-in, call it with no arguments and it will return either a letter, number, punctuation symbol, or a special key name. If the key was none of these, then its code is returned.

You can use this plug-in to create a very simple input function, like this:

```
What is your name? <b><span id='name'></span></b>

<script>
window.onload = function()
{
   input('name')

   function input(id)
   {
      var interrupt = setInterval(simpleInterrupt, INTERVAL)
```

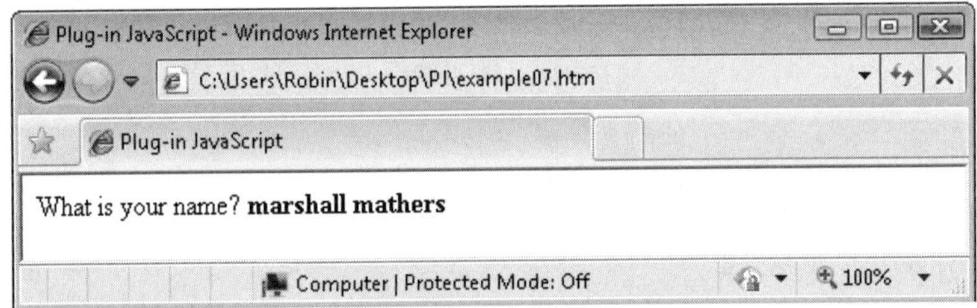

Figure 3-7 This plug-in can build an input function.

```
        function simpleInterrupt()
        {
           var k = GetLastKey()

           if (k == 'Enter')
           {
              k = '.'
              clearInterval(interrupt)
           }
           O(id).innerHTML += k
        }
    }
}
</script>
```

To make this work, a span is created in which the input will be placed. Then the JavaScript code makes a call to a new function called `input()`, passing the ID of the span. The `input()` function then sets up a repeating interrupt using `setInterval()` to the subfunction `simpleInterrupt()`.

The `simpleInterrupt()` function then calls `GetLastKey()` each time it is called. If the value is ever 'Enter', it means the user has pressed the Enter key and `k` is assigned the value '.' (a period), and the interrupt is disabled using `clearInterval()`, with the interrupt ID previously assigned to `interrupt`.

Finally, the `innerHTML` property of the object indicated by `id` has the latest key value returned appended to it. If the value is the empty string, then nothing is appended.

All your code has to do then is look at the end of the string to see if it is the period character to indicate that the user has pressed Enter. Your code then removes that character and uses the remainder of the string. Alternatively, you can use a different end of input marker. Whatever you do, if you want to create your own input routine rather than use a ready-made one such as an `<input type='text'>` tag, you have to go through all these swings and roundabouts of interrupt driven calls, because that's the way JavaScript works. However, at least you now have a way of doing so when you need it.

For a bit of fun, if you store the input somewhere hidden rather than in a span, you can check for a sequence of characters to be entered—much like entering cheat codes into a game—and if a recognizable sequence is entered, you can trigger a bonus feature.

The Plug-in

```
function GetLastKey()
{
   var k = KEY_PRESS
   KEY_PRESS = ''
   return k
}
```

PLUG-IN 8 PreventAction()

This plug-in is for preventing an object's drag or select event (or both) from occurring. For example, sometimes you may wish to prevent a section of text from being copied, or at least from being highlighted, and you can easily do that with this plug-in. Figure 3-8 shows one

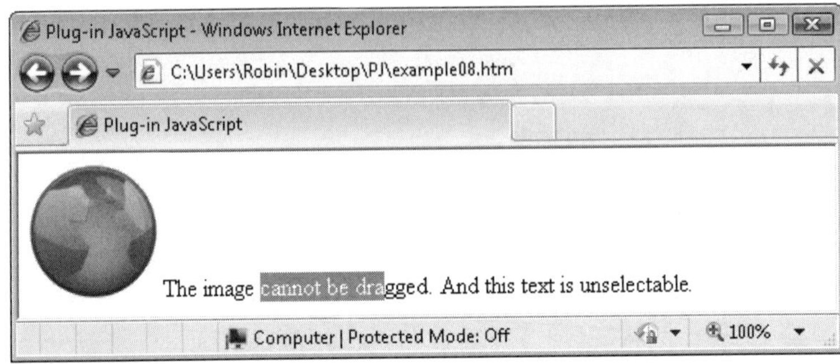

FIGURE 3-8 The image and the second sentence cannot be dragged or selected.

section of text that is being selected, while the second sentence is not selectable. The GIF image is also undraggable.

About the Plug-in

This plug-in takes three arguments and, depending on their values, either prevents or enables certain events to occur. The arguments are as follows:

- **`id`** The ID of an object, such as a div or span section of HTML, a GIF image, or any other object
- **`type`** This argument can have one of three string values: 'drag', 'select', or 'both'. If the value is 'drag', then the object referred to by `id` will either be prevented from being dragged or allowed to be dragged, depending on the value of `onoff`. If it is 'select', then the selection of text will be either prevented or allowed, depending on the value of `onoff`. If it is 'both', then both these events will be either prevented or allowed.
- **`onoff`** This argument should be either `true` or `false`; alternatively, the values `1` or `0` are acceptable. The values `true` or `1` mean the event (or events) in the variable `type` are prevented. If `onoff` is `false` or `0` then the event (or events) are allowed.

Variables, Arrays, and Functions

`ondragstart`	Event of the object passed in `id`
`onselectstart`	Event of the object passed in `id`
`onmousedown`	Event of the object passed in `id`
`MozUserSelect`	Property of the object passed in `id` (only used by Mozilla-based browsers such as Firefox)

How It Works

The plug-in code is divided into two main sections. In the first, the drag event of the object referenced by `id` is managed, while the second half is for handling the `id` object's select event. Each of these halves is again split into two parts. In the first half of each, the events it handles are prevented, while the second half is for re-enabling an event after it has been disabled.

To provide these features, if the browser supports it, either the `ondragstart` or `onselectstart` event of the object in `id` (or both events if the value in `type` is 'both') is assigned an inline, anonymous function that returns the value `false`, which has the effect of cancelling any further action.

If the event is not recognized, then the `onmousedown` event for the object in `id` is caught and set to return `false`. This is not that great a solution because it prevents other `onmousedown` events from being attached, but it does have the effect of preventing the event from occurring.

In the case of Mozilla-based browsers such as Firefox, the special property `MozUserSelect` is set to either 'none' to prevent text from being selected, or 'text' to re-enable it. This is necessary because these browsers will not use the `onselectstart` event, and using this property is less intrusive than capturing the `onmousedown` event.

How To Use It

To prevent the copying and pasting of the contents of a div, for example, you can attach this function to its `onselectstart` event, like this:

```
PreventAction('mydiv', 'select', true)
```

If a user tries to select any text, this plug-in stops the event before it can get going. This is not merely a relatively easy way to prevent people from copying text from your web pages, it also helps prevent text from being inadvertently highlighted when you are using the mouse to drag items about.

You can also use it in to prevent an object from being dragged in the browser or dragged and dropped elsewhere, like this:

```
PreventAction('mygif', 'drag', true)
```

Here's some code that illustrates both of these uses:

```
<img id='gif' src='i1.gif' />
The image cannot be dragged.
<span id='text'>And this text is unselectable</span>

<script>
window.onload = function()
{
   PreventAction('gif',  'drag',   true)
   PreventAction('text', 'select', true)
}
</script>
```

In the HTML section of the example, a GIF image with the name *i1.gif* is displayed and given the ID of 'gif'. This is followed by some regular text and a span with the ID of 'text'.

Below that, in the `<script>` section, the GIF image has its drag property disabled, and the span text is made unselectable. If you try either of these actions they will fail. However, Internet Explorer will allow you to continue the selection within the span if you commence a select action from outside the span. You can work around this bug by setting the whole document as unselectable, like this:

```
PreventAction(document.body, 'select', true)
```

However, this means that nothing at all on your web page can be selected. Other browsers do not have this bug.

The Plug-in

```
function PreventAction(id, type, onoff)
{
   if (type == 'drag' || type == 'both')
   {
      if (onoff == true)
      {
         if (typeof O(id).ondragstart != UNDEF)
            O(id).ondragstart    = function() { return false }
         else O(id).onmousedown = function() { return false }
      }
      else
      {
         if (typeof O(id).ondragstart != UNDEF)
              O(id).ondragstart = ''
         else O(id).onmousedown = ''
      }
   }

   if (type == 'select' || type == 'both')
   {
      if (onoff == true)
      {
         if (typeof O(id).onselectstart != UNDEF)
            O(id).onselectstart = function() { return false }
         else if (typeof S(id).MozUserSelect != UNDEF)
            S(id).MozUserSelect = 'none'
         else O(id).onmousedown = function() { return false }
      }
      else
      {
         if (typeof O(id).onselectstart != UNDEF)
            O(id).onselectstart = ''
         else if (typeof S(id).MozUserSelect != UNDEF)
            S(id).MozUserSelect = 'text'
         else O(id).onmousedown = ''
      }
   }
}
```

PLUG-IN 9 NoPx() and Px()

These plug-ins are short but powerful functions that provide opposing functionality. `NoPx()` removes the 'px' suffix attached to some CSS properties, while `Px()` attaches the 'px' suffix to a property. Figure 3-9 shows the plug-ins in use.

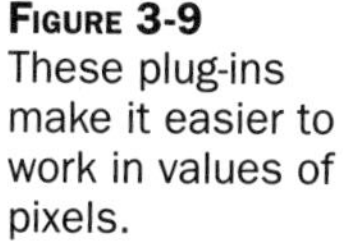

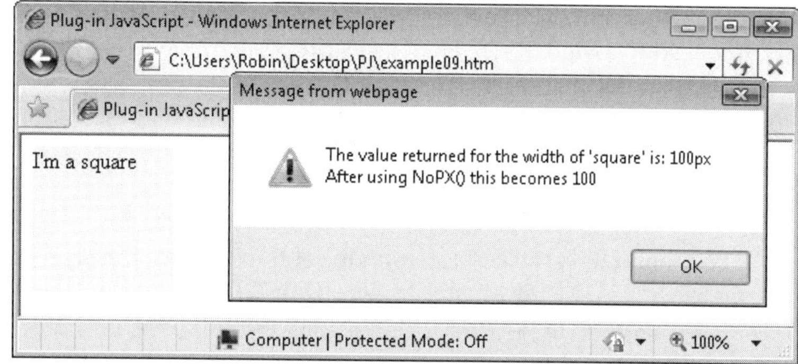

FIGURE 3-9 These plug-ins make it easier to work in values of pixels.

About the Plug-ins

These plug-ins require an object's property to be passed to them. If `NoPx()` is passed a value, then the value returned will be that of the value less any 'px' suffix. If `Px()` is called, then the value returned is that of the value passed to the plug-in, combined with the suffix 'px'. In no case is any property actually changed by these plug-ins, as values are merely derived based on the properties, and it is up to you to use them as required. The plug-ins require the following argument:

- **`value`** The property to be modified

Variables, Arrays, and Functions

`replace()`	JavaScript function for replacing a subsection of a string

How They Work

The `NoPx()` function uses the JavaScript `replace()` function to replace any occurrences of 'px' in the string it is passed, and then returns the result, multiplied by 1 to ensure it is turned from a string into a number.

The `Px()` function adds the suffix 'px' to any value it is passed and then returns the result.

How To Use Them

The `NoPx()` function is very simple in that all it does is replace the substring 'px' (if found) with the empty string in any string it is passed. Thus it can strip away the trailing 'px' suffix that many object properties have. For example, the `style.marginLeft` property is just one of many that end in 'px', so the following call will strip it out:

```
value = NoPx(S(id).marginLeft)
```

In this example the object referred to by `id` is passed to the `S()` function, which returns the style subobject. The `marginLeft` property is then appended to this and the resulting string value, which might look like '10px', for example, is then passed to the `NoPx()` function. In this case, it would return the number 10, which is then assigned to the variable `value`.

The `Px()` function performs the inverse, adding the 'px' suffix to a value. This is useful when you need to assign 'px' to an object's property that needs to know you are working in pixels. For example, the `style.width` property can be used to set the width of an object, but it needs to have 'px' added to it. To save you having to do this you can make the following call instead:

```
S(id).left = Px(135)
```

This command uses the `S()` function to set the width of the object referred to by `id` to 135 pixels, since `Px(135)` evaluates to the string '135px'.

Here's an example of how you might use these plug-ins:

```
<div id='square'>I'm a square</div>

<script>
window.onload = function()
{
   S('square').width           = Px(100)
   S('square').height          = Px(100)
   S('square').backgroundColor = 'yellow'

   alert("The value returned for the width of 'square' is: "    +
      S('square').width + '\nAfter using NoPx() this becomes ' +
      NoPx(S('square').width))
}
</script>
```

The HTML section contains a single div element with some text. In the `<script>` section the div is resized to become 100 pixels wide by 100 high, using the `Px()` function to create the values. The background is also set to yellow so you can see the square.

After this there's a call to the JavaScript `alert()` function in which the value of the object's `width` style property is displayed ('100px'), and that value is passed through the `NoPx()` function and redisplayed. This time it's the number 100.

The Plug-ins

```
function NoPx(value)
{
   return value.replace(/px/, '') * 1
}

function Px(value)
{
   return value + 'px'
}
```

PLUG-IN 10 X() and Y()

This pair of similar functions returns an object's exact horizontal or vertical offset from the left or top of the browser. The plug-in names are so short because they are used very frequently and it saves on typing; it also makes your source code easier to follow. In Figure 3-10 you can see that the left and top edges of the div are inset from the browser edge by 8 pixels.

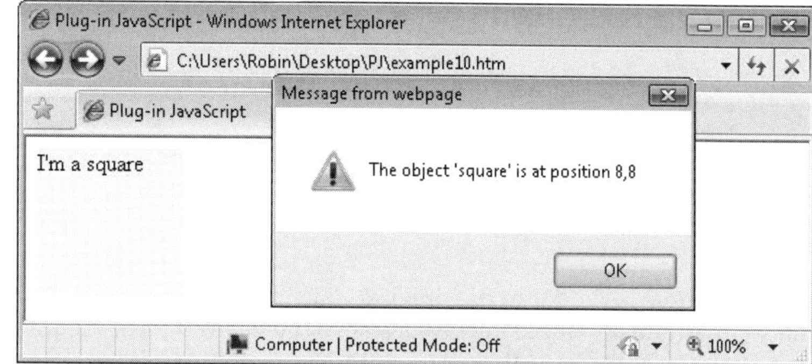

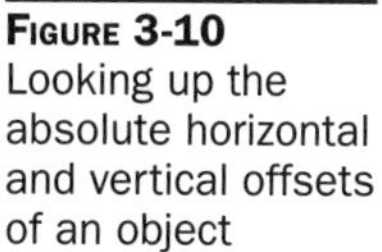

FIGURE 3-10 Looking up the absolute horizontal and vertical offsets of an object

About the Plug-ins

These plug-ins return the absolute horizontal or vertical offsets of an object from the left or top of the browser window. They take this argument:

- **`id`** The object whose offset is to be returned

Variables, Arrays, and Functions

`obj`	Local object copy of the `id` object
`offset`	Local integer used to hold the horizontal or vertical offset
`offsetParent`	The parent offset object
`offsetLeft`	The object's left offset
`offsetTop`	The object's top offset

How They Work

These plug-ins first make a copy of the object represented by `id` in `obj` and set the local variable `offset` to either the `offsetLeft` or `offsetTop` property of the object. This is the amount by which the object is offset from its parent.

Then, in case the parent object is also a subobject, the `if()` and `while()` statements recurse back through all parent objects, adding their offsets in turn to `offset`, until there are no more parent objects. At this point `offset` contains the absolute distance in pixels from the left side or top edge of the browser window to the left or top of the object. This value is then returned.

How To Use Them

To use these plug-ins, pass the ID of an object to them and they will return either the absolute horizontal or absolute vertical position of its left side or top edge in pixels. Here's some code to illustrate their use:

```
<div id='square'>I'm a square</div>

<script>
```

```
window.onload = function()
{
   S('square').width           = Px(100)
   S('square').height          = Px(100)
   S('square').backgroundColor = 'yellow'
   alert("The object 'square' is at position " +
      X('square') + ',' + Y('square'))
}
</script>
```

This example is similar to the previous one in that it creates a square div with the ID 'square', but in this example the object's absolute left and top offsets are returned by the `alert()` statement, with calls to `X()` and `Y()`.

The Plug-ins

```
function X(id)
{
   var obj    = O(id)
   var offset = obj.offsetLeft

   if (obj.offsetParent)
      while(obj = obj.offsetParent)
         offset += obj.offsetLeft

   return offset
}

function Y(id)
{
   var obj    = O(id)
   var offset = obj.offsetTop

   if (obj.offsetParent)
      while(obj = obj.offsetParent)
         offset += obj.offsetTop

   return offset
}
```

PLUG-IN 11 W() and H()

In addition to needing to know the location of an object, as in the previous pair of plug-ins, you often need to know their width and height, which you can determine with these functions. Figure 3-11 shows the plug-ins being used to discover an object's width and height.

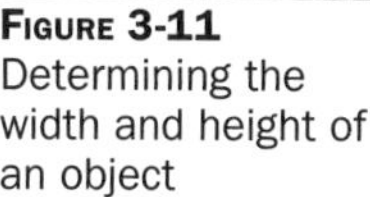

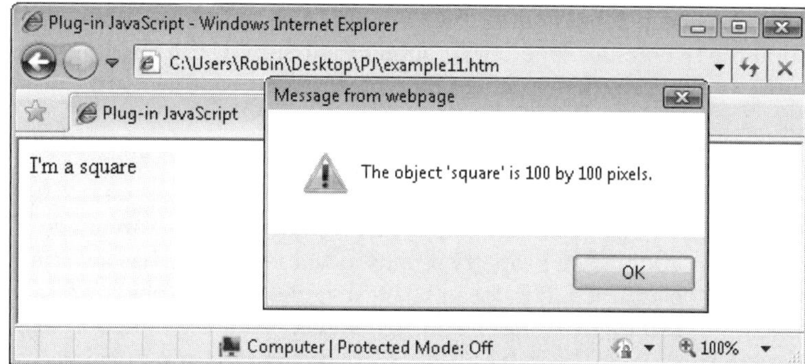

FIGURE 3-11 Determining the width and height of an object

About the Plug-ins

These plug-ins return an object's exact width or height, including any margins and borders. They require the following argument:

- `id` The object whose dimensions are to be returned

Variables, Arrays, and Functions

`offsetWidth`	The object's width
`offsetHeight`	The object's height
`marginLeft`	The object's left margin width
`marginRight`	The objects' right margin width
`marginTop`	The object's top margin width
`marginBottom`	The object's bottom margin width
`borderLeft`	The object's left border width
`borderRight`	The object's right border width
`borderTopWidth`	The object's top border width
`borderBottomWidth`	The object's bottom border width
`border`	The image object's border property
`NoPx()`	The plug-in to remove 'px' suffixes

How They Work

Each function adds together all the properties that affect either an object's width or its height. To return the width of an object, its `offsetWidth` is added to its `marginLeft` and `marginRight` properties, like this:

```
var width = O(id).offsetWidth +
            NoPx(S(id).marginLeft) +
            NoPx(S(id).marginRight)
```

Next, a check is made of its `borderLeftWidth` and `borderRightWidth` properties by adding the two values together to obtain their sum. If the result is greater than 0, then that amount is placed in the variable `bord`. Here is that code section:

```
var bord = NoPx(S(id).borderLeftWidth) +
           NoPx(S(id).borderRightWidth)
```

Next, because an object's border style property overrides an image's border property (even though the border image property retains its value), if `bord` has a value it is subtracted from the value to be returned. If it doesn't have a value, then the object's image border property value, multiplied by two (once for the left and once for the right border), is subtracted from the value to be returned. This is because the `offsetWidth` property already includes the widths of any borders, so they are taken off so as to return only the object and its margin's width. Here is the code for this section:

```
if (bord > 0)            width -= bord
else  if (O(id).border) width -= O(id).border * 2
return width
```

An object's padding width is not returned because none of the plug-ins need to know this value.

To return the height of an object, the same process is used in the `H()` plug-in, with the properties `offsetHeight`, `marginTop`, `marginBottom`, `borderTopWidth`, `borderBottomWidth`, and `border`.

In either case the calculated value is returned.

CAUTION *If you add together the* `H()` *heights of two vertically adjacent boxes (perhaps in order to specify the height of a containing div), if there are margins, the calculated height will be greater than the height the browser actually uses to render both boxes on top of each other, due to vertical margin collapsing, in which only the largest of the two margins is used.*

How To Use Them

To use these plug-ins, pass them the ID of an object whose dimensions you need. Here's some code showing how you might use them:

```
<div id='square'>I'm a square</div>

<script>
window.onload = function()
{
   S('square').width           = Px(100)
   S('square').height          = Px(100)
   S('square').backgroundColor = 'yellow'

   alert("The object 'square' is " +
      W('square') + ' by ' + H('square') + ' pixels.')
}
</script>
```

This example is quite similar to previous ones in that the div called 'square' is created in the HTML section. The difference here is that the `alert()` function displays the width and height of the object using the `W()` and `H()` plug-ins.

NOTE *You may find it interesting to note the use of all the `S()`, `W()`, `H()` and `NoPx()` plug-ins here. Already you can see how these plug-ins are coming together to make your programming much easier. Without the earlier functions to build on, these plug-ins might be two or three times the size, but this way they only use a handful of characters, such as `W('obj')`. Once you get a little further into the book, even more powerful functions will become available to you that would take dozens, if not hundreds, of lines of code to write from scratch.*

The Plug-ins

```
function W(id)
{
   var width    = O(id).offsetWidth +
                  NoPx(S(id).marginLeft) +
                  NoPx(S(id).marginRight)

   var bord     = NoPx(S(id).borderLeftWidth) +
                  NoPx(S(id).borderRightWidth)

   if (bord > 0)           width -= bord
   else if (O(id).border) width -= O(id).border * 2

   return width
}

function H(id)
{
   var height   = O(id).offsetHeight +
                  NoPx(S(id).marginTop) +
                  NoPx(S(id).marginBottom)

   var bord     = NoPx(S(id).borderTopWidth) +
                  NoPx(S(id).borderBottomWidth)

   if (bord > 0)          height -= bord
   else if(O(id).border) height -= O(id).border * 2

   return height
}
```

PLUG-IN 12

Html()

Because you will frequently find yourself needing to write to the `innerHTML` property of objects, I wrote this simple plug-in to keep the code short and improve its readability, as shown in Figure 3-12.

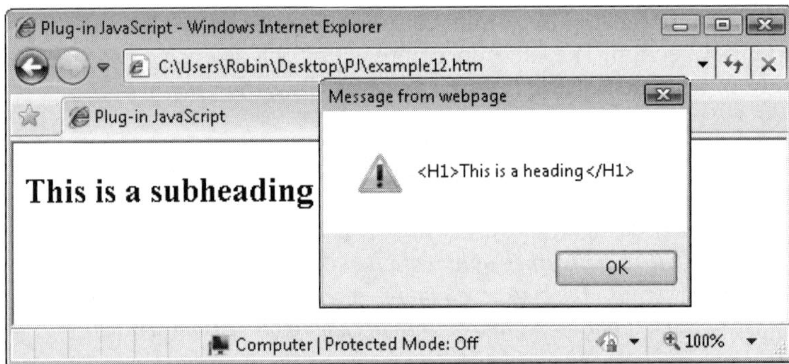

FIGURE 3-12 This plug-in makes it easy to read and write the HTML contents of an object.

About the Plug-in

This plug-in returns the **`innerHTML`** property of the object it is passed. You can use it to either read or write this property. Only the first argument is required to read a value, but both are required to write one:

- **`id`** The ID of the object with the `innerHTML` property to access
- **`value`** The value to assign to the `innerHTML` property

Variables, Arrays, and Functions

`innerHTML`	The property containing the HTML text of an object

How It Works

To read a value, the plug-in uses the `O()` plug-in to reference the object in `id` and return its `innerHTML` property. To write a value, you pass a second argument, `value`, to the plug-in. If the code notices that this argument has been passed, the `innerHTML` property of `id` is changed to `value`. In either case the value of the `innerHTML` property is returned.

How To Use It

You can either read or write to the `innerHTML` property of an object that supports it using this function. To write to it you use a statement such as this:

```
Html('mydiv', 'This is some new text')
```

To read from the property, you use a statement such as this:

```
var contents = Html('mydiv')
```

Here's some code that uses a couple of `alert()` calls so you can see the before and after effects of using the plug-in:

```
<div id='heading'><h1>This is a heading</h1></div>

<script>
```

```
window.onload = function()
{
   alert(Html('heading'))
   Html('heading', '<h2>This is a subheading</h2>')
   alert(Html('heading'))
}
</script>
```

The first section of HTML creates a div with an `<h1>` heading. Then the `<script>` section immediately pops up an alert showing this value by using a call to `Html()`. After that, the value of the object's `innerHTML` property is changed to a subheading, again using `Html()`, and then a second call to the JavaScript `alert()` function redisplays the property, using the `Html()` function—at which time you will see that the contents has changed.

The Plug-in

```
function Html(id, value)
{
   if (typeof value != UNDEF)
      O(id).innerHTML = value
   return O(id).innerHTML
}
```

PLUG-IN 13 SaveState()

After you change the properties for an object, there are times when you might want to restore it to its original state. This plug-in allows you to back up all the most important style properties of an object. Figure 3-13 shows a div being prepared with a few values prior to testing the `SaveState()` plug-in.

About the Plug-in

This plug-in backs up several of the most important style properties of an object, where they can be later retrieved should you need them. It takes the following argument:

- **`id`** The object whose properties are to be backed up

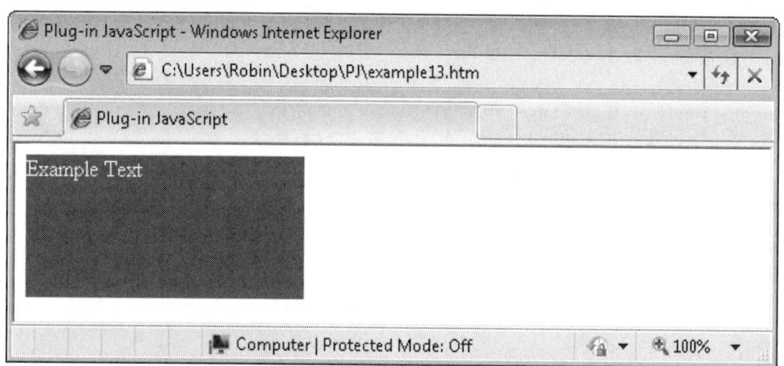

Figure 3-13 Creating a div with which to test saving and restoring states

Variables, Arrays, and Functions

left	The object's `style.left` property
top	The object's `style.top` property
visibility	The object's `style.visibility` property
color	The object's `style.color` property
backgroundColor	The object's `style.backgroundColor` property
display	The object's `style.display` property
opacity	The object's `style.opacity` property
MozOpacity	The object's `style.MozOpacity` property
KhtmlOpacity	The object's `style.KhtmlOpacity` property
filter	The object's `style.filter` property
zIndex	The object's `style.zIndex` property

How It Works

This is a very simple plug-in that creates backup properties for each of the properties. Each new backup property name begins with the string "Save_", and ends with the original property name. The ones you may not know are `MozOpacity`, which is the opacity property used by Mozilla based browsers such as Firefox, and `KhtmlOpacity`, which is used by older versions of the Apple Safari browser.

How To Use It

To create a set of backup properties for an object, pass its ID to the `SaveState()` plug-in, like this:

```
SaveState('myobject')
```

The following code shows a few style settings being made to an object and then its state being saved:

```
<div id='mydiv'>Example Text</div>

<script>
window.onload = function()
{
   S('mydiv').width           = Px(200)
   S('mydiv').height          = Px(100)
   S('mydiv').backgroundColor = 'green'
   S('mydiv').color           = 'white'
   S('mydiv').position        = 'absolute'

   SaveState('mydiv')
}
</script>
```

This creates a green, 200 by 100-pixel rectangle with white text whose position is absolute (and the object is therefore movable). In the next plug-in, you'll see what happens if these values are changed and the saved state is restored.

The Plug-in

```
function SaveState(id)
{
   O(id).Save_left              = S(id).left
   O(id).Save_top               = S(id).top
   O(id).Save_visibility        = S(id).visibility
   O(id).Save_color             = S(id).color
   O(id).Save_backgroundColor = S(id).backgroundColor
   O(id).Save_display           = S(id).display
   O(id).Save_opacity           = S(id).opacity
   O(id).Save_MozOpacity        = S(id).MozOpacity
   O(id).Save_KhtmlOpacity      = S(id).KhtmlOpacity
   O(id).Save_filter            = S(id).filter
   O(id).Save_zIndex            = S(id).zIndex
}
```

PLUG-IN 14

RestoreState()

This is the partner plug-in for `SaveState()`. It will restore an object's major style settings to the way they were when they were saved. Figure 3-14 shows that the div created in the previous plug-in has been modified; its colors are different and it has been moved to the right. An alert box has popped up to let you see this before the `RestoreState()` plug-in is called to restore the div to its original state.

About the Plug-in

This plug-in restores the style properties that have been saved using the `SaveState()` plug-in. It takes this argument:

- **`id`** The object whose style properties are to be restored

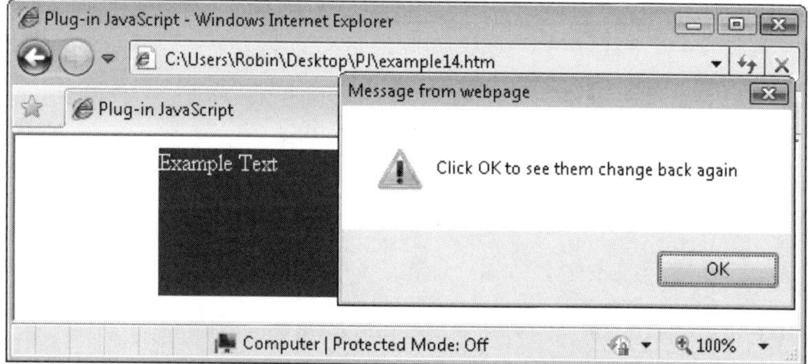

FIGURE 3-14 The SaveState() and RestoreState() plug-ins in action

Variables, Arrays, and Functions

`left`	The object's `style.left` property
`top`	The object's `style.top` property
`visibility`	The object's `style.visibility` property
`color`	The object's `style.color` property
`backgroundColor`	The object's `style.backgroundColor` property
`display`	The object's `style.display` property
`opacity`	The object's `style.opacity` property
`MozOpacity`	The object's `style.MozOpacity` property
`KhtmlOpacity`	The object's `style.KhtmlOpacity` property
`filter`	The object's `style.filter` property
`zIndex`	The object's `style.zIndex` property

How It Works

This plug-in reverses the action of the `SaveState()` plug-in by retrieving the values saved in the properties, beginning with the string 'Save_', and restoring them. If there are any additional properties you need to save and restore, they are very easy to add to these functions.

How To Use It

To use it, just pass this plug-in the ID of an object whose state has already been saved, like this:

```
RestoreState('myobject')
```

The following example extends the previous plug-in to both create a div and then change it twice, the first time by modifying a few of its style properties and the second to change it back by calling `RestoreState()`. In between, the JavaScript `alert()` function is called to give you a chance to view the screen before moving on:

```
<div id='mydiv'>Example Text</div>

<script>
window.onload = function()
{
   S('mydiv').width           = Px(200)
   S('mydiv').height          = Px(100)
   S('mydiv').backgroundColor = 'green'
   S('mydiv').color           = 'white'
   S('mydiv').position        = 'absolute'

   SaveState('mydiv')

   alert('Click OK to see some changes')
```

```
    S('mydiv').backgroundColor = 'blue'
    S('mydiv').color           = 'yellow'
    S('mydiv').left            = Px(100)

    alert('Click OK to see them change back again')

    RestoreState('mydiv')
}
</script>
```

If you enter this example into your browser, the div will start off as white text on green, then it will change to yellow on blue and move to the right, and finally it will return to its original colors and position, all with a single call to `RestoreState()`.

The Plug-in

```
function RestoreState(id)
{
    S(id).left            = O(id).Save_left
    S(id).top             = O(id).Save_top
    S(id).visibility      = O(id).Save_visibility
    S(id).color           = O(id).Save_color
    S(id).backgroundColor = O(id).Save_backgroundColor
    S(id).display         = O(id).Save_display
    S(id).opacity         = O(id).Save_opacity
    S(id).MozOpacity      = O(id).Save_MozOpacity
    S(id).KhtmlOpacity    = O(id).Save_KhtmlOpacity
    S(id).filter          = O(id).Save_filter
    S(id).zIndex          = O(id).Save_zIndex
}
```

PLUG-IN 15 InsVars()

In JavaScript, when you want to create a string of text that also includes the values of different variables, you have to keep closing the string, then use a + sign followed by the variable name, follow it with another +, and then re-open the string—and you have to do this for every single variable. However, this plug-in lets you easily drop the values of variables into any string. Figure 3-15 shows three values being inserted in this manner.

About the Plug-in

This plug-in requires at least two arguments. The first is the string in which to insert various values, and the second, third, and so on, are the values to be inserted, as follows:

- **`string`** The string in which to insert values
- **`value1`** A value to insert in `string`
- **`value2`** As `value1` (etc...)

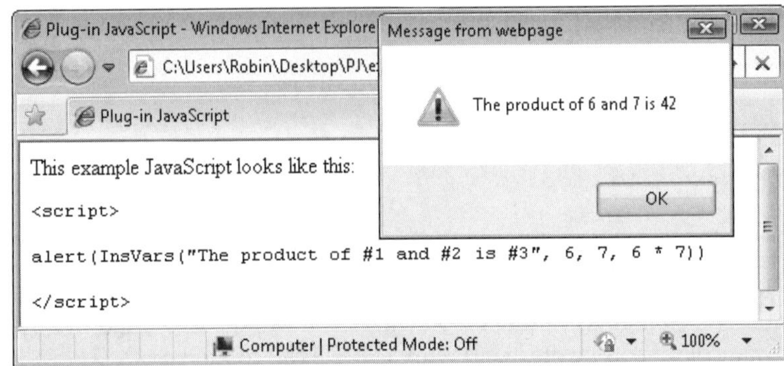

FIGURE 3-15 This plug-in makes it easy to insert values into strings.

Variables, Arrays, and Functions

`tmp`	Local variable containing the string to process
`arguments`	Array of arguments passed to the plug-in
`replace()`	JavaScript function to replace substrings in a string
`regExp()`	JavaScript function to create a regular expression

How It Works

This plug-in makes use of the handy fact that JavaScript passes an array to every function that is called. This array is called `arguments`, and each element of it is one of the values that has been passed to the function.

Therefore, the first element is extracted and placed in `tmp`, a local variable. This is the string in which to make the variable substitutions, like this:

```
var tmp = arguments[0]
```

Then a `for()` loop is used to iterate through each remaining element. If there is a substring with the value '#1' within the string `tmp`, the first value is inserted in its place. The same happens for '#2', '#3', and any number of similar substrings, with each being replaced by the next in line of the values passed to the plug-in, like this:

```
tmp = tmp.replace(new RegExp('#' + j, 'g'), arguments[j])
```

To allow one value to be inserted in many places in a string, a global replace is enabled by using the `RegExp()` object to create a new regular expression with the value 'g' supplied to indicate a global search and/or replace.

Finally, the modified `tmp` string is returned.

How To Use It

To insert values into a string using `InsVars()`, you call it up in the following manner:

```
string = InsVars('The product of #1 and #2 is #3', 6, 7, 6 * 7)
```

This statement will assign the value "The product of 6 and 7 is 42" to `string`. All you have to remember is to use the same number of '#?' tags as there are values to be inserted.

The Plug-in

```
function InsVars()
{
   var tmp = arguments[0]

   for (var j = 1 ; j < arguments.length ; ++j)
      tmp = tmp.replace(new RegExp('#' + j, 'g'), arguments[j])
   return tmp
}
```

PLUG-IN 16

StrRepeat()

Unlike many other languages, JavaScript doesn't come with a function to create a new string from a repeated substring. So here's a plug-in to do the job, as shown in Figure 3-16, in which a cheer is repeated three times.

About the Plug-in

This plug-in creates a repeated string based on a string and a number. It takes these arguments:

- **`str`** A string to repeat
- **`num`** The number of times to repeat the string

Variables, Arrays, and Functions

`tmp`	Local string variable used to store the string as it is assembled
`j`	Local integer variable used for looping

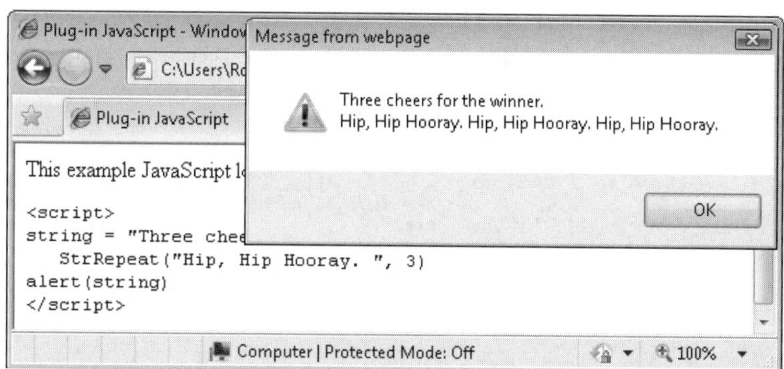

FIGURE 3-16 Using this plug-in to create a cheer.

How It Works

The plug-in uses a `for()` loop to assemble a final string created from `num` copies of `str`, and then returns the new string.

How To Use It

To use this function, pass it a string and a number, like this:

```
string = 'Three cheers for the winner. ' +
   StrRepeat('Hip, Hip Hooray', 3)
alert(string)
```

This code places the repeated cheer into `string` and then displays it using a call to the JavaScript `alert()` function.

The Plug-in

```
function StrRepeat(str, num)
{
   var tmp = ''

   for (var j = 0 ; j < num ; ++j)
      tmp += str

   return tmp
}
```

PLUG-IN 17

HexDec()

The final two plug-ins in this chapter are to do with handling hexadecimal numbers, something you have to do quite often in JavaScript, particularly when managing colors. This one converts a hexadecimal number into decimal, as shown by Figure 3-17.

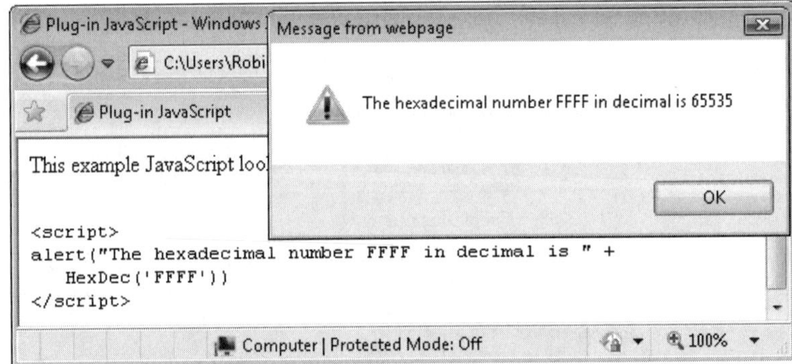

FIGURE 3-17 Converting a number from hexadecimal to decimal

About the Plug-in

This plug-in requires a hexadecimal string to be passed to it, and it then returns that number in decimal. It requires this argument:

- `n` A string containing a hexadecimal number

Variables, Arrays, and Functions

`parseInt()`	JavaScript function to convert a string to a number

How It Works

This plug-in uses the JavaScript function `parseInt()` to convert a hexadecimal string to a decimal number. It does this because the second parameter passed to it is 16. If the second number were 8, for example, it would try to convert from an octal number, and so on.

How To Use It

Pass the `HexDec()` function any string containing a hexadecimal number and it will return decimal number, like this:

```
alert('The hexadecimal number FFFF in decimal is ' +
   HexDec('FFFF'))
```

In this instance the hexadecimal number FFFF is converted to 65,535 in decimal, and the result is displayed using a call to the JavaScript `alert()` function.

The Plug-in

```
function HexDec(n)
{
   return(parseInt(n, 16))
}
```

PLUG-IN 18

DecHex()

This plug-in takes a decimal number and turns it into a hexadecimal string, as shown in Figure 3-18.

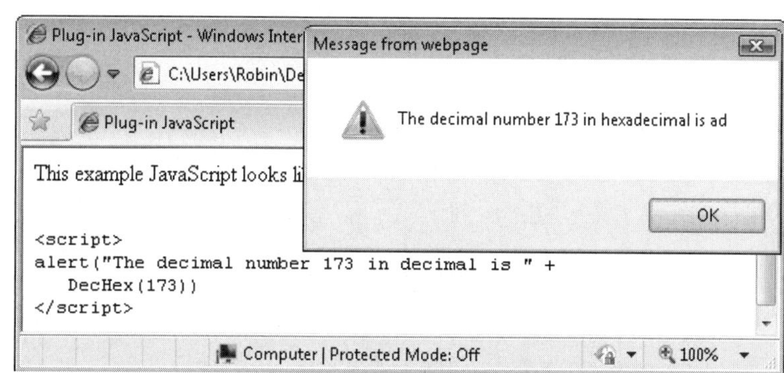

FIGURE 3-18 Converting a number from decimal to hexadecimal

About the Plug-in

This plug-in requires a decimal number to be passed to it, and it then returns that number in the form of a hexadecimal string. It requires this argument:

- **n** A decimal number to be converted into hexadecimal

Variables, Arrays, and Functions

to.String()	JavaScript function for converting a number to a string

How It Works

This plug-in uses two code segments combined into a single statement. The first segment looks like this:

```
n < 16 ? '0' : ''
```

This is known as a ternary expression, in which `n < 16` is an initial test. The `?` symbol then indicates that if the result of the test is true then the value immediately following the `?` should be returned. Otherwise the value following the `:` should be returned. In this example, that means that values of `n` that are lower than 16 will result in the string '0' being returned, while values of `n` that are 16 and above result in '' being returned.

The reason for this is that this plug-in will mostly be used by code that wants to create color triplets for setting a color. These triplets are made up of three groups of two hexadecimal characters, like these: FF0088, 112233, CCCCCC, and so on.

Each of these stands for hexadecimal FF (256 decimal) shades of the colors red green and blue. For example, FF0088 means the intensity values for the given color should be FF red, 00 green and 88 blue, in hexadecimal. Therefore, going back to the code segment, if `n` is less than 16 it becomes a single digit in hexadecimal (a number between 0 and F), and in such cases a leading 0 is added to pad the number up to the required two digits.

Having padded the number with a 0 (if necessary), the number `n` is then passed to the JavaScript `toString()` function with an argument of 16, like this code segment:

```
n.toString(16)
```

This tells it to convert the number to base 16, which is hexadecimal. The results of the two segments are then concatenated and returned. When you put both pieces of code together they look like this:

```
return (n < 16 ? '0' : '') + n.toString(16)
```

How To Use It

To convert a decimal number to hexadecimal, pass it to the `DecHex()` plug-in, like this:

```
alert('The decimal number 173 in hexadecimal is ' + DecHex(173))
```

The value displayed by this statement is 'ad', which is an acceptable hexadecimal number for JavaScript when used as part of a color, so there's usually no need to convert it to uppercase or add any prefix to it.

This now completes the fundamentals of your basic JavaScript toolkit and, of necessity, it's one of the longest chapters in the book. In the next chapter, we'll start adding plug-ins to provide location and positioning features, and then the fun will really start.

The Plug-in

```
function DecHex(n)
{
   return (n < 16 ? '0' : '') + n.toString(16)
}
```

CHAPTER 4

Location and Dimensions

The previous chapter concentrated on providing a basic subset of core functionality. This one does the same, but there are enough plug-ins in the collection now that we can also start to create some interesting effects, including resizing and repositioning objects.

PLUG-IN 19

ResizeWidth()

When creating dynamic web pages you will often need to change the dimensions of objects. You might do this to emphasize a section by enlarging it, you may allow the contents of a page to be rearranged by the user, or you might wish to open up elements such as forms or light boxes, and so forth.

With this plug-in, you can resize the width of any object that has a width property, such as the example div shown in Figure 4-1, which has had its width resized to 300 pixels.

About the Plug-in

This plug-in changes the width of an object. It requires the following arguments:

- **`id`** The ID of an object or the object itself. You can also pass an array of objects and/or object IDs.
- **`width`** The new width for the object. If `id` is an array, all the objects referred to are set to this width.

Variables, Arrays, and Functions

`j`	Local integer loop variable
`overflow`	The object's `style.overflow` property
`width`	The object's `style.width` property
`HID`	Global string variable with the value 'hidden'
`Px()`	Plug-in to add the suffix 'px'

How It Works

This plug-in also offers the multifunctionality of the `O()` and `S()` plug-ins, in which you can pass either the ID of an object or the object itself, and you can even pass an array of IDs and/or objects to change them all at the same time.

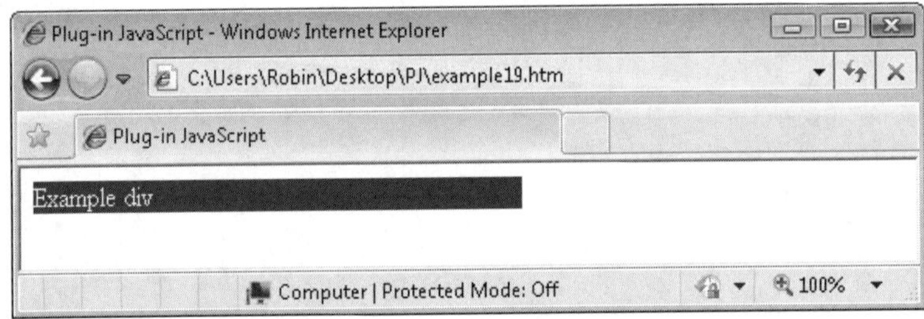

FIGURE 4-1 Resizing the width of an object

It achieves this by taking advantage of the fact that the `S()` plug-in is already set up to deal with an object ID, an object, or an array of objects and/or object IDs. Therefore, all that is necessary is to call `S()` twice; once to set the object's or array of objects' `style.overflow` properties to 'hidden', and then to set the `style.width` properties to the value in `width`.

The variable `HID` is a global variable created by the `Initialize()` plug-in, and it has the value 'hidden'. The `style.overflow` property of the object is set to this value to allow objects to be reduced as well as enlarged and, when reduced, text that would have overflowed is simply ignored.

How To Use It

To use this plug-in pass it an object and a width, like this:

```
ResizeWidth('mydiv', 200)
```

Or you can pass an array of objects, like this:

```
ids = Array('objone', 'objtwo', 'objthree')
ResizeWidth(ids, 480)
```

Here's an example you can try that resets the width of the div to 300 pixels. It also changes the text and background colors so that you can see the change:

```
<div id='example'>Example div</div>

<script>
window.onload = function()
{
   S('example').backgroundColor = 'blue'
   S('example').color           = 'yellow'
   ResizeWidth('example', 300)
}
</script>
```

The Plug-in

```
function ResizeWidth(id, width)
{
   S(id, 'overflow', HID)
   S(id, 'width',    Px(width))
}
```

ResizeHeight()

In the same way that you may need to resize the width of an object, here's a plug-in to resize its height. Figure 4-2 shows the div created in the previous plug-in now increased in height to 100 pixels.

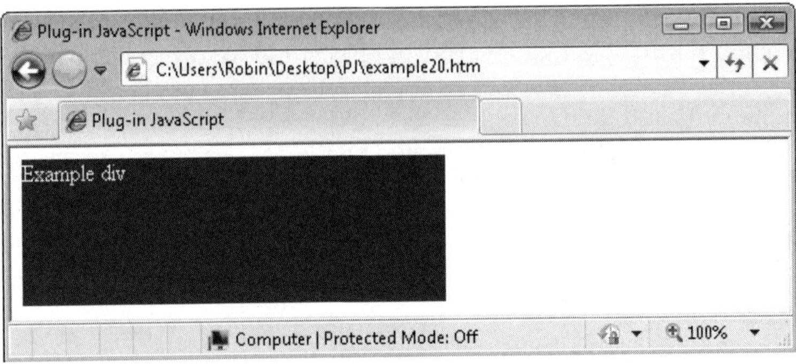

Figure 4-2 Resizing the height of an object

About the Plug-in

This plug-in changes the height of an object. It requires the following arguments:

- **`id`** The ID of an object or the object itself. You can also pass an array of objects and/or object IDs.
- **`height`** The new height for the object. If `id` is an array, all the objects referred to are set to this height.

Variables, Arrays, and Functions

`j`	Local integer loop variable
`overflow`	The object's `style.overflow` property
`height`	The object's `style.height` property
`HID`	Global string variable with the value 'hidden'
`Px()`	Plug-in to add the suffix 'px'

How It Works

This is the companion plug-in to `ResizeWidth()`, and it works in exactly the same manner as the previous one, with the only difference being that the object's `style.height` property is modified instead of `style.width`.

As with `ResizeWidth()`, you can pass either object IDs or objects, and you can also pass an array of IDs and/or objects. For further details on how this plug-in works, please refer to the `ResizeWidth()` plug-in.

How To Use It

To use this plug-in pass it an object and a height, like this:

```
ResizeHeight('mydiv', 100)
```

Or you can pass an array of objects, like this:

```
ids = Array('objone', 'objtwo', 'objthree')
ResizeHeight(ids, 240)
```

Here's an example you can try that modifies the example in the previous plug-in by resizing the div to 100 pixels in height:

```
<div id='example'>Example div</div>

<script>
window.onload = function()
{
   S('example').backgroundColor = 'blue'
   S('example').color           = 'yellow'
   ResizeWidth('example',  300)
   ResizeHeight('example', 100)
}
</script>
```

The Plug-in

```
function ResizeHeight(id, height)
{
   S(id, 'overflow', HID)
   S(id, 'height',   Px(height))
}
```

PLUG-IN 21 Resize()

This simple plug-in combines the previous two into a single function to save on typing and to make your code more compact. With it you can change both the width and height of an object or array of objects, as shown in Figure 4-3.

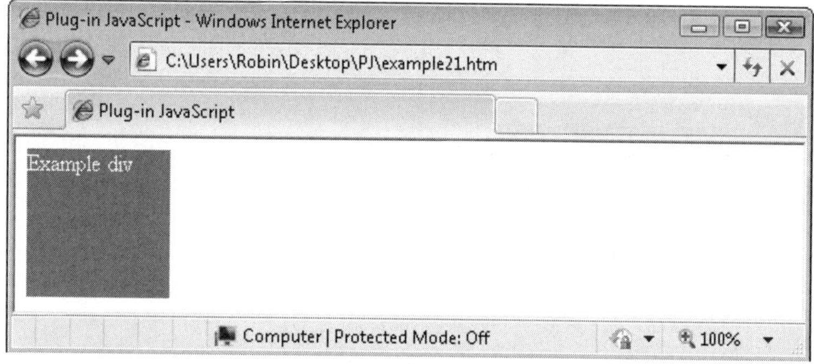

FIGURE 4-3 Resizing both the width and the height of an object

About the Plug-in

This plug-in changes the width and height of an object. It requires the following arguments:

- **`id`** The ID of an object or the object itself. You can also pass an array of objects and/or object IDs.
- **`width`** The new width for the object. If `id` is an array, all the objects referred to are set to this width.
- **`height`** The new height for the object. If `id` is an array, all the objects referred to are set to this height.

Variables, Arrays, and Functions

`ResizeWidth()`	Plug-in to change an object's width
`ResizeHeight()`	Plug-in to change an object's height

How It Works

This plug-in simply makes a call to `ResizeWidth()` followed by one to `ResizeHeight()`.

How To Use It

To use this plug-in, pass it an object along with a width and height, like this:

```
Resize('mydiv', 100, 100)
```

Or you can pass an array of objects, like this:

```
ids = Array('obj1', 'obj2', 'obj3')
Resize (ids, 128, 128)
```

Here's an example you can try that further improves the example in the previous plug-in to resize both the width and height of an object with only a single call:

```
<div id='example'>Example div</div>

<script>
window.onload = function()
{
   S('example').backgroundColor = 'red'
   S('example').color           = 'white'
   Resize('example', 100, 100)
}
</script>
```

The Plug-in

```
function Resize(id, width, height)
{
   ResizeWidth(id,  width)
   ResizeHeight(id, height)
}
```

Position()

This plug-in sets the CSS `style.position` property of an object. This is useful when you wish to control an object's offset from its parent's location, or even completely move it to any absolute position. Figure 4-4 shows a div that has been offset horizontally from its previous position by 100 pixels.

About the Plug-in

This plug in sets the CSS `style.position` property of an object. It requires the following arguments:

- **`id`** An object, an object ID, or an array of objects and/or object IDs
- **`type`** The type of `style.position` property to assign, out of 'absolute', 'fixed', 'relative', 'static' or 'inherit'. You can also use the shorter, global variables (created by the `Initialize()` plug-in) of `ABS`, `FIX`, `REL`, `STA and INH`.

Variables, Arrays, and Functions

`position`	The object's `style.position` property

How It Works

This function uses the capability of the `S()` function that accepts an object, an object ID, or even an array of objects and/or object IDs. Therefore, it simply passes the values in `id` and `type` directly to the `S()` plug-in.

How To Use It

To set an object's `style.position` property using this plug-in, make a call such as:

```
Position('myobject', ABS)
```

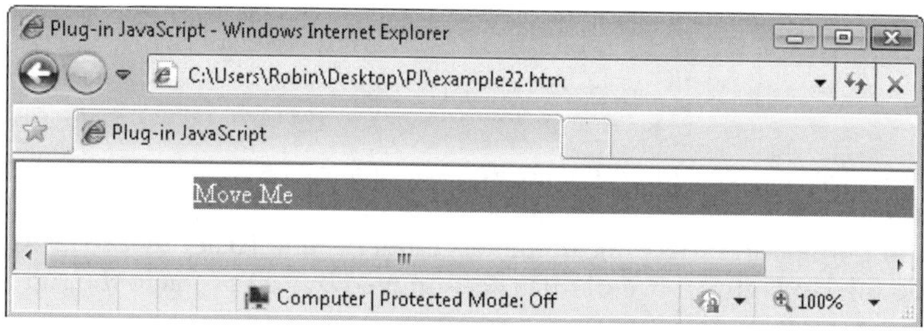

Figure 4-4 This plug-in enables objects to be moved.

For example, to change an object to have an 'absolute' position (using the shorter, global variable `ABS` created by the `Initialize()` plug-in) and then move it, you could use code such as the following:

```
<div id='moveme'>Move Me</div>

<script>
window.onload = function()
{
   S('moveme').backgroundColor = 'red'
   S('moveme').color           = 'white'
   Position('moveme', REL)
   S('moveme').left            = Px(100)
}
</script>
```

This example creates a div called 'moveme', which is then set to white text on a red background, and then the `Position()` plug-in is called to give it a 'relative' position. Finally, its `style.left` property is set to 100 using the `Px()` plug-in, which offsets it horizontally from its parent object by 100 pixels.

CAUTION *As well as the difference in location change between divs that use 'absolute' and 'relative' style positions, you also need to take into account the fact that a div with an 'absolute' style position is automatically shrunk to fit its contents, whereas one with a 'relative' style position will retain its previous width which, by default, extends to the right hand edge of its containing object. If you use a span instead, it will always shrink to fit its contents, regardless of where or how it is positioned.*

The Plug-in

```
function Position(id, type)
{
   S(id, 'position', type)
}
```

PLUG-IN 23

GoTo()

If an object has been set free from the page, for example by using the previous plug-in, `Position()`, then you can move it to another location by changing its `style.left` and `style.top` properties, and this plug-in makes it quicker and easier by providing a single function to do this. In Figure 4-5, a div has been moved by 200 pixels to the right and by 25 pixels down.

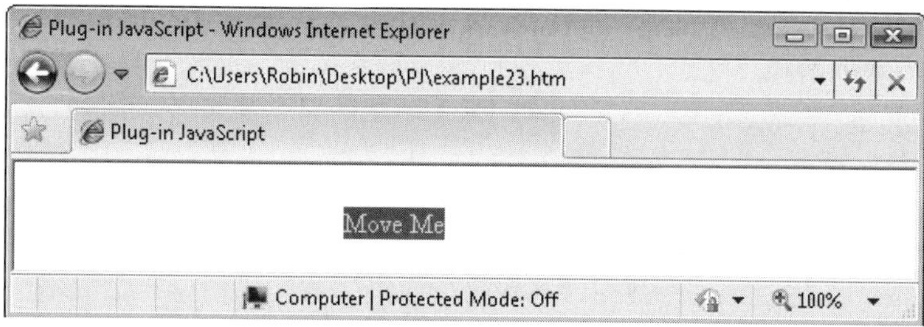

Figure 4-5 The GoTo() plug-in moves an object.

About the Plug-in

This plug-in moves an object (if it is movable) to a new location. It takes the following arguments:

- **`id`** An object, an object ID, or an array of objects and/or object IDs
- **`x`** The horizontal offset, from the left edge of the parent object, to which the object should be moved (or from the browser edge if the object has a `style.position` property of 'fixed' or 'absolute')
- **`y`** The vertical offset, from the top edge of the parent object, to which the object should be moved (or from the browser top if the object has a `style.position` property of 'fixed' or 'absolute')

Variables, Arrays, and Functions

`left`	The object's `style.left` property
`top`	The object's `style.top` property
`Px()`	Plug-in to add the suffix 'px'

How It Works

This plug-in also takes advantage of the `S()` plug-in's capability to manage arrays of objects and/or object IDs, single objects, or object IDs. It makes just two calls: one to set the object's `style.left` property to the value in `x` with the suffix 'px' appended, as is required by the rules of CSS, and the other to do the same but with the `style.top` property using the value in `y`.

How To Use It

To use this plug-in make sure that an object is movable by first issuing a command such as this (using the global variable `REL`, which contains the string 'relative'):

```
Position('advertdiv', REL)
```

The following example gives the div an 'absolute' position (using the global variable ABS) and then moves it:

```
<div id='moveme'>Move Me</div>

<script>
window.onload = function()
{
   S('moveme').backgroundColor = 'green'
   S('moveme').color           = 'cyan'
   Position('moveme', ABS)
   GoTo('moveme', 200, 25)
}
</script>
```

The Plug-in

```
function GoTo(id, x, y)
{
   S(id, 'left', Px(x))
   S(id, 'top',  Px(y))
}
```

PLUG-IN 24

Locate()

This plug-in combines the Position() and GoTo() plug-ins into a very handy single plug-in that is especially useful when first setting up objects on a web page. With it you can set an object's style.position property at the same time as its horizontal and vertical offsets. Figure 4-6 shows this plug-in moving an object with an 'absolute' position to the location 100,40.

About the Plug-in

This plug-in sets an object's style.position property as well as its horizontal and vertical offsets. It requires the following arguments:

- **id** An object, an object ID, or an array of objects and/or object IDs
- **type** The type of style.position property to assign, out of 'absolute', 'fixed', 'relative', 'static', or 'inherit' (or the global variables ABS, FIX, REL, STA and INH)

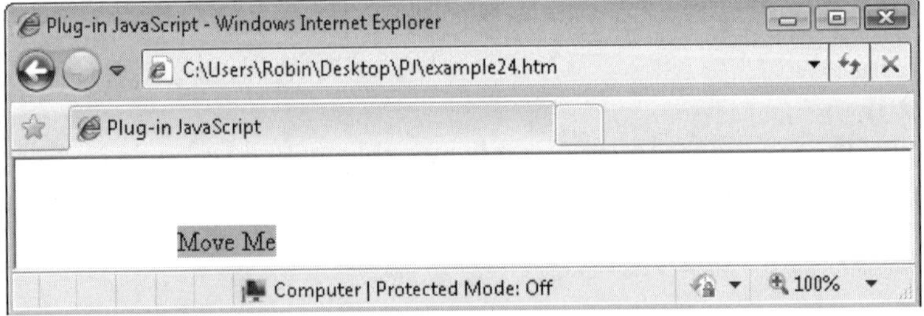

Figure 4-6 Setting an object's position and location at the same time

- **x** The horizontal offset, from the left edge of the parent object (or browser for 'fixed' objects), to which the object should be moved (or from the browser edge if the object has a `style.position` property of 'fixed' or 'absolute')
- **y** The vertical offset, from the top edge of the parent object (or browser for 'fixed' objects), to which the object should be moved (or from the browser top if the object has a `style.position` property of 'fixed' or 'absolute')

Variables, Arrays, and Functions

`Position()`	Plug-in to set an object's `style.position` property
`GoTo()`	Plug-in to move an object to a new location

How It Works

This plug-in draws on the functionality of the plug-ins `Position()` and `GoTo()`, which both allow an object, an object ID, or an array of objects and/or object IDs to be accessed. Therefore, it simply calls each in turn, passing the arguments `id`, `style`, `x`, and `y`, as necessary.

How To Use It

To set an object's `style.position` property and move it to its correct location using this plug-in, you might use code such as the following:

```
<div id='moveme'>Move Me</div>

<script>
window.onload = function()
{
   S('moveme').backgroundColor = 'orange'
   S('moveme').color           = 'black'
   Locate('moveme', ABS, 100, 40)
}
</script>
```

In the preceding you can see the `Locate()` plug-in provides a wide range of functionality with a single call.

NOTE *The absolute position property is always made relative to the first parent element that has a position other than static. A relative position is relative to its containing object, and a fixed property is relative to the browser borders.*

The Plug-in

```
function Locate(id, type, x, y)
{
   Position(id, type)
   GoTo(id, x, y)
}
```

GetWindowWidth()

There are many reasons to need to know the width of the browser window, the most obvious of which is so that you can determine which objects you can display where in a dynamically generated website. This plug-in gives you that exact information, as shown by the alert box in Figure 4-7. It also takes into account any scroll bars that might reduce the available width.

About the Plug-in

This function will tell you the width of the browser window to the nearest pixel. It doesn't require any arguments and returns the width as an integer.

Variables, Arrays, and Functions

`de`	Local object copy of `document.documentElement`
`BROWSER`	Global variable containing the browser name
`barwidth`	Local integer variable set if a vertical scroll bar exists
`scrollHeight`	The `de.scrollHeight` property
`clientHeight`	The `de.clientHeight` property
`innerWidth`	The `window.innerWidth` property
`clientWidth`	The `de.clientWidth` and `document.body.clientWidth` properties

How It Works

This plug-in first copies the `document.documentElement` object into `de` to provide a much shorter name, reducing the amount of code to enter. Next, if the browser is not Internet Explorer as determined by the value in the global variable `BROWSER`, then the local integer variable `barwidth` is set to a value of 17 if the value in `de.scrollHeight` is greater than that in `de.clientHeight`.

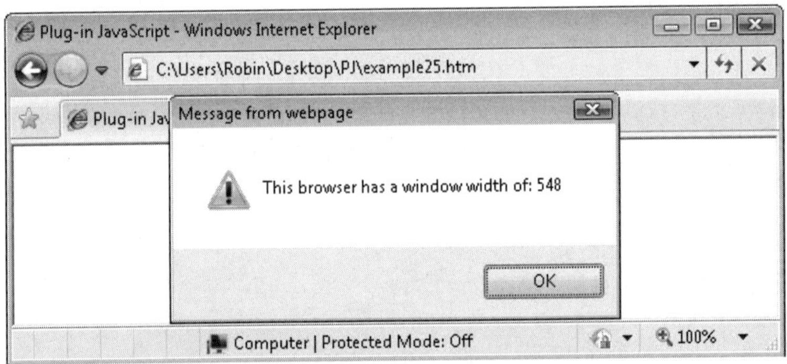

Figure 4-7 Determining the available width of the browser window

The `de.scrollHeight` value is bigger when there is more web page below the bottom that can be scrolled to. In that case, there will be a scroll bar, so `barwidth` is given the value of 17, which is the default width of scrollbars in all browsers. This value is then subtracted from the full window width and the result is returned.

Otherwise, as is often the case if the browser is Internet Explorer, the code simply returns the value of whichever has a value, either `de.clientWidth` or `document.body.clientWidth` (allowing for either strict or quirks mode). This value already takes into account any scroll bar, so no further code is required.

How To Use It

To use this plug-in, simply call it and use the value returned, as in the following example, which passes the returned value to an `alert()` statement, where it is displayed:

```
<script>
window.onload = function()
{
   alert('This browser has a window width of: ' + GetWindowWidth())
}
</script>
```

The Plug-in

```
function GetWindowWidth()
{
   var de = document.documentElement

   if (BROWSER != 'IE')
   {
      var barwidth = de.scrollHeight > de.clientHeight ? 17 : 0
      return window.innerWidth - barwidth
   }

   return de.clientWidth || document.body.clientWidth
}
```

PLUG-IN 26 GetWindowHeight()

This is the companion plug-in to `GetWindowWidth()`. It returns the height of the browser window, bearing in mind any scroll bars. In Figure 4-8 the height of the usable area of this browser has been determined by this plug-in to be 124 pixels.

About the Plug-in

This plug-in takes no arguments and returns the available height of the current window, taking any scroll bars into account.

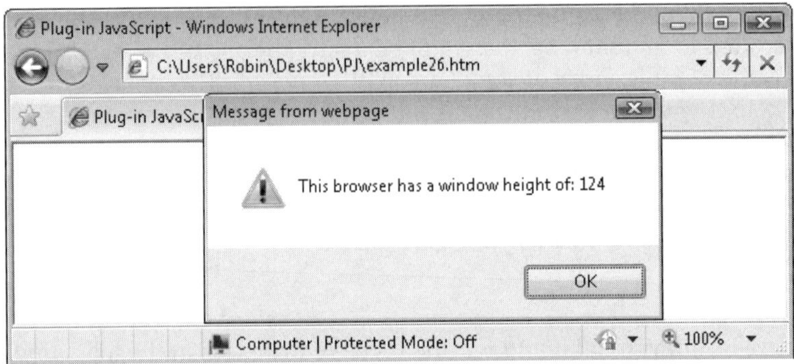

FIGURE 4-8 Determining the usable height of the current browser window

Variables, Arrays, and Functions

`de`	Local object copy of `document.documentElement`
`BROWSER`	Global variable containing the browser name
`barwidth`	Local integer variable set if a vertical scrollbar exists
`scrollWidth`	The `de.scrollWidth` property
`clientWidth`	The `de.clientWidth` property
`innerHeight`	The `window.innerHeight` property
`clientHeight`	The `de.clientHeight` and `document.body.clientHeight` properties

How It Works

This plug-in works in almost the same way as `GetWindowWidth()` except that it returns the available height in the current browser window, taking any scroll bars into account. Please refer to `GetWindowWidth()` for further details.

How To Use It

To use this plug-in, simply call it and use the value returned as in the following example, which passes the returned value to an `alert()` statement where it is displayed:

```
<script>
window.onload = function()
{
   alert('This browser has a window height of: ' + GetWindowHeight())
}
</script>
```

The following plug-in is a good example of how this and the previous plug-in, `GetWindowWidth()`, come in very handy.

The Plug-in

```
function GetWindowHeight()
{
   var de = document.documentElement

   if (BROWSER != 'IE')
   {
      var barwidth = de.scrollWidth > de.clientWidth ? 17 : 0
      return window.innerHeight - barwidth
   }

   return de.clientHeight || document.body.clientHeight
}
```

PLUG-IN 27 GoToEdge()

These plug-ins are starting to come together in such a way that it's now easy to build a plug-in that will move one or more objects to one of the edges of the browser, which is what this one does: it allows you to move objects to the top, left, right, or bottom edges of the browser, as shown in Figure 4-9.

About the Plug-in

This plug-in locates one or more objects at one of the four edges of the browser window. It requires the following arguments:

- **id** An object, an object ID, or an array of objects or object IDs
- **where** The edge to which the object or objects should be moved, out of 'top', 'bottom', 'left', or 'right'
- **percent** The distance from the left or top of the browser depending on the value in where

FIGURE 4-9 Attaching GIF images to different edges of the browser

Variables, Arrays, and Functions

`j`	Local integer for indexing into `id` if its an array
`width`	Local variable containing the width of the browser, less that of `id`
`height`	Local variable containing the height of the browser, less that of `id`
`amount`	Local variable containing `percent` as a percent
`TP`, `BM`, `LT` and `RT`	Global variables with the values 'top', 'bottom', 'left', and 'right'
`GetWindowWidth()`	Plug-in to return the browser width
`GetWindowHeight()`	Plug-in to return the browser height
`W()`	Plug-in to return the width of an object
`H()`	Plug-in to return the height of an object
`GoTo()`	Plug-in to move an object to a new location

How It Works

Like many others, this plug-in supports the passing of an object, an object ID, or an array of objects and/or object IDs. This is managed by the initial `if()` section, which determines whether `id` is an array using the `instanceof` operator. If it is, then each element of the array is recursively passed to the same function, along with the values of `where` and `percent`. Once all have been processed, the function then returns.

After this the three local variables `width`, `height`, and `amount` are assigned values representing the amount of width and height remaining in the browser window (after the width and height of the object are taken into account). This is done by fetching the width and height of the browser window using the `GetWindowWidth()` and `GetWindowHeight()` plug-ins and then subtracting the object's width from one and its height from the other, as determined by calls to `W()` and `H()`.

The variable `amount` is set to `percent /100` so that it can be used as a multiplier. For example, if `percent` has a value of 40, then dividing it by 100 assigns it the value of 0.40, which can then be multiplied by any number to reduce it to 40 percent of its original value. In this case, the multiplier determines how far along an edge the object should appear.

Next, a `switch()` statement tests for the four allowed argument values for `where`, which are 'top', 'bottom', 'left', or 'right'. The shorthand global variable equivalents of `TP`, `BM`, `LT`, and `RT` are used in place of these values to make the code shorter and clearer. A `break` command ends each subsection of the `switch()` statement except for the final one, where it is not required because program flow will continue on the next line down anyway.

Depending on which of the four values has been passed in `where`, the local variables `x` and `y` are set to align the object in `id` right up against the edge specified. The object is also displayed at a position between 0 and 100 percent along (or down), according to the value in `percent`. Finally, a call to `GoTo()` is made to move the object to the new location.

There are many uses for this plug-in; one in particular is a dock bar, similar to the one used at the bottom of the screen on the Apple OS X operating system, with a row or column of expanding and collapsing icons. Plug-in 66, `DockBar()` provides exactly this functionality, for any web page.

How To Use It

To use this plug-in, pass an object to it along with details on where to display it, as in the following example, which displays four different icons, one per edge:

```
<img id='i1' src='i1.gif' />
<img id='i2' src='i2.gif' />
<img id='i3' src='i3.gif' />
<img id='i4' src='i4.gif' />

<script>
window.onload = function()
{
   ids = Array('i1', 'i2', 'i3', 'i4')
   Position(ids, FIX)
   GoToEdge('i1', TP, 50)
   GoToEdge('i2', BM, 10)
   GoToEdge('i3', LT, 33)
   GoToEdge('i4', RT, 66)
}
</script>
```

In the first section of HTML, four GIF images are loaded in, with each given a different ID. Then, in the `<script>` section the array `ids` is populated with these IDs so that the following `Position()` command can set all of them to have a `style.position` of 'fixed'. This means they will stay where they are put, even if the browser page scrolls.

Finally, each image is attached to a different edge using four different calls to `GoToEdge()`. The top one is 50 percent in, the bottom 10 percent in, the left 33 percent down, and the right 66 percent down.

NOTE *As with all of this book's examples, you can download this plug-in and all associated content (such as the images used) from the companion website at* pluginjavascript.com.

The Plug-in

```
function GoToEdge(id, where, percent)
{
   if (id instanceof Array)
   {
      for (var j = 0 ; j < id.length ; ++j)
         GoToEdge(id[j], where, percent)
      return
   }

   var width  = GetWindowWidth()  - W(id)
   var height = GetWindowHeight() - H(id)
   var amount = percent / 100

   switch(where)
   {
      case TP: var x = width * amount
```

```
                var y = 0
                break
        case BM: var x = width * amount
                var y = height
                break
        case LT: var x = 0
                var y = height * amount
                break
        case RT: var x = width
                var y = height * amount
    }

    GoTo(id, x, y)
}
```

PLUG-IN 28 CenterX()

Another very useful function is to center an object, which is what this plug-in does. By using the browser width and object width it moves an object horizontally to exactly the center of the browser. Figure 4-10 shows a div that has been centered horizontally using this plug-in.

About the Plug-in

This plug-in centers an object (or objects) on a horizontal axis. It requires the following argument:

- `id` An object, an object ID, or an array of objects or object IDs

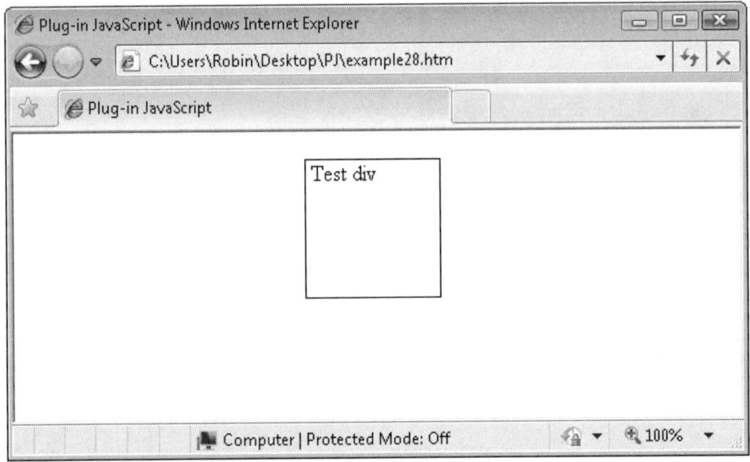

Figure 4-10 Centering a div horizontally

Variables, Arrays, and Functions

j	Local integer variable for indexing into id if it is an array
left	The style.left property of object
SCROLL_X	Global variable containing the number of pixels by which the browser has scrolled horizontally
GetWindowWidth()	The available width of the browser window, taking into account any scroll bars
W()	Plug-in to fetch an object's width
Px()	Plug-in to append the suffix 'px'

How It Works

This plug-in allows arrays of objects and/or object IDs, as well as single objects or object IDs. It does this by using the instanceof operator to tell whether id is an array and, if it is, it iterates through the array using the local variable j as an index, recursively calling itself with the single element values. Upon completion, the if() section of code returns.

In the second part of the plug-in, the S() plug-in sets the object's style.left property to the correct value (using a call to Px() to add the 'px' suffix) to center the object horizontally.

The correct value is determined by looking up the width of the window (less 17 if there's a scroll bar), minus the width of id. This value is then divided by 2. For example, if the window is 600 pixels wide and the object is 100 (and there is no scroll bar), the value is determined by subtracting 100 from 600, which equals 500; and this number is divided by 2 to get a final result of 250. Therefore, an offset of 250 pixels from the left will exactly center an object of 100 pixels width in a 600-pixel wide browser. If there is a scroll bar, the values become 583 – 100 / 2, which equals 241.5. The Math.round() call deals with a fractional result, which in this case is rounded up to 242.

If the browser has not scrolled, this is all the calculation that is needed. However, because the horizontal offset is from the left edge of the document (not the window), if there has been a horizontal scroll the object will be displayed left of center by the amount of the scrolling. Therefore, the global variable SCROLL_X is added to the calculated value in order to place the object exactly between the left and right hand edges of the window.

How To Use It

To center an object, as long as it is capable of being moved, just call CenterX() in the following manner, which creates a simple div and then centers it:

```
<div id='test'> Test div</div>

<script>
window.onload = function()
{
   Locate('test', ABS, 20, 20)
   Resize('test', 100, 100)
   S('test').border = 'solid ' + Px(1)
   CenterX('test')
}
</script>
```

The ` ` entity is there to separate the text from the border, which it otherwise runs into. The `Locate()` call sets the 'test' div to an 'absolute' position using the global variable `ABS` for shorthand. It also locates the div at the position 20,20. The `Resize()` call then turns the div into a 100 by 100-pixel square. Then, in this example, rather than using colors to make the div easy to see, the div has been given a solid border with a call to `S()`.

Finally, a call is made to `CenterX()` and the div is centered horizontally.

The Plug-in

```
function CenterX(id)
{
   if (id instanceof Array)
   {
      for (var j = 0 ; j < id.length ; ++j)
         CenterX(id[j])
      return
   }

   S(id).left = Px(Math.round((GetWindowWidth() - W(id))) / 2 + SCROLL_X)
}
```

PLUG-IN 29 CenterY()

This is the partner plug-in to `CenterX()`, which enables you to center an object vertically. Figure 4-11 shows a div that has been centered using this plug-in.

About the Plug-in

This plug-in centers an object (or objects) on a vertical axis. It requires the following argument:

- **`id`** An object, an object ID, or an array of objects or object IDs

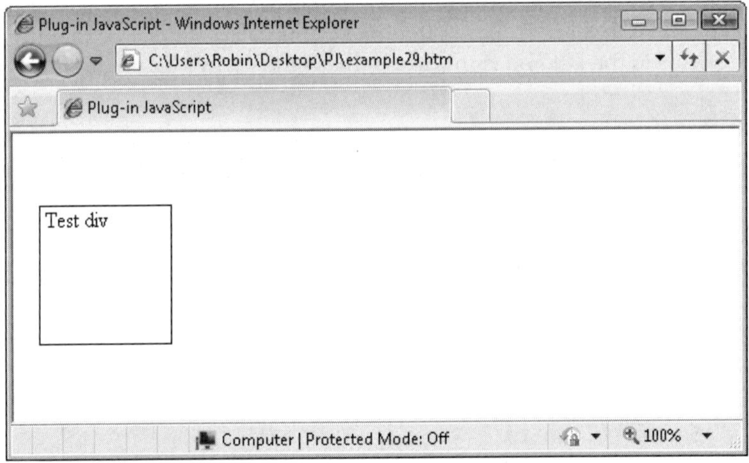

FIGURE 4-11 Centering a div vertically

Variables, Arrays, and Functions

j	Local integer variable for indexing into id if it is an array
top	The style.top property of object
SCROLL_Y	Global variable containing the number of pixels by which the browser has scrolled vertically
GetWindowHeight()	The available height of the browser window, taking into account any scroll bars
H()	Plug-in to fetch an object's height
Px()	Plug-in to append the suffix 'px'

How It Works

This plug-in is almost identical to CenterX(), except that an object is centered along its vertical axis. See the section on CenterX() for more details.

How To Use It

To center an object vertically using this plug-in, you might use code such as the following:

```
<div id='test'> Test div</div>

<script>
window.onload = function()
{
   Locate('test', ABS, 20, 20)
   Resize('test', 100, 100)
   S('test').border = 'solid ' + Px(1)
   CenterY('test')
}
</script>
```

This example creates a div in the HTML section and then, in the <script> section, it sets the object's style.position property to 'absolute' using the Locate() command and the global variable ABS. It also moves the object to location 20,20.

The div is then resized using Resize() to a width and height of 100. After that it is given a single-pixel border to make it stand out and then, on the final line, the CenterY() plug-in is called to center it vertically.

The Plug-in

```
function CenterY(id)
{
   if (id instanceof Array)
   {
      for (var j = 0 ; j < id.length ; ++j)
         CenterY(id[j])
      return
   }

   S(id).top = Px(Math.round((GetWindowHeight() - H(id))) / 2 + SCROLL_Y)
}
```

Center()

More often than not, when you center an object you usually want to do so in both horizontal and vertical directions, so this plug-in brings both the previous ones together into a single function, as shown in Figure 4-12.

About the Plug-in

This plug-in centers an object (or objects) on both its vertical and horizontal axes. It requires the following argument:

- `id` An object, an object ID, or an array of objects or object IDs

Variables, Arrays, and Functions

`CenterX()`	Plug-in to center an object horizontally
`CenterY()`	Plug-in to center an object vertically

How It Works

Since both the `CenterX()` and `CenterY()` plug-ins have been written to take arguments that can be an array of objects and/or object IDs, an object, or an object ID, there is little work for this plug-in to do, so it simply calls each one in turn, passing `id` (whether or not it's an array) to each.

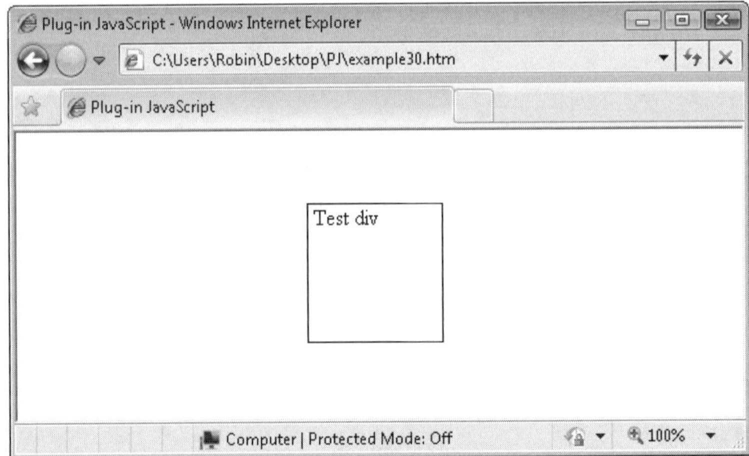

FIGURE 4-12 Centering a div both horizontally and vertically

How To Use It

To fully center an object in both the horizontal and vertical directions you could use code such as the following:

```
<div id='test'>Test div</div>

<script>
window.onload = function()
{
   Locate('test', ABS, 20, 20)
   Resize('test', 100, 100)
   S('test').border = 'solid ' + Px(1)
   Center('test')
}
</script>
```

This example is very similar to the previous two, except that it calls the `Center()` plug-in at the end to fully center the div.

That covers this chapter's plug-ins, and we're about to start really cooking, because in the following chapter we'll begin making objects invisible, and then make them reappear, smoothly fade them in and out, and even more. Along the way I'll show you how to put these effects to good use.

The Plug-in

```
function Center(id)
{
   CenterX(id)
   CenterY(id)
}
```

CHAPTER 5

Visibility

Many of the most impressive effects you'll see on websites are also the simplest. For example, a smooth fade from one image to another is often far more beautiful than other wipe or dissolve transformations. Likewise, instantly revealing or hiding an object, when done well, is clean and easy on the eye.

This chapter focuses on these types of effects, ranging from setting the visibility (or invisibility) of an object to fading objects in and out, fading between objects, and so on. The plug-ins in this chapter also provide the basic functionality required by many later plug-ins—most particularly the menu and navigation plug-ins in Chapter 8.

PLUG-IN 31 Invisible()

To ease into this chapter, we'll begin with a few short and sweet plug-ins that every JavaScript programmer needs in their toolkit. The first one is `Invisible()`, which makes an object disappear from a web page while the space it occupies remains, as opposed to hiding an object, which collapses and causes elements around it to assume its space (see Plug-in 40, `Hide()` for that effect).

Figure 5-1 shows a span with the text "Now you see me…" followed by some plain text not in a div that reads "and soon you won't". An alert window has been raised to let you see these elements before the call to `Invisible()` is made. Figure 5-2 shows what happens after clicking the alert: the shaded text in the span is invisible, but the other text snippet remains in place, demonstrating that the span is still there, just not visible.

About the Plug-in

This plug-in makes an object invisible while retaining the object's position and dimensions. It requires the following argument:

- `id` An object, an object ID, or an array of objects and/or object IDs

Variables, Arrays, and Functions

`visibility`	The `style.visibility` property of the object(s)
`HID`	Global variable with the value 'hidden'

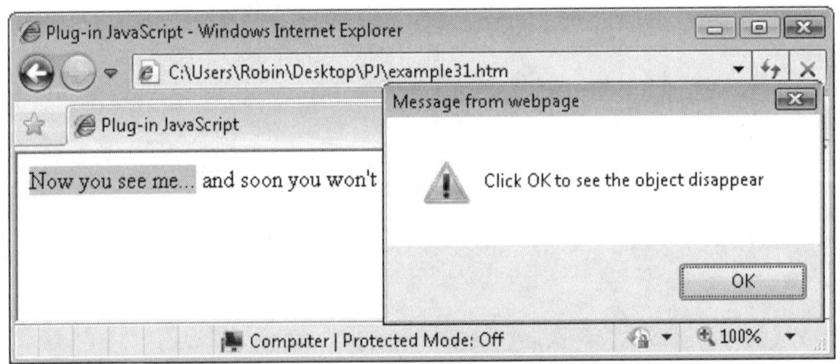

FIGURE 5-1 The shaded area is a span set to disappear when the alert is clicked.

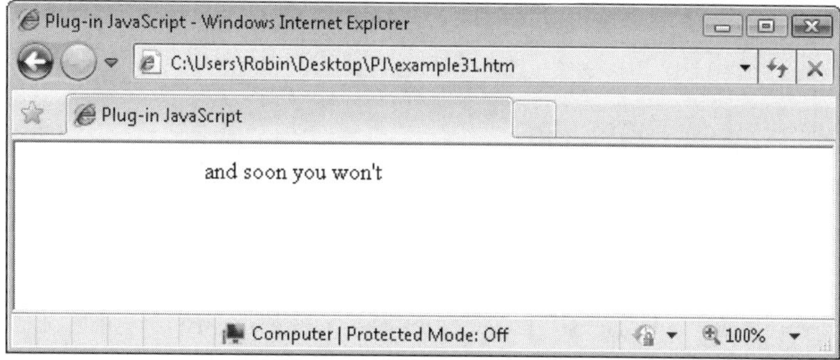

Figure 5-2 After clicking the alert the shaded span becomes invisible.

How It Works

This plug-in makes a call to the `S()` plug-in in such a way that you can pass it an array of objects and/or object IDs, a single object, or an object ID. The `style.visibility` property of the object (or objects) is then set to the value in the global variable `HID`, which is 'hidden'.

How To Use It

To use this plug-in, pass it the object or objects to make invisible. The following example shows one way you might incorporate it:

```
<span id='ghost'>Now you see me...</span> and soon you won't

<script>
window.onload = function()
{
   S('ghost').backgroundColor = 'lightblue'
   Resize('ghost', 128, 32)
   alert('Click OK to see the object disappear')
   Invisible('ghost')
}
</script>
```

This example first creates a span in the HTML section and gives it some text. Following this is more text that isn't included within the span. Then, in the `<script>` section, the span's background color is set to light blue and resized to make it stand out.

Next, an alert is raised to give you the chance to see the initial display before the call to the `Invisible()` plug-in is made. After clicking the alert OK button, the call is made, and the contents of the span becomes invisible.

TIP *When you want to keep your layout unchanged when hiding an object, you should use this plug-in in preference to Plug-in 40,* `Hide()`*. Plug-in 31 preserves an object's dimensions, while Plug-in 40 fully collapses an object, causing elements surrounding it to move in and occupy newly vacant space.*

The Plug-in

```
function Invisible(id)
{
   S(id, 'visibility', HID)
}
```

PLUG-IN 32 Visible()

This is the partner plug-in to `Invisible()`. It makes a previously invisible object visible. Figure 5-3 expands the example in the previous plug-in. Now, when the alert message's OK button is clicked, the invisible text will reappear and the browser will look like Figure 5-1 again (but without the alert window).

About the Plug-in

This plug-in makes an object visible after it has been made invisible. It requires the following argument:

- **`id`** An object, an object ID, or an array of objects and/or object IDs

Variables, Arrays, and Functions

`visibility`	The `style.visibility` property of the object(s)
`VIS`	Global variable with the value 'visible'

How It Works

This plug-in makes a call to the `S()` plug-in in such a way that you can pass it an array of objects and/or object IDs, a single object, or an object ID. Then the `style.visibility` property of the object (or objects) is set to the value in the global variable `VIS`, which is 'visible'.

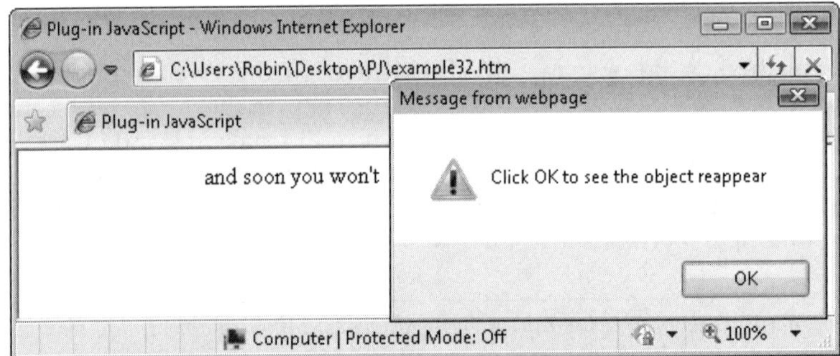

FIGURE 5-3 After clicking OK the hidden text reappears.

How To Use It

To make invisible objects reappear, just pass them to this plug-in. The following example extends the previous plug-in example to make the hidden span reappear:

```
<span id='ghost'>Now you see me...</span> and soon you won't

<script>
window.onload = function()
{
   S('ghost').backgroundColor = 'lightblue'
   Resize('ghost', 128, 32)
   alert('Click OK to see the object disappear')
   Invisible('ghost')
   alert('Click OK to see the object reappear')
   Visible('ghost')
}
</script>
```

Just the final two lines of code in this example are new: an alert, so that you can verify that the span was made invisible, and a call to `Visible()` that is executed after clicking OK, which makes the object reappear.

The Plug-in

```
function Visible(id)
{
   S(id, 'visibility', VIS)
}
```

PLUG-IN 33

VisibilityToggle()

This plug-in inverses the visibility of an object. If it is visible it becomes invisible, or if it is invisible it becomes visible. In Figure 5-4, each time the button is clicked, the text to the right toggles between being visible and invisible.

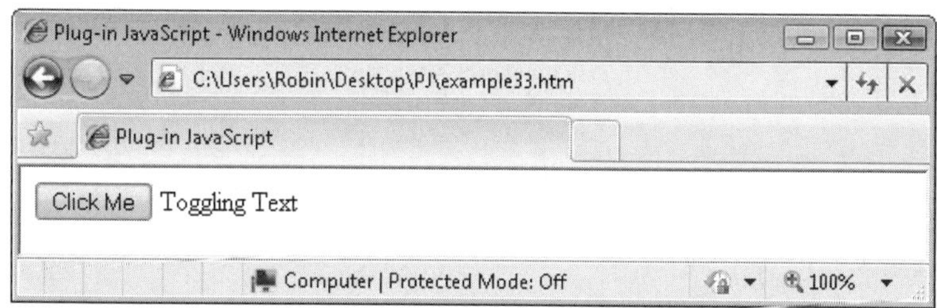

FIGURE 5-4 Attaching a plug-in to a button's click event

About the Plug-in

Each time this plug-in is called, the object or objects passed to it change their visibility to the opposite state. It requires the following argument:

- **id** An object, an object ID, or an array of objects and/or object IDs

Variables, Arrays, and Functions

`j`	Local integer for indexing into `id` if it is an array
`visibility`	The object's `style.visibility` property
`HID`	Global variable with the value 'hidden'
`VIS`	Global variable with the value 'visible'

How It Works

This plug-in uses the recursive trick that many others employ to handle arrays of objects and/or object IDs, as well as single objects and object IDs. It does this using the `instanceof` operator to test whether `id` is an array. If it is, the array is iterated through using the local variable `j` in a `for()` loop, individually calling the function itself recursively for each element of the array. Once it's done, the function returns.

If `id` is not an array, the `S()` plug-in is called, along with the inverse value of the object's `style.visibility` property. This is achieved using the following ternary expression, along with the two global variables `HID` and `VIS`, which stand for the strings 'hidden' and 'visible':

```
S(id).visibility = (S(id).visibility == HID) ? VIS : HID
```

In plain English, this statement equates to "If the current value of the object's `style.visibility` property is 'hidden', then return the value 'visible'; otherwise return the value 'hidden'." Everything after the first equals sign and before the question mark is the test. The value immediately following it is the one to return if the test result is `true`, and the final value is to be returned if the test result is `false`.

All this has the effect of applying the opposite state of the visibility property to the object.

How To Use It

You can call this plug-in directly from within JavaScript, like this:

```
VisibilityToggle('myobject')
```

Or you can pass an array of objects, like this:

```
ids = Array('firstobj', 'secondobj', 'thirdobj')
VisibilityToggle(ids)
```

Alternatively, you can incorporate the call within an HTML statement, as in the following two lines of HTML that cause the text in the span called 'toggle' to switch between being invisible or invisible each time the button is clicked (you could equally attach it to an `onmouseover` or other event too):

```
<input type='submit' value='Click Me'
   onclick="VisibilityToggle('toggle')" />
<span id='toggle'>Toggling Text</span>
```

You will see this plug-in used in a number of the other plug-ins, in various ways.

NOTE *Calling this plug-in from HTML illustrates the main reason why nearly all these plug-ins allow you to pass either an object or an object ID. In the preceding example, the object ID of 'toggle' is passed to the plug-in, but the object* `this` *(which is an object, not the ID of an object) can also be passed, thus telling the plug-in that the HTML object in which the call is embedded is the one to manipulate. This is how rollover and other similar effects are achieved—you'll see more on this in the next plug-in, and in Chapter 8, "Menus and Navigation."*

The Plug-in

```
function VisibilityToggle(id)
{
   if (id instanceof Array)
   {
      for (var j = 0 ; j < id.length ; ++j)
         VisibilityToggle(id[j])
      return
   }

   S(id).visibility = S(id).visibility == HID ? VIS : HID
}
```

PLUG-IN 34

Opacity()

Being able to switch an object from visible to invisible is great, but sometimes you need finer control over an object's visibility. This is referred to in JavaScript by the inverse term: its *opacity*. With this plug-in, you can set the opacity of any object to a value between 0 percent (totally transparent, or invisible) and 100 percent (fully opaque, nothing behind shows through).

Figure 5-5 shows three buttons displayed using the default opacity of 100 percent. In Figure 5-6 each button has been clicked to change its value to 25 percent, 50 percent, or 75 percent, respectively.

About the Plug-in

This plug-in applies the opacity setting supplied to the object or objects it is passed. It requires the following arguments:

- **`id`** An object, an object ID, or an array of objects and/or object IDs
- **`percent`** The amount of opacity to apply to the object or objects, from 0 percent, which is fully transparent, to 100 percent, which is fully opaque.

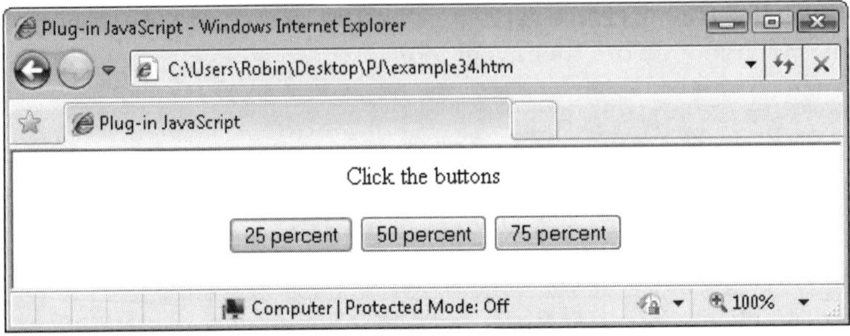

FIGURE 5-5 Three button objects at the default opacity of 100 percent

Variables, Arrays, and Functions

`opacity`	The `style.opacity` property as used by most browsers
`MozOpacity`	The version of the `opacity` property used by Mozilla-based browsers such as Firefox
`KhtmlOpacity`	The version of the `opacity` property used on older versions of the Apple Safari browser
`filter`	Used to implement Microsoft's version of the `opacity` property (and many other properties too)

How It Works

This plug-in makes four different calls in turn because various browsers approach the subject of opacity in different ways. Fortunately, none of the methods clash with each other, so a lot of `if...then...else` code is not necessary.

The first line for most browsers (such as Opera, Google Chrome, and recent versions of Apple Safari) looks like this:

```
S(id, 'opacity', percent / 100)
```

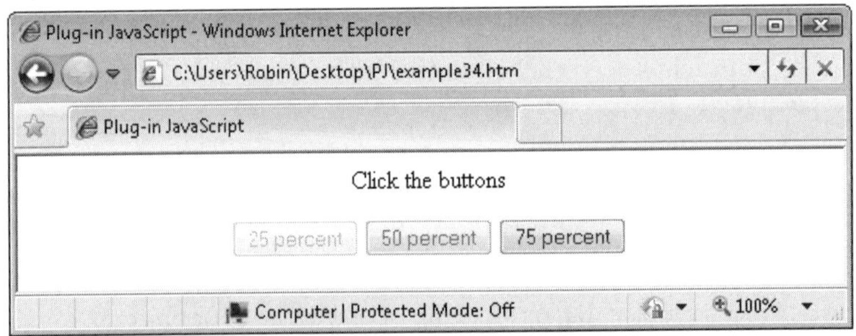

FIGURE 5-6 After being clicked, the buttons are at 25 percent, 50 percent, and 75 percent opacity.

This simply takes the value in `percent`, divides it by 100, and applies it to the `style.opacity` property of `id`. Of course, if `id` is an array, all its elements will have that property updated.

However, Mozilla-based browsers such as Firefox have their own property for this function, so the following line of code performs the equivalent for them by changing the `style.MozOpacity` property. Likewise, the third line is for Safari browsers that use the old rendering engine (before Webkit was introduced) and therefore require the `style.KhtmlOpacity` property be changed.

Finally, Microsoft chose a more complicated approach and includes opacity as part of their nonstandard filters and transitions group of features. The object's filter property is set in the following manner (for a setting of 25 percent, for example):

```
S(id).filter = 'alpha(opacity = 25)'
```

However, because you need to take into account the fact that `id` could be an array, the following version of the call is made, with both the property and setting values also passed to the `S()` plug-in:

```
S(id, 'filter', 'alpha(opacity = 25)')
```

Also, rather than a numeric value, a string has to be assigned to the `filter` property, which requires construction. So, in order to place the value in `percent` into the string, the following code is used (employing the `InsVars()` plug-in from Chapter 3):

```
S(id, 'filter', InsVars("alpha(opacity = '#1')", percent))
```

How To Use It

To change an object's opacity, just pass it along with the object or its ID (or an array of objects and/or object IDs). You can use a JavaScript command like this:

```
Opacity('fadeddiv', 64)
```

Or, you can embed the call within HTML, as in the following example, which creates three clickable buttons:

```
<center>Click the buttons<p>
<input type='submit' value='25 percent' onclick='Opacity(this, 25)' />
<input type='submit' value='50 percent' onclick='Opacity(this, 50)' />
<input type='submit' value='75 percent' onclick='Opacity(this, 75)' />
```

When clicked, the different buttons will change their opacity by the assigned amount (25 percent, 50 percent, or 75 percent, respectively). Notice that none of these HTML elements have been assigned IDs because the keyword `this` has been passed to the `Opacity()` plug-in, thus taking advantage of the fact that this plug-in (like most of them) will accept either an object ID or an object. The `this` keyword directly passes the calling object to the function, which is why no ID name is required.

The Plug-in

```
function Opacity(id, percent)
{
   S(id, 'opacity',       percent / 100)
   S(id, 'MozOpacity',    percent / 100)
   S(id, 'KhtmlOpacity', percent / 100)
   S(id, 'filter',        InsVars("alpha(opacity = '#1')", percent))
}
```

PLUG-IN 35

Fade()

This plug-in makes great use of the previous one, `Opacity()`, by making it possible to smoothly change an object's opacity over time. In Figure 5-7, two images have had their IDs attached to mouse events so that they will fade in and out.

About the Plug-in

This plug-in fades an object from one opacity value to another (either increasing or decreasing it) over a set number of milliseconds. It requires the following arguments:

- **`id`** An object, an object ID, or an array of objects and/or object IDs
- **`start`** The beginning level of opacity
- **`end`** The final level of opacity
- **`msecs`** The number of milliseconds the fade should take
- **`interruptible`** If this option is set, an object's fade can be interrupted and replaced with a new fade on the same object; otherwise, the fade will continue until it has finished.
- **`CB`** This argument is sometimes passed by other plug-ins when a second function is to be called once this one has finished execution. Its value is simply a string variable containing the name of the function to call. Because it is not generally a user passable value, I will no longer mention **`CB`** in the list of arguments, unless it is being used in a different manner.

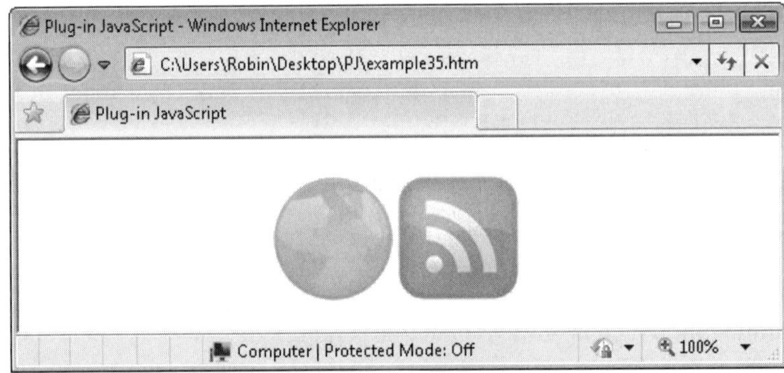

FIGURE 5-7 The left image is slowly fading into the background.

Variables, Arrays, and Functions

j	Local variable for indexing into id if it is an array
stepval	Local variable used in the calculation of the amount of opacity to change in each frame of animation
INTERVAL	Global variable with a default value of 30—the number of milliseconds between each call to the interrupt
FA_Flag	Property of id that is set to true if a fade is in progress, otherwise it is false
FA_Start	Property of id assigned the value of start
FA_End	Property of id assigned the value of end
FA_Level	Property of id containing the current opacity level
FA_Step	Property of id containing the amount by which to change the opacity in each step
FA_Int	Property of id containing the value passed in the interruptible argument
Fadeout	Property of id used by the FadeToggle() plug-in: true if it has been faded out, or false if it has been faded in
FA_IID	Property of id containing the value returned by setInterval()—this value is used by clearInterval() to turn off the DoFade() interrupt attached to id
DoFade()	Plug-in subfunction called every INTERVAL milliseconds until the fade is completed or interrupted—this function updates the opacity of id each time it is called
Opacity()	Plug-in to change the opacity of an object or array of objects
Math.abs()	Function to return an absolute positive value from a number that may be positive or negative
Math.max()	Function to return the largest of two values
Math.min()	Function to return the smallest of two values
setInterval()	Function to start periodic interrupt calls to another function
clearInterval()	Function to stop the interrupts started by SetInterval()

How It Works

This is the first of the really substantial plug-ins. At almost 50 lines of code it isn't short, but don't be put off by it; the coding is straightforward, and you've seen many of its parts before. If you can work through this plug-in, you'll be able to follow them all.

This function works by using interrupts to call a function at regular intervals to change the opacity of an object by a small amount each time (which is how all the transition and animation plug-ins in this book work). To do this, the plug-in comes in two parts. The first part prepares all the variables and initiates the interrupts, and the second part receives the interrupt calls and performs the incremental opacity changes.

Let's start with the first `if()` section of code. There's nothing unusual here; it simply passes `id` back to the same function recursively to be dealt with an element at a time if it's an array:

```
if (id instanceof Array)
{
   for (var j = 0 ; j < id.length ; ++j)
      Fade(id[j], start, end, msecs, interruptible, CB)
   return
}
```

After that, the local variable `stepval` is created, like this:

```
var stepval = Math.abs(start - end) / (msecs / INTERVAL)
```

Its value is calculated by finding the difference between the `start` and `end` opacity values; that is, it subtracts one from the other and then passes the result through the `Math.abs()` function. This gives a positive integer representing the difference, like this:

```
Math.abs(start - end)
```

Then the length of time the fade should take, which has been passed as a value in milliseconds in the variable `msecs`, is divided by `INTERVAL`, which is the number of milliseconds between each frame of the transition (30 by default). The code for that is simple division:

```
(msecs / INTERVAL)
```

The first value (the `start` and `end` difference) is then divided by the second (the timing) and then assigned to the variable `stepval`.

A Specific Case

Let's see what value this calculation comes out as by assuming that `start` has a value of 0, `end` has a value of 100, and `msecs` has a value of 1000. This gives us the following formula:

```
Math.abs(0 - 100) / (1000 / 30)
```

The calculation comes to 100 / (1000 / 30), and the answer is the value 3 . In terms of this code, this means that, if the following three things are `true`:

1. The interrupt is going to take place once every 30 milliseconds,
2. You want the animation to take 1000 milliseconds,
3. There are 100 levels of opacity,

Then the distance between each level of opacity should be 3. In other words, to smoothly fade from a value of 0 to 100 over the course of 1 second, there will be 33.33 steps, separated by 3 levels of opacity.

A Standard Formula

The preceding formula is how almost all the animations and transitions in this book work. They take the value in milliseconds that you supply for their duration, they then divide that by the interval (usually 30 milliseconds), and finally they divide the distance between the start and end points of the animation by the timing value, to find out the amount the animation needs to move on each step, as shown in the following statement:

```
var stepval = Math.abs(start - end) / (msecs / INTERVAL)
```

If a Fade Is Already in Progress

This plug-in has been designed so that you can force it to proceed until it has finished, or you can allow it to be interrupted (but only by another `Fade()` call on the same object). This is so that you can offer `onmouseover` and `onmouseout` routines that will interrupt if you move your mouse again before the transition completes. That way, a partially faded object can be made to fade back to its start point again if you take the mouse away.

Alternatively, sometimes you may need to display an uninterrupted animation on the screen and maybe even chain a few together. You have the option to choose either by setting the `interruptible` argument to `true` if a fade can be interrupted, or `false` if it cannot. You can also use 1 and 0 for these values if you prefer.

The next section of code deals with this by looking at the `FA_Flag` property of `id`. This is a new property given to `id`, which has the value `true` only when a fade is in progress.

NOTE *Assigning new properties directly to objects is a technique used throughout this book. It's a very convenient way of using some object-oriented aspects of JavaScript.*

The next section of code checks whether a fade is already in progress. If it is, the code checks whether the `FA_Int` property of `id` is set (to see whether an interrupt is allowed). If it isn't, the function immediately exits as it cannot be interrupted. Otherwise, the `clearInterval()` function is called to end the currently repeating interrupts, and the object's new `FA_Start` property is set to the current value in `FA_Fade`.

This primes the new fade to start only where the previous one (that was just cancelled) left off, which means that the new fade will ignore the `start` value that was passed. This override ensures a very smooth and natural flow between the two transitions. The following code performs this process:

```
if (O(id).FA_Flag)
{
   if (!O(id).FA_Int) return

   clearInterval(O(id).FA_IID)
   O(id).FA_Start = O(id).FA_Level
}
```

If a Fade Is Not in Progress

If a fade isn't already in progress, the new `id` property `FA_Start` is assigned the value in `start` so that the remaining code can use this value to know where the fade started from.

The id property FA_Level is also set to start because that is the property that will be manipulated to track the opacity level on each interrupt. These statements are placed within an else segment, like this:

```
else
{
   O(id).FA_Start = start
   O(id).FA_Level = start
}
```

The Remaining Assignments

In the final few lines of the setup portion of this plug-in, a few other new properties of id have to be assigned, as follows:

```
O(id).FA_Flag  = true
O(id).FA_End   = end
O(id).FA_Int   = interruptible
```

The first line sets the object's FA_Flag to true, and this is used in other parts of the code to decide whether or not the plug-in can be entered (or reentered). The second line makes a copy of the end value in the new property FA_End, and the last assigns the value in interruptible to the property FA_Int.

Next, the amount by which to change the opacity has to be stored in FA_Step. This is either stepval if the opacity is going to increase, or -stepval if it will be decreasing, as determined by this line:

```
O(id).FA_Step = end > O(id).FA_Start ? stepval : -stepval
```

Assisting the FadeToggle() Plug-in

The FadeToggle() plug-in, which is covered a little later in this chapter, needs a way to know whether an object has been faded in or out. To give it this information, the next new property of id, Fadeout, is set to either true if the object is being faded out, or false if it is being faded in, like this:

```
O(id).Fadeout = end < O(id).FA_Start ? true : false
```

Initiating the Interrupts

The last line of the setup section of the plug-in sets up the repeating interrupts in the following way:

```
O(id).FA_IID   = setInterval(DoFade, INTERVAL)
```

This statement starts off a repeating interrupt that will call the DoFade() subfunction every INTERVAL milliseconds. The value returned by calling setInterval() is saved in the new id property FA_IID, as it is needed later when it's time to cancel the interrupts.

The DoFade() Subfunction

This function is a subfunction of `Fade()` and is known as a private method or private function. Such functions share all the local variables of the parent function, so there's no need to pass them as arguments and, because they can only be used by the parent function, they don't clutter up the namespace.

This makes them ideal to use as interrupt or event driven functions, which is exactly what I have done in this plug-in. Every `INTERVAL` milliseconds (30 by default), `DoFade()` is called up by JavaScript. It has one main job, which is to change the opacity of `id` by just a little. The following line is the one that changes the value for this:

```
O(id).FA_Level += O(id).FA_Step
```

This simply adds the value of the `FA_Step` property of `id` to its `FA_Level` property. If `FA_Step` is positive, the value is therefore added, but if it is negative it is subtracted (for example 100 + –3 is 97, because the first + gets ignored).

If the Final Opacity Has Been Reached

Having derived this new value, it's time to check whether it is the final value wanted, and if so whether the animation has completed. The code to do that is slightly verbose:

```
if (O(id).FA_Level >= Math.max(O(id).FA_Start, O(id).FA_End) ||
    O(id).FA_Level <= Math.min(O(id).FA_Start, O(id).FA_End))
```

Essentially, it checks whether the current opacity value (in `FA_Level`) has reached the final required value (in `FA_End`). If it is the same as or greater than (or less than, in the case of decreasing) the final value, then the following code segment is executed:

```
O(id).FA_Level = O(id).FA_End
O(id).FA_Flag  = false
clearInterval(O(id).FA_IID)
```

In this section, the value of `FA_Level` is set to the exact value in `FA_End`. This must be done because `FA_Level` will often have a fractional value, and one final frame of animation is almost always required to ensure that the correct final opacity level is reached.

After this the `FA_Flag` property of `id` is set to `false` to indicate that the fade has finished. This is immediately followed by a call to `clearInterval()` with the value that was saved in the `FA_IID` property. This cancels any further interrupts.

The CB Argument

The final statement in this `if()` section is as follows:

```
if (typeof CB != UNDEF) eval(CB)
```

It checks the argument passed in `CB` (if any) and uses the `eval()` function to evaluate it. This type of procedure is called a *callback* and is used by the chaining plug-ins. In a nutshell, now that this plug-in has completed running, this call allows any plug-ins that may be chained to follow this one to begin their execution. However, this happens only if the argument `CB` has a value.

This argument is generally passed when you wish to have a second function run when the plug-in has finished executing; you simply pass the function to call in a string as the final parameter to plug-ins that support callbacks natively.

NOTE *Chapter 7 covers callbacks and chaining in much more detail, but I have placed this brief description here due to this being the first plug-in that supports callbacks.*

Changing the Opacity

The last thing this subfunction does is call the `Opacity()` plug-in to set the current opacity value, with this line of code:

```
Opacity(id, O(id).FA_Level)
```

If `clearInterval()` has been called, then that's the end of it; otherwise, `INTERVAL` milliseconds later `DoFade()` will get called again, and a slightly different value for `FA_Level` will be computed and passed to the `Opacity()` plug-in, until the transition has finished.

NOTE *We spent a lot of time going over this particular plug-in because most of the other animation and transition plug-ins work in a similar fashion. Once you understand this one, you will more easily see how the others work.*

How To Use It

To make an object fade, you would use a command such as this:

```
Fade('object', 100, 0, 1000, 0)
```

This will fade the object out starting with full opacity down to being totally transparent, over the course of one second. The final argument of 0 prevents the fade from being interrupted.

You can also embed calls to this plug-in within HTML, like this:

```
<a href='http://abc.com' onmouseover="Fade('object', 75, 100, 500, 1)"
   onmouseout="Fade('object', 100, 75, 500, 1)">My Link</a>
```

If the link was previously given an opacity of 75, then each time the mouse passes over it the link will gradually increase opacity over half a second, darkening it. When the mouse leaves it will fade back to a 75 percent opacity level.

Here's some example code you can try for yourself (or download from the companion website at *pluginjavascript.com* to ensure you have the images):

```
<center><br />
<img id='i1' src='i1.gif' />
<img id='i2' src='i2.gif' />

<script>
window.onload = function()
```

```
{
   O('i1').onmouseover = function() { Fade('i1', 100, 0, 1000, 0) }
   O('i1').onmouseout  = function() { Fade('i1', 0, 100, 1000, 0) }
   O('i2').onmouseover = function() { Fade('i2', 100, 0, 1000, 1) }
   O('i2').onmouseout  = function() { Fade('i2', 0, 100, 1000, 1) }
}
</script>
```

The HTML section sets up two images with the IDs of 'i1' and 'i2'. In the `<script>` section the `onmouseover` and `onmouseout` events of each are attached so that the objects will fade out when the mouse passes over them and fade back in again when the mouse leaves. For the sake of brevity, I used inline, anonymous functions here instead of named functions.

The calls made to `Fade()` for the first image, 'i1', have the interruptible argument set to 0, which means they cannot be interrupted and will always continue to completion. The second image has the interruptible argument set to 1, which allows interruptions.

The Difference between Interruptible and Noninterruptible Calls

Try passing your mouse over the pair of images and note what happens. You will see that the second image smoothly fades in and out as soon as the mouse enters or leaves it, always picking up from the opacity level of the fade that was interrupted.

On the other hand, the first image is harder to control because you can only make it fade out or in from either a fully opaque or a fully transparent state; you cannot interrupt it part way. This also means that if you move the mouse away from the first image before the transition has completed, the mouse will already be out, so there will be no `onmouseout` event to trigger until you move it back in again and wait for the transition to complete, and *then* move the mouse out.

You'll see what I mean as you experiment with the example, and it will become clear how the noninterruptible method is ideal for animations and transitions that you want to always complete, while interruptible ones are best used where user interaction with the mouse is required.

The Plug-in

```
function Fade(id, start, end, msecs, interruptible, CB)
{
   if (id instanceof Array)
   {
      for (var j = 0 ; j < id.length ; ++j)
         Fade(id[j], start, end, msecs, interruptible, CB)
      return
   }

   var stepval = Math.abs(start - end) / (msecs / INTERVAL)

   if (O(id).FA_Flag)
   {
      if (!O(id).FA_Int) return

      clearInterval(O(id).FA_IID)
      O(id).FA_Start = O(id).FA_Level
   }
```

```
   else
   {
      O(id).FA_Start = start
      O(id).FA_Level = start
   }

   O(id).FA_Flag = true
   O(id).FA_End  = end
   O(id).FA_Int  = interruptible
   O(id).FA_Step = end > O(id).FA_Start ? stepval : -stepval
   O(id).Fadeout = end < O(id).FA_Start ? true : false
   O(id).FA_IID  = setInterval(DoFade, INTERVAL)

   function DoFade()
   {
      O(id).FA_Level += O(id).FA_Step

      if (O(id).FA_Level >= Math.max(O(id).FA_Start, O(id).FA_End) ||
          O(id).FA_Level <= Math.min(O(id).FA_Start, O(id).FA_End))
      {
         O(id).FA_Level = O(id).FA_End
         O(id).FA_Flag  = false
         clearInterval(O(id).FA_IID)
         if (typeof CB != UNDEF) eval(CB)
      }

      Opacity(id, O(id).FA_Level)
   }
}
```

PLUG-IN 36 FadeOut()

This plug-in will fade out any object or objects passed to it. In Figure 5-8, each of the images has some text above it that will fade out the image below when the mouse passes over it.

FIGURE 5-8 The right-hand image has been faded out.

About the Plug-in

This plug-in will fade out an object over a period of time specified. It takes the following arguments:

- **`id`** An object, an object ID, or an array of objects and/or object IDs
- **`msecs`** The number of milliseconds the transition should take
- **`interruptible`** If set, the fade out can be interrupted; otherwise it cannot

Variables, Arrays, and Functions

`Fade()`	Plug-in to fade an object between two levels of opacity

How It Works

This plug-in calls the `Fade()` plug-in, but it requires fewer arguments. Because of the way `Fade()` works this plug-in also accepts an object, an object ID, or an array of objects and/or object IDs.

How To Use It

Place a call to `FadeOut()` wherever you would like an object to be faded out. This can be from within HTML in the form of an `onmouseover` or `onclick` event, for example, or you can place the calls within a section of JavaScript code, as in the following example:

```
<center><br />
<span id='sp1'>Mouseover 1</span>
<span id='sp2'>Mouseover 2</span><p>
<img id='i1' src='i1.gif' />
<img id='i2' src='i2.gif' />

<script>
window.onload = function()
{
   O('sp1').onmouseover = function() { FadeOut('i1', 500, 1) }
   O('sp2').onmouseover = function() { FadeOut('i2', 500, 1) }
}
</script>
```

The HTML portion of this example creates two spans to accompany two images. The `<script>` section then attaches to the `onmouseover` events of each span so that the image below each one will fade out if the mouse is passed over the span text.

Once an image has been faded out, you can still pass the mouse over each span and the image will then fade out again. This doesn't look very good, as the images suddenly appear before fading, but it can be corrected with the following plug-in.

The Plug-in

```
function FadeOut(id, msecs, interruptible, CB)
{
   Fade(id, 100, 0, msecs, interruptible, CB)
}
```

FadeIn()

This plug-in is a simple front-end to the `Fade()` plug-in; it fades in an object that has been previously faded out, as can be seen in Figure 5-9.

About the Plug-in

This plug-in will fade in an object over a period of time specified. It takes the following arguments:

- **`id`** An object, an object ID, or an array of objects and/or object IDs
- **`msecs`** The number of milliseconds the transition should take
- **`interruptible`** If set, the fade in can be interrupted; otherwise it cannot

Variables, Arrays, and Functions

`Fade()`	Plug-in to fade an object between two levels of opacity

How It Works

This plug-in calls the `Fade()` plug-in, but it requires fewer arguments. Because of the way `Fade()` works this plug-in also accepts an object, an object ID, or an array of objects and/or object IDs.

How To Use It

You can use this plug-in in much the same way as the previous one: from within HTML or from a JavaScript section of code. The following example is a modified version of the

FIGURE 5-9 The right-hand image has been faded in and the left one has been faded back out.

previous one; this example will fade the images in and out as you pass the mouse over the Mouseover 1 and Mouseover 2 sections:

```
<center><br />
<span id='sp1'>Mouseover 1</span>
<span id='sp2'>Mouseover 2</span><p>
<img id='i1' src='i1.gif' />
<img id='i2' src='i2.gif' />

<script>
window.onload = function()
{
   O('sp1').onmouseover = function() { FadeOut('i1', 500, 1) }
   O('sp2').onmouseover = function() { FadeOut('i2', 500, 1) }
   O('sp1').onmouseout  = function() { FadeIn('i1',  500, 1) }
   O('sp2').onmouseout  = function() { FadeIn('i2',  500, 1) }
}
</script>
```

The main benefit from using this plug-in with `FadeOut()` is that together they require fewer arguments than the `Fade()` plug-in, are easier to remember, and are shorter. They are also used by the next two plug-ins, which toggle an object between being faded out or in and fade smoothly between two objects, respectively.

The Plug-in

```
function FadeIn(id, msecs, interruptible, CB)
{
  Fade(id, 0, 100, msecs, interruptible, CB)
}
```

PLUG-IN 38 FadeToggle()

If you use this plug-in, you don't need to know the current faded out or in state of an object; it tracks the state for you and inverts whatever that state is. Figure 5-10 shows an icon of a house that is being refaded into view with this plug-in.

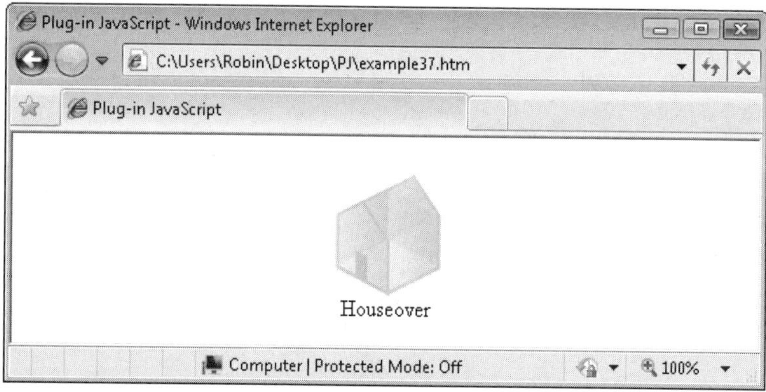

FIGURE 5-10 The house is starting to fade into view.

About the Plug-in

This plug-in either fades an object in or out, depending on its previous state. It requires the following arguments:

- `id` An object, an object ID, or an array of objects and/or object IDs
- `msecs` The number of milliseconds the transition should take
- `interruptible` If set, the fade can be interrupted; otherwise, it cannot

Variables, Arrays, and Functions

`j`	Local variable that iterates through the elements in `id` if it is an array
`Fadeout`	New property given to `id` and set to `true` if it has been faded out
`FadeIn()`	Plug-in to fade an object in
`FadeOut()`	Plug-in to fade an object out

How It Works

This plug-in has to make use of its own code to iterate through `id` if it is an array because of the need to individually check the `Fadeout` property of `id` for each object. It uses the standard form of many prior plug-ins to call the same function recursively with single array elements.

The second half of the plug-in is where the `Fadeout` property is checked. If it is set to `true`, then that value will have been assigned from within the `Fade()` plug-in, discussed earlier in this chapter. When set to `true`, it means that the object has been faded out. If the `Fadeout` property doesn't exist or is set to `false`, then the object has not been faded out.

Therefore, based on the value of `Fadeout`, a decision is made by the `FadeToggle()` plug-in to call either the `FadeIn()` plug-in to fade the object in or the `FadeOut()` plug-in to fade it out.

How To Use It

You can attach this plug-in to an event from within HTML, or you can call it up from a section of JavaScript code. In the following example, the same call to `FadeToggle()` is attached to both the `onmouseover` and the `onmouseout` events of the span:

```
<center><br />
<img id='i1' src='i3.gif' /><br />
<span id='sp1'>Houseover</span>

<script>
window.onload = function()
{
   FadeToggle('i1', 1, 1)
   O('sp1').onmouseover = function() { FadeToggle('i1', 500, 1) }
   O('sp1').onmouseout  = function() { FadeToggle('i1', 500, 1) }
}
</script>
```

Make sure to look at the first call in the <script> section. Notice how it sets a transition time of just 1 millisecond for the fade. This is the recommended way to set up toggleable elements to start up in their inverse state because it causes the transition to occur, but over only a single frame of animation.

This technique is useful if you want the house image to start faded out: the call to `FadeToggle()` accomplishes the first fade out as quickly as possible—faster than the eye can see. When you run the example, you should hardly even notice the image until you pass the mouse over the text.

With the image faded out, the remaining two lines of code attach to the two mouse events. The house will smoothly fade in and out as you pass your mouse over the text because the `interruptible` argument is set to 1 and allows smooth interrupts to the transitions.

The Plug-in

```
function FadeToggle(id, msecs, interruptible, CB)
{
   if (id instanceof Array)
   {
      for (var j = 0 ; j < id.length ; ++j)
         FadeToggle(id[j], msecs, interruptible, CB)
      return
   }

   if (O(id).Fadeout) FadeIn( id, msecs, interruptible, CB)
   else               FadeOut(id, msecs, interruptible, CB)
}
```

PLUG-IN 39

FadeBetween()

This plug-in fades smoothly between two images in a similar manner to a fade transition in a slideshow program. Figure 5-11 shows two overlaid images in the process of fading between each other.

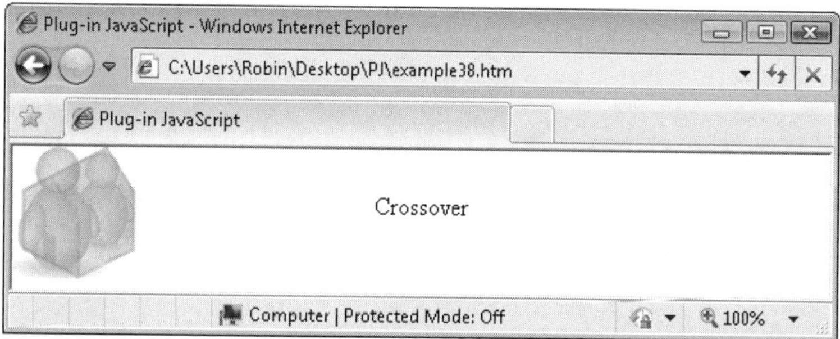

FIGURE 5-11 The house and people icons are fading between each other.

About the Plug-in

This plug-in fades smoothly between two images. It requires the following arguments:

- `id1` An object, an object ID, or an array of objects and/or object IDs
- `id2` An object, an object ID, or an array of objects and/or object IDs
- `msecs` The number of milliseconds the transition should take
- `interruptible` If set, the fade can be interrupted; otherwise, it cannot

Variables, Arrays, and Functions

`FadeOut()`	Plug-in to fade an object out
`FadeIn()`	Plug-in to fade an object in

How It Works

This plug-in calls the `FadeOut()` plug-in for `id1` and the `FadeIn()` plug-in for `id2`. It is also possible to supply an object, an object ID, or an array of objects and/or object IDs to both plug-ins.

How To Use It

To use this plug-in, pass it two IDs, objects, or arrays of objects and/or object IDs, and they will fade from the first object to the second. For the best results, you will probably want to overlay the objects on top of each other so that you can get smooth transitions. However, the plug-in still works fine if you wish to fade between objects in different locations.

The following example illustrates the setting up of your objects and then fading between them:

```
<center><br />
<span id='sp1'>Crossover</span>
<img id='i1' src='i3.gif' />
<img id='i2' src='i4.gif' />

<script>
window.onload = function()
{
   Locate(Array('i1', 'i2'), ABS, 0, 0)
   FadeToggle('i2', 1, 1)
   O('sp1').onmouseover = function() { FadeBetween('i1', 'i2', 500, 1) }
   O('sp1').onmouseout  = function() { FadeBetween('i2', 'i1', 500, 1) }
}
</script>
```

In the HTML section a span is created to which mouse events will be attached and then two GIF images are loaded.

In the `<script>` section the two images are lifted out of the layout by making their position setting 'absolute', then the second image is speedily faded out (over a period of 1 millisecond) so that only the first image is visible.

The mouse events are attached to the `FadeBetween()` plug-in so that passing your mouse over the span text smoothly fades between the images over a period of half a second. The first `FadeBetween()` call fades from the first image to the second, while the second call fades back again.

The Plug-in

```
function FadeBetween(id1, id2, msecs, interruptible, CB)
{
   FadeOut(id1, msecs, interruptible, CB)
   FadeIn( id2, msecs, interruptible, CB)
}
```

PLUG-IN 40 Hide()

This plug-in is different from Plug-in 31, `Invisible()`, in that when called it completely collapses the object down to a 0 by 0 pixel space. The object is still there so that it can be unhidden, but it is not visible. Because it occupies no space, other elements will often move in to occupy the freed up space. This makes it perfect for menuing and similar features.

In Figure 5-12, a row of three buttons has been created, each of which is attached by its `onclick` event to a call to the `Hide()` plug-in. In Figure 5-13, the middle button is hidden after being clicked, and the other buttons have moved in to take up the vacant space.

About the Plug-in

This plug-in will hide an object, effectively removing it from a web page. It requires the following argument:

- **`id`** An object, an object ID, or an array of objects and/or object IDs

Variables, Arrays, and Functions

`HI_Flag`	New property assigned to `id` and set to `true` when `id` is hidden
`display`	The `style.display` property of `id`

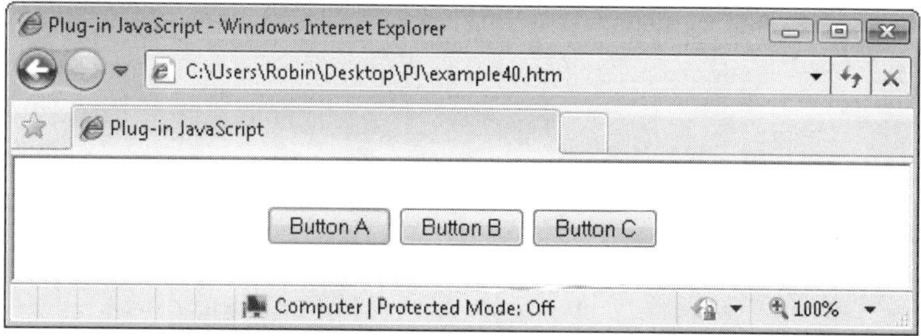

FIGURE 5-12 Three buttons created with click events to hide them

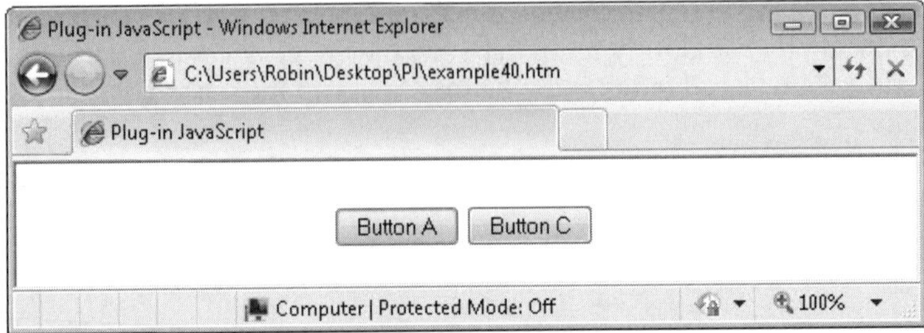

FIGURE 5-13 The middle button has been clicked and is now hidden.

How It Works

This plug-in makes a call to the `S()` plug-in using the assignment version of the call, so that `id` can be an object, an object ID, or an array of objects and/or object IDs. Each object has its `style.display` property set to 'none', which hides it. Additionally, a call to `O()` is made with the arguments `HI_Flag` and `true`, which sets the new object property `Hi_Flag` to `true` so that other plug-ins can tell that the object has been hidden. This call also supports arrays.

Finally, any callback function contained in `CB` is evaluated with the `eval()` function, but only if the argument `CB` (explained in Chapter 7) has a value.

How To Use It

To hide an object, pass it to the `Hide()` plug-in, either from inside a section of JavaScript code, or from within HTML. The follow example creates three buttons, each of which can be clicked to make it hide:

```
<br /><center>
<input id='a' type='submit' value=' Button A ' />
<input id='b' type='submit' value=' Button B ' />
<input id='c' type='submit' value=' Button C ' />

<script>
window.onload = function()
{
   O('a').onclick = function() { Hide('a') }
   O('b').onclick = function() { Hide('b') }
   O('c').onclick = function() { Hide('c') }
}
</script>
```

Alternatively, the input tags could be written as follows, and then no `<script>` section is necessary:

```
<input type='submit' value=' Button A ' onclick='Hide(this)' />
<input type='submit' value=' Button B ' onclick='Hide(this)' />
<input type='submit' value=' Button C ' onclick='Hide(this)' />
```

Or, one button can hide another, like this:

```
<input id='a' type='submit' value=' Button A ' onclick="Hide('b')" />
<input id='b' type='submit' value=' Button B ' onclick="Hide('a')" />
```

The previous two lines each hide the other button, so whichever is clicked first will stay displayed, since the other button will now be hidden and therefore can't be clicked.

In the following plug-in you'll see how `Hide()` can be combined with `Show()` for creating dynamic web page interaction.

The Plug-in

```
function Hide(id, CB)
{
   S(id, 'display', 'none')
   O(id, 'HI_Flag', true)
   if (typeof CB != UNDEF) eval(CB)
}
```

PLUG-IN 41

Show()

This is the partner plug-in for `Hide()`. With it you can reveal an object that has previously been hidden. In Figure 5-14 the two plug-ins have been combined to create a mouseover menu of limericks.

About the Plug-in

This plug-in will show an object, restoring its dimensions and location and moving back any elements that had moved in to take its space. It requires the following argument:

- **`id`** An object, an object ID, or an array of objects and/or object IDs

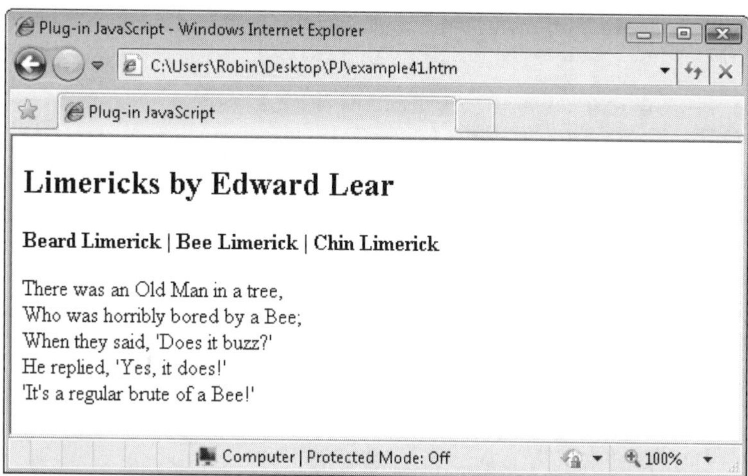

FIGURE 5-14 Different limericks appear as the mouse passes each heading.

Variables, Arrays, and Functions

HI_Flag	New property assigned to id and set to true when id is hidden or false when it is not
display	The style.display property of id

How It Works

This plug-in makes a call to the S() plug-in using the assignment version of the call so that id can be an object, an object ID, or an array of objects and/or object IDs. Each object has its style.display property set to 'block', which restores its full width and height. Additionally, a call to O() is made with the arguments HI_Flag and false, which sets the new object property HI_Flag to false, so that other plug-ins can tell that the object is not hidden. This call also supports arrays.

Finally, any callback function contained in CB is evaluated with the eval() function, but only if the argument CB (explained in Chapter 7) has a value.

How To Use It

Now that you have both Hide() and Show() in your toolkit, you can start to create some professional results, as in the following example, which features a simple mouseover menu of headings that call up different sections of HTML when the mouse passes over them:

```
<h2>Limericks by Edward Lear</h2><b>

<span id='h1'>Beard Limerick</span> |
<span id='h2'>Bee Limerick</span> |
<span id='h3'>Chin Limerick</span></b><p>

<div id='l1'>There was an Old Man with a beard,<br />
Who said, 'It is just as I feared!<br />
Two Owls and a Hen,<br />
Four Larks and a Wren,<br />
Have all built their nests in my beard!'</div>

<div id='l2'>There was an Old Man in a tree,<br />
Who was horribly bored by a Bee;<br />
When they said, 'Does it buzz?'<br />
He replied, 'Yes, it does!'<br />
'It's a regular brute of a Bee!'</div>

<div id='l3'>There was a Young Lady whose chin,<br />
Resembled the point of a pin;<br />
So she had it made sharp,<br />
And purchased a harp,<br />
And played several tunes with her chin.</div>

<script>
window.onload = function()
```

```
{
   Hide(Array('l1', 'l2', 'l3'))
   O('h1').onmouseover = function() { Show('l1') }
   O('h1').onmouseout  = function() { Hide('l1') }
   O('h2').onmouseover = function() { Show('l2') }
   O('h2').onmouseout  = function() { Hide('l2') }
   O('h3').onmouseover = function() { Show('l3') }
   O('h3').onmouseout  = function() { Hide('l3') }
}
</script>
```

This is all pretty straightforward. The HTML section is in two parts. The first displays a header along with the three spans containing subheadings, and the second displays three divs, each containing a different limerick.

The `<script>` section then hides all three of the divs with a single call to `Hide()` in which an array of object IDs is passed. Then follows six statements that attach either the `Hide()` or `Show()` plug-in to the `onmouseover` or `onmouseout` events of the subheadings via the use of anonymous inline functions.

Whenever the mouse is passed over any subheading, the matching div will be displayed using a call to `Show()`. As soon as the mouse passes out of the subheading, a matching call to `Hide()` is made to remove it again.

Placing the JavaScript within HTML

As you will have noticed, my preference when creating such interactive sections of a web page is to proceed using strong separation between HTML and JavaScript. I find that it makes the HTML much more readable and far easier to update. However, if you prefer to embed JavaScript calls within HTML, you could replace the three span lines with the following:

```
<span id='h1' onmouseover="Show('l1')" onmouseout="Hide('l1')">Beard
   Limerick</span> |
<span id='h2' onmouseover="Show('l2')" onmouseout="Hide('l2')">Bee
   Limerick</span> |
<span id='h3' onmouseover="Show('l3')" onmouseout="Hide('l3')">Chin
   Limerick</span></b><p>
```

If you *do* choose this method of attaching to the mouse events, you can remove the final six statements from the `<script>` section, but you will still need to keep the initial `Hide()` statement in order to hide all the divs away on page load.

The Plug-in

```
function Show(id, CB)
{
   S(id, 'display', 'block')
   O(id, 'HI_Flag', false)
   if (typeof CB != UNDEF) eval(CB)
}
```

HideToggle()

This chapter's final plug-in combines the `Hide()` and `Show()` plug-ins into a single plug-in that will toggle the value of an object from one state to the other, without you having to know which state it was in to begin with. Figure 5-15 shows an informational paragraph that, when clicked, will replace itself with another, simply by issuing a single call to this plug-in.

About the Plug-in

This plug-in will make an object hidden if it is shown or show it if it is hidden. It requires the following argument:

- `id` An object, an object ID, or an array of objects and/or object IDs

Variables, Arrays, and Functions

`j`	Local variable to iterate through `id` if it is an array
`HI_Flag`	Flag set by the `Hide()` and `Show()` plug-ins. If `true` an object is hidden, if `false` or unset it is shown.
`display`	The `style.display` property of `id`
`Show()`	Plug-in to show an object that has been hidden
`Hide()`	Plug-in to hide an object

How It Works

This plug-in uses the usual code you have seen a few times to iterate through `id` if it happens to be an array. It determines this with the `instanceof` operator and, if it *is* an array, the local variable `j` iterates through `id` using a `for()` loop, passing each individual element of the array back to the same function recursively. Once the array has been processed, the function returns.

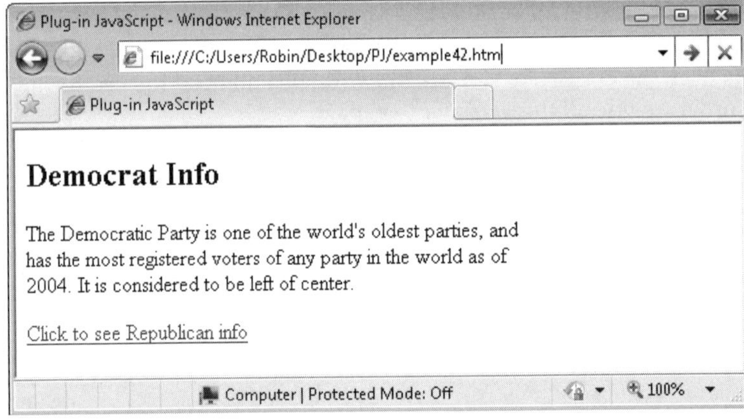

FIGURE 5-15 Toggling between sets of info

If `id` is not an array, the `display` property of `id` is inspected. If its value is not 'none', the object is visible, so the `Hide()` plug-in is called. Otherwise, the object is visible, so the `Show()` plug-in is called.

How To Use It

To use this plug-in, pass it an object to be hidden or shown. As in most cases, you can also pass an object ID or an array of objects and/or object IDs. The following example illustrates creating a couple of different elements and toggling between them:

```
<div id='democrat'><h2>Democrat Info</h2>
The Democratic Party is one of the world's oldest parties, and<br />
has the most registered voters of any party in the world as of<br />
2004. It is considered to be left of center.<p>
<a id='democrat' href='#'>Click to see Republican info</a></div>

<div id='republican'><h2>Republican Info</h2>
The Republican Party is often called the Grand Old Party or the<br />
GOP, despite being the younger of the two major parties.  It is<br />
considered to be right of center.<p>
<a id='republican' href='#'>Click to see Democrat info</a></div>

<script>
window.onload = function()
{
   Hide('republican')
   O('democrat').onclick   = toggle
   O('republican').onclick = toggle

   function toggle()
   {
      HideToggle(Array('democrat', 'republican'))
   }
}
</script>
```

In the HTML section, two divs are created, one for information on the U.S. Democratic Party, and the other for the U.S. Republican Party. After the informational text (taken from Wikipedia) each div also includes a link with which the alternate information can be displayed.

In the `<script>` section, the second div (with the ID of 'republican') is hidden so that only one div is shown. The other div could be hidden instead, but *one* of them must be hidden to start with in order for the toggling to work.

Then two attachments are made, one to each `onclick` event of the divs. They simply attach the function `toggle()` to the events, remembering that by leaving out the brackets the *function* is attached to the event, rather than the *value returned* by the function being attached.

Finally, the `toggle()` function calls the `HideToggle()` plug-in, passing it both of the div IDs. Since one is shown and one is hidden, toggling them both replaces one with the other.

The Plug-in

```
function HideToggle(id, CB)
{
   if (id instanceof Array)
   {
      for (var j = 0 ; j < id.length ; ++j)
         HideToggle(id[j], CB)
      return
   }

   if (S(id).display != 'none') Hide(id, CB)
   else Show(id, CB)
}
```

CHAPTER 6

Movement and Animation

From this point on, the plug-ins really start to get interesting as most of the core functions have now been covered. Using the tools already outlined, the plug-ins in this chapter enable you to slide objects around the screen, deflate, and inflate objects over time, and zoom objects in a variety of ways. With all of this, you can create some very impressive effects with only a few lines of code.

PLUG-IN 43

Slide()

This plug-in allows you to slide an object from one place to another over time, making it useful for sliding elements in on demand, hiding and revealing objects, or creating animation effects. Figure 6-1 shows an image in the process of sliding from the bottom left to the top right of the browser.

About the Plug-in

This plug-in moves an object from one location to another over a period of time. It supports single objects only (not arrays) because if there were more than one object, only the topmost one would be seen. Therefore, you can pass only an object or an object ID to this plug-in. It requires the following arguments:

- **`id`** Either an object or an object ID—it cannot be an array of objects
- **`frx`**, **`fry`** The top left corner of the initial position for `id`
- **`tox`**, **`toy`** The top left corner of the final position for `id`
- **`msecs`** The number of milliseconds the animation should take
- **`interruptible`** If `true` (or 1), this plug-in can be interrupted by a new call on the same object; if `false` (or 0), the call is uninterruptible

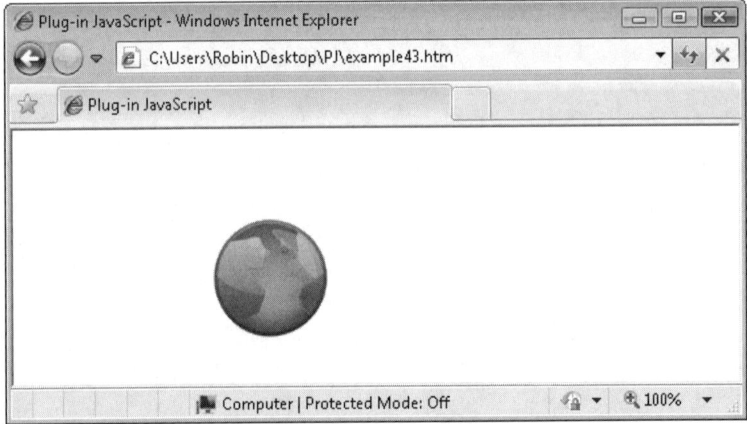

FIGURE 6-1 This plug-in smoothly slides objects over time.

Variables, Arrays, and Functions

`stepx`	Local variable containing the amount by which to move horizontally in each step
`stepy`	Local variable containing the amount by which to move vertically in each step
`count`	Local variable to count the steps
`len1`	Local variable containing the start to end distance
`len2`	Local variable containing the new start to end distance after an animation is interrupted and given now coordinates
`SL_Flag`	New property assigned to `id`: `true` when a slide is in progress, otherwise `false` or unset
`SL_Int`	New property assigned to `id`: `true` if the previous call to this plug-in set the slide to uninterruptible
`SL_IID`	New property assigned to `id` with which the repeating interrupts can be stopped
`INTERVAL`	Global variable with the value 30
`Distance()`	Subfunction to calculate the distance between two locations
`DoSlide()`	Subfunction to perform the sliding animation
`GoTo()`	Plug-in to move an object to a new location
`setInterval()`	Function to set another function to be called repeatedly
`clearInterval()`	Function to stop the interrupts created by `setInterval()`

How It Works

The first section of code tests for the existence of the `SL_Flag` property of `id`. If it has a value of `true` (or 1) then a slide on `id` is already in progress. This is the statement used:

```
if (O(id).SL_Flag)
```

Next, the property of `id`, `SL_Int` is tested. If it is `false` then the previous call to `Slide()` for this `id` set this variable to indicate that the function could not be interrupted, so the function returns.

Otherwise, interrupting the plug-in is allowed, so the current slide is stopped by calling `clearInterval()`, passing it the `SL_IID` property of `id`, as returned by `SetInterval()`. The code to do this is as follows:

```
if (!O(id).FL_Int) return
else clearInterval(O(id).SL_IID)
```

Next, because the plug-in has been interrupted, it's necessary to allow the interrupting slide to commence from wherever the previous one was halted. What's more, because the coordinates of the halted object will not be the start coordinates passed to the interrupting call, it's necessary to ensure that the interrupting call moves at the same speed as the one specified in the call.

For example, if the call to `Slide()` specifies an animation time of 1000 milliseconds, but it interrupts another slide and discovers that the object is now only one third of the distance from the destination (instead of the 100 percent it would have been if this was the first `Slide()` call on the object), then the new slide should only take one-third of 1000 milliseconds to move, or 333 milliseconds.

Using the Pythagorean Theorem

To calculate the new distance to travel, and, therefore, determine the speed of the new slide, the plug-in uses the Pythagorean theorem, which states that on a right angled triangle, the volume of the square on the hypotenuse is equal to the sum of the volumes of the squares on the other two sides.

This works because if you draw a line between any two points, on a two-dimensional surface such as a browser, you can draw a horizontal line from one point and a vertical line from the other so that they meet each other at a single coordinate to create a right angled triangle, with the longest edge being the line connecting the two locations.

Therefore, using the Pythagorean theorem, the distance between the requested start and end locations is determined by passing the results of `tox - frx` and `toy - fry` to the subfunction `Distance()`, like this:

```
var len1 = Distance(tox - frx, toy - fry)
```

The `Distance()` subfunction looks like this:

```
function Distance(x, y)
{
   x = Math.max(1, x)
   y = Math.max(1, y)
   return Math.round(Math.sqrt(Math.abs(x * x) + Math.abs(y * y)))
}
```

The variable `x` is the length of one short side of the triangle, while `y` is the length of the other short side. If either value is 0, then it is changed to 1, otherwise division-by-zero errors may occur.

Each value is then multiplied by itself to determine the volumes of the squares, and they are then converted to absolute values, since they could be negative numbers. These figures are then added together to give their combined volume, which is also the volume of the square on the long side of the triangle.

Finally, to discover the length of the triangle's longest side, the square root of this new volume is returned—the distance in pixels between the locations `frx,fry` and `tox,toy`.

With the distance now stored in `len1`, the values of `frx` and `fry` are overridden with those of the actual coordinates of the object, by looking them up with the `X()` and `Y()` plug-ins using the following code. The plug-in will use this new start location, overriding the one passed to it by the calling code:

```
frx = X(id)
fry = Y(id)
```

The preceding process is then repeated to discover the distance between the new start location of `frx,fry` and the final location of `tox,toy` and this distance is then placed in the variable `len2`, like this:

```
var len2 = Distance(tox - frx, toy - fry)
```

It is now possible to adjust the value of `msecs` (the length of time the animation should take in milliseconds) by multiplying it by the result of dividing `len2` by `len1`, like this:

```
msecs *= len2 / len1
```

For example, if the original length is 240 pixels and the new length is 200 pixels, then the preceding statement is the equivalent of

```
msecs *= 200 / 240
```

or:

```
msecs *= 0.833
```

Therefore, the length of time the animation should take will become 833 milliseconds. This formula also works when the interrupting call discovers that the actual location of the object is further away than the start position it has specified. If that is the case, `msecs` will end up being multiplied by a value larger than 1, which will extend the time that should be taken.

Determining the Movement Distance for Each Step

Next, the plug-in computes the distance between the start and end positions (whether as originally requested by the calling code, or modified due to interrupting a previous slide) and divides the horizontal and vertical differences into the number of steps required to make the animation last for the number of milliseconds specified in `msecs` (which again could be the original value, or a new value computed from interrupting a previous slide). The following code calculates these step values:

```
var stepx = (tox - frx) / (msecs / INTERVAL)
var stepy = (toy - fry) / (msecs / INTERVAL)
```

To explain how these two lines of code work, I have determined that the value in `INTERVAL` (which is 30 by default) is the optimal time in milliseconds between animation frames. Therefore, the following calculation calculates the number of steps required to make an animation last `msecs` milliseconds (if each step happens every `INTERVAL` milliseconds):

```
(msecs / INTERVAL)
```

TIP *Always ensure you pass the `msecs` argument a value greater than zero because this plug-in (and all of the animation and transition plug-ins) does not check for it having a value of zero, which will cause errors and halt the animation.*

The distance between the start and end locations is determined by subtracting the end from the start, as in these two calculations:

```
(tox - frx)
(toy - fry)
```

If the start is before the end then the result of a calculation is a negative number, otherwise it is positive. The results are then divided by the result of the previous calculation to divide the distance by the steps required to determine the amount of movement for each axis, for each step of animation.

Setting Up the Repeating Interrupts

The last four lines of the setup portion of the plug-in set the local variable `count` to zero; it will count each step, and inform the plug-in when it's time to stop. Then the new `SL_Int` property of `id` is set to the value in `interruptible`. This causes any call that attempts to interrupt the slide to be prevented unless it has the value `true` or 1. Next, the new `SL_Flag` property of `id` is given the value `true` to tell this and any other plug-ins that a slide is currently in progress on the object `id`.

Finally, `setInterval()` is called, passing it the `DoSlide` function name and the value in `INTERVAL`. Because the brackets are left off the end of the function name, the function itself is passed to `setInterval()`. If brackets were placed after the name then the *result* of calling the `DoSlide()` function would be passed to `setInterval()`, which is another value altogether.

This statement has the effect of initiating an interrupt call to the `DoSlide()` function every `INTERVAL` (30 by default) milliseconds. The value returned by the function is stored in `SL_IID` (`IID` stands for Interrupt ID), so that it can be used as an argument to `clearInterval()` when the slide has completed (or if it is interrupted). The code to do all this is as follows:

```
var count      = 0
O(id).SL_Int   = interruptible
O(id).SL_Flag  = true
O(id).SL_IID   = setInterval(DoSlide, INTERVAL)
```

Performing the Slide

The portion of code that performs the animation is the `DoSlide()` subfunction. Subfunctions retain access to the main function's local variables and are, therefore, a neat way to create a repeating interrupt without having to keep passing the arguments required.

The first thing the subfunction does is call the `GoTo()` plug-in to move the object to its next location, as follows:

```
GoTo(id, frx + stepx * count, fry + stepy * count)
```

The two values `stepx` and `stepy` were calculated earlier in the plug-in, so this simply takes the value in `frx` and adds to it the result of multiplying `stepx` by `count` (the current step number). The same is also calculated for the vertical location.

Next, an `if()` section of code is entered, in which the value of `count` is tested against the result of the calculation `msecs / INTERVAL`. The current value of `count` is tested, but the suffix of ++ then increments `count` after making the test so that it has its new value ready for the next time the subfunction is called. The statement looks like this:

```
if (count++ >= (msecs / INTERVAL))
{
   ...
}
```

If `count` is greater than or equal to `msecs / INTERVAL`, the object has reached its final destination and the animation is complete, so the following four lines of code (shown as ... in the previous `if()` segment) are executed:

```
O(id).SL_Flag = false
GoTo(id, tox, toy)
clearInterval(O(id).SL_IID)
if (typeof CB != UNDEF) eval(CB)
```

The first line sets the `SL_Flag` property of `id` to `false` to indicate no slide is running on `id`. Then a `GoTo()` call ensures that the object has ended in exactly the correct position, by passing it the values of `tox` and `toy`. This is necessary because the values of `stepx` and `stepy` will usually be floating point numbers and, therefore, the final location as calculated using them could be a tiny bit off. The `tox` and `toy` arguments for this call ensure that any imprecision is not an issue.

After this, the `clearInterval()` function is called with an argument of `SL_IID`, the property of `id` that was created from the result of calling `setInterval()`. This turns off the repeated interrupts.

Finally, any callback function contained in `CB` is evaluated with the `eval()` function, but only if the argument `CB` (explained in Chapter 7) has a value.

How To Use It

To slide an object from one place to another it must first be released from its default location by giving its `style.position` property a value such as 'absolute'. The following example moves an object from the coordinates 0,100 to 450,0 over the course of 1500 milliseconds (1.5 seconds):

```
<img id='globe' src='i1.gif'>

<script>
window.onload = function()
{
   Position('globe', ABS)
   Slide('globe', 0, 100, 450, 0, 1500, 0)
}
</script>
```

The HTML section displays an image and gives it the ID 'globe'. Then, in the `<script>` section, the image is given an 'absolute' position using the `Position()` plug-in and is then animated with a single call to `Slide()`. The final argument passed is for whether the animation is interruptible and, in this case, it is not.

Let's look at another example that responds to mouse events and allows interruption by adding a couple of commands to the `<script>` section of the previous example:

```
O('globe').onmouseover = function()
   { Slide(this, 450, 0,  450, 50, 500, 1) }
O('globe').onmouseout  = function()
   { Slide(this, 450, 50, 450, 0,  500, 1) }
```

Now when you pass the mouse over the globe it will move from the position 450,0 to 450,50. When you move the mouse away, it will slide back to 450,0. As you'll see, it doesn't matter where you interrupt the slide, it always maintains the correct speed. Notice that the keyword `this` tells `Slide()` which object to slide.

However, if you interrupt one slide with another that has a different distance to go or a different length of time specified, then the interrupted and interrupting speeds will not match. I recommend you to generally disallow interrupting a slide with a dissimilar one. as with the first `Slide()` call in the example, which you cannot interrupt.

The Plug-in

```
function Slide(id, frx, fry, tox, toy, msecs, interruptible, CB)
{
   if (O(id).SL_Flag)
   {
      if (!O(id).SL_Int) return
      else clearInterval(O(id).SL_IID)

      var len1  = Distance(tox - frx, toy - fry)
      frx       = X(id)
      fry       = Y(id)
      var len2  = Distance(tox - frx, toy - fry)
      msecs    *= len2 / len1
   }

   var stepx = (tox - frx) / (msecs / INTERVAL)
   var stepy = (toy - fry) / (msecs / INTERVAL)

   var count      = 0
   O(id).SL_Int   = interruptible
   O(id).SL_Flag  = true
   O(id).SL_IID   = setInterval(DoSlide, INTERVAL)

   function Distance(x, y)
   {
      x = Math.max(1, x)
      y = Math.max(1, y)
      return Math.round(Math.sqrt(Math.abs(x * x) + Math.abs(y * y)))
   }

   function DoSlide()
   {
      GoTo(id, frx + stepx * count, fry + stepy * count)

      if (count++ >= (msecs / INTERVAL))
```

```
        {
           O(id).SL_Flag = false
           GoTo(id, tox, toy)
           clearInterval(O(id).SL_IID)
           if (typeof CB != UNDEF) eval(CB)
        }
     }
  }
```

PLUG-IN 44

SlideBetween()

This plug-in is swaps the positions of two objects by sliding them past each other. This is a great effect for swapping requested objects into a chosen location. For example, Figure 6-2 shows a collection of photos that can be individually displayed by passing the mouse over the associated title. When you do this, the previous photograph is swapped with the new one and they slide past each other, the old one returning to the stack of pictures and the new one moving to the main viewing area.

About the Plug-in

This plug-in takes the positions of two objects and then swaps the two by sliding the objects past each other. It takes the following arguments:

- **`id`** Either an object, or an object ID—it cannot be an array of objects
- **`msecs`** The number of milliseconds the animation should take
- **`interruptible`** If `true` (or 1), this plug-in can be interrupted by a new call on the same objects; otherwise, if `false` (or 0), the call is uninterruptible

FIGURE 6-2 This plug-in creates smooth and impressive swap effects.

Variables, Arrays, and Functions

SL_Flag	Property of both id1 and id2—true if a slide is in progress
SL_Int	Property of both id1 and id2—true if a slide can be interrupted
t1	Local temporary variable to store a copy of id1's SB_X property
t2	Local temporary variable to store a copy of id1's SB_Y property
x1	Local temporary variable to store a copy of id1's SB_X property
y1	Local temporary variable to store a copy of id1's SB_Y property
x2	Local temporary variable to store a copy of id2's SB_X property
y2	Local temporary variable to store a copy of id2's SB_Y property
SB_X	Property of both id1 and id2 containing their horizontal locations
SB_Y	Property of both id1 and id2 containing their vertical locations

How It Works

This plug-in first checks whether either of the objects passed to it is currently being used in a slide animation by testing their SL_Flag properties. If so, both objects then have their SL_Int properties tested. If neither has a value of true or 1, then the slide may not be interrupted and the function returns. The code to do this is as follows:

```
if (O(id1).SL_Flag || O(id2).SL_Flag)
{
   if (!O(id1).SL_Int || !O(id2).SL_Int)
      return
```

If the function is interruptible, then the locations of each object require swapping so that they can return to their start locations. This behavior has been chosen because the only details passed to the plug-in are the object IDs. Therefore, if an interrupting call to SlideBetween() is requested on an object, the only different action it can take is to reverse the current slide.

To do this, the temporary variables t1 and t2 are given the current horizontal and vertical locations of id1. Then id1 is given the position of id2. Finally, id2 is given the position stored in t1 and t2, using the following statements:

```
var t1        = O(id1).SB_X
var t2        = O(id1).SB_Y
O(id1).SB_X = O(id2).SB_X
O(id1).SB_Y = O(id2).SB_Y
O(id2).SB_X = t1
O(id2).SB_Y = t2
```

If a slide is not currently in progress on either object, copies are made of the current horizontal and locations of each object. These are created as new properties of each object (rather than local variables) so that interrupting calls (if allowed) can have access to them, as follows:

```
else
{
   O(id1).SB_X = X(id1)
   O(id1).SB_Y = Y(id1)
```

```
    O(id2).SB_X = X(id2)
    O(id2).SB_Y = Y(id2)
}
```

Next, although not necessary, temporary copies are made of the locations of each object in the short named variables `x1`, `x2`, `y1`, and `y2`. This is so that the final two statements are easier to read and can fit on single lines. The four lines that do it look like this:

```
var x1 = O(id1).SB_X
var y1 = O(id1).SB_Y
var x2 = O(id2).SB_X
var y2 = O(id2).SB_Y
```

The final statements that start the animations going with calls to the `Slide()` plug-in are as follows:

```
Slide(id1, x1, y1, x2, y2, msecs, interruptible, CB)
Slide(id2, x2, y2, x1, y1, msecs, interruptible, CB)
```

The first statement sets up `id1` to move from its location to that of `id2`, and the second sets `id2` up to move from its location to that of `id1`.

How To Use It

There are many ways you can use this plug-in. All you need is a single line of code to smoothly swap two objects, like the following, which swaps `object1` and `object2` by sliding them past each other over the course of 1000 milliseconds (1 second):

```
SlideBetween(object1, object2, 1000, 0)
```

The final argument of 0 specifies that the animation may not be interrupted and must proceed until it completes.

Here's an example of how you could use this plug-in to create a simple but effective way to display photographs:

```
Choose a photo:
<span id='m1'>Landscape</span>,
<span id='m2'>Museum</span>,
<span id='m3'>Parrots</span>,
<span id='m4'>Steps</span>,
<span id='m5'>Pyramid</span>
<div id='b1'></div>
<div id='b2'></div>
<div id='b3'></div>
<div id='b4'></div>
<div id='b5'></div>
<img id='p1' src='photo1.jpg' />
<img id='p2' src='photo2.jpg' />
<img id='p3' src='photo3.jpg' />
<img id='p4' src='photo4.jpg' />
<img id='p5' src='photo5.jpg' />
```

```
<script>
window.onload = function()
{
   Locate(Array('b1', 'b2', 'b3', 'b4', 'b5'), 'absolute',  2, 50)
   Locate('p1', ABS, 330, 50)
   Locate('p2', ABS, 335, 55)
   Locate('p3', ABS, 340, 60)
   Locate('p4', ABS, 345, 65)
   Locate('p5', ABS, 350, 70)

   swap('m1', 'p1', 'b1')
   swap('m2', 'p2', 'b2')
   swap('m3', 'p3', 'b3')
   swap('m4', 'p4', 'b4')
   swap('m5', 'p5', 'b5')

   function swap(o1, o2, o3)
   {
      O(o1).onmouseover = function() { SlideBetween(o2, o3, 200, 1) }
      O(o1).onmouseout  = function() { SlideBetween(o2, o3, 200, 1) }
   }
}
</script>
```

The HTML section of this example displays some text and five headings that describe five photographs. Each heading is given an ID and placed in its own span tag. Underneath this, five empty divs are created with unique IDs. These will be used as objects with which to swap the photographs. Finally, the photographs are displayed, with each one having a unique ID assigned to it.

In the `<script>` section, the first statement sets all the blank divs to have a position property of 'absolute' and places them all at the location 2,50. Then the photos are also made 'absolute' and placed in their locations. I chose to give them slightly different coordinates to show them as a stack of images.

After this, five calls to a new function called `swap()` are made to attach to the image's mouse events. The `swap()` function takes three arguments, `o1`, `o2`, and `o3`, for the three objects passed to it. The `o1` object is one of the heading divs, which then has its `onmouseover` and `onmouseout` events attached to by inline, anonymous functions that call the `SlideBetween()` plug-in, passing `o2` and `o3` (the two objects to swap) to it, and a time period of 200 milliseconds that the swap should take.

All this has the effect of swapping a photo with its blank companion div when the mouse passes over its heading. It swaps them back when the mouse passes out of the heading. Because the final argument passed to `SlideBetween()` is a 1, the animations are interruptible, so if you move the mouse away before a picture has finished sliding, it will simply slide back to its position in the stack of images.

I have deliberately only given you the guts of how this works so you can see how to easily create your own functions. With suitable CSS and graphics, you can use these techniques to create very impressive dynamic effects.

The Plug-in

```
function SlideBetween(id1, id2, msecs, interruptible, CB)
{
   if (O(id1).SL_Flag || O(id2).SL_Flag)
   {
      if (!O(id1).SL_Int || !O(id2).SL_Int)
         return

      var t1       = O(id1).SB_X
      var t2       = O(id1).SB_Y
      O(id1).SB_X = O(id2).SB_X
      O(id1).SB_Y = O(id2).SB_Y
      O(id2).SB_X = t1
      O(id2).SB_Y = t2
   }
   else
   {
      O(id1).SB_X = X(id1)
      O(id1).SB_Y = Y(id1)
      O(id2).SB_X = X(id2)
      O(id2).SB_Y = Y(id2)
   }

   var x1 = O(id1).SB_X
   var y1 = O(id1).SB_Y
   var x2 = O(id2).SB_X
   var y2 = O(id2).SB_Y

   Slide(id1, x1, y1, x2, y2, msecs, interruptible, CB)
   Slide(id2, x2, y2, x1, y1, msecs, interruptible, CB)
}
```

PLUG-IN 45 Deflate()

With this plug-in you can make an object shrink down over time until it is no longer visible. You can also specify whether to deflate (or shrink) the width, height, or both. Figure 6-3 shows three images, each of which is in the process of being deflated with this plug-in. The first is shrinking horizontally, the last vertically, and the middle one is deflating in both dimensions.

About the Plug-in

This plug-in takes an object and over a specified time period shrinks it down until it is no longer visible. The following are the required arguments:

- **id** An object, an object ID, or an array of objects and/or object IDs
- **w** If `true` or 1, the object's width will shrink
- **h** If `true` or 1, the object's height will shrink

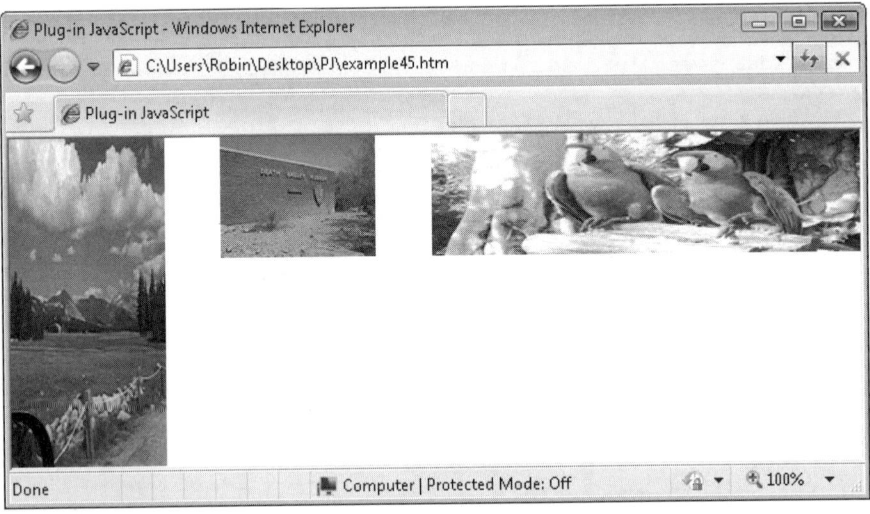

Figure 6-3 Three different types of deflation supported by this plug-in

- **`msecs`** The number of milliseconds the animation should take
- **`interruptible`** If `true` (or 1), this plug-in can be interrupted by a new call on the same object; otherwise, if `false` (or 0), the call is uninterruptible

Variables, Arrays, and Functions

`j`	Local variable to index into `id` if it is an array
`stepw`	Local variable containing the amount of horizontal change per frame
`steph`	Local variable containing the amount of vertical change per frame
`width`	Local variable containing the width to which `id` should be changed at each step
`height`	Local variable containing the height to which `id` should be changed at each step
`overflow`	The object's `style.overflow` object, which is set to `HID` ('hidden') to prevent an object's contents overflowing as it shrinks
`DF_Flag`	Property of `id` that is `true` if a `Deflate()` call is in progress
`DF_Int`	Property of `id` containing `true` if the deflation is interruptible
`DF_IID`	Property of `id` used to clear an interrupt with `clearInterval()`
`DF_OldW`	Property of `id` containing the unshrunk width of `id`
`DF_OldH`	Property of `id` containing the unshrunk height of `id`
`DF_Count`	Property if `id` that counts the number of frames in the animation
`Deflated`	Property of `id` set to `true` if it has been deflated—used by the `DeflateToggle()` plug-in

`INTERVAL`	Global variable with the value 30
`HID`	Global variable with the value 'hidden'
`setInterval()`	Function to set up repeating interrupts
`clearInterval()`	Function to stop repeating interrupts
`DoDeflate()`	Subfunction to perform the animation
`W()`	Plug-in to fetch an object's width
`H()`	Plug-in to fetch an object's height
`Resize()`	Plug-in to resize an object

How It Works

This plug-in has a few different parts. The first part tests whether `id` is an array; if it is, it calls itself recursively with each element of `id` using the following code:

```
if (id instanceof Array)
{
   for (var j = 0 ; j < id.length ; ++j)
      Deflate(id[j], w, h, msecs, interruptible, CB)
   return
}
```

This allows many objects to be deflated at once, as long as they are passed to `Deflate()` in an array.

Next, the code has to take into account the fact that when only one dimension of an image is changed, most browsers will automatically modify the other one to keep the image at the same aspect ratio. However, in this case that feature is not wanted, so if either the horizontal or vertical width is not to be changed (as decided by the values in the `w` and `h` arguments), that dimension is given a fixed value representing its current length to replace its default value of 'auto'. This allows one dimension to be altered and the other will not change:

```
if (!w) ResizeWidth( id, W(id))
if (!h) ResizeHeight(id, H(id))
```

Next, if a deflate animation is already in progress on `id` (as determined by its `DF_Flag` property having a value of `true` or 1), its `DF_Int` property is checked. This contains `true` or 1 if the animation may be interrupted; if it is not `true` or 1, the function returns. Otherwise, if any deflate interrupt is currently running, it is stopped with a call to `clearInterval()`. The code for these two actions is as follows:

```
if (O(id).DF_Flag)
{
   if (!O(id).DF_Int) return
   else clearInterval(O(id).DF_IID)
}
```

Otherwise, if this is the first time the id object has been used by the Deflate() plug-in, there are some properties that need assigning, as follows:

```
else
{
   if (w) O(id).DF_OldW   = W(id)
   if (h) O(id).DF_OldH   = H(id)
   O(id).DF_Count = msecs / INTERVAL
}
```

In this section, the properties DF_OldW and DF_OldH are assigned the current width and height of the object so that they can be restored later—but only those dimensions that are to be resized have this value saved.

Also, the DF_Count property is assigned the result of msecs / INTERVAL, which is the number of steps in the animation. This variable will later count down one step at a time to zero (in the DoDeflate() subfunction), and each time its value will be multiplied by the values in stepw and/or steph to calculate the correct width and/or height of id for each step of the animation.

Next, some properties have to be assigned a certain value (whether or not this is the first time id has been used with this plug-in) by the following statements:

```
var stepw = O(id).DF_OldW / (msecs / INTERVAL)
var steph = O(id).DF_OldH / (msecs / INTERVAL)

S(id).overflow = HID
O(id).Deflated = true
O(id).DF_Flag  = true
O(id).DF_Int   = interruptible
O(id).DF_IID   = setInterval(DoDeflate, INTERVAL)
```

First, the horizontal and vertical distances for each step of the animation are assigned to stepw and steph. This determines the amount of horizontal and vertical shrinkage required in each step to ensure the animation lasts msecs milliseconds.

The next statement ensures that the contents of the id object will not overflow its boundaries during resizing by setting the style.overflow property of id to HID (which stands for 'hidden'). This is not an issue when resizing images, but it certainly is when the object is a div or span that contains multiple items such as text and images.

The Deflated property is then set to true to indicate the object's current deflated/inflated state to this and other plug-ins, such as DeflateToggle(). The DF_Flag is also set to true to tell this and any other plug-ins that a Deflate() call is now in progress on id.

Next, DF_Int is given the value in interruptible so that if the plug-in is called again on id while the animation is still running, this value can be tested and, if not true or 1, the plug-in will not be interrupted.

The final statement in this part of the code uses setInterval() to set up an interrupt call to DoDeflate() every INTERVAL milliseconds. The result of making this call is a value that can later be passed to clearInterval() to cancel the interrupts. It is saved in the DF_IID property of id.

The DoDeflate() Subfunction

Once initialized by the main part of the plug-in, the `DoDeflate()` subfunction is called every `INTERVAL` milliseconds, and each time it shrinks the object a little more, like this:

```
if (w) ResizeWidth( id, stepw * O(id).DF_Count)
if (h) ResizeHeight(id, steph * O(id).DF_Count)
```

These two lines calculate the new width and/or height of `id` and then resize either or both.

Next, a check is made to see if this was the final resize and whether the animation can now stop. This is done by checking the value of `DF_Count`, which is decremented after each frame of animation.

When the Animation Is Finished

If the `DF_Count` property is less than 1, the animation has completed and the `DF_Flag` property of `id` is set to `false` to indicate that there is now no deflate operation running on `id`.

Finally, the width and/or height of the dimension(s) being resized are set to zero to complete the transition.

In the final two lines of the plug-in, the `clearInterval()` function is called to prevent any further interrupts. Any callback function contained in `CB` is evaluated with the `eval()` function, but only if the argument `CB` (explained in Chapter 7) has a value. The code for these actions is as follows:

```
if (O(id).DF_Count-- < 1)
{
   O(id).DF_Flag = false

   if (w) ResizeWidth(id, 0)
   if (h) ResizeHeight(id, 0)

   clearInterval(O(id).DF_IID)
   if (typeof CB != UNDEF) eval(CB)
}
```

TIP *The double-hyphen (`--`) operator following `DF_Count` is a handy way of telling JavaScript to decrement the variable, but only* after *its current value has been used in the `if()` statement, thus saving an extra line of code.*

How To Use It

Using `deflate()` is a great way to make an object disappear smoothly and is much more fun than just fading it out or hiding it. Here's some example code illustrating the three different types of effects supported by this plug-in:

```
<span id='d'>Mouseover Me</span>

<img id='p1' src='photo1.jpg' />
<img id='p2' src='photo2.jpg' />
<img id='p3' src='photo3.jpg' />
```

```
<script>
window.onload = function()
{
   Locate('p1', ABS, 0,   0)
   Locate('p2', ABS, 160, 0)
   Locate('p3', ABS, 320, 0)
   Deflate('p1', 1, 0, 2000, 0)
   Deflate('p2', 1, 1, 2000, 0)
   Deflate('p3', 0, 1, 2000, 0)
}
</script>
```

The HTML section of this example places three images on the screen and assigns them unique IDs. The `<script>` section then uses the `Locate()` plug-in to give them all a position of 'absolute' and places them overlapping each other, along the top of the browser.

The final three lines call up a different `Deflate()` effect on each, which is achieved by passing different values of the second and third parameters. The first image shrinks only in a horizontal direction because the two width and height parameters are 1 and 0. The middle image has width and height parameters of 1 and 1, so it shrinks in both directions. The last image has width and height parameters of 0 and 1 and shrinks only in a vertical direction.

The final two parameters of 2000 and 0 cause the animations to take 2000 milliseconds each (although they run concurrently), and the 0 specifies that they are not interruptible.

The Plug-in

```
function Deflate(id, w, h, msecs, interruptible, CB)
{
   if (id instanceof Array)
   {
      for (var j = 0 ; j < id.length ; ++j)
         Deflate(id[j], w, h, msecs, interruptible, CB)
      return
   }

   if (!w) ResizeWidth( id, W(id))
   if (!h) ResizeHeight(id, H(id))

   if (O(id).DF_Flag)
   {
      if (!O(id).DF_Int) return
      else clearInterval(O(id).DF_IID)
   }
   else
   {
      if (w) O(id).DF_OldW   = W(id)
      if (h) O(id).DF_OldH   = H(id)
      O(id).DF_Count = msecs / INTERVAL
   }

   var stepw = O(id).DF_OldW / (msecs / INTERVAL)
   var steph = O(id).DF_OldH / (msecs / INTERVAL)
```

```
    S(id).overflow = HID
    O(id).Deflated = true
    O(id).DF_Flag  = true
    O(id).DF_Int   = interruptible
    O(id).DF_IID   = setInterval(DoDeflate, INTERVAL)

    function DoDeflate()
    {
       if (w) ResizeWidth( id, stepw * O(id).DF_Count)
       if (h) ResizeHeight(id, steph * O(id).DF_Count)

       if (O(id).DF_Count-- < 1)
       {
          O(id).DF_Flag = false
          if (w) ResizeWidth( id, 0)
          if (h) ResizeHeight(id, 0)
          clearInterval(O(id).DF_IID)
          if (typeof CB != UNDEF) eval(CB)
       }
    }
}
```

PLUG-IN 46 Reflate()

This is the companion plug-in to `Deflate()`. With it, you can expand a deflated object back to its original dimensions over a specified period of time, with a choice of three different animation types. In Figure 6-4, a div has been added to the example in the `Deflate()` plug-in with which you can deflate or reflate the objects.

FIGURE 6-4 Both the plug-ins Deflate() and Reflate() are attached to mouse events.

About the Plug-in

This plug-in takes an object (or an array of objects) and reinflates it to its original dimensions after it was deflated using the `Deflate()` plug-in. You can call this plug-in only on objects that have been previously deflated, otherwise the call will be ignored. It takes the following arguments:

- **`id`** An object, an object ID, or an array of objects and/or object IDs
- **`w`** If `true` or 1, the object's width will expand to its original value
- **`h`** If `true` or 1, the object's height will expand to its original value
- **`msecs`** The number of milliseconds the animation should take
- **`interruptible`** If `true` (or 1), this plug-in can be interrupted by a new call on the same object; otherwise, if `false` (or 0), the call is uninterruptible

Variables, Arrays, and Functions

`j`	Local variable to index into `id` if it is an array
`stepw`	Local variable containing the amount of horizontal change per frame
`steph`	Local variable containing the amount of vertical change per frame
`width`	Local variable containing the width to which `id` should be changed at each step
`height`	Local variable containing the height to which `id` should be changed at each step
`DF_Flag`	Property of `id` that is `true` if a `Deflate()` call is in progress
`DF_Int`	Property of `id` containing `true` if the deflation is interruptible
`DF_IID`	Property of `id` that clears an interrupt with `clearInterval()`
`DF_OldW`	Property of `id` containing the unshrunk width of `id`
`DF_OldH`	Property of `id` containing the unshrunk height of `id`
`DF_Count`	Property of `id` that counts the number of frames in the animation
`Deflated`	Property of `id` set to `true` if it has been deflated—used by the `DeflateToggle()` plug-in
`INTERVAL`	Global variable with the value 30
`setInterval()`	Function to set up repeating interrupts
`clearInterval()`	Function to stop repeating interrupts
`DoReflate()`	Subfunction to perform the animation
`Resize()`	Plug-in to resize an object

How It Works

This plug-in works in a very similar way to the `Deflate()` plug-in with two main differences. First, if the `Deflated` property of `id` is not `true`, the plug-in returns because the object cannot be reinflated. Here is the piece of code that does that:

```
if (!O(id).Deflated) return
```

Second, instead of `DF_Count` counting down from the maximum step count to zero, it counts upward from 0 and so is initialized to a value of zero in this plug-in (as opposed to the value it is assigned with `msecs / INTERVAL` in the `Deflate()` plug-in). The `DoReflate()` subfunction uses the following statement to increment the `DF_Count` property each frame of the animation (instead of decrementing, as in the `DoDeflate()` subfunction of `Deflate()`):

```
if (O(id).DF_Count++ >= msecs / INTERVAL)
```

The `Deflated` property of `id` that indicates whether an object is deflated or inflated is set to `false` by this plug-in (rather than `true`, as with `Deflate()`), but the rest of the code is virtually the same, so please read the details on `Deflate()` for further details.

How To Use It

You should call this plug-in on an object only after the object has been deflated using the `Deflate()` plug-in. If you try to use it on an object that hasn't yet been deflated, the plug-in will simply return.

The following example is expanded from the one in the `Deflate()` plug-in section. It has a div inserted before the images that you can pass the mouse over to either deflate or reflate the images:

```
<span id='d'>Mouseover Me</span>

<img id='p1' src='photo1.jpg' />
<img id='p2' src='photo2.jpg' />
<img id='p3' src='photo3.jpg' />

<script>
window.onload = function()
{
   Locate('p1', ABS, 0,   30)
   Locate('p2', ABS, 160, 30)
   Locate('p3', ABS, 320, 30)

   O('d').onmouseover = down
   O('d').onmouseout  = up

   function down()
   {
      Deflate('p1', 1, 0, 2000, 1)
      Deflate('p2', 1, 1, 2000, 1)
      Deflate('p3', 0, 1, 2000, 1)
   }
```

```
   function up()
   {
      Reflate('p1', 1, 0, 2000, 1)
      Reflate('p2', 1, 1, 2000, 1)
      Reflate('p3', 0, 1, 2000, 1)
   }
}
</script>
```

This example replaces the direct calls to the `Deflate()` plug-in with a pair of new functions, `down()` and `up()`. These are attached to the `onmouseover` and `onmouseout` events of the span displaying the text "Mouseover Me", so that when you move the mouse over the text the objects deflate, and when you move it away, they inflate.

The calls to the two plug-ins have their final parameter set to 1. This is the `interruptible` argument, and, therefore, interrupting of the plug-ins has been enabled. This means that the example is very responsive and the animations occur immediately upon moving the mouse in or out of the span, taking into account the current amount of deflation or reflation to smoothly inverse the previous animation.

The Plug-in

```
function Reflate(id, w, h, msecs, interruptible, CB)
{
   if (id instanceof Array)
   {
      for (var j = 0 ; j < id.length ; ++j)
         Reflate(id[j], w, h, msecs, interruptible, CB)
      return
   }

   if (!O(id).Deflated) return
   else if (O(id).DF_Flag)
   {
      if (!O(id).DF_Int) return
      else clearInterval(O(id).DF_IID)
   }
   else O(id).DF_Count = 0

   var stepw  = O(id).DF_OldW / (msecs / INTERVAL)
   var steph  = O(id).DF_OldH / (msecs / INTERVAL)

   O(id).DF_Flag   = true
   O(id).Deflated = false
   O(id).DF_Int    = interruptible
   O(id).DF_IID    = setInterval(DoReflate, INTERVAL)

   function DoReflate()
   {
      if (w) ResizeWidth( id, stepw * O(id).DF_Count)
      if (h) ResizeHeight(id, steph * O(id).DF_Count)

      if (O(id).DF_Count++ >= msecs / INTERVAL)
```

```
        {
            O(id).DF_Flag = false
            if (w) ResizeWidth( id, O(id).DF_OldW)
            if (h) ResizeHeight(id, O(id).DF_OldH)
            clearInterval(O(id).DF_IID)
            if (typeof CB != UNDEF) eval(CB)
        }
    }
}
```

PLUG-IN 47

DeflateToggle()

If you use this plug-in, you don't need to keep track of which objects have or haven't been deflated, and it saves on extra code, too. In Figure 6-5 the example in the `Reflate()` plug-in section has been updated to use this plug-in.

About the Plug-in

This plug-in toggles an object between being deflated or inflated. It takes the following arguments:

- **`id`** An object, an object ID, or an array of objects and/or object IDs
- **`w`** If `true` or 1, the object's width will deflate or reflate
- **`h`** If `true` or 1, the object's height will deflate or reflate
- **`msecs`** The number of milliseconds the animation should take
- **`interruptible`** If `true` (or 1), this plug-in can be interrupted by a new call on the same object; otherwise, if `false` (or 0), the call is uninterruptible

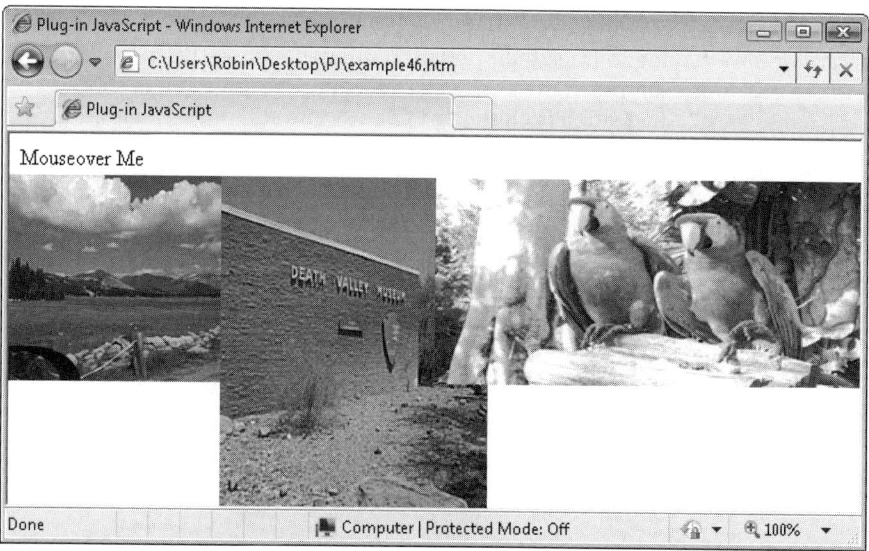

Figure 6-5 The images automatically toggle between being inflated and deflated.

Variables, Arrays, and Functions

`j`	Local variable for indexing into `id` if it is an array
`Deflated`	Property of `id` that is `true` if `id` is deflated
`Deflate()`	Plug-in to deflate an object to 0 width by 0 height
`Reflate()`	Plug-in to reflate an object to its original dimensions

How It Works

This plug-in uses the standard recursive techniques of many of the others to determine whether `id` is an array and if it is, to pass each element of the array recursively back to the same function to be dealt with individually, as follows:

```
if (id instanceof Array)
{
   for (var j = 0 ; j < id.length ; ++j)
      DeflateToggle(id[j], w, h, msecs, interruptible, CB)
   return
}
```

After that there are just two statements, the first of which tests the `Deflated` property of `id`. If it is `true`, the object has been (or is in the process of being) deflated, so the `Reflate()` plug-in is called. Otherwise, the object is inflated (or is in the process of being reinflated), so the `Deflate()` plug-in is called, like this:

```
if (O(id).Deflated) Reflate(id, w, h, msecs, interruptible, CB)
else                Deflate(id, w, h, msecs, interruptible, CB)
```

How To Use It

You can use this plug-in to replace having to call both of the `Deflate()` and `Reflate()` plug-ins and to save having to track their deflated/inflated states. The following code is similar to the previous example in the `Reflate()` section, except that it is shorter because it uses `DeflateToggle()` instead of both the `Deflate()` and `Reflate()` plug-ins:

```
<span id='d'>Mouseover Me</span>

<img id='p1' src='photo1.jpg' />
<img id='p2' src='photo2.jpg' />
<img id='p3' src='photo3.jpg' />

<script>
window.onload = function()
{
   Locate('p1', ABS, 0,   30)
   Locate('p2', ABS, 160, 30)
   Locate('p3', ABS, 320, 30)
   Deflate('p2', 1, 0, 1, 1)

   O('d').onmouseover = toggle
   O('d').onmouseout  = toggle
```

```
   function toggle()
   {
      DeflateToggle('p1', 1, 1, 2000, 1)
      DeflateToggle('p2', 1, 0, 2000, 1)
      DeflateToggle('p3', 0, 1, 2000, 1)
   }
}
</script>
```

For variety, I added a call to `Deflate()` just after those to the `Locate()` plug-in so that the second picture will start off deflated. Notice that I passed a value of 1 millisecond for the call (the fastest allowed) so that, for all intents and purposes, it is instant.

Try passing your mouse in and out of the Mouseover Me text and watch how the pictures toggle their deflated/inflated states as you do so, smoothly changing between each animation type as soon as you move the cursor in and out.

To become fully acquainted with what this plug-in can do for you, you might want to change the animation length from 2000 milliseconds to other values, change the `interruptible` argument to 0, change the animation types by varying the `w` and `h` parameters, or use different images in varying locations.

TIP *Remember that the second and third arguments (`w` and `h`, which specify whether the width and/or height is to be modified) must be the same for all deflates, inflates, and toggles on an object for it to correctly deflate and inflate. For example, if you deflate just the width of an object and then try to inflate just its height then nothing will happen since the height has not been deflated. In this case only the object's width can be inflated.*

The Plug-in

```
function DeflateToggle(id, w, h, msecs, interruptible, CB)
{
   if (id instanceof Array)
   {
      for (var j = 0 ; j < id.length ; ++j)
         DeflateToggle(id[j], w, h, msecs, interruptible, CB)
      return
   }

   if (O(id).Deflated) Reflate(id, w, h, msecs, interruptible, CB)
   else                Deflate(id, w, h, msecs, interruptible, CB)
}
```

PLUG-IN 48 DeflateBetween()

This plug-in provides similar functionality to the `FadeBetween()` plug-in, except that it resizes a pair of objects in a choice of three different ways (height, width, or width and height), rather than simply fading from one to the other. This plug-in is good for creating professional slideshow effects, or for swapping content. In Figure 6-6, two images have been

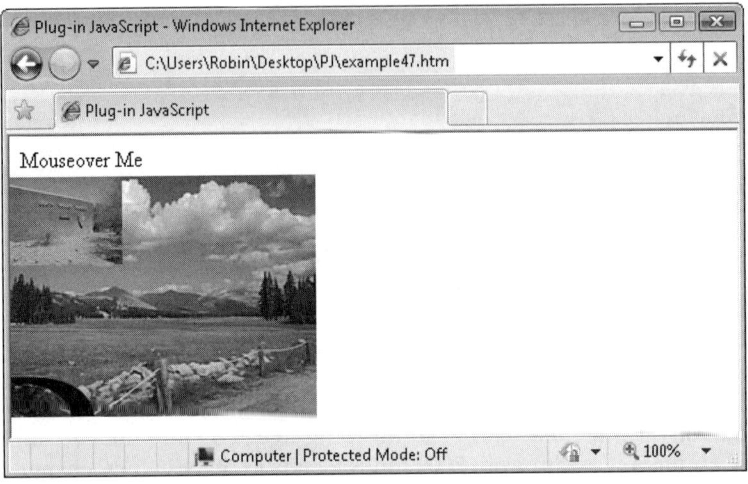

FIGURE 6-6 Swapping two objects by deflating one and inflating the other

overlaid on each other and, while the larger one deflates, the smaller picture inflates and will soon be as large as the original image, which will have disappeared by the time the original smaller picture reaches that size.

About the Plug-in

This plug-in swaps two objects by deflating one and inflating the other at the same time. It requires these arguments:

- **`id1`** An object, an object ID, or an array of objects and/or object IDs
- **`id2`** An object, an object ID, or an array of objects and/or object IDs
- **`w`** If `true` or 1, the object's width will deflate or reflate
- **`h`** If `true` or 1, the object's height will deflate or reflate
- **`msecs`** The number of milliseconds the animation should take
- **`interruptible`** If `true` (or 1), this plug-in can be interrupted by a new call on the same object; otherwise, if `false` (or 0), the call is uninterruptible

Variables, Arrays, and Functions

`Deflate()`	Plug-in to deflate an object to zero width and height
`Reflate()`	Plug-in to reinflate and object to its previous dimensions

How It Works

This plug-in simply makes one call to `Deflate()` for the first object and another to `Reflate()` for the second.

How To Use It

To use this plug-in, you need to ensure that the second object has already been deflated. Ideally, you will have also released each object from its position in the HTML by giving it a position style of 'absolute' or 'relative'. You will probably also have overlaid the objects on each other.

The following example does all of this and features a span that you can pass your mouse over to initiate the swaps:

```
<span id='d'>Mouseover Me</span>

<img id='p1' src='photo1.jpg' />
<img id='p2' src='photo2.jpg' />

<script>
window.onload = function()
{
   Locate(Array('p1', 'p2'), ABS, 0, 30)
   Deflate('p2', 1, 1, 1, 0)

   O('d').onmouseover = swap1
   O('d').onmouseout  = swap2

   function swap1()
   {
      DeflateBetween('p1', 'p2', 1, 1, 1000, 1)
   }

   function swap2()
   {
      DeflateBetween('p2', 'p1', 1, 1, 1000, 1)
   }
}
</script>
```

The HTML section creates a span with the text "Mouseover Me" and also displays two images, All three items are given unique IDs.

In the `<script>` section, both of the images are given a position style setting of 'absolute' and located at 0 pixels across, and 30 down using calls to the `Locate()` plug-in. The second image is then deflated using the `Deflate()` plug-in, over the shortest time possible (1 millisecond), which is virtually instantaneous.

Finally, the `onmouseover` and `onmouseout` events of the div are attached, in order, to the `swap1()` and `swap2()` functions, which call the `DeflateBetween()` plug-in to either swap from image 1 to image 2, or from image 2 to image 1.

The transitions are given 1000 milliseconds (or 1 second) to complete. Because the `interruptible` parameter is set to 1, you can pass your mouse in and out of the Mouseover Me text to instantly change between displaying one image or the other.

You may want to try changing the `w` and `h` arguments to see the various different effects you can achieve.

The Plug-in

```
function DeflateBetween(id1, id2, w, h, msecs, interruptible, CB)
{
   Deflate(id1, w, h, msecs, interruptible, CB)
   Reflate(id2, w, h, msecs, interruptible, CB)
}
```

PLUG-IN 49 Zoom()

This plug-in is similar in some ways to the `Deflate()` and `Reflate()` plug-ins but it can do much more, including zooming in and out using the center of an object as the focus, padding margins during zooms to retain the same width and height (ensuring other objects don't get disturbed by the resizing), and specifying end widths and heights.

In Figure 6-7, four icons are displayed, each of which is attached by its mouse events to the `Zoom()` plug-in so that when the mouse passes over them they enlarge, and when it moves away they shrink back down. In the figure the second icon is currently zoomed up.

About the Plug-in

This plug-in will zoom an object over a period of time between two supplied sets of width and height. It can also pad the object to retain its overall dimensions and supports three different styles of zoom. It requires the following arguments:

- **`id`** An object, an object ID, or an array of objects and/or object IDs
- **`w`** If `true` or 1, the object's width will be zoomed
- **`h`** If `true` or 1, the object's height will be zoomed
- **`fromw`** The width from which the object should be zoomed
- **`fromh`** The height from which the object should be zoomed
- **`tow`** The width to which the object should be zoomed

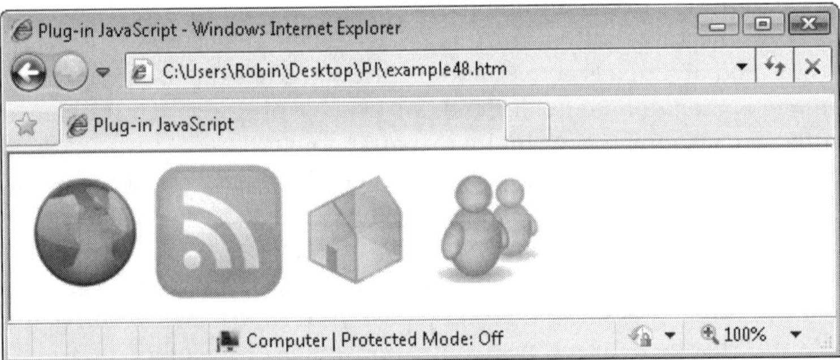

FIGURE 6-7 Zooming icons when the mouse passes over them

- **toh** The height to which the object should be zoomed
- **msecs** The number of milliseconds the animation should take
- **pad** If greater than 0, the object will be padded with CSS padding (so that it always keeps the same dimensions); otherwise, if it is –1, no padding is required and `id` may not be moved during a zoom. If pad is 0 or `null` then, as well as not applying padding, the object will be moved during resizing so as to remain centered.
- **interruptible** If `true` (or 1), this plug-in can be interrupted by a new call on the same object; otherwise, if `false` (or 0), the call is uninterruptible

Variables, Arrays, and Functions

`j`	Local variable for indexing into `id` if it is an array
`tox`	Local variable containing the final horizontal offset
`toy`	Local variable containing the final vertical offset
`midx`	Local variable containing the horizontal center offset
`midy`	Local variable containing the vertical center offset
`width1`	Local variable containing the amount of padding for the left of the object
`width2`	Copy of `width1` containing the amount of padding for the right of the object
`height1`	Local variable containing the amount of padding for the top of the object
`height2`	Copy of `height1` containing the amount of padding for the bottom of the object
`stepw`	Local variable containing the amount of change in width for each step
`steph`	Local variable containing the amount of change in height for each step
`INTERVAL`	Global variable containing the value 30
`HID`	Global variable containing the value 'hidden'
`ZO_W`	Property of `id` containing its current width
`ZO_H`	Property of `id` containing its current height
`ZO_Flag`	Property of `id` set to `true` if a zoom is in progress
`ZO_Int`	Property of `id` set to `true` if a zoom may be interrupted
`ZO_Count`	Property of `id` containing the current frame number of the animation
`ZO_IID`	Property of `id` containing the value required to cancel the interrupts with `clearInterval()`

`paddingLeft`	The `style.paddingLeft` property of `id`
`paddingTop`	The `style.paddingTop` property of `id`
`paddingRight`	The `style.paddingRight` property of `id`
`paddingBottom`	The `style.paddingBottom` property of `id`
`overflow`	The `style.overflow` property of `id`
`setInterval()`	Function to start repeated interrupts to another function
`clearInterval()`	Function to stop repeated interrupts
`Math.max()`	Function to return the maximum out of two values
`Math.floor()`	Function to remove any numbers after the decimal point in a floating point number and return an integer
`Math.round()`	Function to round a floating point number either up or down to the nearest integer
`DoZoom()`	Subfunction to perform the zoom animation
`ZoomPad()`	Subfunction to pad an object while zooming so that it retains the same dimensions
`NoPx()`	Plug-in to remove the 'px' suffix of a property
`Px()`	Plug-in to add the 'px' suffix to a value
`W()`	Plug-in to return an object's width
`H()`	Plug-in to return an object's height
`X()`	Plug-in to return an object's horizontal offset
`Y()`	Plug-in to return an object's vertical offset
`GoTo()`	Plug-in to move an object to a new location
`Resize()`	Plug-in to resize the dimensions of an object

How It Works

This plug-in is quite long because it has to achieve a number of different objectives, but if you follow this explanation you'll see how it breaks down into easily digestible chunks. However, you don't need to understand how this function works if you just want to use it, so please don't be put off by this extended commentary.

You should be fully familiar with the first section of code by now because it checks whether `id` is an array, and if it is, passes each element recursively to the same function to be dealt with individually, as follows:

```
if (id instanceof Array)
{
   for (var j = 0 ; j < id.length ; ++j)
      Zoom(id[j], w, h, fromw, fromh, tow, toh,
         msecs, pad, interruptible, CB)
   return
}
```

After this, copies of the object's current x and y coordinates need saving (if they haven't already been saved), like this:

```
if (typeof O(id).ZO_X == UNDEF)
{
   O(id).ZO_X = X(id)
   O(id).ZO_Y = Y(id)
}
```

The typeof operator checks whether the property ZO_X is already defined; if it isn't, it assigns values it and the property ZO_Y, taken from the plug-ins X() and Y().

If a Zoom Is Not Currently in Progress

Next, the plug-in checks whether a zoom is currently in progress on id by looking at its ZO_Flag property. If a zoom is not in progress, then three variables require initializing prior to starting the zoom, as follows:

```
if (!O(id).ZO_Flag)
{
   O(id).ZO_W     = Math.max(fromw, tow)
   O(id).ZO_H     = Math.max(fromh, toh)
   O(id).ZO_Count = 0
}
```

The first two statements assign whichever value is larger out of the start and destination widths and heights in fromw, tow, fromh, and toh to the ZO_W and ZO_H properties of id. This sets default values for the width and height of a zoom should only one of the dimensions be set to change (therefore, the nonchanging dimension will retain this value). The ZO_Count property is also initialized to zero.

If a Zoom Is in Progress

If a zoom is in progress, the ZO_Int property is inspected. If it is not true, the plug-in may not be interrupted, so it returns. Next, the repeating interrupts are stopped by calling the clearInterval() function. Also, because the only useful action an interrupt can do to a zoom in progress is to reverse the direction of zooming, the ZO_Count property of id is set to its inverse. Here is the section of code that does this:

```
else
{
   if (!O(id).ZO_Int) return
   else clearInterval(O(id).ZO_IID)

   O(id).ZO_Count = (msecs / INTERVAL) - O(id).ZO_Count
}
```

If the zoom can't be interrupted then the plug-in returns. Otherwise the current repeating interrupts are cancelled.

The final statement is based on the result of msecs / INTERVAL being the number of steps required to make the zoom last for msecs milliseconds. Therefore, if the ZO_Count property has a value of 10 out of 34 (for example), then for the zoom to reverse there will be only 10 steps remaining to return to the starting zoom level.

Setting Up the Variables

After this, a few local variables require setting up (whether or not a zoom is currently running), using this code:

```
var maxw  = Math.max(fromw, tow)
var maxh  = Math.max(fromh, toh)
var stepw = (tow - fromw) / (msecs / INTERVAL)
var steph = (toh - fromh) / (msecs / INTERVAL)
```

The first two statements use the `Math.max()` function to determine the maximum width and height an object will be at either the start or end of the zoom, and places these values in `maxw` and `maxh`. Then the horizontal and vertical distance between each frame of the zoom is calculated and placed in `stepw` and `steph`.

The last four statements of the initial setup process are these:

```
S(id).overflow = HID
O(id).ZO_Flag  = true
O(id).ZO_Int   = interruptible
O(id).ZO_IID   = setInterval(DoZoom, INTERVAL)
```

The first one ensures that the object will not overflow outside its boundaries if it is made smaller than the contents. This isn't applicable to images but must be done for objects such as divs and spans that can contain many different elements. The overflowing is prevented by setting `id`'s `style.overflow` property to the value in `HID`, which is 'hidden'.

Next, the `ZO_Flag` property is set to `true` to indicate to this and other plug-ins that a zoom is in progress on `id`. The `ZO_Int` property is also assigned the value in `interruptible`, which will be `true` if this zoom can be interrupted.

Finally, the `setInterval()` function is called in such a way that the `DoZoom()` subfunction will be called every `INTERVAL` milliseconds. The result returned by the function is placed in `ZO_IID` so that it can later be used to cancel the interrupts using a call to `clearInterval()`.

The DoZoom() Subfunction

The job of the `DoZoom()` subfunction is to perform the resizing required by changing the object's dimensions just a little each time it is called. The first three lines calculate the new width and height and perform the resizing as follows:

```
if (w) O(id).ZO_W = Math.round(fromw + stepw * O(id).ZO_Count)
if (h) O(id).ZO_H = Math.round(fromh + steph * O(id).ZO_Count)
Resize(id, O(id).ZO_W, O(id).ZO_H)
```

In the first line, if the argument `w` is `true`, then horizontal resizing is allowed so the `ZO_W` property of `id` is assigned the new value required for the object's width. This value is calculated by multiplying `stepw` (the amount of change for each step of the animation) by `ZO_Count` (the number of this animation step) and adding it to the value of the `fromw` argument (the original width of the object). If the zoom is reducing `id`, then a negative value is added to `fromw`, otherwise a positive value is added.

The second line does exactly the same, but for the object's height and places the result in `id`'s `ZO_H` property. If either `w` or `h` is not `true`, then that dimension is not to be resized during the zoom, and the value previously assigned to either the `ZO_W` or `ZO_H` property earlier in the plug-in will be the default used. The third line performs the resizing by calling the Resize() plug-in.

After this, the values required to center the object are placed in midx and midy, like this:

```
var midx = O(id).ZO_X + Math.round((maxw - O(id).ZO_W) / 2)
var midy = O(id).ZO_Y + Math.round((maxh - O(id).ZO_H) / 2)
```

These are calculated by taking the maximum width and height of the object and then subtracting its current width and height from them. These values are then divided by 2 to obtain the offset from the top left of the object, which has been stored in the ZO_X and ZO_T properties of id.

When the Pad Argument Is True

If the pad argument is greater than zero, the calling code of this plug-in will pad out id as it changes dimensions so that it will retain the same overall size, and, therefore, elements resting against it will also stay aligned where they are. Without this setting, as the width and height of id changes, any objects surrounding it might move about to take the new dimensions into account. The following line of code calls the ZoomPad() subfunction to create the padding required:

```
if (pad > 0) ZoomPad(Math.max(fromw, tow),
   Math.max(fromh, toh), O(id).ZO_W, O(id).ZO_H)
```

This finds the maximum width and height that the object will be out of its start and end values of fromw, tow, fromh, and toh, by using the Math.max() function. The object will then have its padding adjusted so that if it is going to zoom larger, padding is placed around it in advance, into which the resizing can grow. Or, if it will be reducing, then no padding is added, but as the object reduces, more and more padding is added to make up for the reduction in size. The overall result is that when pad is greater than zero, id will always have the same overall dimensions (when you add its width and height to its padding).

Otherwise, if pad doesn't have a value of –1, id is moved to keep it centered (if pad is –1, no padding is required and no moving of id is wanted).

If This Plug-in Has Been Called by the DockBar() Plug-in

Next, there's an interesting piece of code used only by the DockBar() plug-in, covered in Chapter 8. It looks like this:

```
else if (O(id).DB_Parent)
   GoToEdge(O(id).DB_Parent, O(id).DB_Where, 50)
```

This code examines the DB_Parent property of id. If it is true, the plug-in has been called from DockBar(), in which case the GoToEdge() plug-in from Chapter 4 is called to keep id up against the edge to which it has been assigned by the value in the DB_Where property.

If this plug-in isn't being used as part of the DockBar() plug-in, then it's necessary to keep id centered (unless the pad argument is –1, in which case centering is disabled). Of course, if id has not been lifted up from the page by making it have an 'absolute', 'relative', or other position style property, then any attempt to change its location will be ignored (in which case the best way to keep the object centered is to set pad to true).

However, if the object does have a set x and y coordinate, then each time it reduces or enlarges, its top left corner will require moving slightly to keep its center in the middle, although an object that is using padding will not change position as it will always have the same overall dimensions.

When the Animation Has Completed

To check whether the zoom has completed, the following `if()` statement is used:

```
if (++O(id).ZO_Count >= (msecs / INTERVAL))
```

This statement increments the `ZO_Count` property of `id` and then checks whether it is greater than or equal to the result of `msecs / INTERVAL` (which gives the number of steps in the animation). If it isn't, then the contents of the `if()` statement are ignored and the subfunction returns and will be called up again in `INTERVAL` milliseconds time.

Otherwise, the zoom has finished and the following statements are executed:

```
var endx      = O(id).ZO_X + Math.round((maxw - tow) / 2)
var endy      = O(id).ZO_Y + Math.round((maxh - toh) / 2)
O(id).ZO_Flag = false
Resize(id, tow, toh)
clearInterval(O(id).ZO_IID)
```

The first two lines calculate the final top x and y locations for the object and place them in `endx` and `endy`. The next line sets the `ZO_Flag` property of `id` to `false` to indicate that no zoom is running on `id`. Next, the object is resized to its final width and height in `tow` and `toh`, and the repeating interrupts are stopped by calling `clearInterval()`, passing it the property `ZO_IID` that was stored when `setInterval()` was called.

After this, if padding is being used, `ZoomPad()` is called to update the padding; otherwise, if `pad` is not –1, the `GoTo()` plug-in is called to ensure that `id` is located exactly at its final position in `endx` and `endy`:

```
if (pad > 0) ZoomPad(fromw, fromh, tow, toh)
else if (pad != -1) GoTo(id, endx, endy)
```

Then, if this plug-in is being called by the `DockBar()` plug-in, `id` is moved to its final place at the required edge:

```
if (O(id).DB_Parent) GoToEdge(O(id).DB_Parent, O(id).DB_Where, 50)
```

The final statement checks whether the `CB` argument has been passed, and if so it calls `eval()` to execute it, as explained in Chapter 7:

```
if (typeof CB != UNDEF) eval(CB)
```

The ZoomPad() Subfunction

The `ZoomPad()` subfunction applies sufficient CSS padding to `id` in order to ensure that the object always has the same overall dimensions. It takes four arguments, `frw`, `frh`, `padw`, and `padh`. The variables `frw` and `frh` contain the initial width and height of `id`, and `padw` and `padh` contain the overall required width and height for `id`.

Therefore, if frw is less than padw or frh is less than padh, some padding must be applied. This is calculated by subtracting padw from frw and padh from frh. Along the way, padw and padh are passed through the Math.round() function to return integer values.

Then left and top are given the new padding width and height to be given to the left and top of id. The variables right and bottom are also assigned these values, which will apply the padding width and height to the right and bottom of id. This is the code used, which simply divides each padding value by two:

```
var left   = Math.max(0, frw - Math.round(padw)) / 2
var right  = left
var top    = Math.max(0, frh - Math.round(padh)) / 2
var bottom = top
```

If the amount of padding to add to either the width or height of id is an odd number, then left and/or top (being half that number) will have a fractional part of .5.

For example, if 5 pixels width padding is required, then left will have a value of 2.5, as will right. This is because left contains the padding to add to one side of id, right contains the amount to add to the other, top contains the amount of padding to add to the top, and bottom contains the amount to add to the bottom of id.

However, because most browsers don't allow floating point values for these properties (although, strangely, some do), left is compared with the value of Math.floor(left), which returns the value passed to it, less any fractional part. So if left has a value of 2.5, Math.floor(left) returns 2.

Therefore, if the following code finds that left does have a fractional part, it removes it and then gives that value plus 1 to right so that, in the current example, if left was 2.5 then now it will have a value of 2, and right will be 3:

```
if (left != Math.floor(left))
{
   left  = Math.floor(left)
   right = left + 1
}
```

The next five lines of code are the same, except they set up top and bottom padding amounts, like this:

```
if (top != Math.floor(top))
{
   top    = Math.floor(top)
   bottom = top + 1
}
```

The final four statements actually set all the object's padding values, like this:

```
S(id).paddingLeft   = Px(left)
S(id).paddingRight  = Px(right)
S(id).paddingTop    = Px(top)
S(id).paddingBottom = Px(bottom)
```

How To Use It

Thankfully, using this plug-in is a great deal simpler than describing it. To zoom an object either up or down all you need to do is pass the object to `Zoom()`, along with start and end dimensions, like this:

```
Zoom(myobject, 1, 1, 100, 100, 20, 20, 1000, 0, 0)
```

This statement will zoom `myobject` from a width and height of 100 pixels each to just 20 each. You can also get fancy and turn a horizontal rectangle into a vertical one, like this:

```
Zoom(myobject, 1, 1, 100, 10, 10, 100, 1000, 0, 0)
```

This will change `myobject` from being 100 by 10 pixels to 10 by 100 pixels over the course of 1000 milliseconds.

The following example displays four 86 by 86 pixel icons at a width and height of 70 by 70 pixels. You can then pass your mouse over them to zoom them up to their original size and back down again:

```
<img id='i1' src='i1.gif' />
<img id='i2' src='i2.gif' />
<img id='i3' src='i3.gif' />
<img id='i4' src='i4.gif' />

<script>
window.onload = function()
{
   ids = Array('i1', 'i2', 'i3', 'i4')
   Zoom(ids, 1, 1, 86,86, 70,70, 1, 1, 0)
   O(ids, 'onmouseover', 'up')
   O(ids, 'onmouseout',  'down')

   function up()
   {
      Zoom(this, 1, 1, 70, 70, 86, 86, 200, 1, 1)
   }

   function down()
   {
      Zoom(this, 1, 1, 86, 86, 70, 70, 200, 1, 1)
   }
}
</script>
```

The first four lines of HTML display the icons and give them unique IDs. The `<script>` section then creates the array `ids` out of these IDs, which is used in the following line to zoom down all the icons from 86 by 86 pixels to 70 by 70. It passes a value of 1 millisecond so that the change is virtually instantaneous.

Then the `O()` plug-in attaches the `up()` and `down()` functions to all these icons' `onmouseover` and `onmouseout` events en masse. In these functions, the calls to `Zoom()` set the `pad` argument to `true` so that all the icons are padded as they zoom and, therefore, retain the same overall dimensions (so keeping the surrounding icons from moving about during the zooms).

The `interruptible` argument is set to `true` so that each zoom can be smoothly interrupted and reversed as you pass your mouse over and away from each icon.

If you wish to experiment, try changing the values of the `pad` and `interruptible` arguments to `false` or zero and see what happens when you toggle the values of the `w` and `h` arguments (as long as at least one remains `true` or 1) to change the types of zooms.

The Plug-in

```
function Zoom(id, w, h, fromw, fromh, tow, toh,
   msecs, pad, interruptible, CB)
{
   if (id instanceof Array)
   {
      for (var j = 0 ; j < id.length ; ++j)
         Zoom(id[j], w, h, fromw, fromh, tow, toh,
            msecs, pad, interruptible, CB)
      return
   }

   if (typeof O(id).ZO_X == UNDEF)
   {
      O(id).ZO_X = X(id)
      O(id).ZO_Y = Y(id)
   }

   if (!O(id).ZO_Flag)
   {
      O(id).ZO_W     = Math.max(fromw, tow)
      O(id).ZO_H     = Math.max(fromh, toh)
      O(id).ZO_Count = 0
   }
   else
   {
      if (!O(id).ZO_Int) return
      else clearInterval(O(id).ZO_IID)


      O(id).ZO_Count = (msecs / INTERVAL) - O(id).ZO_Count
   }

   var maxw  = Math.max(fromw, tow)
   var maxh  = Math.max(fromh, toh)
   var stepw = (tow - fromw) / (msecs / INTERVAL)
   var steph = (toh - fromh) / (msecs / INTERVAL)

   S(id).overflow = HID
   O(id).ZO_Flag  = true
   O(id).ZO_Int   = interruptible
   O(id).ZO_IID   = setInterval(DoZoom, INTERVAL)
```

```
function DoZoom()
{
   if (w) O(id).ZO_W = Math.round(fromw + stepw * O(id).ZO_Count)
   if (h) O(id).ZO_H = Math.round(fromh + steph * O(id).ZO_Count)

   Resize(id, O(id).ZO_W, O(id).ZO_H)

   var midx = O(id).ZO_X + Math.round((maxw - O(id).ZO_W) / 2)
   var midy = O(id).ZO_Y + Math.round((maxh - O(id).ZO_H) / 2)

   if (pad > 0) ZoomPad(Math.max(fromw, tow),
      Math.max(fromh, toh), O(id).ZO_W, O(id).ZO_H)
   else if (pad != -1) GoTo(id, midx, midy)

   if (O(id).DB_Parent)
      GoToEdge(O(id).DB_Parent, O(id).DB_Where, 50)

   if (++O(id).ZO_Count >= (msecs / INTERVAL))
   {
      var endx      = O(id).ZO_X + Math.round((maxw - tow) / 2)
      var endy      = O(id).ZO_Y + Math.round((maxh - toh) / 2)
      O(id).ZO_Flag = false

      Resize(id, tow, toh)
      clearInterval(O(id).ZO_IID)

      if (pad > 0) ZoomPad(fromw, fromh, tow, toh)
      else if (pad != -1) GoTo(id, endx, endy)

      if (O(id).DB_Parent)
         GoToEdge(O(id).DB_Parent, O(id).DB_Where, 50)
      if (typeof CB != UNDEF) eval(CB)
   }

   function ZoomPad(frw, frh, padw, padh)
   {
      var left   = Math.max(0, frw - Math.round(padw)) / 2
      var right  = left
      var top    = Math.max(0, frh - Math.round(padh)) / 2
      var bottom = top

      if (left != Math.floor(left))
      {
         left  = Math.floor(left)
         right = left + 1
      }

      if (top != Math.floor(top))
      {
         top    = Math.floor(top)
         bottom = top + 1
      }
```

```
            S(id).paddingLeft   = Px(left)
            S(id).paddingRight  = Px(right)
            S(id).paddingTop    = Px(top)
            S(id).paddingBottom = Px(bottom)
        }
    }
}
```

ZoomDown()

This plug-in zooms an object down over time from its current size to zero dimensions. It does this in such a way that the object can also be zoomed back up again with the following plug-in, `ZoomRestore()`. Figure 6-8 shows four icons that have had their `onmouseover` events attached to this plug-in and that are in varying states of zooming after the mouse has swept across them.

About the Plug-in

This plug-in takes an object and zooms it down until it has zero dimensions. It requires the following arguments:

- **`id`** An object, an object ID, or an array of objects and/or object IDs
- **`w`** If `true` or 1, the object's width will be zoomed down
- **`h`** If `true` or 1, the object's height will be zoomed down
- **`msecs`** The number of milliseconds the animation should take
- **`pad`** If 0, the object will be moved during resizing so as to remain centered. If greater than 0, the object will be padded with CSS padding to retain its original dimensions as it zooms down. If –1, no padding will be applied and the object will not be moved during resizing.
- **`interruptible`** If `true` (or 1), this plug-in can be interrupted by a new call on the same object; otherwise, if `false` (or 0), the call is uninterruptible

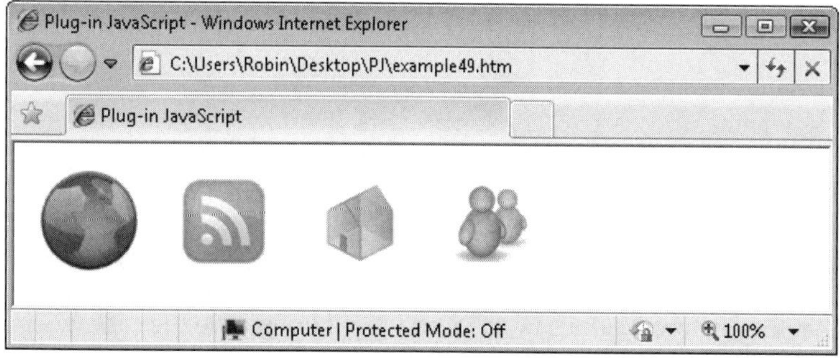

Figure 6-8 These icons are in varying states of zooming down.

Variables, Arrays, and Functions

j	local variable for indexing into id if it is an array
ZO_Flag	Property of id that contains true if a zoom on id is in process
ZO_Int	Property of id that contains true if a zoom is interruptible
ZO_OldW	Property of id containing its previous width
ZO_OldH	Property of id containing its previous height
Zoomdown	Property of id that contains true if it has been zoomed down
Zoom()	Plug-in to zoom an object from one size to another

How It Works

This plug-in starts off with the familiar code to iterate through id if it is an array and recursively call itself with each element to process it individually, as follows:

```
if (id instanceof Array)
{
   for (var j = 0 ; j < id.length ; ++j)
      ZoomDown(id[j], w, h, msecs, pad, interruptible, CB)
   return
}
```

Next, the plug-in checks whether a zoom is already in process on id and, if so, it checks whether that zoom is interruptible, like this:

```
if (O(id).ZO_Flag && !O(id).ZO_Int) return
```

If there is a zoom in action (as determined by the ZO_Flag property of id) and it cannot be interrupted (as determined by id's ZO_Int property) then the plug-in returns. Otherwise the following code is executed:

```
else if (!O(id).ZO_OldW)
{
   O(id).ZO_OldW = W(id)
   O(id).ZO_OldH = H(id)
   O(id).ZO_X    = X(id)
   O(id).ZO_Y    = Y(id)
}
```

This checks whether the ZO_OldW property exists. If it doesn't, id has not been zoomed down before so its current width and height are stored in its ZO_OldW and ZO_OldH properties. These values are obtained using the W() and H() plug-ins. Also, the coordinates of the object are read from X(id) and Y(id) and stored in the ZO_X and ZO_Y properties.

The first of the final three statements sets the Zoomdown property of id to true to indicate that the object is (or is in the process of being) zoomed down. Then the object's location is reset to the stored values in ZO_X and ZO_Y (to handle the case where an object has an odd dimension length and sometimes gets disturbed by a pixel), and the Zoom()

plug-in is called, passing it the original width and height of id, the new zero width and height values, and the value of pad and interruptible, as follows:

```
O(id).Zoomdown = true
GoTo(id, O(id).ZO_X, O(id).ZO_Y)
Zoom(id, w, h, O(id).ZO_OldW, O(id).ZO_OldH, 0, 0,
   msecs, pad, interruptible, CB)
```

How To Use It

To use this function, you pass it an object (or array of objects) and specify the type of zoom down you want (whether to zoom down the horizontal or vertical axis, or both), along with the number of milliseconds it should take, whether to use padding and whether the zoom should be interruptible, like this:

```
ZoomDown(myobject, 1, 1, 1000, 0, 0)
```

This zooms down myobject from whatever its current dimensions are in both the horizontal and vertical directions, over a period of 1000 milliseconds. The final two values specify that no padding should be used and that the zoom should not be interruptible.

Here's an example in which four icons are displayed, which have their onmouseover events attached to this plug-in:

```
<img id='i1' src='i1.gif' />
<img id='i2' src='i2.gif' />
<img id='i3' src='i3.gif' />
<img id='i4' src='i4.gif' />

<script>
window.onload = function()
{
   ids = Array('i1', 'i2', 'i3', 'i4')
   O(ids, 'onmouseover', 'down')


   function down()
   {
      ZoomDown(this, 1, 1, 500, 1, 1)
   }
}
</script>
```

The first section of HTML displays the images and assigns them unique IDs. The <script> section creates the array ids out of the ID names and then passes it to the O() plug-in, which attaches the down() function to their onmouseover events.

The function down() simply calls ZoomDown() to zoom each icon down when the mouse passes over it. You will notice that once an icon has been zoomed down you can still pass the mouse over the empty space it leaves to activate another zoom. This is because the previous width and height values of each object are stored by the ZoomDown() plug-in.

Rather than allowing this messy behavior, you can attach the following plug-in, `ZoomRestore()`, to the icons, so that they will zoom back up when the mouse moves away.

The Plug-in

```
function ZoomDown(id, w, h, msecs, pad, interruptible, CB)
{
   if (id instanceof Array)
   {
      for (var j = 0 ; j < id.length ; ++j)
         ZoomDown(id[j], w, h, msecs, pad, interruptible, CB)
      return
   }

   if (O(id).ZO_Flag && !O(id).ZO_Int) return
   else if (!O(id).ZO_OldW)
   {
      O(id).ZO_OldW = W(id)
      O(id).ZO_OldH = H(id)
      O(id).ZO_X    = X(id)
      O(id).ZO_Y    = Y(id)
   }

   O(id).Zoomdown = true
   GoTo(id, O(id).ZO_X, O(id).ZO_Y)
   Zoom(id, w, h, O(id).ZO_OldW, O(id).ZO_OldH, 0, 0,
      msecs, pad, interruptible, CB)
}
```

PLUG-IN 51 ZoomRestore()

This is the partner plug-in for `ZoomDown()`. With it you can restore a previously zoomed down object over time to its original dimensions. In Figure 6-9, four icons have been displayed with their `onmouseover` events attached to the `ZoomDown()` plug-in and their `onmouseout` events attached to this plug-in.

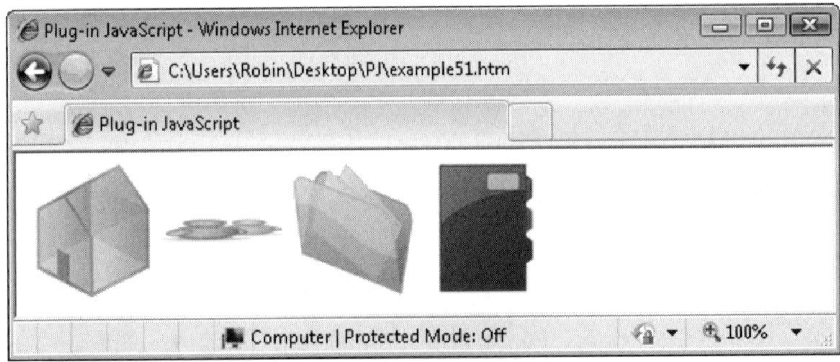

FIGURE 6-9 The icons can now be zoomed down and back up with the mouse.

About the Plug-in

This plug-in takes an object that has been zoomed down and over time zooms it back to its original dimensions. It takes the following arguments:

- **`id`** An object, an object ID, or an array of objects and/or object IDs
- **`w`** If `true` or 1, the object's width will be zoomed up
- **`h`** If `true` or 1, the object's height will be zoomed up
- **`msecs`** The number of milliseconds the animation should take
- **`pad`** If 0, the object will be moved during resizing so as to remain centered. If greater than 0, the object will be padded with CSS padding to retain its original dimensions as it zooms down. If –1, no padding will be applied and the object will not be moved during resizing.
- **`interruptible`** If `true` (or 1), this plug-in can be interrupted by a new call on the same object; otherwise, if `false` (or 0), the call is uninterruptible

Variables, Arrays, and Functions

`j`	Local variable for indexing into `id` if it is an array
`ZO_Flag`	Property of `id` that contains `true` if a zoom on `id` is in process
`ZO_Int`	Property of `id` that contains `true` if a zoom is interruptible
`ZO_OldW`	Property of `id` containing its previous width
`ZO_OldH`	Property of `id` containing its previous height
`Zoomdown`	Property of `id` that contains `true` if it has been zoomed down
`Zoom()`	Plug-in to zoom an object from one size to another

How It Works

This plug-in begins with the familiar code to iterate through `id` if it is an array and recursively call itself with each element to process it individually, as follows:

```
if (id instanceof Array)
{
   for (var j = 0 ; j < id.length ; ++j)
      ZoomRestore(id[j], w, h, msecs, pad, interruptible, CB)
   return
}
```

Next, the plug-in checks whether a zoom is already in process on `id` and if so it checks whether that zoom is interruptible, like this:

```
if ((O(id).ZO_Flag && !O(id).ZO_Int) || !O(id).Zoomdown)
    return
```

If there is a zoom in action (as determined by the `ZO_Flag` property of `id`,) and it cannot be interrupted (as determined by `id`'s `ZO_Int` property) then the plug-in returns.

The Zoomdown property of id is also checked, because if it is not true then the object is not zoomed down, so the plug-in also returns.

The final two statements set the Zoomdown property of id to false to indicate that the object is (or is in the process of being) zoomed up, and then the Zoom() plug-in is called, passing it the current zero width and height of id, the object's previously saved original width and height values in the ZO_OldW and ZO_OldH properties, and the value of pad and interruptible, as follows:

```
O(id).Zoomdown = false
Zoom(id, w, h, 0, 0, O(id).ZO_OldW, O(id).ZO_OldH,
   msecs, pad, interruptible, CB)
```

How To Use It

To use this function, you pass it an object (or array of objects) that has already been zoomed down and specify the type of zoom up you want (whether to zoom the horizontal or vertical axis, or both), along with the number of milliseconds it should take, whether to use padding, and whether the zoom should be interruptible, like this:

```
ZoomRestore(myobject, 1, 1, 1000, 0, 0)
```

This restores the dimensions of myobject over a period of 1000 milliseconds from zero width and height, back to its original values. The final two values specify that no padding should be used, and that the zoom should not be interruptible.

The following examples extend the previous plug-in, ZoomDown(), to restore the icons back to their original sizes when the mouse moves away from them:

```
<img id='i1' src='i3.gif' />
<img id='i2' src='i4.gif' />
<img id='i3' src='i5.gif' />
<img id='i4' src='i6.gif' />

<script>
window.onload = function()
{
   ids = Array('i1', 'i2', 'i3', 'i4')
   O(ids, 'onmouseover', 'down')
   O(ids, 'onmouseout',  'up')

   function down()
   {
      ZoomDown(this, 0, 1, 500, 1, 1)
   }

   function up()
   {
      ZoomRestore(this, 0, 1, 500, 1, 1)
   }
}
</script>
```

For this example I set the horizontal w argument of the calls to 0 so that only the height of the objects is allowed to be resized. This has the effect of making the icons appear to spin around their horizontal axes if you let them zoom all the way down and back up again. You could alternatively set the vertical h argument to zero instead (but not both), and then the icons would appear to spin around their vertical axes.

The Plug-in

```
function ZoomRestore(id, w, h, msecs, pad, interruptible, CB)
{
   if (id instanceof Array)
   {
      for (var j = 0 ; j < id.length ; ++j)
         ZoomRestore(id[j], w, h, msecs, pad, interruptible, CB)
      return
   }

   if ((O(id).ZO_Flag && !O(id).ZO_Int) || !O(id).Zoomdown)
       return

   O(id).Zoomdown = false
   Zoom(id, w, h, 0, 0, O(id).ZO_OldW, O(id).ZO_OldH,
      msecs, pad, interruptible, CB)
}
```

PLUG-IN 52 ZoomToggle()

The final plug-in in this chapter brings the last few zooming plug-ins together into a single one that can zoom both down and up, in three different ways. In Figure 6-10, four icons have been displayed, each of which is attached to this plug-in and set to zoom around its vertical axis when the mouse passes in and out.

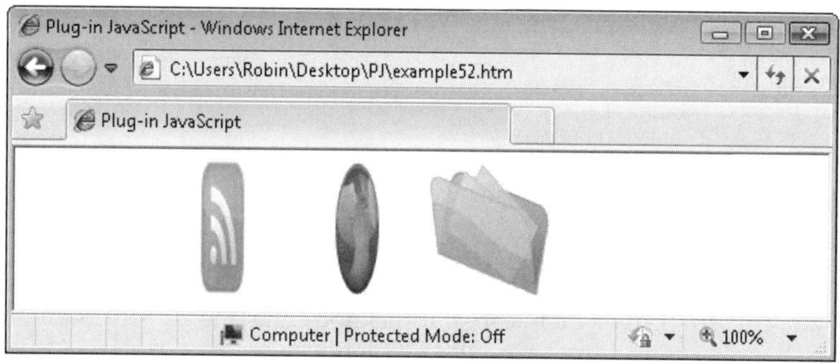

FIGURE 6-10 The ZoomToggle() plug-in being used on four different icons

About the Plug-in

This plug-in toggles the zoomed down state of an object. If it is zoomed down then the object is restored to its original dimensions; otherwise, the object is zoomed down to zero width and height. It requires the following arguments:

- **id** An object, an object ID, or an array of objects and/or object IDs
- **w** If `true` or 1, the object's width will be zoomed
- **h** If `true` or 1, the object's height will be zoomed
- **msecs** The number of milliseconds the animation should take
- **pad** If 0, the object will be moved during resizing so as to remain centered. If greater than 0, the object will be padded with CSS padding to retain its original dimensions as it zooms down. If –1, no padding will be applied and the object will not be moved during resizing.
- **interruptible** If `true` (or 1), this plug-in can be interrupted by a new call on the same object; otherwise, if `false` (or 0), the call is uninterruptible

Variables, Arrays, and Functions

`j`	Local variable for indexing into `id` if it is an array
`ZO_Flag`	Property of `id` that contains `true` if a zoom on `id` is in process
`ZO_Int`	Property of `id` that contains `true` if a zoom is interruptible
`Zoomdown`	Property of `id` that contains `true` if it has been zoomed down
`ZoomDown()`	Plug-in to zoom an object down to zero width and height
`ZoomRestore()`	Plug-in to zoom an object back to its original dimensions

How It Works

This plug-in begins with the familiar code to iterate through `id` if it is an array and recursively call itself with each element to process it individually, as follows:

```
if (id instanceof Array)
{
   for (var j = 0 ; j < id.length ; ++j)
      ZoomRestore(id[j], w, h, msecs, pad, interruptible, CB)
   return
}
```

Next, the `ZO_Flag` property of `id` is tested. If it is `true`, a zoom is currently in progress on `id` so the `ZO_Int` property is then tested. If it is not `true`, the current zoom may not be interrupted, so the plug-in returns, using the following code:

```
if (O(id).ZO_Flag && !O(id).ZO_Int) return
```

The final two statements check the Zoomdown property of id. If it is not true, the object is not zoomed down so the ZoomDown() plug-in is called; otherwise, the object is zoomed down so the ZoomRestore() plug-in is called, as follows:

```
if (!O(id).Zoomdown) ZoomDown(id, w, h, msecs, pad, interruptible, CB)
else                 ZoomRestore(id, w, h, msecs, pad, interruptible, CB)
```

How To Use It

To use this plug-in, you don't need to keep track of an object's zoom down state because you can just call it and the plug-in will decide whether an object requires zooming down or up. All you need to do is specify whether the zoom can occur in the horizontal or vertical direction (or both), the speed of the zoom, whether to pad the object, and if the zoom should be interruptible, like this:

```
ZoomToggle(myobject, 1, 0, 750, 0, 0)
```

This statement will toggle the zoom down state of the object myobject and allows the zoom to progress only on its width (so the object will appear to rotate about its vertical axis). The zoom will take 750 milliseconds, will not pad myobject, and is not interruptible.

The following example is similar to those in the last couple of plug-ins in that four icons are displayed and their zoom states can be controlled by passing the mouse in and out of them:

```
<img id='i1' src='i6.gif' />
<img id='i2' src='i2.gif' />
<img id='i3' src='i1.gif' />
<img id='i4' src='i5.gif' />

<script>
window.onload = function()
{
   ids = Array('i1', 'i2', 'i3', 'i4')
   ZoomToggle(Array('i1', 'i3'), 1, 1, 1, 1, 0)
   O(ids, 'onmouseover', 'toggle')
   O(ids, 'onmouseout',  'toggle')

   function toggle()
   {
      ZoomToggle(this, 1, 0, 500, 1, 1)
   }
}
</script>
```

There is an extra call to ZoomToggle() just after the ids array is assigned, which toggles the zoom down state of the first and third icons. This means that the ZoomToggle() effect can be easily seen as you pass your mouse over the icons, and some zoom into view while others zoom down. I have chosen to allow the zoom to occur only on an object's width so that the icons appear to be spinning around their vertical axes.

In Chapter 7, I'll show how you can connect or chain a set of plug-ins together, among other goodies, so that each one is called only when the previous one has finished. This allows for some very creative and professional-looking animation effects and also further extends user interaction.

NOTE *Don't forget that while I have concentrated on images in this chapter, all the plug-ins will work on any type of object, so you can slide, deflate, and zoom chunks of HTML or anything that can be placed in or is a visible object.*

The Plug-in

```
function ZoomToggle(id, w, h, msecs, pad, interruptible, CB)
{
   if (id instanceof Array)
   {
      for (var j = 0 ; j < id.length ; ++j)
         ZoomToggle(id[j], w, h, msecs, pad, interruptible, CB)
      return
   }

   if (O(id).ZO_Flag && !O(id).ZO_Int) return

   if (!O(id).Zoomdown) ZoomDown(id, w, h, msecs, pad, interruptible, CB)
   else                 ZoomRestore(id, w, h, msecs, pad, interruptible, CB)
}
```

CHAPTER 7

Chaining and Interaction

In this chapter I'll show you how you can chain together many of the plug-ins in this book to form sequences of actions or animations. These can be animations you write to create stunning opening effects, or they can be small chains to perform simple actions such as moving menu elements.

Chaining is also useful for ensuring that one action will follow another. This can be very hard to do in JavaScript because it is event driven, and therefore plug-ins called at the same time will normally run in parallel with each other. However, by adding what is known as a *callback* function at the end of many of the plug-ins, one plug-in can be set to call another when it completes—hence the term chaining.

You'll also learn how you can use callbacks (like a mini, two-part chain) on those functions that support chaining.

PLUG-IN 53 Chain(), NextInChain(), and CallBack()

These plug-ins are a suite of functions that enable you to line up a sequence of plug-in calls to run in sequence, with each one calling the next when it has finished. This is a great way to create amazing animation effects in JavaScript that you might think can only be done in programs such as Java or Flash. Figure 7-1 shows a ball that has been set to bounce around the screen by chaining together four calls to the `Slide()` plug-in.

About the Plug-ins

The `Chain()` plug-in accepts an array of plug-in calls and then pushes them onto a stack so that each call can be popped off one at a time and executed when the previous one finishes. It requires the following argument:

- **`calls`** An array of strings containing a sequence of plug-ins to call

Table 7-1 lists the plug-ins that have the ability to call other plug-ins via a callback.

FIGURE 7-1 A ball is made to bounce around the screen

Chain()	DeflateToggle()	FadeToggle()	Repeat()	While()
CallBack()	Fade()	Hide()	Show()	Zoom()
ChainThis()	FadeBetween()	HideToggle()	Slide()	ZoomDown()
Deflate()	FadeIn()	Pause()	SlideBetween()	ZoomRestore()
DeflateBetween()	FadeOut()	Reflate()	WaitKey()	ZoomToggle()

TABLE 7-1 The Plug-ins That Support the Chaining of Other Plug-ins

Table 7-2 lists the plug-ins that can be called by another plug-in via a callback. You should not include any other plug-in calls within a chain sequence (unless you use the `ChainThis()` plug-in, discussed later), as they will not call up any remaining plug-ins in a chain, so a sequence may be interrupted. However, you can always include your own plug-ins in a chain if you place a call to `NextInChain()` after the final instruction has executed.

CAUTION *Never attempt to insert any of the* `Chain()`, `Repeat()`, *or* `While()` *plug-ins into a chain or you'll get "out of memory," recursion, and possibly other errors. These functions can only be used for creating chains that* don't *contain calls to themselves.*

The `NextInChain()` and `CallBack()` plug-ins are generally not expected to be called directly, although you can do so using the information that follows.

Variables, Arrays, and Functions

j	Local variable to iterate through the `calls` array
CHAIN_CALLS	Global array in which chained plug-ins are stored prior to their execution.
push()	Function to push a value onto an array
pop()	Function to pop a value off an array
eval()	Function to evaluate a string as JavaScript code

How They Work

The `Chain()` plug-in takes the plug-ins stored in the `calls` array and pushes them all onto the global `CHAIN_CALLS` array. Because the last item pushed onto an array is always the

ChainThis()	FadeIn()	Reflate()	ZoomDown()
Deflate()	FadeOut()	Show()	ZoomRestore()
DeflateBetween()	FadeToggle()	Slide()	ZoomToggle()
DeflateToggle()	Hide()	SlideBetween()	
Fade()	HideToggle()	WaitKey()	
FadeBetween()	Pause()	Zoom()	

TABLE 7-2 The Plug-ins That Support Being Chained or Using Callbacks

first one out when using the JavaScript `push()` and `pop()` functions, they would all come out in the reverse order if the elements were pushed onto the array in the order they were encountered. Therefore, the `calls` array is traversed from end to start, pushing each element in turn onto `CHAIN_CALLS`, like this:

```
function Chain(calls)
{
   for (var j = calls.length ; j >= 0 ; --j)
      if (calls[j])
         CHAIN_CALLS.push(calls[j])

   NextInChain()
}
```

The first line is the one that iterates backward through the `calls` array. The second checks that there is something stored in that element and, if there is, the third pushes it onto the `CHAIN_CALLS` global array.

Finally, the `NextInChain()` plug-in (discussed next) is called to start executing the chain.

NOTE *The `push()` and `pop()` JavaScript functions create what is known as a LIFO stack, which stands for* Last In First Out. *With such a system the most recently pushed element is popped off first, and the first element pushed onto the stack is the last one popped off it. But in the case of the `Chain()` plug-in a FIFO* (First In First Out) *stack is required, which is achieved by pushing the contents of the calls array onto the stack in reverse order, so that the sequence in which the stack of calls is executed is the same as in the array originally passed to the `Chain()` plug-in.*

The NextInChain() Plug-in

The `NextInChain()` plug-in simply examines the global `CHAIN_CALLS` array and, if it has any chained calls left to run, pops the next one off and passes it to the `CallBack()` plug-in to execute it, like this:

```
if (CHAIN_CALLS.length)
   CallBack(CHAIN_CALLS.pop())
```

The CallBack() Plug-in

This plug-in allows you to attach a plug-in to be called after the current one finishes execution, like this:

```
var insert = expr.lastIndexOf(')')
var left   = expr.substr(0, insert)
var right  = expr.substr(insert)
var middle = "'NextInChain()'"

if (expr.substr(insert - 1, 1) != '(')
   middle = ', ' + middle

eval(left + middle + right)
```

This code works by passing the name of a plug-in to be called in the `CB` argument for a function call that supports it. It does this by taking the expression passed to it and then inserting the next call in the chain into this expression as its final argument.

To do this the string variables `left`, `right` and `middle` are first created, with `left` containing all the expression up to the insertion point, `middle` a string containing a reference to the `'NextInChain()'` plug-in, and `right` the remainder of the expression after the insertion point. The reference to `'NextInChain()'` uses single quotes within double quotes to ensure that when the string is evaluated, the single quoted string will be processed as a string, and not the result of calling the function named in the string.

Then, if the character immediately preceding the final ')' is not a '(' this means that the expression passed to `CallBack()` includes arguments, so the variable `middle` has a comma and space prepended to it, to act as a variable separator. Otherwise, it keeps its assigned value of `'NextInChain()'`. Finally the three values of `left`, `middle`, and `right` are concatenated and passed to the `eval()` function.

When a plug-in is called up this way it will notice that the `CB` argument is not empty and will therefore evaluate it. In this instance the `NextInChain()` plug-in will be called.

NOTE *The reason for passing the name of a function (or an expression) in* `CB` *this way, rather than simply having the plug-in just call* `NextInChain()`*, is to let you pass expressions of your own to be executed as a callback. To do this you place an expression (or function call) in a string and pass it in the* `CB` *argument to any plug-in that accepts it (listed in Table 7-1). Your expression will then be evaluated when the called plug-in completes.*

The ChainThis() Plug-in

This plug-in allows you to take a plug-in or function that is not chainable (which you can determine by checking Table 7-2) and then use it within a chain. The code is quite simple and looks like this:

```
eval(expr)
NextInChain()
```

For example, suppose that for one of the instructions in a chain you want to move an object using the following statement:

```
GoTo('myobject', x / 2, y + 100)
```

You can make this call chainable by turning it into a string using the `InsVars()` plug-in and `ChainThis()`, as follows:

```
string = InsVars("ChainThis('GoTo(\"myobject\", #1, #2)')",
   x / 2, y + 100)
```

The `InsVars()` plug-in makes it easy to insert variables into a string by using tokens such as #1 and #2 as place holders for them and passing the variables or expressions after the main string.

If you then pass the string `string` to `Chain()` (or `Repeat()` or `While()`) as one of the elements in a chain, the `GoTo()` call will be executed when its turn comes up, and the program flow will pass onto the next item in the chain (if any).

This technique only works well with functions that work procedurally from start to end in a single process. If you use `ChainThis()` on a function that does its job using events or interrupts, you will usually get very unexpected results.

NOTE *You may find with the `InsVars()` plug-in that you use up the main two levels of quotation marks, both double and single, and need a third level of quotation. This is easily accomplished by using the \ escape character before a quotation mark, like this: `\"` or this: `\'`. In fact, you will see that the previous example statement uses this technique when passing the "myobject" ID to `GoTo()`, because the double quote has already been used for the outside of the string and the single quote is used for the substring being passed to `CallBack()`.*

How To Use Them

To use the `Chain()` plug-in, you need to create an array of plug-in calls to be chained together, and each call must be assembled into a string before it is placed into the array. For example, assume you wish to add the following call to a chain:

```
FadeOut(myobject, 1000, 0)
```

To do so, you must first convert it to a string, like this:

```
string1 = 'FadeOut(' + myobject + ', 1000, 0)'
```

Or, if you have a more complicated call, like this:

```
Slide('a', width / 2, height / 2 - 50, width / 2 -20, height / 2, 500, 0)
```

then it would need to be turned into a string, like this:

```
string2 = "Slide('" + a + "', " + width / 2 + ", " + height / 2 - 50 + ", "
+ width / 2 -29 + ", " + "height / 2, 500, 0)"
```

Obviously this quickly gets very messy, so it's almost always much easier to make use of Plug-in 15, `InsVars()`, as in these two simpler versions of the preceding statements:

```
string1 = InsVars('FadeOut('#1', 1000, 0)', myobject)
string2 = InsVars("Slide('#1', #2, #3, #4, #5, 500, 0",
   ball, width / 2, height / 2 - 50, width / 2 -20, height / 2)
```

In these two lines the argument list has simply been placed at the end of the main string, with each value position replaced with a #1, #2, and so on, for each value to be inserted.

The two strings can then be placed in a chain, and the first item in the chain started, using the following statement:

```
Chain(Array(string1, string2))
```

The first statement places the strings in an array which it then passes to the `Chain()` plug-in. Here's an example that uses these techniques to make a ball bounce around the browser:

```
<img id='ball' src='ball.png' />

<script>
window.onload = function()
```

```
{
   Position('ball', ABS)
   width  = GetWindowWidth()
   height = GetWindowHeight()
   r      = width  - 100
   b      = height - 100
   x      = width  / 2 - 50
   y      = height / 2 - 50

   ch1 = InsVars("Slide('ball', #1, #2, #3, #4, 500, 0)", 0, y, x, 0)
   ch2 = InsVars("Slide('ball', #1, #2, #3, #4, 500, 0)", x, 0, r, y)
   ch3 = InsVars("Slide('ball', #1, #2, #3, #4, 500, 0)", r, y, x, b)
   ch4 = InsVars("Slide('ball', #1, #2, #3, #4, 500, 0)", x, b, 0, y)

   Chain(Array(ch1, ch2, ch3, ch4))
}
</script>
```

The HTML section displays a 100 by 100 pixel image of a ball, then the first line of the `<script>` section sets the ball's property style to 'absolute' so that it can be moved about.

After this the width and height of the browser are calculated and stored in `width` and `height`, then the right and bottom positions required to place the ball against these edges are placed in `r` and `b`. These values are simply the width and height of the browser less the ball's width and height of 100 pixels each.

The variables `x` and `y` are also calculated to set them to coordinates that place the ball exactly in the center of the browser (bearing in mind its width and height of 100 pixels).

Next, four `Slide()` plug-in calls are assembled into strings using the `InsVars()` plug-in. In turn, the calls slide the ball from the center left of the browser to the top middle, then to the center right, then to the bottom middle, and finally back to the center left of the browser.

These call strings are then placed in an array and passed to the `Chain()` plug-in to get the ball rolling (so to speak).

NOTE *Because of the way chaining has been implemented with a single global array, you can have only one chain of plug-ins running at a time. You can sometimes carefully create a chain that interleaves two or more separate sets of plug-ins so that a number of different animations appear to be running concurrently. However, you will need to use trial and error to get the best results with this technique.*

Using the CallBack() Function Directly

The `CallBack()` plug-in achieves its functionality by adding the name of a function to call back after the current one has finished execution. You can also do this, as long as the plug-in you call supports chaining, as detailed in Table 7-2.

For example, if you would like to have the `Hide()` plug-in called immediately after a `Deflate()`, you can use code such as this:

```
Deflate(myobject, 1, 1, 500, 0, 'Hide(myobject)')
```

This calls up the `Deflate()` plug-in, passing it `myobject`, with the required parameters to deflate it over 500 milliseconds and without the possibility of the plug-in being interrupted. However, there is a final argument, which is a call to `Hide()`, placed within a string so that the string, not the result of executing the function, is passed.

You will need to tweak the syntax slightly if you are passing object IDs rather than objects within a callback, like this:

```
Deflate('myobject', 1, 1, 500, 0, "Hide('myobject')")
```

This way, after the double quotes are stripped off by the `eval()` function that will eventually execute this callback string, the single quotes will remain to indicate that `myobject` is a string that is an object ID, and not the name of an object.

This procedure is a quick and easy way to create a two-part chain without having to assemble a chain. Remember, however, that it works only on plug-ins that can be inserted into a chain.

The Plug-ins

```
function Chain(calls)
{
   for (var j = calls.length ; j >= 0 ; --j)
      if (calls[j])
         CHAIN_CALLS.push(calls[j])

   NextInChain()
}

function NextInChain()
{
   if (CHAIN_CALLS.length)
      CallBack(CHAIN_CALLS.pop())
}

function CallBack(expr)
{
   var insert = expr.lastIndexOf(')')
   var left   = expr.substr(0, insert)
   var right  = expr.substr(insert)
   var middle = "'NextInChain()'"

   if (expr.substr(insert - 1, 1) != '(')
      middle = ', ' + middle

   eval(left + middle + right)
}

function ChainThis(expr)
{
   eval(expr)
   NextInChain()
}
```

Repeat()

As well as chaining plug-ins together, you can make one or more plug-ins repeat a specified number of times using the `Repeat()` plug-in. In a medium such as a book it's not possible to capture the motion in these examples, so Figure 7-2 shows the ball (slightly grayed out) as it was captured on different repetitions of an animation created using this plug-in.

About the Plug-in

This plug-in allows you to repeat a chain of actions as many times as you like. It requires the following arguments:

- **`number`** The number of times the chain should be repeated
- **`calls`** An array of strings containing a sequence of plug-ins to call

Variables, Arrays, and Functions

`j`	Local variable used for counting the repeats
`temp`	Local copy of the `calls` array
`concat()`	Function to merge two or more arrays
`Chain()`	Plug-in used to chain a group of plug-ins together

How It Works

This plug-in takes the `calls` array and duplicates it enough times so that there are `number` copies of the calls, like this:

```
var temp = calls
for (var j = 1 ; j < number ; ++j)
   calls = calls.concat(temp)
Chain(calls)
```

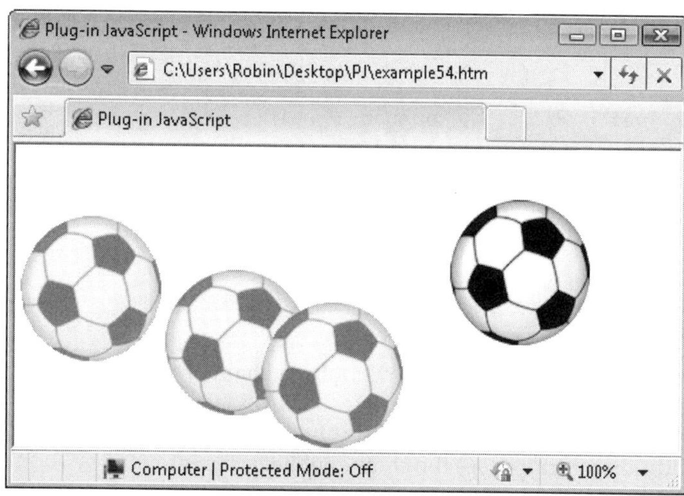

FIGURE 7-2 You can repeat a chain multiple times.

First, the local array `temp` is assigned a copy of `calls`, then the `concat()` function merges the contents of `temp` with `calls`, until there are `number` copies altogether. Finally, the `Chain()` plug-in is called to start the first call running.

How To Use It

Using this plug-in is the same as calling `Chain()` except that you also pass an additional parameter to specify the number of times the chain should repeat.

The following example slightly modifies the one in the `Chain()` and `NextInChain()` plug-ins section to make the ball bounce around the browser 10 times:

```
<img id='ball' src='ball.png' />

<script>
window.onload = function()
{
   Position('ball', ABS)
   width  = GetWindowWidth()
   height = GetWindowHeight()
   r      = width  - 100
   b      = height - 100
   x      = width  / 2 - 50
   y      = height / 2 - 50

   ch1 = InsVars("Slide('ball', #1, #2, #3, #4, 500, 0)", 0, y, x, 0)
   ch2 = InsVars("Slide('ball', #1, #2, #3, #4, 500, 0)", x, 0, r, y)
   ch3 = InsVars("Slide('ball', #1, #2, #3, #4, 500, 0)", r, y, x, b)
   ch4 = InsVars("Slide('ball', #1, #2, #3, #4, 500, 0)", x, b, 0, y)

   Repeat(10, Array(ch1, ch2, ch3, ch4))
}
</script>
```

The Plug-in

```
function Repeat(number, calls)
{
   var temp = calls

   for (var j = 1 ; j < number ; ++j)
      calls = calls.concat(temp)

   Chain(calls)
}
```

PLUG-IN 55 While()

Sometimes you may find it convenient for a chain of plug-ins to keep repeating while a certain condition is `true`; for example, if no key has been pressed or the mouse hasn't been clicked. With this plug-in you can supply a test condition along with a chain and, as long as the condition returns `true`, the chain will keep repeating.

Figure 7-3 shows an animation of a sailing ship that slowly fades into view and sails across the browser, then fades out again. Before each trip the global variable KEY_PRESS is checked and the animation repeats until the space bar is pressed.

About the Plug-in

This plug in takes an expression and an array of statements to chain if the expression evaluates to true. It requires the following parameters:

- **expr** A string containing an expression that can be evaluated to either true or false
- **calls** An array of strings containing a sequence of plug-ins to place in a chain

Variables, Arrays, and Functions

temp	Local string variable used for reconstructing a string from the array in calls
j	Local variable for iterating through the calls array
eval()	Function to evaluate a JavaScript expression
replace()	Function to replace parts of a string
substr()	Function to return part of a string
push()	Function to push a value onto an array
InsVars()	Plug-in for inserting values into a string
Chain()	Plug-in for chaining sequences of plug-ins together

How It Works

This plug-in resides within an if() statement and completes only if the string value passed in expr evaluates to true, like this:

```
if (eval(expr))
```

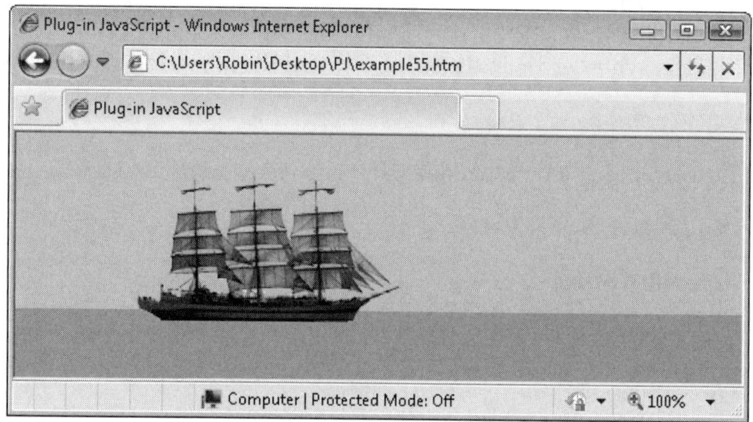

FIGURE 7-3 The ship keeps on sailing until the space bar is pressed.

If it does, the local string `temp` is created and the `calls` array is iterated through using the local variable `j` as an index into it. This is done because the way the chain keeps repeating is to continually pass an entire chain as a single statement of a new chain. To understand this, consider the following pseudo code:

```
if expr is true then…
   Add this statement to a chain
   Also add this statement
   And then add this statement
   Now add all of the above including the if statement to the chain
```

What is happening here is the same as what the code in the `While()` plug-in does. It first evaluates the expression and if it is `true` it sends all the statements it has been passed to the `Chain()` plug-in. Then it also sends all of the preceding statements, so that when the first sequence has finished executing, the `if()` statement and associated calls will come up once again and will be passed once more to the `While()` plug-in to deal with.

The next time around, if `expr` evaluates to `false`, the `While()` plug-in will finish. But if it still evaluates to `true`, then all the statements are again sent to `Chain()`, followed by all the code required to make it start over again. And so the process continues, going round and round until `expr` evaluates to `false`, if it ever does.

How the Additional Call to While() Is Added to a Chain

In essence, what the preceding does is add a call to `While()` as one of the items in a chain. To do this, each element in `calls` is extracted from the array and appended to the string `temp`.

This is because the `Chain()` plug-in, which will be called later, does not accept array elements that are themselves arrays. Instead, such elements must be a string value that will later be converted into an array by a call to `eval()` (by the `NextInChain()` plug-in, which occurs when it is the statement's turn to be executed). The code that creates `temp` is as follows:

```
var temp = ''
for (var j = 0 ; j < calls.length ; ++j)
   temp += '"' + calls[j].replace(/"/g, '\\\"') + '",'
```

Each time round the loop the value in `calls[j]` is extracted, the `replace()` function is used to escape any double quotes, changing them from `"` to `\"`. Because a double quote is also added to the start and end of each string section (followed by a comma), any double quotes that appear inside the strings and are not escaped will clash with the outside quotes and create a syntax error, in the same way that the following statement would fail:

```
string = "She said "Hello""
```

The correct version of this statement with escaped double quotes is:

```
string = "She said \"Hello\""
```

The Assembled String

Let's assume that `calls` contains the following two strings:

```
FadeOut('obj', 50, 0)
FadeIn("Obj", 50, 0)
```

After processing through the previous code it will be turned into the following string:

```
"FadeOut('obj', 50, 0)","FadeIn(\"Obj\", 50, 0)",
```

Now we have a string that can be merged with another string containing the word `Array()` to look like the following (once the final comma is removed):

```
Array("FadeOut('obj', 50, 0)","FadeIn(\"Obj\", 50, 0)")
```

The `eval()` function can then evaluate this string back into an array. As I mentioned, the final comma needs removing, and this is done by the following line of code, which uses the `substr()` function to trim it off:

```
temp = temp.substr(0, temp.length -1)
```

The new string in `temp` is now ready to convert into the final string to be added to the `calls` array as part of the chain, which is done with the following statement:

```
calls.push(InsVars("While('#1', Array(#2))", expr, temp))
```

This uses the `InsVars()` plug-in to insert the value in `expr` and the string just assembled in `temp` into the string that is passed to the `push()` call.

In the case of the previous `calls.push()` statement, if the contents of `expr` is simply the number 1 (an expression that will always be `true`), the entire new string would look like this:

```
While('1', Array("FadeOut('obj', 50, 0)","FadeIn(\"Obj\", 50, 0)"))
```

As you can see, this is a perfectly formatted call to the `While()` plug-in itself and, in fact, it will always be identical to the call that your code made to the plug-in in the first case.

How To Use It

Using this plug-in is much simpler than explaining its workings. All you have to do is make a call to `While()`, passing it an expression as a string and an array of calls to be chained if the expression evaluates to `true`, like this:

```
var c = 0
While("c++ < 3", Array("FadeIn('obj', 50, 0)", "FadeOut('obj', 50, 0)"))
```

Here the variable `c` is assigned the value 0, then `While()` is called, passing it the expression `c++ < 3`. Each time the chain repeats, the value of `c` will be incremented until it is 3, at which point the expression will evaluate as `false`, so the `While()` will finish. In this instance, the object '`obj`' will pulsate three times and then be invisible.

Here's a much more interesting example that animates a ship sailing on the sea, including effects such as fading in and out:

```
<div id='sea'></div>
<img id='ship' src='ship1.png' />

<script>
```

```
window.onload = function()
{
   width  = GetWindowWidth()
   height = GetWindowHeight()
   x      = width  - 200
   y      = height - 150

   Locate('sea', ABS, 0, height - 50)
   Resize('sea', width, 50)
   S(document.body).backgroundColor = '#b7d4dc'
   S('sea').backgroundColor         = '#90a5a6'
   Locate('ship', ABS, 0, y)

   While("KEY_PRESS != ' '",
      Array(
         "FadeIn('ship', 500, 0)",
         InsVars("Slide('ship', #1, #2, #3, #4, 5000,0)", 0, y, x, y),
         "FadeOut('ship', 500, 0)",
         InsVars("CallBack('GoTo(\"ship\", #1, #2)')", 0, y)
      )
   )
}
</script>
```

The two lines of HTML set up a div to represent the sea and display an image of a sailing ship. Next, the `<script>` section starts off by obtaining the width and height of the browser and setting `x` and `y` to values for the sailing ship to use in a call to the `Slide()` plug-in.

After this, the sea is given the property style of 'absolute' so that it can be placed in an exact location, and is then resized so that it takes up the bottom 50 pixels of the browser. To represent the sky and sea colors, the `document.body` object has its background color changed, while the 'sea' object also has its background color changed. Finally, the ship is located at its start position of `0,y`.

The final part of this example is the `While()` statement, which passes the following expression:

```
"KEY_PRESS != ' '"
```

`KEY_PRESS` is a global variable that is automatically set to whatever the value of the last key pressed happens to be, so this expression will return `true` until the space bar is pressed.

The first three statements in the chain of calls are pretty obvious; they fade the ship in, move it across the browser, and then fade it out. However, the final call is a little more interesting because it's an example of using the `CallBack()` plug-in to turn a nonchainable plug-in (in this case `GoTo()`) into a chainable one, for just this single call.

It uses the `InsVars()` plug-in to insert the variables and values into the string containing the `GoTo()` call. This string is then placed within a call to `CallBack()` and becomes chainable.

Therefore, the fourth statement moves the ship back to the start position ready for its next voyage—if the space bar still hasn't been pressed.

NOTE *Because the expression passed to the* `While()` *statement is tested only at the start of each chain of calls, an entire chain will always execute before it can be stopped. If you need more precise control than this you can always empty the global array* `CHAIN_CALLS` *(which contains all the items in a chain). This will stop a chain after the current statement has finished and can be done by issuing the statement* `CHAIN_CALLS.length = 0`*. If you need an even speedier reaction to user input, a* `While()` *statement is not your best choice of plug-in, and you should be looking at creating some event-driven code.*

The Plug-in

```
function While(expr, calls)
{
   if (eval(expr))
   {
      var temp = ''

      for (var j = 0 ; j < calls.length ; ++j)
         temp += '"' + calls[j].replace(/"/g, '\\\"') + '",'

      temp = temp.substr(0, temp.length -1)
      calls.push(InsVars("While('#1', Array(#2))", expr, temp))
      Chain(calls)
   }
}
```

PLUG-IN 56 Pause()

There are often times during an animation when you need it to stop for a while, and you can do this with the `Pause()` plug-in. With it, you can specify a period of time in milliseconds until the next plug-in in a chain is called. In Figure 7-4, the example from the previous plug-in, `While()`, has a few extra commands inserted into the chain, which zoom

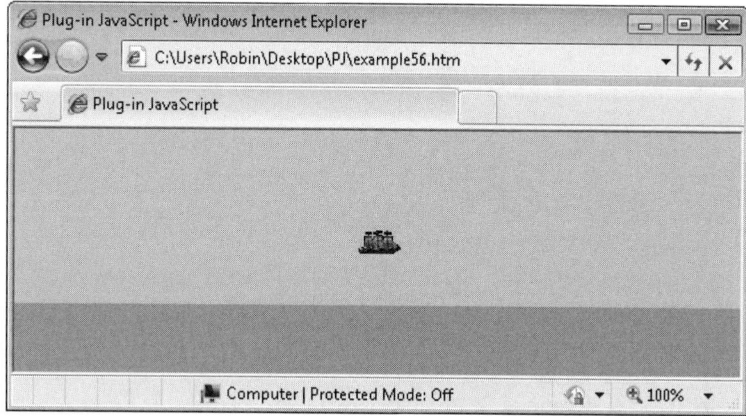

FIGURE 7-4 Inserting time delays into chains

the ship down when it reaches the center of the browser and then pause for 1 second before zooming it back again to resume its journey.

About the Plug-in

This plug-in pauses between commands in a chain for the length of time specified. It takes the following argument:

- **`wait`** Length of time to pause in milliseconds

Variables, Arrays, and Functions

`setTimeout()`	Function to create a single interrupt at some point in the future
`NextInChain()`	Plug-in to run the next command in a chain (if there is one)

How It Works

This plug-in is quite straightforward. It simply makes a call to the `SetTimeout()` function to make it call the `NextInChain()` plug-in after `wait` milliseconds have expired.

Because commands within a chain are linked together via the `NextInChain()` plug-in, this is the only means by which the next command in a chain can be run. By setting the timeout to occur at a future time, the chain will not continue execution until that timeout occurs and `NextInChain()` is called.

Unlike the `setInterval()` function, `setTimeout()` sets up a single interrupt and then forgets all about it once it has occurred, so there is no need to clear it.

How To Use It

To use this plug-in, insert a string such as the following, which will create an event 1.5 seconds in the future to resume execution of the chain, into an array of chain commands:

```
"Pause(1500)"
```

Here's a fun example that illustrates the use of `Pause()` by zooming down the ship in the previous plug-in, `While()`, when it reaches the center of the browser, then pausing for a second before zooming it back in again, letting the ship continue on its course:

```
<div id='sea'></div>
<img id='ship' src='ship.png' />

<script>
window.onload = function()
{
   width  = GetWindowWidth()


   height = GetWindowHeight()
   x      = width  - 200
   y      = height - 150
   mid    = width / 2 - 100
```

```
    Locate('sea', ABS, 0, height - 50)
    Resize('sea', width, 50)
    S(document.body).backgroundColor = '#b7d4dc'
    S('sea').backgroundColor         = '#90a5a6'
    Locate('ship', ABS, 0, y)

    While("KEY_PRESS != \" \"",
       Array(
          "FadeIn('ship', 500, 0)",
          InsVars("Slide('ship', 0, #1, #2, #1, 2500,0)", y, mid),
          "ZoomDown('ship', 1, 1, 250, 0, 0)",
          "Pause(1000)",
          "ZoomRestore('ship', 1, 1, 250, 0, 0)",
          InsVars("Slide('ship', #1, #2, #3, #2, 2500,0)", mid, y, x),
          "FadeOut('ship', 500, 0)",
          InsVars("CallBack('GoTo(\"ship\", 0, #1)')", y)
       )
    )
}
</script>
```

The changes from the previous example are highlighted in bold. As you can see, the main difference is the insertion of a call to `Pause()` between calls to `ZoomDown()` and `ZoomRestore()`. The `Slide()` command for moving the ship has also been split into two halves, and the variable `mid` is used for the midpoint of the ship's journey.

NOTE *Where you already know values and they do not require calculating with an expression (or taking them from a variable), there is no need to use the `InsVars()` plug-in to insert them into a string because you can simply put the values in the string yourself, as I did with the `FadeIn()`, `ZoomDown()`, `Pause()`, `ZoomRestore()`, and `FadeOut()` calls.*

The Plug-in

```
function Pause(wait)
{
   setTimeout("NextInChain()", wait)
}
```

WaitKey()

This plug-in is useful for inserting a pause in a chain that waits until a key is pressed. In Figure 7-5, the chain has been paused and is using this plug-in to wait for a keypress.

About the Plug-in

This plug-in halts execution of a chain until a key is pressed. It requires no arguments.

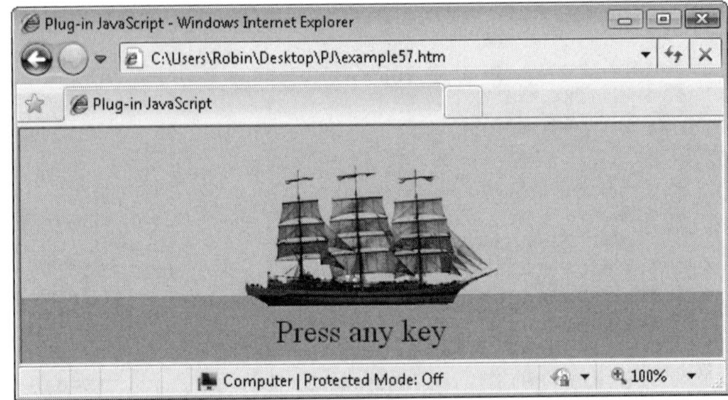

FIGURE 7-5 A chain waits for a keypress

Variables, Arrays, and Functions

`KEY_PRESS`	Global variable containing the value of the last key pressed
`INTERVAL`	Global variable containing the value 30
`GetLastKey()`	Plug-in to return the value of the last key pressed
`NextInChain()`	Plug-in to run the next command in a chain
`DoWaitKey()`	Subfunction to wait for a keypress before allowing a chain to continue execution
`SetTimeout()`	Function to create a single call to another function at a future time

How It Works

This plug-in first calls the `GetLastKey()` function, which removes any key that has been pressed and leaves the global variable `KEY_PRESS` containing the empty string. Next, the `setTimeout()` function is called to create an interrupt call to the `DoWaitKey()` subfunction in `INTERVAL` milliseconds. Here is the code for these two statements:

```
GetLastKey()
setTimeout(DoWaitKey, INTERVAL)
```

When the `DoWaitKey()` subfunction is called, it checks the value of `KEY_PRESS` and, if it is no longer the empty string, the `NextInChain()` plug-in is called to allow the next command in a chain to run (if there is one).

Otherwise, if no key has been pressed, another call to `setTimeout()` is made, which calls `DoWaitKey()` after another `INTERVAL` milliseconds to see if a key has been pressed, using this code:

```
if (KEY_PRESS != '') NextInChain()
else setTimeout(DoWaitKey, INTERVAL)
```

Therefore, if there is a keypress, after calling `NextInChain()` the subfunction returns and will not be called again unless a new call is made to `WaitKey()`, otherwise `DoWaitKey()` will be repeatedly called every `INTERVAL` milliseconds until a key is pressed.

How To Use It

To use this plug-in, you will need to insert it as a string within an array of chain commands, as follows:

```
"WaitKey()"
```

You can then choose to ignore the key that was pressed or have a later command in the chain use the `GetLastKey()` plug-in to return the key and use it.

The following example replaces the somewhat zany zooming down and back up of the previous example in the `Pause()` plug-in section, with a "Press any key" message that fades in, waits for a keypress, and then fades out again—allowing the ship to sail on its way:

```
<div id='sea'></div>
<img id='ship' src='ship.png' />
<span id='note'><font size='5'>Press any key</font></span>

<script>
window.onload = function()
{
   width  = GetWindowWidth()
   height = GetWindowHeight()
   x      = width  - 200
   y      = height - 150
   mid    = width / 2 - 100

   Locate('sea', ABS, 0, height - 50)
   Resize('sea', width, 50)
   S(document.body).backgroundColor = '#b7d4dc'
   S('sea').backgroundColor         = '#90a5a6'
   Locate('ship', ABS, 0, y)
   Locate('note', ABS,0, y + 115)
   CenterX('note')
   Opacity('note', 0)

   While("KEY_PRESS != ' '",
      Array(
         "FadeIn('ship', 500, 0)",
         InsVars("Slide('ship', 0, #1, #2, #1, 2500,0)", y, mid),
         "FadeIn('note', 1000, 0)",
         "WaitKey()",
         "FadeOut('note', 1000, 0)",
         InsVars("Slide('ship', #1, #2, #3, #2, 2500,0)", mid, y, x),
         "FadeOut('ship', 500, 0)",
         InsVars("CallBack('GoTo(\"ship\", 0, #1)')", y)
      )
   )
}
</script>
```

The differences between this and the last example are highlighted in bold. In the HTML section, a new span has been added with the message text. In the `<script>` section, the span is moved to the location where it will later be displayed, and its opacity is set to zero to make it invisible.

Finally, within the chain of commands the previous zoom instructions have been replaced with calls to `FadeIn()`, `WaitKey()`, and `FadeOut()`.

If you press any key except the space bar when the message is displayed, the ship will then proceed on its way and continue repeating in a loop. However, if the key you press *is* the space bar, then the expression at the start of the `While()` command will evaluate to `true`, and the chain will stop repeating.

The Plug-in

```
function WaitKey()
{
   GetLastKey()
   setTimeout(DoWaitKey, INTERVAL)

   function DoWaitKey()
   {
      if (KEY_PRESS != '') NextInChain()
      else setTimeout(DoWaitKey, INTERVAL)
   }
}
```

PLUG-IN 58 Flip()

This plug-in provides a professional flip effect that will appear to spin an object around to reveal its reverse side. Three different spin effects are provided, making this a great way to provide interesting visual effects and offer more information on your web pages.

In Figure 7-6, the photograph of Albert Einstein is attached to a mouse event so that when the mouse passes over the image, it flips to reveal more information. It's not possible to show you the effect in the medium of a book, but think of the image as a trading or similar type of card with a picture on the front and further information on the back. Figure 7-7 shows the "reverse" of the image as the mouse is held over it.

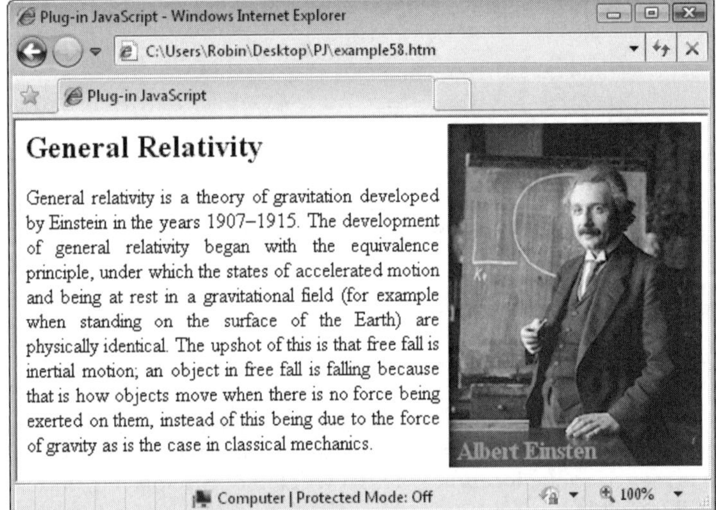

FIGURE 7-6 The image in this web page is reversible when moused over.

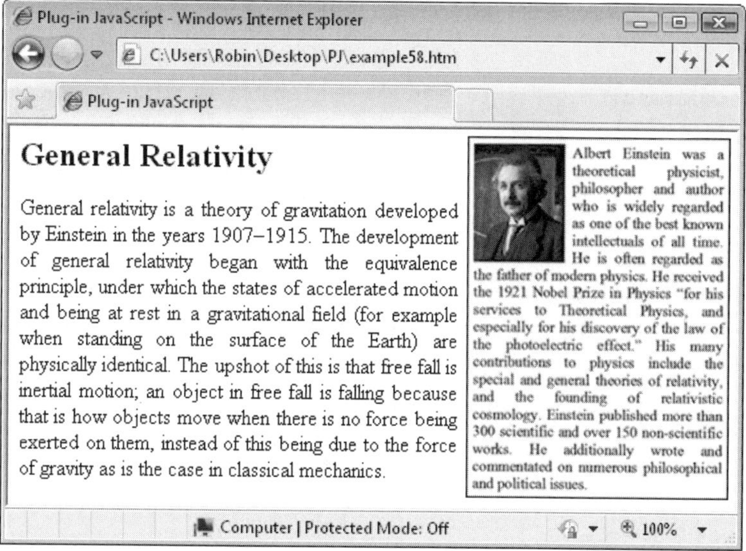

Figure 7-7 When the mouse is passed over the image, it smoothly flips over.

About the Plug-in

This plug-in takes two objects and then animates them so that they appear to flip over as if they are attached back to back. It requires these arguments:

- `id1` An object or object ID—it may not be an array
- `id2` An object or object ID—it may not be an array
- `w` If `true` or 1, the width will be flipped
- `h` If `true` or 1, the height will be flipped
- `msecs` The number of milliseconds the flip should take
- `pad` If set, the objects will be padded to retain their overall dimensions during the flip

Variables, Arrays, and Functions

`swap`	Local string variable containing a command string suitable for `InsVars()` to add a call to `VisibilityToggle()` to a chain
`fast`	Local string variable containing a command string suitable for `InsVars()` to add a 1 millisecond call to `ZoomToggle()` to a chain
`slow`	Local string variable containing a command string suitable for `InsVars()` to add a call of length `msecs / 2` to `ZoomToggle()` to a chain

`ZO_Flag`	Property of either or both `id1` and `id2`, which is set if a zooms already in operation on an object
`CallBack()`	Plug-in to enable any command to be added to a chain
`VisibilityToggle()`	Plug-in to toggle the visibility of an object
`ZoomToggle()`	Plug-in to toggle the zoom state of an object
`Chain()`	Plug-in to start a chain of calls executing

How It Works

This function first checks the state of both `id1` and `id2`'s `ZO_Flag` property. If either is `true`, a zoom is already in operation on an object, so the function returns, like this:

```
if (O(id1).ZO_Flag || O(id2).ZO_Flag) return
```

Next, three local string variables are created as a way to keep the code tidy and stop any lines wrapping around. They are also efficient as each string is used twice. These are the assignments:

```
var swap = "ChainThis('VisibilityToggle(\"#1\")')"
var fast = "ZoomToggle('#1', #2, #3,  1, #4, 0)"
var slow = "ZoomToggle('#1', #2, #3, #4, #5, 0)"
```

The variable `swap` is assigned a string suitable for enabling the `VisibilityToggle()` plug-in to be used in a chain (by implementing it via the `ChainThis()` plug-in). The strings `fast` and `slow` contain strings to place calls to the `ZoomToggle()` plug-in, one of them taking 1 millisecond (and therefore being virtually instantaneous) and the other taking a specified time.

The `#1`, `#2`, and so on within the strings are variable or value place holders. When these strings are passed to the `InsVars()` plug-in, these place holders will be replaced by the values or variables also passed to it.

The final call in the plug-in is to the `Chain()` plug-in, passing it a sequence of six commands, which are all passed through the `InsVars()` plug-in to combine the strings with the variables, like this:

```
Chain(Array(
      InsVars(slow, id1, w, h, msecs / 2, pad),
      InsVars(fast, id2, w, h,            pad),
      InsVars(swap, id2                      ),
      InsVars(slow, id2, w, h, msecs / 2, pad),
      InsVars(swap, id1                      ),
      InsVars(fast, id1, w, h,            pad)
))
```

I have spaced out the code into columns so that you can more clearly see the values being passed. The sequence of commands performs the following six steps:

1. **Zoom `id1` down over half the time specified in `msecs`** This performs the first half of the flip animation.
2. **Zoom `id2` down over the course of 1 millisecond** This ensures that `id2` is quickly zoomed down so that can be zoomed up shortly at normal speed.

3. **Toggle `id2`'s visibility (from hidden to visible)** After `id2` has been zoomed down, this makes it safe to make it visible ready for zooming up.
4. **Zoom `id2` up over half the time specified in `msecs`** This performs the second half of the flip animation.
5. **Toggle `id1`'s visibility (from visible to hidden)** This tidies up after the flip by making `id1` invisible.
6. **Zoom `id1` up over the course of 1 millisecond** Once invisible, `id1` is zoomed back up again, and the objects are then in a state where the flip can be reversed.

How To Use It

To create a flip animation, you need to first have two objects of equal dimensions. They must then be overlaid on each other with the second object's visibility property turned off, using code such as this:

```
ids = Array('a', 'b')
Locate(ids, ABS, 10, 10)
VisibilityToggle('b')
Flip('a', 'b', 1, 0, 1000, 0)
```

This code takes two objects that have been given the IDs of 'a' and 'b', places their names in the array `ids`, and then locates them at the absolute position 10,10 with a call to the `Locate()` plug-in. Object 'b' then has its visibility turned off by the `VisibilityToggle()` plug-in. Finally, the `Flip()` plug-in is called with the two objects and set to flip only the width (so that the flip will twist around the vertical axis). A time of 1000 milliseconds is specified and padding is not used.

Here's an example that creates a mini web page on the subject of general relativity with a photo of Albert Einstein that flips when you pass the mouse over it, revealing more information on the reverse side:

```
<img id='a' src='einstein1.png' />
<img id='b' src='einstein2.png' />
<div id='c'><font size='5'><b>General Relativity</b></font>
<p align='justify'>General relativity is a theory of gravitation
developed by Einstein in the years 1907-1915. The development of
general relativity began with the equivalence principle, under which
the states of accelerated motion and being at rest in a gravitational
field (for example when standing on the surface of the Earth) are
physically identical. The upshot of this is that free fall is inertial
motion; an object in free fall is falling because that is how objects
move when there is no force being exerted on them, instead of this
being due to the force of gravity as is the case in classical
mechanics.</p></div>

<script>
window.onload = function()
{
   Hide('c')
   width  = GetWindowWidth()
```

```
    Resize('c', width - 220, 260)
    Show('c')
    ids = Array('a', 'b')
    Locate(ids, ABS, width - 205, 5)
    Resize(ids, 200, 264)
    VisibilityToggle('b')
    O('a').onmouseover = function() { Flip('a', 'b', 1, 0, 250, 0) }
    O('b').onmouseout  = function() { Flip('b', 'a', 1, 0, 250, 0) }
}
</script>
```

The HTML section displays the two images along with a div containing the article text. The `<script>` section then hides the text with a call to `Hide()` because it is going to be resized; if it didn't do this, the Internet Explorer browser would return the wrong browser width in the next command as it would prepare for possibly requiring a scroll bar. After resizing the article text, the `Show()` plug-in is called to display it again and, now that it has its dimensions reduced to fit within the current window, Internet Explorer will not try to leave a gap for a scroll bar in case it should need it.

Next, the `ids` array is populated with the image IDs and is passed to the `Locate()` plug-in to place them at the top right corner of the browser. The `Resize()` plug-in is also called because, unfortunately, odd widths and heights sometimes cause a slight 1-pixel disturbance to animations depending on the browser used (something to do with the way they handle rounding), so ensuring that both dimensions of objects passed to `Flip()` are even is the easiest way to get the best results. It also ensures that both images have the same dimensions and will flip neatly.

Next, the second object is set to invisible before setting up the mouse events to call `Flip()`. This *must* be done because the two images are overlaid on each other and could have varying `zIndex` values, so you must ensure the correct one is at the front by making the other one invisible.

In the final two lines, the `onmouseover` event of object 'a' is attached to a flip from object 'a' to 'b', while the `onmouseout` event of object 'b' is attached to a flip from object 'b' to 'a'.

Before any flips, object 'a' will be visible, so passing the mouse over it will start the flip. After the flip has finished, object 'b' will be visible and the mouse will still be over it (unless the user quickly moved it away), which is why the `onmouseout` even of object 'b' is attached: so the animation will flip back again when the mouse moves away.

Objects as well as images

Although images give the best flip results, you can pass any kind of object such as a div or table and so on, to the `Flip()` plug-in. This means you could, for example, have an e-mail button that flips over when the mouse passes over it to reveal a small form for entering your e-mail address to subscribe to newsletters. If you do this, text and objects will flow in and out of the object rather than rotate the way an image does, so you get a slightly different—but still interesting—effect.

You can also use `Flip()` to swap sections of HTML according to the selection of radio button or clicking of links. And don't forget that you can flip objects horizontally and vertically, or you can even do both at the same time to create a zoom-away-and-back-again effect. Try changing the values in the `Flip()` calls of the last two lines of the example and see what different results you get.

NOTE *As already mentioned, when using objects that have an odd value for one or more dimensions you may see a slight one pixel jitter occur either horizontally or vertically during a flip. This happens because there are differences between the way different browsers round fractional numbers and is fixed by the plug-in remembering the object's positions before a flip and restoring them afterwards. Even though it's almost imperceptible, if you wish to avoid this tiny disturbance, you should work only with dimensions that have even values. It's quite easy to ensure this with a call to the* `Resize()` *plug-in prior to using* `Flip()`.

The Plug-in

```
function Flip(id1, id2, w, h, msecs, pad)
{
   if (O(id1).ZO_Flag || O(id2).ZO_Flag) return

   var swap = "ChainThis('VisibilityToggle(\"#1\")')"
   var fast = "ZoomToggle('#1', #2, #3,  1, #4, 0)"
   var slow = "ZoomToggle('#1', #2, #3, #4, #5, 0)"

   Chain(Array(
      InsVars(slow, id1, w, h, msecs / 2, pad),
      InsVars(fast, id2, w, h,            pad),
      InsVars(swap, id2                      ),
      InsVars(slow, id2, w, h, msecs / 2, pad),
      InsVars(swap, id1                      ),
      InsVars(fast, id1, w, h,            pad)
   ))
}
```

PLUG-IN 59 HoverSlide()

This plug-in places an object on one of the edges of the browser with a small portion of it revealed and the remainder hidden. When you pass your mouse over it, the object slides out into the window to reveal itself and then slides back in again when you move the mouse away.

Figure 7-8 shows an object that has been attached to the top of a browser, showing only the keys of a piano. In Figure 7-9, the mouse has passed over the keyboard and slid the object into the browser to reveal itself.

About the Plug-in

This plug-in places an object across one edge of a browser boundary with most of it unseen, outside the browser, and a small area showing that you can pass the mouse over to make the object slide in and out. It requires the following arguments:

- **`id`** Either an object or an object ID—this cannot be an array of objects
- **`where`** The edge to which the object should be attached out of 'top', 'left', 'right', and 'bottom'

FIGURE 7-8 An object is attached to the browser top showing only its bottom.

- `offset` The amount by which the object should be offset from the left or top of the edge—if `offset` is a number, the amount is an exact offset in pixels, but if it is a string prefaced with a % symbol (such as "%50"), then the object is to be placed that percent along the edge
- `showing` The number of pixels by which the object must poke into the browser
- `msecs` The number of milliseconds it should take for the object to slide either in or out

FIGURE 7-9 After moving the mouse over the object, it slides into view.

Variables, Arrays, and Functions

w & h	Local variables containing the furthest positions along and down an edge that id can be placed
o	Local variable containing the position in pixels along or down the edge at which to display id
t	Local variable containing the portion of the object in pixels that isn't displayed when id is slid out
u	Local variable containing the number of steps in the animation
x, y	Local variable containing the coordinates of the top left corner of id
s	Local variable containing the amount by which to move id for each step when it is sliding
ox, oy	Local variables used while updating the HS_X and HS_Y properties of id
HS_X, HS_Y	Properties of id containing its top left coordinates
HS_IID	Property of id used for clearing repeating interrupts set up by setInterval()
INTERVAL	Global variable containing the value 30
TP, BM, LT, RT	Global variables standing for 'top', 'bottom', 'left', and 'right'
onmouseover	Event attached to id when the mouse passes over it
onmouseout	Event attached to id when the mouse passes out of it
Math.max()	Function to return the maximum of two values
Math.min()	Function to return the minimum of two values
setInterval()	Function to start repeating interrupts
clearInterval()	Function to end repeating interrupts
substr()	Function to return part of a string
GetWindowWidth()	Plug-in to return the width of the browser
GetWindowHeight()	Plug-in to return the height of the browser
W()	Plug-in to return the width of an object
H()	Plug-in to return the height of an object
GoTo()	Plug-in to move an object to a new location
SlideIn()	Subfunction to start id sliding into the browser
SlideOut()	Subfunction to start id sliding out of the browser
DoSlideIn()	Sub-subfunction to perform the slide in animation
DoSlideOut()	Sub-subfunction to perform the slide out animation

How It Works

This plug-in begins by finding the farthest possible position along or down an edge that id can be placed, by taking the browser width, subtracting the width of id from it, and placing the result into w. The variable h is also calculated for the vertical edges, as follows:

```
var w = GetWindowWidth()  - W(id)
var h = GetWindowHeight() - H(id)
```

Next, the variable o is set to zero if offset is a number or, if offset is a string beginning with the % character, o is given the value resulting from dividing the numeric part of the argument by 100. In the first instance, the value of zero will indicate later that an exact offset in pixels has been passed in offset, but in the second case, a percentage distance along the edge has been specified for where id should be located, and that value is now in o. Here is the code that does this:

```
var o = offset[0] != '%' ? 0 : offset.substr(1) / 100
```

If the Left or Right Edge Has Been Chosen

Next, the plug-in needs to determine which edge is going to be used, so it first tests the value where against the global variables LT and RT (which contain the strings 'left' and 'right'). If it is one of these, then the following code is executed:

```
var t = W(id) - showing
var u = Math.min(t, msecs / INTERVAL)
var x = where == LT ? -t : w + t
var y = o ? h * o : offset
var s = t / u
```

This assigns the amount of id that isn't shown by default to t, then u is assigned the number of steps the animation requires to complete in msecs milliseconds. After this, the x and y coordinates are determined by checking the where argument again to see if it contains 'left' (the value of LT). If it does, it means the left edge is being used, so x is set to -t, which places id sufficiently off screen so that only showing pixels of the object are visible. Otherwise, x is set to move the object off the right hand edge of the screen in a similar fashion.

The y variable is similarly calculated, being set either to the value in offset if o is zero (in other words, an absolute offset along the edge was requested), or set to h * o because o is a fractional value representing the percent along the edge that the object should be located, and h is the maximum distance down the edge that the object may appear.

Finally, s, the step distance by which id should be moved for each frame of a slide, is calculated by dividing t (the amount of id that isn't shown by default) by u (the number of steps required to make the animation last msecs milliseconds). These variables will all be used during the animation stages of the plug-in.

If the Top or Bottom Edge Has Been Chosen

If either the top or bottom edge has been chosen for the object's placement, a very similar set of calculations is made to obtain the values required for t, u, x, y, and s, as follows:

```
var t = H(id) - showing
var u = Math.min(t, msecs / INTERVAL)
var x = o ? w * o : offset
var y = where == TP ? -t : h + t
var s = t / u
```

Setting Up the Events

The final few lines of code in the setup section move `id` to the location `x,y`; store a copy of each in the `HS_X` and `HS_Y` properties; and set up the `onmouseover` and `onmouseout` events to call up the `SlideIn()` and `SlideOut()` subfunctions, respectively:

```
GoTo(id, x, y)
O(id).HS_X = x
O(id).HS_Y = y
O(id).onmouseover = SlideIn
O(id).onmouseout  = SlideOut
```

The SlideIn() Subfunction

The job of this function is to slide the object into view when the mouse passes over any part of it. The first thing it does is cancel any previously running regular interrupts (for instance, if the object was in the process of sliding out) with a call to `clearInterval()`, and then it sets up a new regular interrupt to the `DoSlideIn()` sub-subfunction, like this:

```
if (O(id).HS_IID) clearInterval(O(id).HS_IID)
O(id).HS_IID = setInterval(DoSlideIn, INTERVAL)
```

This sub-subfunction is where all the animation takes place. First, though, to make use of smaller, more manageable variable names, `ox` and `oy` are given the values in the `HS_X` and `HS_Y` properties of `id`. These are the location of the top left corner of `id`:

```
var ox = O(id).HS_X
var oy = O(id).HS_Y
```

Next, a group of `if... else if...` statements test for whether the edge being used is the top, bottom, left, or right by checking the argument `where` against the global variables `TP`, `BM`, `LT`, and `RT`. Then, as long as `id` still has further to move, the value of either `ox` or `oy` is incremented or decremented by the step value in `s`. Otherwise, if there is no further movement to make, the `clearInterval()` function is called to stop the repeating interrupts, like this:

```
if      (where == TP && oy < 0) oy = Math.min(0, oy + s)
else if (where == BM && oy > h) oy = Math.max(h, oy - s)
else if (where == LT && ox < 0) ox = Math.min(0, ox + s)
else if (where == RT && ox > w) ox = Math.max(w, ox - s)
else clearInterval(O(id).HS_IID)
```

Finally, the object is moved to the new location in `ox` and `oy`, and the `HS_X` and `HS_Y` properties are assigned these values, as follows:

```
GoTo(id, ox, oy)
O(id).HS_X = ox
O(id).HS_Y = oy
```

The SlideOut() Subfunction

The job of this function is to slide the object away again when the mouse passes out of it. The first thing it does is cancel any previously running regular interrupts (for instance, if the object was in the process of sliding in) with a call to `clearInterval()`. Then it sets up a new regular interrupt to the `DoSlideOut()` sub-subfunction, like this:

```
if (O(id).HS_IID) clearInterval(O(id).HS_IID)
O(id).HS_IID = setInterval(DoSlideOut, INTERVAL)
```

As with the similar function `DoSlideIn()`, copies of the properties used are first placed into shorter variable names, like this:

```
var ox = O(id).HS_X
var oy = O(id).HS_Y
```

Then, if the movement hasn't completed, the values of `ox` and `oy` are modified as necessary depending upon which edge is being used; otherwise the repeating interrupt is cancelled, as follows:

```
if      (where == TP && oy > y) oy = Math.max(y, oy - s)
else if (where == BM && oy < y) oy = Math.min(y, oy + s)
else if (where == LT && ox > x) ox = Math.max(x, ox - s)
else if (where == RT && ox < x) ox = Math.max(x, ox + s)
else clearInterval(O(id).HS_IID)
```

Finally, the object is moved to the new location in `ox` and `oy`, and the `HS_X` and `HS_Y` properties are assigned these values, as follows:

```
GoTo(id, ox, oy)
O(id).HS_X = ox
O(id).HS_Y = oy
```

NOTE *HoverSlide() is one of the more complicated plug-ins, but it does create great effects, so it's worth reading the preceding explanation through a few times if any parts aren't clear at first.*

How To Use It

To use the `HoverSlide()` plug-in, you pass it an object and then tell it where the object should be placed (out of the 'top', 'bottom', 'left', or 'right' edges), whereabouts on the edge to place it, how much of the object to allow showing, and the speed of the sliding animation in milliseconds, as in these two examples:

```
HoverSlide('myobject', 'top', '%50', 60, 1000)
HoverSlide('myobject2', 'right', 15, 20, 1000)
```

The first statement places an object at the top edge of the browser, exactly 50 percent along, with 60 pixels showing, and with a sliding time of 1 second. The second one does the same for another object, but it is attached to the right edge starting 15 pixels down and has only 20 pixels showing.

Before you call the plug-in, it's important to give the object a style position of either 'absolute' or 'fixed', as in these statements:

```
Position(object, FIX)
Position('mydiv', ABS)
```

The first of these has a fixed position (`FIX`) and places the object in the browser so that even if you scroll right through the web page, the object will remain on screen exactly where it was placed. The second has an absolute position (`ABS`) and places the object absolutely within a web page so that it will start off looking exactly the same as a fixed object but will move with the page when you scroll it.

Here's a fun example using a fixed object to create a dynamic menu for a music store:

```
<table id='a' width='375' height='160'
   cellpadding='0' cellspacing='0' bgcolor='black'>
   <tr height='20'>
      <td colspan='3'>
         <font color='white' face='Verdana' size='5'>
            <center>
               <b>I'll Be Bach Music Store</b>
            </center>
         </font>
      </td>
   </tr>
   <tr height='80'>
      <td width='150' align='right'>
         <img src='instruments.png'>
      </td>
      <td>
          
      </td>
      <td width='315' valign='middle'>
         <center>
            <font face='Verdana' color='yellow'>
               <u>New! - Special Offers</u><br />
               <u>View our Guestbook</u><br />
               <u>Follow us on Twitter</u><br />
               <u>Read our Blog</u>
            </font>
         </center>
      </td>
   </tr>
   <tr height='60'>
      <td colspan='3'>
         <img id='a' src='piano.png' />
      </td>
   </tr>
</table>
```

```
<br /><br /><br />
<font face='Verdana'>
   <center>
      <font color='purple' size=5>
         <b>The "I'll Be Bach" Music Store</b>
      </font>
   </center>
   <br />
   We pride ourselves in having the widest selection of instruments of
   any music store, ranging from pianos, violins, flutes, and other
   classical and band instruments, to the latest electric guitars,
   keyboards, synthesizers and mixing equipment.
</font>

<script>
window.onload = function()
{
   Position('a', FIX)
   HoverSlide('a', 'top', '%50', 60, 300)
}

</script>
```

The vast majority of this example is plain HTML, which is intentional, because I wanted to illustrate how easy it is to set up such a feature on your website with only a couple of lines of JavaScript; the first one of which sets the style position of the object, and the second displays the object with just the piano keyboard graphic image showing. By the way, the links shown in the slide in menu are, of course, only for illustrative purposes and cannot be clicked.

For an even more interesting effect, you could try changing the opacity of the div, like this:

```
Opacity('a', 80)
```

Now that you have available the full power of chaining and other interactive techniques, in the next chapter I'll show you some amazing menu and navigation effects that will really help your web pages to stand out from the crowd.

The Plug-in

```
function HoverSlide(id, where, offset, showing, msecs)
{
   var w = GetWindowWidth()  - W(id)
   var h = GetWindowHeight() - H(id)
   var o = offset[0] != '%' ? 0 : offset.substr(1) / 100

   if (where == LT || where == RT)
   {
      var t = W(id) - showing
      var u = Math.min(t, msecs / INTERVAL)
```

```
      var x = where == LT ? -t : w + t
      var y = o ? h * o : offset
      var s = t / u
   }
   else
   {
      var t = H(id) - showing
      var u = Math.min(t, msecs / INTERVAL)
      var x = o ? w * o : offset
      var y = where == TP ? -t : h + t
      var s = t / u
   }

   GoTo(id, x, y)
   O(id).HS_X = x
   O(id).HS_Y = y
   O(id).onmouseover = SlideIn
   O(id).onmouseout  = SlideOut

   function SlideIn()
   {
      if (O(id).HS_IID) clearInterval(O(id).HS_IID)
      O(id).HS_IID = setInterval(DoSlideIn, INTERVAL)

      function DoSlideIn()
      {
         var ox = O(id).HS_X
         var oy = O(id).HS_Y

         if      (where == TP && oy < 0) oy = Math.min(0, oy + s)
         else if (where == BM && oy > h) oy = Math.max(h, oy - s)
         else if (where == LT && ox < 0) ox = Math.min(0, ox + s)
         else if (where == RT && ox > w) ox = Math.max(w, ox - s)
         else clearInterval(O(id).HS_IID)

         GoTo(id, ox, oy)
         O(id).HS_X = ox
         O(id).HS_Y = oy
      }
   }

   function SlideOut()
   {
      if (O(id).HS_IID) clearInterval(O(id).HS_IID)
      O(id).HS_IID = setInterval(DoSlideOut, INTERVAL)

      function DoSlideOut()
      {
         var ox = O(id).HS_X
         var oy = O(id).HS_Y
```

```
            if      (where == TP && oy > y) oy = Math.max(y, oy - s)
            else if (where == BM && oy < y) oy = Math.min(y, oy + s)
            else if (where == LT && ox > x) ox = Math.max(x, ox - s)
            else if (where == RT && ox < x) ox = Math.max(x, ox + s)
            else clearInterval(O(id).HS_IID)

            GoTo(id, ox, oy)
            O(id).HS_X = ox
            O(id).HS_Y = oy
        }
    }
}
```

CHAPTER 8

Menus and Navigation

As websites try to offer a better look and feel than their competitors, new ways of navigating through large numbers of pages are being devised all the time. Menus and navigation are probably the areas that make the most use of JavaScript for this purpose.

In the early days of JavaScript, the interaction was mainly limited to instant changes of location and color as the mouse passed over a menu, but nowadays savvy web users expect much more fluid and appealing designs with fades, transitions, and more.

The plug-ins in this chapter give you a variety of solutions that you can use as-is, or you can build them up into more sophisticated systems. They range from sliding menus to pop-up and down menus, folding and context menus, and even a dock bar similar to the one used in Mac OS X.

HoverSlideMenu()

This plug-in expands on the final one in Chapter 7, `HoverSlide()`, to build a complete menu system, rather than just a single slideable menu. With it you can select a group of objects that will be attached to one of the edges of the browser and which will slide into view when the mouse passes over the part showing. In Figure 8-1, two almost identical sets of objects containing links have been attached to the top and bottom of the browser.

About the Plug-in

This plug-in takes an array of objects and then lines them all up along one of the browser edges where they become a collection of slide in menus. The following arguments are required:

- **`ids`** An array of objects and/or object IDs
- **`where`** The edge the objects should be attached to, either 'top', 'left', 'right', or 'bottom'
- **`offset`** How far along the edge to locate the objects—if `offset` begins with a `%` symbol, the position will be that percent from the start, otherwise it will be `offset` pixels from the start
- **`showing`** The number of pixels to leave showing of each object so the mouse can pass over them to cause the menu to slide in

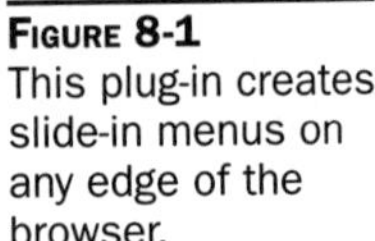

FIGURE 8-1 This plug-in creates slide-in menus on any edge of the browser.

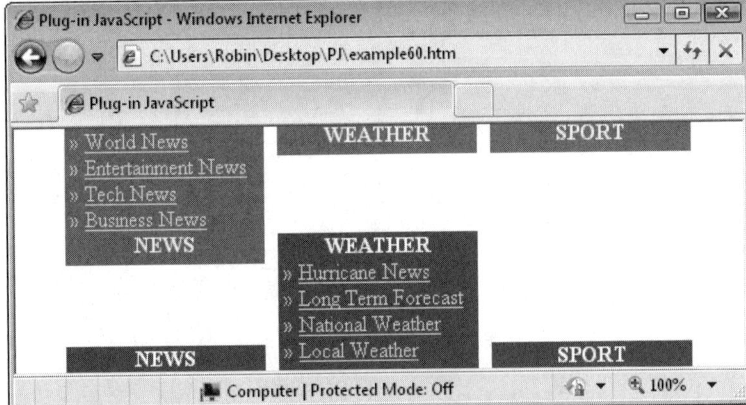

- **gap** The number of pixels to leave between each object
- **msecs** The number of milliseconds each object should take to slide in or out

Variables, Arrays, and Functions

`len`	Local variable containing the number of objects in `ids`
`total`	Local variable containing the total width or height that all the objects take up when brought together, including gaps
`start`	Local variable containing the position along or down an edge that the first object should be placed
`a`	Local array containing the width or height of each object
`jump`	Local variable containing the progressive width of each object and the gaps while positioning the objects
`j`	Local variable for indexing into the `a` array to save the width or height of each object
`TP` & `BM`	Global variables containing the values 'top' and 'bottom'
`W()`	Plug-in to return the width of an object
`H()`	Plug-in to return the height of an object
`GetWindowWidth()`	Plug-in to return the width of the browser
`GetWindowHeight()`	Plug-in to return the height of the browser
`HoverSlide()`	Plug-in to slide an object in and out from a browser edge

How It Works

The first thing this plug-in does is assign values to some local variables, like this:

```
var len   = ids.length
var total = gap * (len - 1)
var start = (offset[0] != '%') ? 0 : offset.substr(1) / 100
var a     = []
var jump  = 0
```

The variable `len` is assigned the number of items in the `ids` array, and `total` is assigned the width in pixels of all the gaps. Next, `start` is set to either 0 or the value of `offset / 100` if it begins with the character `%`. Later, if `start` is 0, the value in `offset` will be used to align the objects in their required positions at exact positions. Otherwise, `start` contains a percentage value for the start point.

After this, the array `a` is created to hold the widths of the objects and `jump` is initialized to 0; it will store the current widths and gaps so far, as each object is given its location.

Next, there are two sections of code, the first of which is executed if either the top or bottom of the browser is to be used for the menu:

```
if (where == TP || where == BM)
{
   for (var j = 0 ; j < len ; ++j)
```

```
    {
       a[j]    = W(ids[j])
       total += a[j]
    }

    start = start ? (GetWindowWidth() - total) * start : offset * 1
}
```

The first line compares the where argument with TP and BM (global variables containing the values 'top' and 'bottom'). If where is one of these values, the menu will be laid out horizontally, so the for() loop places all the widths of the objects in the a array by fetching them with the W() plug-in. The variable total is also incremented by this value so that when the loop has finished it will contain the sum of all the object widths and all the gap widths (the latter having been assigned earlier).

Then, if start is not zero, it contains the percentage value that was previously assigned, so the width of the browser, as returned by GetWindowWidth() less the value in total, is multiplied by start (which is a fractional value less than 1), and the result is placed in start. This value represents the percent offset from the start of the edge. However, if start is 0, then offset contains the exact number of pixels the menus should be located from the edge. Because this value may be a string, it is multiplied by 1 to turn it into an integer. The result is then placed in start.

The second part of the if() statement repeats the procedure, substituting values applicable for the left or right hand edge of the screen, like this:

```
else
{
   for (var j = 0 ; j < len ; ++j)
   {
      a[j]    = H(ids[j])
      total += a[j]
   }

   start = start ? (GetWindowHeight() - total) * start : offset * 1
}
```

Finally, another for() loop iterates through the ids array and calls the HoverSlide() plug-on for each object, placing them all in their correct positions based on the value of start, plus that in jump. Initially, jump is zero so there is no additional offset, but as each object is added to the menu, jump is incremented by the previous object width and the size of the gap, so that each additional object is located at the correct distance from the previous one.

How To Use It

To use this plug-in, you need to create an object for each of the sliding menu parts. A div is perfect for the job. Fill each with the images, links, and any other contents you need, and make sure the edge of the div is a suitable tab that will make people want to pass their mouse over it. Now all you need to do is call the plug-in, like this:

```
HoverSlideMenu(ids1, 'top', '%50', 20, 10, 200)
```

In this example, the objects in the array ids are passed to the plug-in, telling it to place the menus at the browser top, 50 percent along the edge (therefore in the middle), with 20 pixels poking into the browser, 10 pixels space between each object, and a slide in and out time of 200 milliseconds.

Here's an example that places such a set of menus at the top of the screen:

```
<div id='m1'>
 &raquo; <u>World News</u><br />
 &raquo; <u>Entertainment News</u><br />
 &raquo; <u>Tech News</u><br />
 &raquo; <u>Business News</u><br />
<center><b><font color='yellow'>NEWS</font></b></center></div>

<div id='m2'>
 &raquo; <u>Hurricane News</u><br />
 &raquo; <u>Long Term Forecast</u><br />
 &raquo; <u>National Weather</u><br />
 &raquo; <u>Local Weather</u><br />
<center><b><font color='yellow'>WEATHER</font></b></center></div>

<div id='m3'>
 &raquo; <u>Football News</u><br />
 &raquo; <u>Baseball News</u><br />
 &raquo; <u>Soccer News</u><br />
 &raquo; <u>Hockey News</u><br />
<center><b><font color='yellow'>SPORT</font></b></center></div>

<script>
window.onload = function()
{
   ids = Array('m1', 'm2', 'm3')
   Hide(ids)
   Resize(ids, 150, 100)
   Position(ids, FIX)
   S(ids, 'backgroundColor', 'red')
   S(ids, 'color', 'cyan')
   Show(ids)
   HoverSlideMenu(ids, 'top', '%50', 21, 10, 200)
}
</script?>
```

This example creates three divs and places simulated links in them using `<u>` tags—in the real world you might use `<a href...>` tags here. Each object is also given a unique ID. Also the `»` HTML entity creates pairs of right pointing brackets.

Then, in the `<script>` section, the `ids` array is populated with the object names and the `Hide()` plug-in makes them invisible so they will display neatly when the menus have been created—and you shouldn't see them jump around. It also helps to hide any content that might make some browsers return a value that makes room for a potential horizontal scroll bar, thus ensuring that everything centers correctly.

After resizing the objects, setting style positions, and assigning their colors, it's then safe to show the objects again with `Show()`. In fact, you *must* do so in order for the plug-in to be able to look up their dimensions. Finally, the `HoverSlideMenu()` plug-in is called and the menus are displayed.

NOTE *It isn't necessary to give all objects the same dimensions—they will still line up neatly, spaced from each other by the value passed in the* gap *argument. You can also specify a value of 0 for the gap if you want all the menus to align directly next to each other. Also, don't forget that if you use a style position of 'absolute', your menus will scroll with the page, but if you use 'fixed' they will stay where you put them, even if the page is scrolled.*

The Plug-in

```
function HoverSlideMenu(ids, where, offset, showing, gap, msecs)
{
   var len   = ids.length
   var total = gap * (len - 1)
   var start = (offset[0] != '%') ? 0 : offset.substr(1) / 100
   var a     = []
   var jump  = 0

   if (where == TP || where == BM)
   {
      for (var j = 0 ; j < len ; ++j)
      {
         a[j]   = W(ids[j])
         total += a[j]
      }

      start = start ? (GetWindowWidth() - total) * start : offset * 1
   }
   else
   {
      for (var j = 0 ; j < len ; ++j)
      {
         a[j]   = H(ids[j])
         total += a[j]
      }

      start = start ? (GetWindowHeight() - total) * start : offset * 1
   }

   for (var j = 0 ; j < len ; ++j)
   {
      HoverSlide(ids[j], where, start + jump, showing, msecs)
      jump += a[j] + gap
   }
}
```

PLUG-IN 61 PopDown()

With this function, you can remove an object from the browser using a variety of different transitions. This plug-in is especially good for menu effects, as you'll see in other plug-ins in this chapter. Figure 8-2 shows four avatars from the resource website *art.eonworks.com*.

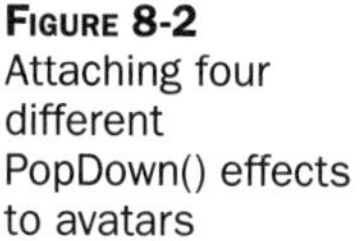
FIGURE 8-2 Attaching four different PopDown() effects to avatars

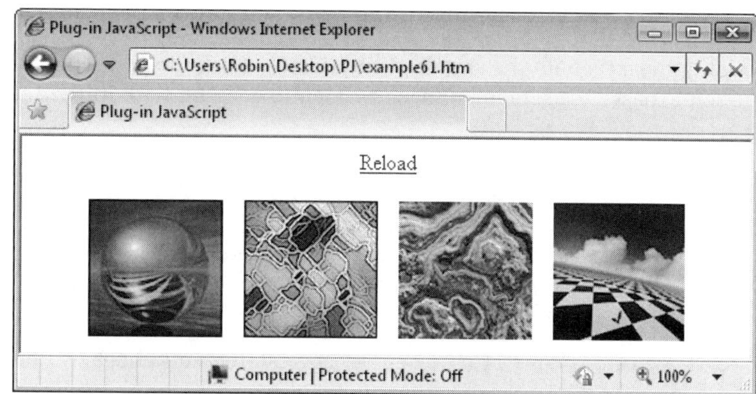

Each avatar has a different `PopDown()` style attached to its `onmouseover` event and will disappear in different ways as you pass your mouse over them.

About the Plug-in

This plug-in takes an object and then removes it from the browser in one of a variety of styles. It requires the following arguments:

- **`id`** An object or object ID or an array of objects and/or object IDs
- **`type`** The type of pop-down—out of 'fade', 'inflate', 'zoom', or 'instant'
- **`w`** If `true` or 1, the width of the object (where applicable) will reduce
- **`h`** If `true` or 1, the height of the object (where applicable) will reduce
- **`msecs`** The number of milliseconds the transition should take, except for the type 'instant', which uses no timing
- **`interruptible`** If `true` or 1, the plug-in can be interrupted with another call on the same object

Variables, Arrays, and Functions

`j`	Local variable for iterating though `id` if it is an array
`PO_IsUp`	Property of `id` that is `false` if it is popped down, otherwise it is popped up
`FadeOut()`	Plug-in to fade out an object over time
`Deflate()`	Plug-in to reduce an object's dimensions over time
`ZoomDown()`	Plug-in to zoom down an object around its center point
`Hide()`	Plug-in to hide an object so it does not appear in the browser
`InsVars()`	Plug-in to insert values into a string

How It Works

This plug-in starts with the standard code that iterates through `id` if it is an array and recursively passes each element back to itself to be dealt with individually, as follows:

```
if (id instanceof Array)
{
   for (var j = 0 ; j < id.length ; ++j)
      PopDown(id[j], type, w, h, msecs, interruptible)
   return
}
```

Next, a group of four `if()` … `else if()` statements check for the different types of pop-down requested in the argument type, like this:

```
if (type == 'fade')
{
   FadeOut(id, msecs, interruptible,
      InsVars("Hide('#1')", id))
}
else if() …
```

This first section calls the `FadeOut()` plug-in and passes the callback function name of `Hide()`, with `id` as its argument, so that the object will be hidden after it has faded. The other sections call up `Deflate()` and `ZoomDown()` in the same way and with the same callback string, with the final section simply calling the `Hide()` plug-in when the type of pop-down requested is 'instant'.

Finally, the `PO_IsUp` property of `id` is set to `false` to indicate to other plug-ins that the object is (or is on the process of being) popped down.

How To Use It

Using this plug-in is as simple as passing an object (or an array of objects), along with the pop-down type you want, out of 'fade', 'inflate', 'zoom', or 'instant'. If `type` is either 'inflate' or 'zoom', you also need to specify whether the width or height (or both) dimensions should be modified. If `type` is either 'fade' or 'instant', you can pass any values for these arguments, such as 0 or `null`, as they will be ignored. Finally, you specify the length of time in milliseconds the pop-down should take (if it's not 'instant') and whether the plug-in can be interrupted.

Here's an example that displays four images and attaches a different style of pop-down to each:

```
<center><a href=example61.htm>Reload</a><br /><br />
<img id='a1' src='avatar1.jpg' />   
<img id='a2' src='avatar2.jpg' />   
<img id='a3' src='avatar3.jpg' />   
<img id='a4' src='avatar4.jpg' /></center>

<script>
window.onload = function()
{
   O('a1').onmouseover = function() { PopDown('a1','fade',    1,1,500,0) }
```

```
   O('a2').onmouseover = function() { PopDown('a2','inflate',1,0,500,0) }
   O('a3').onmouseover = function() { PopDown('a3','zoom',    1,1,500,0) }
   O('a4').onmouseover = function() { PopDown('a4','instant',1,1,500,0) }
}
</script>
```

The HTML section centers a group of four images and gives them unique IDs. A link is also made to reload the page. Next, in the `<script>` section, four different calls to `PopDown()` are attached to the different `onmouseover` events of the images.

When you pass your mouse over any image it will pop down and then hide, and the other images will all move in to take up the space it previously occupied. This is why there is the "Reload" link above them, so that you can reload the example and watch it again.

Take some time to play with each type of pop-down and note what's different about them. For example, the `Deflate()` plug-in reduces the object's dimensions in real time, causing the other objects to reposition as the object is deflating, whereas the `ZoomDown()` plug-in first zooms the object down and then collapses its width and height. You may also wish to experiment with the `w` and `h` arguments to see how they change the type of pop-down effect.

The Plug-in

```
function PopDown(id, type, w, h, msecs, interruptible)
{
   if (id instanceof Array)
   {
      for (var j = 0 ; j < id.length ; ++j)
         PopDown(id[j], type, w, h, msecs, interruptible)

      return
   }

   if (type == 'fade')
   {
      FadeOut(id, msecs, interruptible,
         InsVars("Hide('#1')", id))
   }
   else if (type == 'inflate')
   {
      Deflate(id, w, h, msecs, interruptible,
         InsVars("Hide('#1')", id))
   }
   else if (type == 'zoom')
   {
      ZoomDown(id, w, h, msecs, 1, interruptible,
         InsVars("Hide('#1')", id))
   }
   else if (type == 'instant') Hide(id)

   O(id).PO_IsUp = false
}
```

PopUp()

This is the partner plug-in for PopDown(). With it, you can pop an object up that has previously been popped down. Figure 8-3 extends the one in the PopDown() plug-in by providing four spans, which you can pass the mouse over and out of to pop an object down and back up again.

About the Plug-in

This plug-in takes an object and then restores its state using one of a variety of styles. It requires the following arguments:

- **id** An object or object ID or an array of objects and/or object IDs
- **type** The type of pop-up, out of 'fade', 'inflate', 'zoom', or 'instant'
- **w** If true or 1, the width of the object (where applicable) will expand
- **h** If true or 1, the height of the object (where applicable) will expand
- **msecs** The number of milliseconds the transition should take, except for the type 'instant', which uses no timing
- **interruptible** If true or 1, the plug-in can be interrupted with another call on the same object

Variables, Arrays, and Functions

j	Local variable for iterating though id if it is an array
PO_IsUp	Property of id that is false if it is popped down, otherwise it is popped up
FadeIn()	Plug-in to fade in an object over time
Reflate()	Plug-in to expand an object's dimensions over time
ZoomRestore()	Plug-in to zoom up an object around its center point
Hide()	Plug-in to show an object that has been hidden
InsVars()	Plug-in to insert values into a string

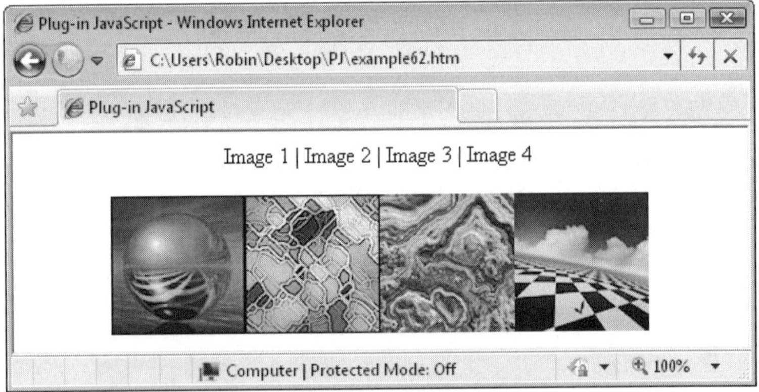

Figure 8-3 With this plug-in you can pop objects back up again.

How It Works

This plug-in has the usual code at the start that iterates through `id` if it is an array and recursively passes each element back to itself to be dealt with individually, as follows:

```
if (id instanceof Array)
{
   for (var j = 0 ; j < id.length ; ++j)
      PopUp(id[j], type, w, h, msecs, interruptible)
   return
}
```

Next, since the object will previously have been hidden using the `Hide()` plug-in, it is shown by calling `Show()`:

```
Show(id)
```

This is all that needs to be done at this point if `type` is 'instant'. If it isn't, a group of `if() … else if()` statements call one of the `FadeIn()`, `Reflate()`, or `ZoomRestore()` plug-ins, depending on the value in `type`, as follows:

```
if (type == 'fade')
   FadeIn(id, msecs, interruptible)
else if (type == 'inflate')
   Reflate(id, w, h, msecs, interruptible)
else if (type == 'zoom')
   ZoomRestore(id, w, h, msecs, 1, interruptible)
```

Finally, the `PO_IsUp` property of `id` is set to `true` to indicate to other plug-ins that the object is (or is in the process of being) popped up.

```
O(id).PO_IsUp = true
```

How To Use It

You use this plug-in in the same manner as `PopDown()` to restore an object to its original state. Following is an example that expands on the `PopDown()` plug-in to make the images pop both down and up again:

```
<center>
<span id='l1'>Image 1</span> |
<span id='l2'>Image 2</span> |
<span id='l3'>Image 3</span> |
<span id='l4'>Image 4</span>

<br /><br /><div id='d'>
<img id='a1' src='avatar1.jpg' align='left' />
<img id='a2' src='avatar2.jpg' align='left' />
<img id='a3' src='avatar3.jpg' align='left' />
<img id='a4' src='avatar4.jpg' align='left' /></div></center>
```

```
<script>
window.onload = function()
{
   Position('d', 'absolute')
   CenterX('d')

   O('l1').onmouseover = function() { PopDown('a1','fade',    1,1,500,1) }
   O('l2').onmouseover = function() { PopDown('a2','inflate',1,0,500,1) }
   O('l3').onmouseover = function() { PopDown('a3','zoom',    1,1,500,1) }
   O('l4').onmouseover = function() { PopDown('a4','instant',1,1,500,1) }

   O('l1').onmouseout  = function() { PopUp('a1','fade',    1,1,500,1) }
   O('l2').onmouseout  = function() { PopUp('a2','inflate',1,0,500,1) }
   O('l3').onmouseout  = function() { PopUp('a3','zoom',    1,1,500,1) }
   O('l4').onmouseout  = function() { PopUp('a4','instant',1,1,500,1) }
}
</script>
```

As well as displaying the four images, the HTML section now includes four spans that you can pass the mouse over and out of to make the associated images pop down and back up again. The images have their alignment set to make them line up beside each other, and they are placed in a div that is centered by a statement in the `<script>` section.

Also, in the `<script>` section, there are four more statements that attach `PopUp()` plug-ins to the `onmouseout` events of the spans.

The Plug-in

```
function PopUp(id, type, w, h, msecs, interruptible)
{
   if (id instanceof Array)
   {
      for (var j = 0 ; j < id.length ; ++j)
         PopUp(id[j], type, w, h, msecs, interruptible)
      return
   }

   Show(id)

   if (type == 'fade')
      FadeIn(id, msecs, interruptible)
   else if (type == 'inflate')
      Reflate(id, w, h, msecs, interruptible)
   else if (type == 'zoom')
      ZoomRestore(id, w, h, msecs, 1, interruptible)

   O(id).PO_IsUp = true
}
```

PLUG-IN 63 PopToggle()

With this plug-in, you can cut down on a lot of code by calling it whenever you want to reverse the pop-down or up state of an object. Figure 8-4 shows the result of optimizing the code from the `PopUp()` plug-in section to use only this plug-in.

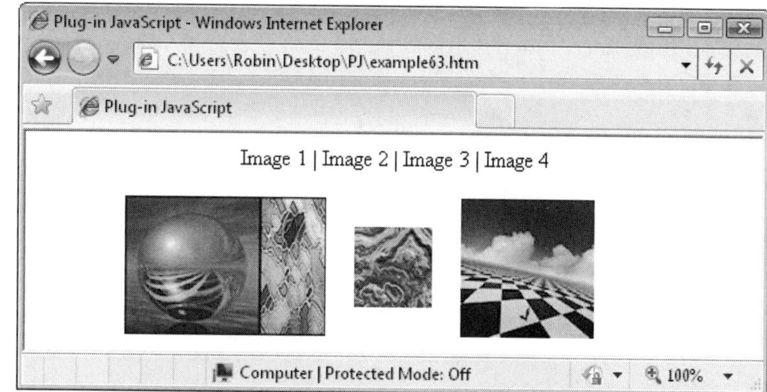

FIGURE 8-4 With PopToggle() you can substantially optimize your code.

About the Plug-in

This plug-in takes an object and then toggles its state between popped up and down using one of a variety of styles. It requires the following arguments:

- **`id`** An object or object ID or an array of objects and/or object IDs
- **`type`** The type of pop-up or pop-down, out of 'fade', 'inflate', 'zoom', or 'instant'
- **`w`** If true or 1, the width of the object (where applicable) will be modified
- **`h`** If true or 1, the height of the object (where applicable) will be modified
- **`msecs`** The number of milliseconds the transition should take, except for the type 'instant', which uses no timing
- **`interruptible`** If `true` or 1, the plug-in can be interrupted with another call on the same object

Variables, Arrays, and Functions

`j`	Local variable for iterating though `id` if it is an array
`PO_IsUp`	Property of `id` that is `false` if it is popped down, otherwise it is popped up
`PopDown()`	Plug-in to pop down an object
`PopUp()`	Plug-in to pop up an object

How It Works

This plug-in starts with the code used by many plug-ins to iterate through `id` if it is an array and recursively pass each element back to itself to be processed individually, like this:

```
if (id instanceof Array)
{
   for (var j = 0 ; j < id.length ; ++j)
      PopToggle(id[j], type, w, h, msecs, interruptible)
   return
}
```

Next, the PO_IsUp property of id is tested to see whether it has a value. If its type is UNDEF (or 'undefined') then it doesn't, and the object has to be popped down (since it hasn't been popped down yet), so PO_IsUp is set to true, like this:

```
if (typeof O(id).PO_IsUp == UNDEF)
   O(id).PO_IsUp = true
```

Then a check is again made on PO_IsUp now that it must have a value of either true or false. If it is true, the PopDown() plug-in is called; otherwise, the object is already popped down so the PopUp() plug-in is called, as follows:

```
if (O(id).PO_IsUp) PopDown(id, type, w, h, msecs, interruptible)
else               PopUp(id, type, w, h, msecs, interruptible)
```

How To Use It

To use this plug-in, pass it an object and the type of pop-up and down effect to use, out of 'fade', 'inflate', 'zoom', or 'instant'. Then decide whether the width, height, or both dimensions will resize (if applicable), how long the transition should take, and whether it can be interrupted, like this:

```
PopToggle('object', 'inflate', 0, 1, 500, 0)
```

Here's an example that rewrites the code used in the previous pop-in example to significantly shorten it:

```
<center>
<span id='l1'>Image 1</span> |
<span id='l2'>Image 2</span> |
<span id='l3'>Image 3</span> |
<span id='l4'>Image 4</span>

<br /><br /><div id='d'>

<img id='a1' src='avatar1.jpg' align='left' />
<img id='a2' src='avatar2.jpg' align='left' />
<img id='a3' src='avatar3.jpg' align='left' />
<img id='a4' src='avatar4.jpg' align='left' /></div></center>

<script>
window.onload = function()
{
   Position('d', ABS)
   CenterX('d')

   O('l1').onmouseover = O('l1').onmouseout = fade
   O('l2').onmouseover = O('l2').onmouseout = inflate
   O('l3').onmouseover = O('l3').onmouseout = zoom
   O('l4').onmouseover = O('l4').onmouseout = instant
```

```
    function fade()    { PopToggle('a1', 'fade',    1, 1, 500, 1) }
    function inflate() { PopToggle('a2', 'inflate', 1, 0, 500, 1) }
    function zoom()    { PopToggle('a3', 'zoom',    1, 1, 500, 1) }
    function instant() { PopToggle('a4', 'instant', 1, 1, 500, 1) }
}
</script>
```

The HTML section is unchanged, but the `<script>` uses a technique I haven't shown you yet, which is to assign both the `onmouseover` and `onmouseout` events to the same function, using a single statement, like this:

```
O('l1').onmouseover = O('l1').onmouseout = fade
```

This works because these events are readable as well as writable, so the `onmouseout` event is first assigned to the `fade()` function, and the `onmouseover` event is then assigned to the value in the `onmouseout` event.

This means only four statements are used in place of eight. Likewise, because `PopToggle()` can replace both the `PopDown()` and `PopUp()` plug-ins, only four functions are required to manage eight actions.

In fact, the functions can be attached to the events using inline, anonymous functions, but the line lengths would become rather long and less easy to edit.

The Plug-in

```
function PopToggle(id, type, w, h, msecs, interruptible)
{
   if (id instanceof Array)
   {
      for (var j = 0 ; j < id.length ; ++j)
         PopToggle(id[j], type, w, h, msecs, interruptible)
      return
   }

   if (typeof O(id).PO_IsUp == UNDEF)
      O(id).PO_IsUp = true

   if (O(id).PO_IsUp) PopDown(id, type, w, h, msecs, interruptible)
   else                  PopUp(id, type, w, h, msecs, interruptible)
}
```

FoldingMenu()

Using the pop-up and down features of the preceding plug-ins, it's possible to create professional looking folding menus, which is what this plug-in offers. With it, you can create a wide variety of different folding menus with different transition styles. For example, Figure 8-5 shows a folding menu with four headings, each with different sets of contents.

FIGURE 8-5 Creating a folding menu side bar.

About the Plug-in

The plug-in requires a pair of arrays of heading and contents objects and then displays a folding menu based on the styles and actions you supply. It takes the following arguments:

- **`headings`** An array of objects and/or object IDs
- **`contents`** An array of objects and/or object IDs
- **`action`** The menu action type, either 'hover' or 'click'
- **`type`** The type of transitions to use, out of 'fade', 'inflate', 'zoom', or 'instant'
- **`multi`** If `true` or 1, more than one contents section can be open at a time
- **`w`, `h`** If `type` is 'inflate' or 'zoom', these arguments specify whether the width, height, or both dimensions will be modified during transitions
- **`msecs1`** The transition time in milliseconds of popping down
- **`msecs2`** The transition time in milliseconds of popping up
- **`interruptible`** If `true` or 1, the `PopUp()` and `PopDown()` plug-in can be interrupted by another call on the same `id`

Variables, Arrays, and Functions

`j`	Local variable for iterating through the `headings` array
`FO_C`	Property of each heading containing the object in the `contents` array to which it refers
`PO_IsUp`	Property of each object in the contents array, which is `false` when an object is popped down, otherwise the object is popped up
`cursor`	Property of each heading's style object used for changing the mouse pointer when over the heading

`onmouseover`	Event of each heading
`onmouseout`	Event of each heading
`slice()`	Function to return a subsection of an array
`PopUp()`	Plug-in to pop up an object
`PopDown()`	Function to pop down an object
`PopToggle()`	Function to toggle the popped state of an object
`DoFoldingMenu()`	Subfunction to perform the transition

How It Works

The first thing this plug-in does is pop down all the objects in the contents array except for the first one, which must remain popped up—and which has its `PO_IsUp` property set to `true` to indicate this, as follows:

```
PopDown(contents.slice(1), type, w, h, 1, 0)
O(contents[0]).PO_IsUp = true
```

The `slice()` function is used with a value of 1 to pass to `PopDown()` all elements from the second element onward (because the first element of an array is 0). The `msecs` argument to `PopDown()` is 1 so that the transition is set to take only 1 millisecond and is, therefore, virtually instantaneous.

Next, the `headings` and `contents` arrays are iterated though in a `for()` loop, using `j` as an index into them, like this:

```
for (var j = 0 ; j < headings.length ; ++j)
{
   O(headings[j]).FO_C    = contents[j]
   S(headings[j]).cursor = 'pointer'

   if (action == 'hover') O(headings[j]).onmouseover = DoFoldingMenu
   else                   O(headings[j]).onclick     = DoFoldingMenu
}
```

Each heading has its `FO_C` property assigned the object in the associated contents array. This will pop up and down the contents associated with a heading. Then each heading has it cursor property set to 'pointer', so that the mouse pointer will change when it passes over the heading.

After that the `action` argument is tested. If it is 'hover', the `DoFoldingMenu()` subfunction is attached to the current heading's `onmouseover` event so that it will be called up by passing the mouse over it.

Otherwise, the subfunction is attached to the current heading's `onclick` event so that it will only be called up when the heading is clicked.

The DoFoldingMenu Subfunction

Once all the various properties and events are set up for the plug-in, the `DoFoldingMenu()` subfunction will be called up whenever a change to the menus is required.

When this happens, the first statement in the function checks the `multi` argument. If it is `true` or 1, it means that more than one set of contents can be popped up at a time; in fact, all of them can be up (or down) at the same time.

By setting the `multi` argument, each `onmouseover` or `onclick` event of a heading will toggle the pop-up or pop-down state of the associated contents object with the `PopToggle()` plug-in, like this:

```
if (multi) PopToggle(this.FO_C, type, w, h, msecs1, interruptible)
```

If `multi` is not set, then only one contents object can be popped up at a time, so when a new one is selected to be popped up the previously popped up one must be popped down. This is worked out by iterating through the headings array in a `for()` loop, like this:

```
for (j = 0 ; j < headings.length ; ++j)
   if (O(O(headings[j]).FO_C).PO IsUp && O(headings[j]) != this)
      PopDown(O(headings[j]).FO_C, type, w, h, msecs1, interruptible)
```

The variable `j` iterates through each element in the `headings` array and checks each one's associated contents object `PO_IsUp` property. If it is `true` or 1, the contents object is currently popped up, so the heading object is compared with `this`, which refers to the current heading that was either clicked or had the mouse passed over it. If they match, they are one and the same and nothing happens since the currently selected contents object will be set to a popped up state a couple of lines later in the code.

However, if the `contents` object that has been found to be popped up is different from the current heading's `contents` object, then it is the one that was previously popped up, so it is popped down with a call to `PopDown()`. The time setting used here is from the argument `msecs1`.

Finally, the currently selected `contents` object is set to a popped up state (if it isn't already popped up), like this:

```
if (!O(this.FO_C).PO_IsUp)
   PopUp(this.FO_C, type, w, h, msecs2, interruptible)
```

This pop-up action is given its own time setting in `msecs2` so that different folding effects can be achieved by using differing values for `msecs1` and `msecs2`.

How To Use It

There are two main ways to use this plug-in. The first is within an accordion or folding menu, and the other is to separate out the headings from the contents to have the control objects in a different place from the displayed contents. The first is most suited to being operated by mouse clicks because, as the transitions occur, new elements could pass under the mouse cursor, and if `onmouseover` were used, unwanted selections could be made.

Here's an example of an accordion-style menu driven by mouse clicks:

```
<span id='h1'><b>News</b></span><br /><div id='c1'>
  &raquo; <a href='local.htm'>Local News</a><br/ >
  &raquo; <a href='world.htm'>World News</a><br/ >
  &raquo; <a href='entertainment.htm'>Entertainment News</a><br/ >
```

```
  &raquo; <a href='business.htm'>Business News</a><br/ >
  &raquo; <a href='technology.htm'>Technology News</a><br/ ></div>

<span id='h2'><b>Sport</b></span><br /><div id='c2'>
  &raquo; <a href='football.htm'>Football</a><br/ >
  &raquo; <a href='baseball.htm'>Baseball</a><br/ >
  &raquo; <a href='hockey.htm'>Hockey</a><br/ >
  &raquo; <a href='soccer.htm'>Soccer</a><br/ ></div>

<span id='h3'><b>Weather</b></span><br /><div id='c3'>
  &raquo; <a href='movies.htm'>Movies</a><br/ >
  &raquo; <a href='music.htm'>Music</a><br/ >
  &raquo; <a href='televison.htm'>Television</a><br/ ></div>

<span id='h4'><b>Links</b></span><br /><div id='c4'>
  &raquo; <a href='index.htm'>Home Page</a><br/ >
  &raquo; <a href='articles.htm'>Articles</a><br/ >
  &raquo; <a href='videos.htm'>Videos</a><br/ >
  &raquo; <a href='podcasts.htm'>Podcasts</a><br/ ></div>

<script>
window.onload = function()
{
   headings = Array('h1', 'h2', 'h3', 'h4')
   contents = Array('c1', 'c2', 'c3', 'c4')

   FoldingMenu(headings, contents, 'click', 'inflate', 0,1,1,200,300,1)
}
</script>
```

I designed this and most other plug-ins in such a way that they do not rely on you using CSS other than to style the menus in the way you want them. Of course, CSS can be used to apply different styles when the mouse passes over, but the goal of this book is to enable you to set up objects in standard HTML that you control with a small section of JavaScript.

Therefore, the HTML in this example creates four heading spans, each of which has a span section of links underneath, although this contents could be any HTML or objects, such as images and so on. In addition to the four headings, there are four contents sections.

I have specifically chosen spans here because browsers automatically know their dimensions based on their contents. Divs are different in that their width is effectively infinite (at least to the browser edge), so you cannot deflate a div's width dimension unless you set it, for example, using the `ResizeWidth()` plug-in.

The `<script>` section is very simple. Two arrays are created, one for the headings and one for the contents. Next, the `FoldingMenu()` plug-in is called, with an `action` argument of 'click', a `style` argument of 'inflate', and a `multi` argument of 0. The `w` and `h` arguments are set to 0 and 1 so that only the height of an object will be adjusted during transitions.

After this, `msecs1` and `msecs2` are set to 200 and 300 so that popping down will take 200 milliseconds and popping up will take 300. This provides a more interesting effect than if they are given the same values. I recommend you try altering them yourself, giving first `msecs1` the larger value and then `msecs2`. You'll find you can create a wide range of interesting effects.

You can also have a lot of fun by changing the `type` to another value such as 'fade', 'zoom', or 'instant'; you may also want to experiment with modifying the `w` and `h` arguments to change the width and height (or both). Don't forget that you can also change `multi` to `true` or 1 and have a quite different type of menu, in which the headings toggle their contents between being popped up and down.

Using the 'hover' Action

If you plan to offer a hover effect, you'll need to lay out your HTML slightly differently so that when objects pop up they don't do so under the mouse and then cause an automatic (and unwanted) mouseover event to occur—which could result in popping up the wrong section.

Here's one way you can modify the HTML to use the 'hover' action of the `FoldingMenu()` plug-in:

```
<span id='h1'><b>News</b></span> |
<span id='h2'><b>Sport</b></span> |
<span id='h3'><b>Weather</b></span> |
<span id='h4'><b>Links</b></span><br />

<span id='c1'>
  &raquo; <a href='local.htm'>Local News</a>
  <a href='world.htm'>World News</a>
  <a href='entertainment.htm'>Entertainment News</a>
  <a href='business.htm'>Business News</a>
  <a href='technology.htm'>Technology News</a></span>

<span id='c2'>
  &raquo; <a href='football.htm'>Football</a>
  <a href='baseball.htm'>Baseball</a>
  <a href='hockey.htm'>Hockey</a>
  <a href='soccer.htm'>Soccer</a></span>

<span id='c3'>
  &raquo; <a href='movies.htm'>Movies</a>
  <a href='music.htm'>Music</a>
  <a href='televison.htm'>Television</a></span>

<span id='c4'>
  &raquo; <a href='index.htm'>Home Page</a>
  <a href='articles.htm'>Articles</a>
  <a href='videos.htm'>Videos</a>
  <a href='podcasts.htm'>Podcasts</a></span>

<script>
window.onload = function()
{
   headings = Array('h1', 'h2', 'h3', 'h4')
   contents = Array('c1', 'c2', 'c3', 'c4')

   FoldingMenu(headings, contents, 'click', 'inflate', 0,1,1,200,300,1)
}
</script>
```

The script section is identical to the previous example; only the HTML has been changed to place all the headings at the top, with the contents sections underneath them as shown in Figure 8-6.

The Plug-in

```
function FoldingMenu(headings, contents, action, type, multi,
   w, h, msecs1, msecs2, interruptible)
{
   PopDown(contents.slice(1), type, w, h, 1, 0)
   O(contents[0]).PO_IsUp = true

   for (var j = 0 ; j < headings.length ; ++j)
   {
      O(headings[j]).FO_C   = contents[j]
      S(headings[j]).cursor = 'pointer'

      if (action == 'hover') O(headings[j]).onmouseover = DoFoldingMenu
      else                   O(headings[j]).onclick     = DoFoldingMenu
   }

   function DoFoldingMenu()
   {
      if (multi) PopToggle(this.FO_C, type, w, h, msecs1, interruptible)
      else
      {
         for (j = 0 ; j < headings.length ; ++j)
            if (O(O(headings[j]).FO_C).PO_IsUp && O(headings[j]) != this)
               PopDown(O(headings[j]).FO_C, type, w, h,
                  msecs1, interruptible)

         if (!O(this.FO_C).PO_IsUp)
            PopUp(this.FO_C, type, w, h, msecs2, interruptible)
      }
   }
}
```

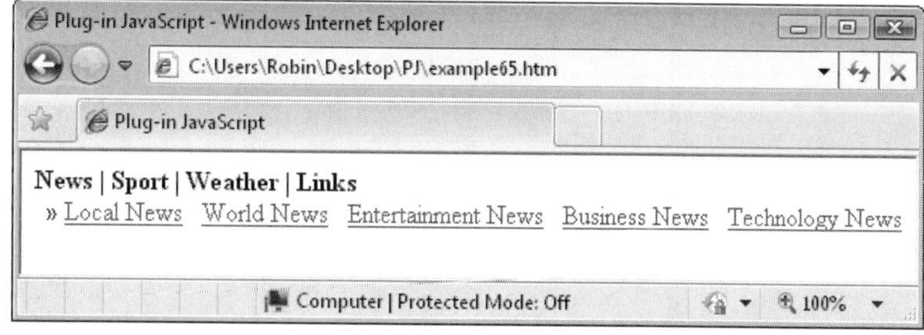

FIGURE 8-6 The plug-in is now used to create 'hover' action menus.

ContextMenu()

With this plug-in, you can replace the standard mouse right-click menu with your own. Much more than a way to block casual users from viewing the source of a page, the `ContextMenu()` plug-in lets you create entire sections of HTML and pop them up at the mouse cursor position when the user clicks the right mouse button. In Figure 8-7, a simple menu for a hardware store has been popped up with a right-click.

About the Plug-in

This plug-in requires an object that, when right-clicked, should pop up a menu, which you also pass to it. It takes the following arguments:

- **`id`** An object to which the right-click should be attached—generally, you will attach to the `document` object, but you can be more specific and attach different context menus to different objects (arrays of objects are not supported)
- **`contents`** An object containing the menu to be displayed
- **`type`** The type of transition effect for popping the menu up and down, out of 'fade', 'inflate', 'zoom', or 'instant'
- **`w`** If applicable and this argument is `true` or 1, the object's width will be modified during the transition
- **`h`** If applicable and this argument is `true` or 1, the object's height will be modified during the transition
- **`msecs`** The number of milliseconds the pop-up transition should take

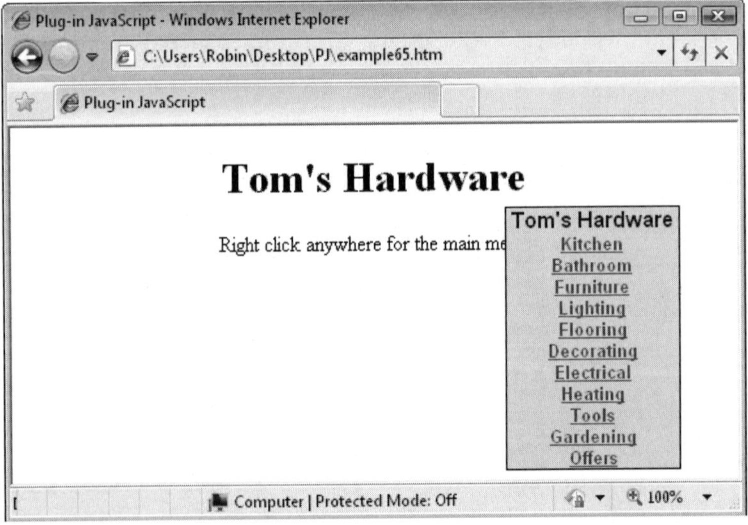

FIGURE 8-7 Now you can create your own right-click menus.

Variables, Arrays, and Functions

x, y	Local variables containing the left and top edges of the location of content
MOUSE_X, MOUSE_Y	Global variables containing the current mouse x and y coordinates
PO_IsUp	Property of id that is false if it is popped down, otherwise it is popped up
FA_Flag	Property of id set by the Fade() plug-in when a fade is in progress on id
DF_Flag	Property of id set by the Deflate or Inflate() plug-in when a deflate or reflate is in progress on id
zIndex	Style property of contents containing its depth location from front (highest) to back (lowest)
Context_IID	Property of id returned by calling setInterval() to later be used by clearInterval()
SetInterval()	Function to start repeating interrupts
clearInterval()	Function to stop repeating interrupts
Locate()	Plug-in to set an object's style position and coordinates
PopUp()	Plug-in to pop up a previously popped down object
PopDown()	Plug-in to pop down an object
W(), H()	Plug-ins to return the width and height of an object
ContextUp()	Subfunction to pop up contents when the mouse is right-clicked
ContextDown()	Subfunction of ContextUp() to check whether the mouse has moved out of the space occupied by contents and if so to remove it

How It Works

This plug-in first releases the contents object from its position in the HTML document by using the Locate() plug-in to give it a style position of ABS (a global variable with the value 'absolute'). Next, it moves it off screen to a location thousands of pixels away, removing it from the browser as quickly as possible so as not to appear within your page.

Next, contents is popped down, ready to be popped up when required, and the oncontextmenu event of id is attached to the ContextUp() subfunction, which will pop up contents when id is right-clicked. Here are the three lines of code that do this:

```
Locate(contents, ABS, -10000, -10000)
PopDown(contents, type, 1, 1, 1, 0)
O(id).oncontextmenu = ContextUp
```

The ContextUp() Subfunction

The purpose of this subfunction is to react to a right-click event on `id`. The first thing it does, though, is check whether it can go ahead by examining the state of flags created by the `PopUp()`, `PopDown()`, `Fade()`, `Deflate()`, and `Reflate()` plug-ins, like this:

```
if (O(contents).PO_IsUp ||
    O(contents).FA_Flag ||
    O(contents).DF_Flag) return false
```

If any of these flags is `true`, then either `contents` is already popped up, or one of the transition types is already in action on `contents`, so the plug-in returns.

If the plug-in can proceed, it next sets the local variables `x` and `y` to the current coordinates of the mouse cursor and then moves the popped down contents to that location with a call to `GoTo()`. It calls `PopUp()` to pop it up, like this:

```
var x = MOUSE_X
var y = MOUSE_Y
GoTo(contents, x, y)
PopUp(contents, type, w, h, msecs, 1)
```

Next, it's necessary to ensure that any objects that have been created or had their `zIndex` property changed since the `contents` div was created will not appear in front of it, so the object's `zIndex` property is set to the value in `ZINDEX` plus 1. `ZINDEX` is the global variable that tracks the highest `zIndex` property so far used by an object, so adding 1 to this value ensures that `contents` will appear on top of every other object in the browser. Here's the statement that does this:

```
S(contents).zIndex = ZINDEX + 1
```

The plug-in needs a way to determine whether the mouse has moved out of the area occupied by `contents`, and therefore whether it needs to be popped down. You might think that attaching to the `onmouseout` event of `contents` would do the trick but, sadly, it won't do so reliably and in all cases. The reason for this is if you include a form input or other elements within `contents`, when the mouse passes over them the browser will think it has passed out of being over the contents object and will prematurely trigger the `onmouseout` event.

Therefore, it is necessary to track the position of the mouse and pop the object down only if it moves out of the object's bounds. To do this, a repeating interrupt is created to call up the subfunction `ContextDown()` every `INTERVAL` milliseconds to see whether the mouse is still inside the object, as follows:

```
O(id).Context_IID = setInterval(ContextDown, INTERVAL)
```

Finally, the `return` statement returns a value of `false` to tell the browser to cancel pulling up the standard right-click menu:

```
return false
```

The ContextDown Sub-subfunction

This function monitors the position of the mouse by checking the `MOUSE_X` and `MOUSE_Y` global variables:

```
if (MOUSE_X < x || MOUSE_X > (x + W(contents)) ||
    MOUSE_Y < y || MOUSE_Y > (y + H(contents)))
```

If the mouse pointer is not within the bounds of `contents`, the object is popped down and the repeating interrupts are stopped with a call to `clearInterval()`, passing it the value in the property `Context_IID` that was saved when `setInterval()` was called. Also, the property `PO_IsUp` is set to `false` because `contents` has now been popped down:

```
PopDown(contents, type, w, h, msecs, 1)
clearInterval(O(id).Context_IID)
O(contents).PO_IsUp = false
```

If the mouse is still within the bounds of `contents`, the function returns to be called again in another `INTERVAL` milliseconds.

NOTE *With a little tweaking, this plug-in could easily be adapted to create a slight buffer around the context menu so the menu won't disappear if the mouse goes slightly outside the boundary.*

How To Use It

To use this plug-in, use HTML (and CSS if you wish) to create an attractive menu (or whatever object you want the right-click to call up), and pass it to the plug-in, along with the object to which it should be attached, the type of pop-up transition to use, and the time the transition should take.

Here's an example that creates a simple menu for a hardware store:

```
<center><h1>Tom's Hardware</h1>
Right click anywhere for the main menu</center>

<span id='menu'><center>
<font face='Arial' size='2'><b>
<font size='3' color='#0b0d7d'>
 Tom's Hardware </font><br />
<a href='#'>Kitchen</a><br />
<a href='#'>Bathroom</a><br />
<a href='#'>Furniture</a><br />
<a href='#'>Lighting</a><br />
<a href='#'>Flooring</a><br />
<a href='#'>Decorating</a><br />
<a href='#'>Electrical</a><br />
<a href='#'>Heating</a><br />
<a href='#'>Tools</a><br />
<a href='#'>Gardening</a><br />
<a href='#'>Offers</a>
</b></font></center></span>
```

```
<script>
window.onload = function()
{
   S('menu').backgroundColor = '#abeceb'
   S('menu').border          = 'solid 1px'
   ContextMenu(document, 'menu', 'fade', 0, 0, 300)
}
</script>
```

The HTML section displays a simple heading and instructional sentence, followed by a span with the ID 'menu', which contains a few links. Of course, the links go nowhere because they only contain a # symbol, but they display as if they do.

The `<script>` section sets the background color of the menu, gives it a solid border, and then calls up `ContextMenu()` to prepare the browser for handling right-clicks.

You might want to play with this example by trying different `style` arguments such as 'inflate', 'zoom', and 'instant'. You can also play with the `w` and `h` arguments, as well as the timing in `msecs`.

Something else you can try is to create an object and attach the menu to that rather than the entire `document`. Or, try making a couple of different menus for different objects—once you have this plug-in in your web toolkit, you are on your way to creating some highly dynamic and interactive websites.

The Plug-in

```
function ContextMenu(id, contents, type, w, h, msecs)
{
   Locate(contents, ABS, -10000, -10000)
   PopDown(contents, type, 1, 1, 1, 0)
   O(id).oncontextmenu = ContextUp

   function ContextUp()
   {
      if (O(contents).PO_IsUp ||
          O(contents).FA_Flag ||
          O(contents).DF_Flag) return false


      var x = MOUSE_X
      var y = MOUSE_Y
      GoTo(contents, x, y)
      PopUp(contents, type, w, h, msecs, 1)
      S(contents).zIndex = ZINDEX + 1
      O(id).Context_IID  = setInterval(ContextDown, INTERVAL)
      return false

      function ContextDown()
      {
         if (MOUSE_X < x || MOUSE_X > (x + W(contents)) ||
             MOUSE_Y < y || MOUSE_Y > (y + H(contents)))
         {
            PopDown(contents, type, w, h, msecs, 1)
            clearInterval(O(id).Context_IID)
```

```
                O(contents).PO_IsUp = false
            }
        }
    }
}
```

PLUG-IN 66 DockBar()

This plug-in adds a dock bar to the browser similar to the one used by Mac OS X. It's easily configurable and can be attached to any of the browser's four edges. Figure 8-8 shows six dock bar icons attached to the bottom edge of a browser using this plug-in, with one in the process of zooming up.

About the Plug-in

This plug-in takes a containing object and list of elements within the object and turns them into a dock bar that you can affix to any edge of the browser. It requires the following arguments:

- **`id`** A containing object such as a div or span that holds the individual dock bar elements—this cannot be an array
- **`items`** An array of objects located within `id`, usually comprising images
- **`where`** The edge to which the bar should be attached, out of 'top', 'bottom', 'left', or 'right'
- **`increase`** The percentage by which an item should enlarge when the mouse passes over it
- **`msecs`** The number of milliseconds the transition should take

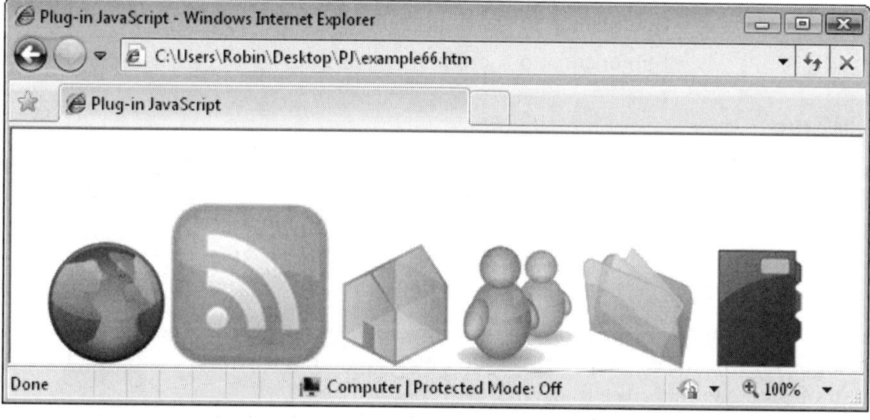

FIGURE 8-8 Use this plug-in to create impressive dock bars.

Variables, Arrays, and Functions

j	Local variable used for iterating through the items array
oldw, oldh	Local variables containing the original width and height of an item
TP, BM	Global variables containing the strings 'top' and 'bottom'
verticalAlign	Style property of the elements of the items array
align	Property of the elements of the items array
cursor	Style property of the elements of the items array to set the mouse cursor icon
DB_Parent	Property of each element of the items array containing a copy of id
DB_Where	Property of each element of the items array containing a copy of where
DB_Name	Property of each element of the items array containing a copy of the element
DB_OldW, DB_OldH	Properties of each element of the items array containing the original width and height of the element
DB_NewW, DB_NewH	Properties of each element of the items array containing the enlarged width and height of the element
onmouseover	Event of each element of the items array used for attaching to DockUp()
onmouseout	Event of each element of the items array used for attaching to DockDown()
Math.round()	Function to turn a floating point number into an integer
Position()	Plug-in to change the style position of an object
GoToEdge()	Plug-in to move an object to a browser edge
Zoom()	Plug-in to zoom an object down or up
DockUp()	Subfunction to zoom up an object
DockDown()	Subfunction to zoom down an object

How It Works

This plug-in starts by releasing the containing object in id from the browser and giving it a style position of 'fixed' to ensure that the dock bar will stay in place even if the browser is scrolled, as follows (FIX being a global variable with the value 'fixed'):

```
Position(id, FIX)
```

Then all the elements in the items array are iterated through in a for() loop with the local variable j as the index pointer, and the first statements within the loop set the alignment of each element, like this:

```
for (var j = 0 ; j < items.length ; ++j)
{
```

```
if (where[1] == TP || where == BM)
   S(items[j]).verticalAlign = where
else       O(items[j]).align = where
```

If the argument `where` has either of the values 'top' or 'bottom' (tested by the global variables `TP` and `BM`), then the `verticalAlign` style property of the element is set to the value in `where`. Otherwise, `where` must have a value of either 'left' or 'right' so the `align` property of the element is given that value.

Next, each element's original width and height is extracted from the `W()` and `H()` plug-ins and placed in the local variables `oldw` and `oldh`, like this:

```
var oldw = W(items[j])
var oldh = H(items[j])
```

After that, the cursor to display whenever the mouse is over an element is set to 'pointer' and several properties are created, as follows:

```
S(items[j]).cursor    = 'pointer'
O(items[j]).DB_Parent = id
O(items[j]).DB_Where  = where
O(items[j]).DB_OldW   = oldw
O(items[j]).DB_OldH   = oldh
O(items[j]).DB_NewW   = Math.round(oldw + oldw * increase / 100)
O(items[j]).DB_NewH   = Math.round(oldh + oldh * increase / 100)
```

This causes information about the element and the containing object it is located within to be stored as new properties of the elements. These properties can then be referenced by the following `DockUp()` and `DockDown()` subfunctions and also be referenced from within the `Zoom()` plug-in which this one relies on.

First, the `id` object is copied to the `DB_Parent` property. Next, the value in `where` is copied so that `Zoom()` will know where to place the element as it zooms it, and `oldw` and `oldh` are added as properties to tell `Zoom()` where to zoom up from. The width and height that an element should be zoomed up to are also calculated by increasing the original width and height by the percentage value in `increase` and placed in the `DB_NewW` and `DB_NewH` properties.

The final two statements in this loop attach the `DockUp()` and `DockDown()` subfunctions to the element's `onmouseover` and `onmouseout` events, respectively, as follows:

```
O(items[j]).onmouseover = DockUp
O(items[j]).onmouseout  = DockDown
```

Finally, in the setup section of code, the containing object `id` is moved to the edge indicated by the value in `where`, like this:

```
GoToEdge(id, where, 50)
```

The DockUp() and DockDown() Subfunctions

These two functions trigger either the popping up or the popping down of an element by passing the various properties of the pseudo object `this` to the `Zoom()` plug-in; `this` being a keyword that represents the object that triggered the event that called the function.

The two functions are very similar and simply swap the positions of the original and larger dimensions of the element. Here's the statement that zooms an object up:

```
Zoom(this, 1, 1, O(this).DB_OldW, O(this).DB_OldH,
   O(this).DB_NewW, O(this).DB_NewH, msecs, 0, 1)
```

And this one zooms it back down again:

```
Zoom(this, 1, 1, O(this).DB_NewW, O(this).DB_NewH,
   O(this).DB_OldW, O(this).DB_OldH, msecs, 0, 1)
```

How To Use It

To use this plug-in to create a dock bar, you first need to create an HTML object to contain the various elements. Usually a simple span or div is all you need. Next, place the elements that comprise the dock bar in that container. Generally, you will want to use images, but you can use other objects if you wish.

Here's an example that creates a six-icon dock bar:

```
<span id='dock'>
<img id='i1' src='i1.gif' />
<img id='i2' src='i2.gif' />
<img id='i3' src='i3.gif' />
<img id='i4' src='i4.gif' />
<img id='i5' src='i5.gif' />
<img id='i6' src='i6.gif' />
</span>

<script>
window.onload = function()
{
   Position('dock', FIX)
   ids = Array('i1', 'i2', 'i3', 'i4', 'i5', 'i6')
   DockBar('dock', ids, 'bottom', 32, 256)
}
</script>
```

As you can see, it's all very simple and easy to assemble. I placed only the images in the span, but you will probably want to enclose each image within an `<a href... >... </a>` pair of tags to give them a click action.

In this instance, I placed the dock bar at the bottom, but a quick change to the `where` argument from 'bottom' to 'top' will move it to the top of the browser.

If you wish to place a dock bar on the left or right edge of the browser, you'll need to slightly alter the HTML, like this:

```
<span id='dock'>
<img id='i1' src='i1.gif' /><br clear='all' />
<img id='i2' src='i2.gif' /><br clear='all' />
<img id='i3' src='i3.gif' /><br clear='all' />
<img id='i4' src='i4.gif' /><br clear='all' />
```

```
<img id='i5' src='i5.gif' /><br clear='all' />
<img id='i6' src='i6.gif' />
</span>
```

Notice that all I added are some `<br clear='all' />` statements to ensure that the elements line up one below the other. Now you can change the `where` argument in the `<script>` section to either 'left' or 'right' to attach the dock bar to the left or right edge.

TIP *You can apply a background or gradient to the enclosing span to provide a greater effect.*

The Plug-in

```
function DockBar(id, items, where, increase, msecs)
{
   Position(id, FIX)

   for (var j = 0 ; j < items.length ; ++j)
   {
      if (where == TP || where == BM)
         S(items[j]).verticalAlign = where
      else       O(items[j]).align = where

      var oldw = W(items[j])
      var oldh = H(items[j])

      S(items[j]).cursor     = 'pointer'
      O(items[j]).DB_Parent = id
      O(items[j]).DB_Where  = where
      O(items[j]).DB_OldW   = oldw
      O(items[j]).DB_OldH   = oldh
      O(items[j]).DB_NewW   = Math.round(oldw + oldw * increase / 100)
      O(items[j]).DB_NewH   = Math.round(oldh + oldh * increase / 100)

      O(items[j]).onmouseover = DockUp
      O(items[j]).onmouseout  = DockDown
   }

   GoToEdge(id, where, 50)

   function DockUp()
   {
      Zoom(this, 1, 1, O(this).DB_OldW, O(this).DB_OldH,
         O(this).DB_NewW, O(this).DB_NewH, msecs, 0, 1)
   }

   function DockDown()
   {
      Zoom(this, 1, 1, O(this).DB_NewW, O(this).DB_NewH,
         O(this).DB_OldW, O(this).DB_OldH, msecs, 0, 1)
   }
}
```

PLUG-IN 67 RollOver()

You've almost certainly seen and used rollover images that change as the mouse passes over them, but what about making rollover objects do the same? That's what this plug-in does. With it, rollovers can contain HTML, images, and anything else you like, making it much more powerful than simple image rollovers.

Figure 8-9 shows an advertisement from a classified ads site.

When you mouse over the ad, it rolls over to show the new details in Figure 8-10.

About the Plug-in

This plug-in takes two objects that can be images, divs, or spans containing HTML and/or images. It creates a rollover so that the second object is displayed when the mouse passes across the first. It requires the following arguments:

- **`ro1`** An object or object ID or an array of objects and or object IDs—if it is an array, then `ro2` must also be an array with the same number of elements
- **`ro2`** An object or object ID or an array of objects and or object IDs—this should only be an array if `ro1` is an array

Variables, Arrays, and Functions

`a`	Local array containing the objects in `ro1` and `ro2`
`w, h`	Local variable containing the width and height of the objects
`x, y`	Local variable containing the top left corner coordinates of the objects
`iid`	Local variable containing the result of calling `setInterval()` used later for calling `clearInterval()`
`MOUSE_X, MOUSE_Y`	Global variables containing the current horizontal and vertical positions of the mouse pointer
`Hide()`	Plug-in to hide an object
`HideToggle()`	Plug-in to toggle the hidden/shown state of an object
`Locate()`	Plug-in to move an object to another location and assign it a style position property such as 'relative' or 'absolute', and so on
`onmouseover`	Event of `ro1` that calls up the `DoRoll()` subfunction
`DoRoll()`	Subfunction to perform a rollover from `ro1` to `ro2` and then set up a repeating interrupt to the `RollCheck()` sub-subfunction to see if the mouse has moved away yet
`RollCheck()`	Sub-subfunction that returns every `INTERVAL` milliseconds when it is called unless the mouse has moved away from `ro2`, in which case the objects are rolled back again

How It Works

This plug-in supports arrays as well as single objects and is almost unique among all the plug-ins in that, if the first argument is an array, then the second one must also be an array.

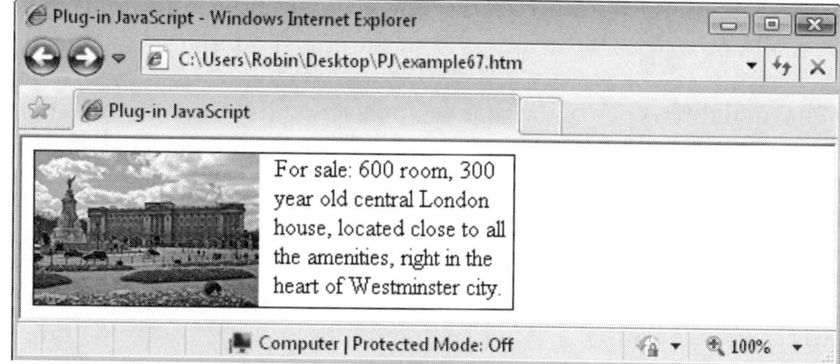

FIGURE 8-9 A rollover has been attached to this "for sale" classified ad.

Usually, if the first argument is an array the second argument, a single object, is assigned to all elements of the array, but this plug-in requires either two single objects or two arrays.

In the former case, the first object is rolled over with the second. In the latter case, each element of the first array will roll over with each matching element in the second array.

The first few lines of code facilitate recursively passing on the elements of both arrays as individual items back to the same function to be processed as individual items (there is no error checking, so make sure you pass two matching arrays or two objects):

```
if (ro1 instanceof Array)
{
   for (var j = 0 ; j < id.length ; ++j)
      RollOver(ro1[j], ro2[j])
   return
}
```

Next, the local array a is assigned elements ro1 and ro2 to make them easier for later functions to access them. Then the width and height and horizontal and vertical locations of the objects are saved in the local variables w, h, x, and y, like this:

```
var a = Array(ro1, ro2)
var w = W(ro1) + 1
var h = H(ro1) + 1
var x = X(ro1)
var y = Y(ro1)
```

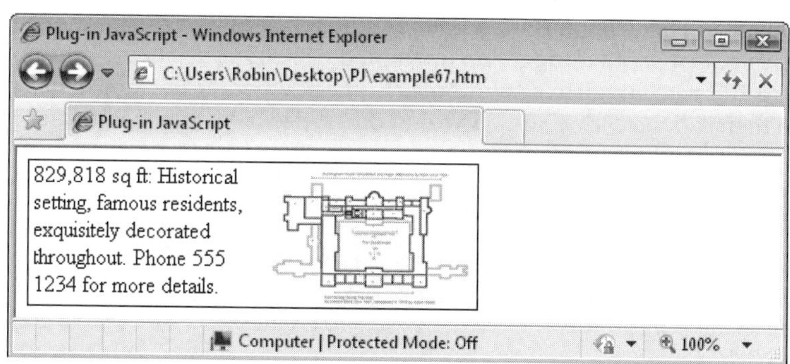

FIGURE 8-10 When the mouse passes over, the second object is displayed.

The width and height each have a pixel added to resolve issues in some browsers where there might otherwise be an anomaly at the edge boundary, which could cause the rollover to cycle rapidly.

The final three lines of the main setup section hide `ro2` so that only `ro1` is visible, then both `ro1` and `ro2` are located relative to their enclosing object at an offset of 0,0, so that they are on top of each other. Finally, an `onmouseover` event attaches the `DoRoll()` subfunction to the `onmouseover` event of `ro1`, as follows:

```
Hide(ro2)
Locate(a, REL, 0, 0)
O(ro1).onmouseover = DoRoll
```

The DoRoll() Subfunction

This function swaps the two objects' visibility properties so that `ro2` becomes visible and `ro1` becomes hidden. Then it sets up a repeating interrupt to call the `RollCheck()` sub-subfunction every `INTERVAL` milliseconds, like this:

```
HideToggle(a)
var iid = setInterval(RollCheck, INTERVAL)
```

The local variable `iid` is give the value returned by `setInterval()`, which will later be used by `clearInterval()` to cancel the repeating interrupts.

The RollCheck() Sub-subfunction

This function simply checks whether the mouse has moved out of the space occupied by the objects. If it has, it swaps the two objects back so that `ro1` is visible and `ro2` is again hidden. Then it cancels the repeating interrupts with a call to `clearInterval()`, like this:

```
if (MOUSE_X < x || MOUSE_X > x + w ||
    MOUSE_Y < y || MOUSE_Y > y + h)
{
   HideToggle(a)
   clearInterval(iid)
}
```

Why Not Use onmouseout Instead of RollCheck()?

Much as I would like to use `onmouseout` instead of `RollCheck()`, it's not possible to do so on an object that contains many different items because passing the mouse cursor between these items will often trigger an unwanted `onmouseout` event. Therefore the simplest, and also a 100 percent reliable solution, is to check whether the mouse has moved out of the area and then call the code that you would otherwise have attached to an `onmouseout` event.

How To Use It

To use this plug-in, you need to prepare two objects that have the same width and height. You can then pass them as arguments. Or, if you prefer, you can create several sets of matching pairs to use as rollovers and pass two arrays to the plug-in. This saves repeated calls to the plug-in if you have many sets to create.

Here's an example that uses two single objects to create a rollover effect for a classified ad:

```
<div id='r1'>
<img id='p1' src='palace.png' align='left'>
For sale: 600 room, 300 year old central London house, located
close to all the amenities, right in the heart of Westminster city.</div>

<div id='r2'>
<img id='p2' src='plan.png' align='right'>
829,818 sq ft: Historical setting, famous residents, exquisitely
decorated throughout. Phone 555 1234 for more details.</div>

<script>
window.onload = function()
{
   rolls = Array('r1', 'r2')
   S(rolls, 'border', 'solid 1px')
   Resize(rolls, 320, 100)
   S('p1').paddingRight = Px(10)
   S('p2').paddingLeft  = Px(10)
   RollOver('r1', 'r2')
}
</script>
```

The HTML section creates two divs and places some text and an image in each. Then the `<script>` section creates the array `rolls`, which adds a border to each object and resizes them both to 320 by 100 pixels.

A couple of calls to the `S()` plug-in sets up some padding around the images so that the text doesn't align right up against them, and then the `RollOver()` plug-in is called to combine the two objects into a single rollover.

The Plug-in

```
function RollOver(ro1, ro2)
{
   if (ro1 instanceof Array)
   {
      for (var j = 0 ; j < id.length ; ++j)
         RollOver(ro1[j], ro2[j])
      return
   }

   var a = Array(ro1, ro2)
   var w = W(ro1) + 1
   var h = H(ro1) + 1
   var x = X(ro1)
   var y = Y(ro1)

   Hide(ro2)
   Locate(a, REL, 0, 0)
   O(ro1).onmouseover = DoRoll

   function DoRoll()
   {
```

```
            HideToggle(a)
            var iid = setInterval(RollCheck, INTERVAL)

            function RollCheck()
            {
               if (MOUSE_X < x || MOUSE_X > x + w ||
                   MOUSE_Y < y || MOUSE_Y > y + h)
               {
                  HideToggle(a)
                  clearInterval(iid)
               }
            }
        }
    }
```

PLUG-IN 68 Breadcrumbs()

This plug-in provides an automatic trail of "breadcrumbs" leading from a website's home page to the current page. With it, users can backtrack to any location between the current page and the home page with a single click. Figure 8-11 shows the plug-in being used on a page in a local file system on a Windows PC.

About the Plug-in

This plug-in returns the HTML to create a breadcrumb trail from the current web page back to the home page. It requires the following argument:

- `spacer` A string of characters to place between each breadcrumb

Variables, Arrays, and Functions

`parts`	Local array containing the URL of the current page split into parts
`crumbs`	Local array that builds the breadcrumbs
`title`	Local variable containing the title of the current web page, if any
`url`	Local variable containing the URL of the website
`display`	Local variable containing the main HTML to return to
`j`	Local variable for iterating through different arrays
`push()`	Function to push a value onto an array
`InsVars()`	Plug-in to insert values into a string

How It Works

This plug-in fetches the path to the current page from `self.location.href` and splits it at the `?` character (if there is one) to extract the main URL from any query string. Then the half before the `?` is split again at every / character, with the result being placed in the array `parts`.

After that, the `crumbs` array is created, which will be built up to contain the path. It is assigned an initial value of `parts[0]` (which will be `http:` or `ftp:` and so on), followed by the string '//', like this:

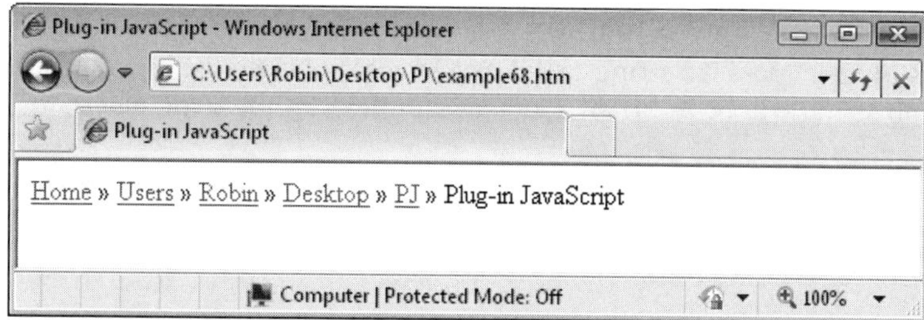

FIGURE 8-11 Breadcrumbs provide a quick and easy website navigation aid.

```
var parts  = self.location.href.split('?')[0].split('/')
var crumbs = Array(parts[0] + '//')
```

Next a `for()` loop iterates through all but the first two elements of the `parts` array to reassemble the URL into the `crumbs` array using the `push()` function, as follows:

```
for (var j = 2 ; j < parts.length ; ++j)
{
   if (parts[j] == '') crumbs[0] += '/'
   else crumbs.push(parts[j])
}
```

The next three lines of code extract the title of the page (if any), the main URL of the website, and the first breadcrumb, named 'Home', like this:

```
var title   = document.title ? document.title : parts[j - 1]
var url     = crumbs[0] + crumbs[1]
var display = InsVars("<a href='#1'>Home</a>", url)
```

The `InsVars()` plug-in inserts the value in `url` into the string `display`, replacing the `#1`. If no title is found, the filename of the current page is used instead. Then, if no argument was supplied for the spacer to place between each breadcrumb, `spacer` is given the default value of a single space:

```
if (typeof spacer == UNDEF) gap = ' '
```

After this, another `for()` loop extracts each element from the `crumbs` array and attaches it (prefaced with a / character) to the `display` string with suitable HTML anchor tags, like this:

```
for (j = 2 ; j < crumbs.length - 1 ; ++j)
{
   url     += '/' + crumbs[j]
   display += spacer + InsVars("<a href='#1'>#2</a>", url, crumbs[j])
}
```

Finally, the contents of `display` is returned, prepended to another `spacer` string, followed by the page title:

```
return display + spacer + title
```

How To Use It

To use this plug-in, pass it a string to use as a spacer between the breadcrumbs, and the breadcrumb string will be returned. Here's a simple example to do just that:

```
<div id='bc'></div>

<script>
window.onload = function()
{
   O('bc').innerHTML = Breadcrumbs(" &raquo; ")
}
</script>
```

The HTML section creates a div in which the result will be placed, while the `<script>` section makes a single call and places the result into the `innerHTML` property of the div. Because simple, plain HTML is returned, you can use CSS to style the returned string to make it fit with your web page design.

The Plug-in

```
function Breadcrumbs(spacer)
{
   var parts  = self.location.href.split('?')[0].split('/')
   var crumbs = Array(parts[0] + '//')

   for (var j = 2 ; j < parts.length ; ++j)
   {
      if (parts[j] == '') crumbs[0] += '/'
      else crumbs.push(parts[j])
   }

   var title   = document.title ? document.title : parts[j - 1]
   var url     = crumbs[0] + crumbs[1]
   var display = InsVars("<a href='#1'>Home</a>", url)

   if (typeof spacer == UNDEF) gap = ' '

   for (j = 2 ; j < crumbs.length - 1 ; ++j)
   {
      url     += '/' + crumbs[j]
      display += spacer + InsVars("<a href='#1'>#2</a>", url, crumbs[j])
   }

   return display + spacer + title
}
```

PLUG-IN 69 BrowserWindow()

Didn't you just hate pop-ups before browsers came with blockers? In my view, there is nothing wrong with the concept of pop-ups, it's just that it was too easy for websites to inundate you with them, and once everyone started using them it turned into a nightmare.

However, when I set up an Internet radio station in the 1990s, I used pop-ups to good effect by implementing them as an audio player console so that people could listen to the radio while they continued to surf in the main browser window. Perhaps partly due to the novelty, most of the website's visitors kept these pop-ups open for long periods as they listened to our shows.

Even though they have a bad name nowadays, pop-ups do have plenty of sensible uses, such as providing alerts and instant message notifications, for example. This plug-in provides a versatile in-browser pop-up that's more user friendly than opening a new browser window pop-up—which will generally only get blocked anyway. It also gives the user full control, as it can be moved around the browser window and is easily dismissible.

With this plug-in, you can ask a user for their login details, display private messages from another user in a forum, provide a selection of options, and so on. Or, as in Figure 8-12, you can pop up a window to provide further details when a user clicks a link. The great thing about it is that the user has full control. They can keep the widow raised and move it around to reveal any content it was covering, or they can simply close it.

About the Plug-in

This plug-in creates an in-browser pop-up window that can be moved about by the user and also popped back down again. It requires the following arguments:

- `id` An object or object ID identifying the main container—this may not be an array
- `headerid` An object or object ID identifying the draggable header
- `closeid` An object or object ID identifying the close button
- `x` & `y` The top left coordinates of the pop-up

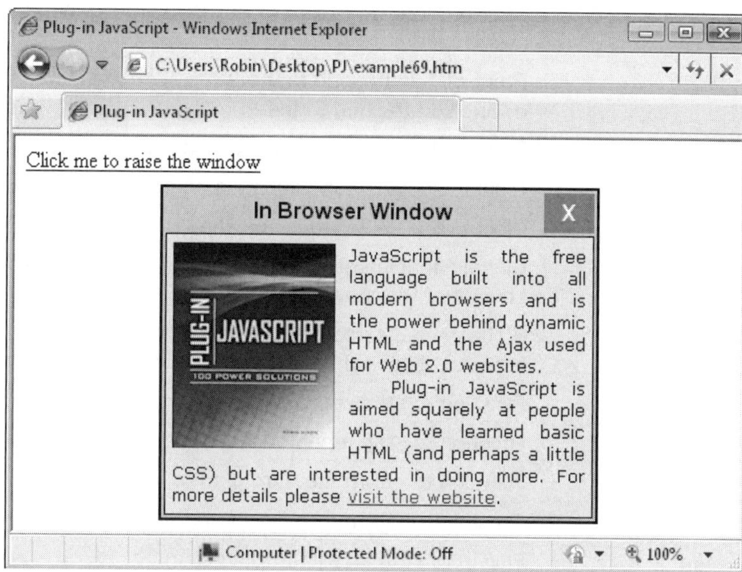

FIGURE 8-12 Creating an in-browser pop-up window

- **bounds** If true, the pop-up is forced to stay within the browser window, otherwise it may be moved off the edges
- **type** The type of transition to use when popping the pop-up up or down, either 'fade', 'inflate', 'zoom', or 'instant'
- **w & h** If type is either 'inflate' or 'zoom', w and h specify which dimension(s) will be modified, otherwise these values will be ignored
- **msecs** The number of milliseconds a pop-up or pop-down should take (unless type is 'instant')
- **interruptible** If true, the pop-up can be interrupted by a pop-down call during its pop-up transition

Variables, Arrays, and Functions

browserw, browserh	Local variables containing the width and height of the browser
borderw, borderh	Local variables containing the total widths of the left and right and top and bottom borders of the pop-up
popupw, popuph	Local variables containing the width and height of the pop-up
xoffset, yoffset	Local variables of the BWMove() subfunction containing the differences between the pop-up location and the current mouse positions
x, y	Local variables of the DoBWMove() sub-subfunction containing the differences between the current and saved mouse positions
r, b	Local variables of the DoBWMove() sub-subfunction containing the right and bottom maximum allowable coordinates for the pop-up if bounds is true
cursor	Style property of closeid set to 'pointer' when the mouse passes over it
onclick	Event of id attached to the BWToFront() subfunction and event of closeid attached to the BWCloseWindow() subfunction
onmousedown	Event of headerid attached to the BWMove() subfunction
MOUSE_X, MOUSE_Y	Global variables containing the coordinates of the mouse cursor
MOUSE_DOWN	Global variable set to true when the mouse button is down
MOUSE_IN	Global variable set to true when the mouse cursor is within the bounds of the browser
SCROLL_X, SCROLL_Y	Global variables containing the number of pixels the document has been scrolled in the horizontal and vertical directions
setInterval()	Function to start repeated interrupts
clearInterval()	Function to stop repeated interrupts
Math.max()	Function to return the maximum of two values
Math.min()	Function to return the minimum of two values
PreventAction()	Plug-in to stop an event from occurring

GoTo()	Plug-in to move an object to a new location
PopUp()	Plug-in to pop up a previously popped down object
PopDown()	Plug-in to pop down and object
BWToFront()	Subfunction to bring a pop-up window to the front
BWCloseWindow()	Subfunction to close a pop-up window
BWMove()	Subfunction to prepare to move a pop-up when it is dragged
DoBWMove()	Sub-subfunction to move a pop-up when it is dragged

How It Works

The first thing this plug-in does is move the pop-up to its correct location and initiate the pop-up process, like this:

```
GoTo(id, x, y)
PopUp(id, type, w, h, msecs, interruptible)
```

Next, some local variables are assigned values to keep track of the browser's dimensions, the borders (if any) of the pop-up, and its width and height, as follows:

```
var browserw = GetWindowWidth()
var browserh = GetWindowHeight()
var borderw  = NoPx(S(id).borderLeftWidth) +
               NoPx(S(id).borderRightWidth)
var borderh  = NoPx(S(id).borderTopWidth)  +
               NoPx(S(id).borderBottomWidth)
var popupw   = W(id)
var popuph   = H(id)
```

The mouse cursor is then set to become a pointer when it passes over the `closeid` object, which is used as the close button. After that, the `BWToFront()` subfunction is assigned to the `onclick` event of the pop-up so that whenever you click anywhere on the pop-up, if it is partially obscured by another, it is brought to the front.

In addition, the `closeid` object is assigned to the `BWCloseWindow()` subfunction so that clicking the close button will pop the window down, and the `BWMove()` subfunction is attached to the `headerid` object so that you can click and drag the header to move the pop-up about, like this:

```
S(closeid).cursor        = 'pointer'
O(id).onclick            = BWToFront
O(closeid).onclick       = BWCloseWindow
O(headerid).onmousedown = BWMove
```

The last couple of lines in the main setup section of code use the `PreventAction()` plug-in to disable the 'select' event on the `headerid` and `closeid` objects. If this is not done, dragging the pop-up quickly may highlight parts of the header text because the pop-up will drag behind the pointer. This unsightly behavior is prevented like this:

```
PreventAction(headerid, 'select', true)
PreventAction(closeid,  'select', true)
```

The BWToFront() and BWCloseWindow() Subfunctions

The `BWToFront()` function simply changes the style `zIndex` property of the pop-up so that it is brought to the front, like this:

```
S(id).zIndex = ++ZINDEX
```

Every time an in-browser window such as `id` is clicked, this function is called, moving it to the front, and updating the value in `ZINDEX`.

The `BWCloseWindow()` function pops the pop-up down, like this:

```
PopDown(id, type, w, h, msecs, interruptible)
```

The BWMove Subfunction

The job of this function is to prepare the pop-up for being dragged around. First, the pop-up is brought to the front with a call to `BWToFront()` and the mouse cursor is changed to the operating system's icon for moving a window, like this:

```
BWToFront()
S(headerid).cursor = 'move'
```

Next, it makes copies of the current difference between the top left corner of the pop-up and the current mouse position, placing them in `xoffset` and `yoffset`, and `setInterval()` is called to create repeating interrupts to the `DoBWMove()` sub-subfunction every 10 milliseconds to allow the object to be dragged about, as follows:

```
var xoffset = MOUSE_X - X(id)
var yoffset = MOUSE_Y - Y(id)
var iid     = setInterval(DoBWMove, 10)
```

The DoBWMove() Sub-subfunction

This is the function that actually moves the pop-up about. It starts by giving the local variables `x` and `y` the difference between the current mouse location and the location that was stored in `xoffset` and `yoffset` when `BWMove()` was initially called, like this:

```
var x = MOUSE_X - xoffset
var y = MOUSE_Y - yoffset
```

Then the `bounds` argument is tested. If it is `true` or 1, then the pop-up must stay within the main browser window, and the farthest horizontal and vertical locations the pop-up may go to are placed in the local variables `r` and `b` (for right and bottom). These values are then used to calculate the new values of `x` and `y`, using the `Math.min()` and `Math.max()` functions to ensure the pop-up stays in bounds, like this:

```
var r = browserw - popupw - borderw + SCROLL_X
var b = browserh - popuph - borderh + SCROLL_Y
x     = Math.max(0, Math.min(x, r))
y     = Math.max(0, Math.min(y, b))
```

Next, the current mouse position is tested to see whether it is outside the bounds of the browser window or if the mouse button is no longer down. In any of these cases, dragging of the pop-up must be terminated so the `clearInterval()` function is called to stop the repeating interrupts and the mouse cursor icon for the `headerid` object is restored to the default, like this:

```
if (MOUSE_X < 0 || MOUSE_X > (browserw + SCROLL_X) ||
    MOUSE_Y < 0 || MOUSE_Y > (browserh + SCROLL_Y) ||
    !MOUSE_DOWN || !MOUSE_IN)
{
   clearInterval(iid)
   S(headerid).cursor = 'default'
}
```

Finally, whether or not the interrupts have been stopped, a call is made to `GoTo()` to update the location of the pop-up, like this:

```
GoTo(id, x, y)
```

If the interrupts have not been turned off, `DoBWMove()` will be called again in another 10 milliseconds, and so on, until dragging the object has stopped.

The use of `SCROLL_X` and `SCROLL_Y` means that, as long as they have the style `position` property of 'absolute', these windows can be made to pop up anywhere within a document, not just within the viewable area.

How To Use It

To use this plug-in, you must first create an object that will be the main container for the plug-in. This can be a div, a span, or even a table. Then you need to place a couple of different elements within this container, namely a header which will drag the pop-up about and a close button for dismissing the pop-up. Once this is done, you can place anything else you want in your pop-up and it will be ready to be called up.

Following is an example that uses a table to create the various elements. Many people will say this is not the correct use for tables and that I should use CSS. However, my aim in this example is to avoid styling as much as possible and provide the bare bones to keep it easy to follow. A simple table is easy to understand and uses less code than CSS styling would take:

```
<div id='click'><u>Click me to raise the window</u></div>

<table id='window' bgcolor='lightblue' cellpadding='5'>
   <tr>
      <td id='header' width='310' align='center'>
         <font face='Arial'><b>In Browser Window</b></font>
      </td>
      <td id='close' width='20' bgcolor='red' align='center'>
         <font face='Arial' color='white'><b>X</b></font>
      </td>
   </tr>
   <tr>
      <td id='content' colspan='2' bgcolor='#eeeeee'>
         <img id='image' src='pijsmall.png' align='left' />
         <font face='Verdana' size='2'>
```

```
            JavaScript is the free language built into all modern
            browsers and is the power behind dynamic HTML and the Ajax
            used for Web 2.0 websites. <br />    Plug-in
            JavaScript is aimed squarely at people who have learned
            basic HTML (and perhaps a little CSS) but are interested
            in doing more. For more details please <a href=
            'http://pluginjavascript.com' target='New'>visit the
            website</a>.
         </font>
      </td>
   </tr>
</table>

<script>
window.onload = function()
{
   Hide('window')
   x = (GetWindowWidth()  - 330) / 2
   y = (GetWindowHeight() - 245) / 2

   S('window').border = 'solid 2px'
   Position('window', ABS)
   PopDown('window', 'fade', null, null, 1, false)
   Resize('window', 330, 245)

   S('click').cursor       = 'pointer'
   S('image').paddingRight = Px(10)
   S('content').border     = 'solid 1px'
   S('content').textAlign  = 'justify'

   O('click').onclick = function()
   {
      BrowserWindow('window', 'header', 'close', x, y, true,
         'fade', null, null, 500, false)
   }
}
</script>
```

The HTML section starts by creating a div that you can click to raise the pop-up. Underneath this is a table with three sections: a header, a close button, and a content section.

The `<script>` section of code starts by calculating the correct coordinates to place the pop-up in the center of the browser, gives the pop-up a solid border of 2 pixel's width, and uses the `Position()` plug-in to give the pop-up a style `position` of 'absolute', which releases is from its place within the HTML so that it can be moved anywhere within the document. You can use a style `position` of 'fixed' if you prefer to limit the pop-up to staying only within the browser's viewport into the document.

The `PopDown()` plug-in is then called with a value of 1 millisecond to quickly hide the pop-up away. It's important to use the transition type of 'fade' to later pop the window up because the transition types must match or you will get strange errors.

The window is then resized to ensure that it is of set dimensions and, to prevent content overflowing from the pop-up, its `overflow` style property is set to 'hidden'.

Next, four style properties are set to give the first div a mouse pointer cursor, to give a little padding to the image, to provide a 1 pixel border between the header and the content, and to set the text to full justification. None of these things are necessary, but they are included to show how you can add a little styling from JavaScript as easily as you can from a `<style>` section of HTML.

Finally, the `onclick` event of the div is set to call the `BrowserWindow()` plug-in.

NOTE *Because I used a table as the container object for this pop-up, it does not handle the 'deflate' or 'zoom' transitions at all well, since table dimensions are fixed and will not collapse on demand. If you wish to create a pop-up window that uses either of these transition types, you will need to build your container object using divs, spans, and CSS.*

The Plug-in

```
function BrowserWindow(id, headerid, closeid, x, y, bounds,
   type, w, h, msecs, interruptible)
{
   GoTo(id, x, y)
   PopUp(id, type, w, h, msecs, interruptible)

   var browserw = GetWindowWidth()
   var browserh = GetWindowHeight()
   var borderw  = NoPx(S(id).borderLeftWidth) +
                  NoPx(S(id).borderRightWidth)
   var borderh  = NoPx(S(id).borderTopWidth)   +
                  NoPx(S(id).borderBottomWidth)
   var popupw   = W(id)
   var popuph   = H(id)

   S(closeid).cursor        = 'pointer'
   O(id).onclick            = BWToFront
   O(closeid).onclick       = BWCloseWindow
   O(headerid).onmousedown = BWMove

   PreventAction(headerid, 'select', true)
   PreventAction(closeid,  'select', true)

   function BWToFront()
   {
      S(id).zIndex = ++ZINDEX
   }

   function BWCloseWindow()
   {
      PopDown(id, type, w, h, msecs, interruptible)
   }

   function BWMove()
   {
      BWToFront()
      S(headerid).cursor = 'move'
```

```
        var xoffset = MOUSE_X - X(id)
        var yoffset = MOUSE_Y - Y(id)
        var iid     = setInterval(DoBWMove, 10)

        function DoBWMove()
        {
           var x = MOUSE_X - xoffset
           var y = MOUSE_Y - yoffset

           if (bounds)
           {
              var r = browserw - popupw - borderw + SCROLL_X
              var b = browserh - popuph - borderh + SCROLL_Y
              x     = Math.max(0, Math.min(x, r))
              y     = Math.max(0, Math.min(y, b))
           }

           if (MOUSE_X < 0 || MOUSE_X > (browserw + SCROLL_X) ||
               MOUSE_Y < 0 || MOUSE_Y > (browserh + SCROLL_Y) ||
               !MOUSE_DOWN || !MOUSE_IN)
           {
              clearInterval(iid)
              S(headerid).cursor = 'default'
           }

           GoTo(id, x, y)
        }
     }
  }
```

CHAPTER 9

Text Effects

This chapter provides you with a wide range of plug-ins offering text manipulation features. For example, you can enable text scrolling, either to the left or right, and you can choose how many times the scroll should repeat and its speed.

There are also typewriter and "matrix" effects to make text appear and disappear, as well as color fading text, flying text into position, and even fancy ripple effects for drawing attention to important text.

TextScroll()

With this plug-in, you can scroll selected text either left or right at a speed of your choosing and for a set number of times. Figure 9-1 shows two phrases. The top one is scrolling left over the course of three seconds, and the bottom is scrolling right over a period of one second.

About the Plug-in

This plug-in takes an object that contains text and then scrolls it. It requires the following arguments:

- **`id`** An object, object ID, or array of objects and/or object IDs
- **`dir`** The direction of scrolling, either 'left' or 'right'
- **`number`** The number of times to repeat the scroll, with 0 indicating infinite repeats
- **`msecs`** The number of milliseconds a full scroll should take

Variables, Arrays, and Functions

`j`	Local variable for iterating through `id` if it is an array
`copy`	Local copy of the HTML contents if `id`
`len`	Local variable containing the length of `copy`
`freq`	Local variable containing the period in milliseconds between each call to `DoTextScroll()`
`ctr1, ctr2`	Local counters for counting the characters in a string and the number of scroll iterations
`iid`	Local variable returned from the call to `setInterval()`, to be used when calling `clearInterval()`
`innerText`	Property of `id` in non-Firefox browsers containing the object's text
`textContent`	Property of `id` in Firefox browsers containing the object's text
`TS_Flag`	Property of `id` that is `true` when a scroll is in progress on it
`LT`	Global variable with the value 'left'
`Math.round()`	Function to turn a floating point number into an integer
`substr()`	Function to return a substring
`SetInterval()`	Function start repeating interrupts
`clearInterval()`	Function to stop repeating interrupts
`DoTextScroll()`	Subfunction to perform the text scrolling
`Html()`	Plug-in to return the HTML content of an object

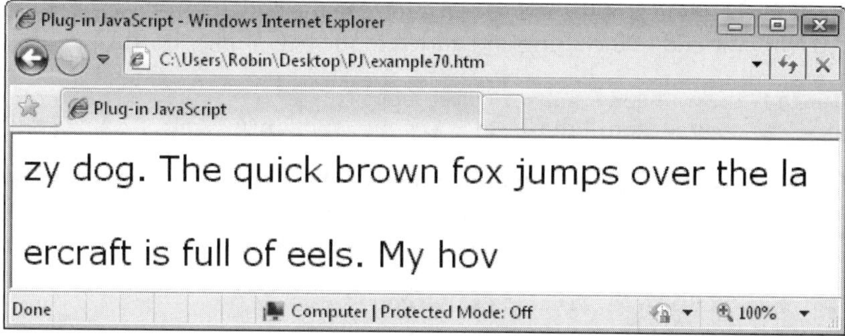

FIGURE 9-1 Scrolling text is easy with this plug-in.

How It Works

This plug-in begins by iterating through `id` if it is an array, recursively calling itself to individually deal with each element, like this:

```
if (id instanceof Array)
{
   for (var j = 0 ; j < id.length ; ++j)
      TextScroll(id[j], dir, number, msecs)
   return
}
```

The `TS_Flag` property of `id` is then tested. If it's true, a scroll is already operating on the object so the function returns. Otherwise, the property is set to `true` to indicate that a scroll is in action on the `id`, as follows:

```
if (O(id).TS_Flag) return
else O(id).TS_Flag = true
```

Next, some local variables are set up to hold the text content of `id`, the length of the text, the frequency at which the `DoTextScroll()` subfunction must be called in order for the scroll to take `msecs` milliseconds, a couple of counters and, finally, the repeating interrupts are set up with a call to `setInterval()`, with these statements:

```
var copy = Html(id)
var len  = copy.length
var freq = Math.round(msecs / len)
var ctr1 = 0
var ctr2 = 0
var iid  = setInterval(DoTextScroll, freq)
```

The DoTextScroll Subfunction

This function is called repeatedly at a frequency that will ensure that a full scroll of the text will take `msecs` milliseconds. It first determines whether to scroll left or right by checking the `dir` argument and then modifying the string `copy` accordingly. If scrolling left, characters are removed from the beginning of the string and added to the end. If scrolling right, characters are removed from the end of the string and added to the beginning, like this:

```
if (dir == LT) copy = copy.substr(1) + copy[0]
else           copy = copy[len - 1]  + copy.substr(0, len - 1)
```

Another test must then be made due to differences between browsers. If the browser supports the `innerText` property of an object, then that is assigned the value in `copy`; otherwise, the `textContent` property is assigned the value, as follows:

```
if (O(id).innerText) O(id).innerText = copy
else                 O(id).textContent = copy
```

Next, an `if()` statement increments `ctr1`. If the incremented value equals the value in `len`, then the contents of the statement are executed because a full scroll has completed; otherwise, the function returns to be called again in `freq` milliseconds. The code looks like this:

```
if (++ctr1 == len)
{
```

Inside the statement, `ctr1` is reset to 0, ready for the next scroll (if there is one). Then `ctr2` is incremented in another `if()` statement. If that value equals the one in the argument `number`, all scrolling is complete, and the `TS_Flag` property of `id` is set to `false` and the repeated interrupts are stopped with a call to `clearInterval()`, like this:

```
ctr1 = 0

if (++ctr2 == number)
{
   O(id).TS_Flag = false
   clearInterval(iid)
}
```

How To Use It

To use this plug-in, you pass it an object, such as a div or span that has some text in it, tell it whether to scroll left or right, and decide how many times the scroll should repeat and how long it should take.

Here's an example that creates two divs with different sentences in the HTML section, and then in the `<script>` section scrolls them in different directions, a different number of times, and at differing speeds:

```
<font face='Verdana' size='5'>
<div id='t1'>The quick brown fox jumps over the lazy dog. </div><br />
<div id='t2'>My hovercraft is full of eels. </div>
</font>

<script>
window.onload = function()
```

```
{
   TextScroll('t1', LT, 2, 1000)
   TextScroll('t2', RT, 1, 2000)
}
</script>
```

The divs have IDs of `t1` and `t2`, respectively, and the `LT` and `RT` arguments are global variables with the values 'left' and 'right'.

The Plug-in

```
function TextScroll(id, dir, number, msecs)
{
    if (id instanceof Array)
   {
      for (var j = 0 ; j < id.length ; ++j)
         TextScroll(id[j], dir, number, msecs)
      return
   }

   if (O(id).TS_Flag) return
   else O(id).TS_Flag = true

   var copy = Html(id)
   var len  = copy.length
   var freq = Math.round(msecs / len)
   var ctr1 = 0
   var ctr2 = 0
   var iid  = setInterval(DoTextScroll, freq)

   function DoTextScroll()
   {
      if (dir == LT) copy = copy.substr(1) + copy[0]
      else           copy = copy[len - 1]  + copy.substr(0, len - 1)

      if (O(id).innerText) O(id).innerText = copy
      else                 O(id).textContent = copy

      if (++ctr1 == len)
      {
         ctr1 = 0

         if (++ctr2 == number)
         {
            O(id).TS_Flag = false
            clearInterval(iid)
         }
      }
   }
}
```

TextType()

This plug-in emulates an old-fashioned typewriter or a teletype machine by outputting the text contents of an object one character at a time, over a period of time specified by you. Figure 9-2 shows a phrase being displayed with this plug-in.

About the Plug-in

This plug-in takes an object that contains text and then displays it one character at a time. It requires the following arguments:

- `id` An object, object ID, or array of objects and/or object IDs
- `number` The number of times to repeat the process, with 0 indicating infinite repeats
- `msecs` The number of milliseconds it should take to type out the text

Variables, Arrays, and Functions

`j`	Local variable that iterates through `id` if it is an array
`html`	Local variable containing the HTML content of `id`
`len`	Local variable containing the length of `html`
`freq`	Local variable containing the period in milliseconds between each call to `DoTextScroll()`
`ctr1`, `ctr2`	Local counters for counting the characters in a string and the number of scroll iterations
`iid`	Local variable returned from the call to `setInterval()`, to be used when calling `clearInterval()`
`str`	Substring of `html` used for displaying the characters so far "typed"
`innerText`	Property of `id` in non-Firefox browsers containing the object's text
`textContent`	Property of `id` in Firefox browsers containing the object's text
`TT_Flag`	Property of `id` that is `true` when a call to `TextType()` is already in progress on it
`Math.round()`	Function to turn a floating point number into an integer
`substr()`	Function to return a substring
`SetInterval()`	Function to start repeating interrupts
`clearInterval()`	Function to stop repeating interrupts
`Html()`	Plug-in to return the HTML content of an object
`DoTextType()`	Subfunction to perform the "typing"

Figure 9-2 You can emulate a teletype machine or typewriter with this plug-in.

How It Works

This plug-in begins by iterating through `id` if it is an array, recursively calling itself to individually process each element, like this:

```
if (id instanceof Array)
{
   for (var j = 0 ; j < id.length ; ++j)
      TextType(id[j], number, msecs)
   return
}
```

The `TT_Flag` property of `id` is then tested. If it's true, a call to this plug-in is already operating on the object, so it returns. Otherwise, the property is set to `true` to indicate that a call is in progress on the `id`, as follows:

```
if (O(id).TT_Flag) return
else O(id).TT_Flag = true
```

Next, some local variables are set up to hold the text content of `id`, the length of the text, the frequency at which the `DoTextType()` subfunction must be called in order for the typing to take `msecs` milliseconds, a couple of counters and, finally, the repeating interrupts are set up with a call to `setInterval()`, with these statements:

```
var html = Html(id)
var len  = html.length
var freq = Math.round(msecs / len)
var ctr1 = 0
var ctr2 = 0
var iid  = setInterval(DoTextType, freq)
```

The DoTextType() Subfunction

This function starts by assigning the characters so far typed to the local variable `str`. Next, an underline character is placed at the end to simulate a cursor, like this:

```
var str = html.substr(0, ctr1) + '_'
```

After that, the ctr1 counter is tested against the value in len. If they match, the text has completed being typed; otherwise, there is more yet to be typed, so ctr1 is incremented, like this:

```
if (ctr1++ == len)
{
```

Inside the if() statement, ctr1 is reset to 0 ready for the next repeat (if there is one) and ctr2 is incremented within another if() statement and compared with the value in the number argument. If they match, then all repeats have finished and the TT_Flag property of id is set to false, the repeating interrupts are cancelled with a call to clearInterval(), and the final underline character (which was previously appended to str) is stripped from it using a call to substr(), as follows:

```
ctr1 = 0

if (++ctr2 == number)
{
   O(id).TT_Flag = false
   clearInterval(iid)
   str = str.substr(0, len)
}
```

Next, because different browsers use different properties for the value, if the browser supports the innerText property, it is assigned the value in str; otherwise, the textContent property of id is assigned the value, like this:

```
if (O(id).innerText) O(id).innerText   = str
else                 O(id).textContent = str
```

Then the function returns and, if the repeating interrupts have not been cleared, it will be called up again in another freq milliseconds.

How To Use It

To use this plug-in, put some text in a container, such as a div or span, and pass that container to the plug-in along with the number of repeats required and the length of time it should take to complete the typing.

Here's a simple example that types out a simple phrase once, over a period of five seconds:

```
<font face='Courier New' size='6'><b>
<div id='text'>The quick brown fox jumps over the lazy dog.</div>
</b></font>

<script>
window.onload = function()
{
   TextType('text', 1, 5000)
}
</script>
```

The Plug-in

```
function TextType(id, number, msecs)
{
    if (id instanceof Array)
   {
      for (var j = 0 ; j < id.length ; ++j)
         TextType(id[j], number, msecs)
      return
   }

   if (O(id).TT_Flag) return
   else O(id).TT_Flag = true

   var html = Html(id)
   var len  = html.length
   var freq = Math.round(msecs / len)
   var ctr1 = 0
   var ctr2 = 0
   var iid  = setInterval(DoTextType, freq)

   function DoTextType()
   {
      var str = html.substr(0, ctr1) + '_'

      if (ctr1++ == len)
      {
         ctr1 = 0

         if (++ctr2 == number)
         {
            O(id).TT_Flag = false
            clearInterval(iid)
            str = str.substr(0, len)
         }
      }

      if (O(id).innerText) O(id).innerText   = str
      else                 O(id).textContent = str
   }
}
```

PLUG-IN 72 MatrixToText()

This plug-in provides an effect similar to the one used in the *Matrix* movies to make text slowly appear from a random collection of characters. Figure 9-3 shows some text halfway through being revealed using this plug-in.

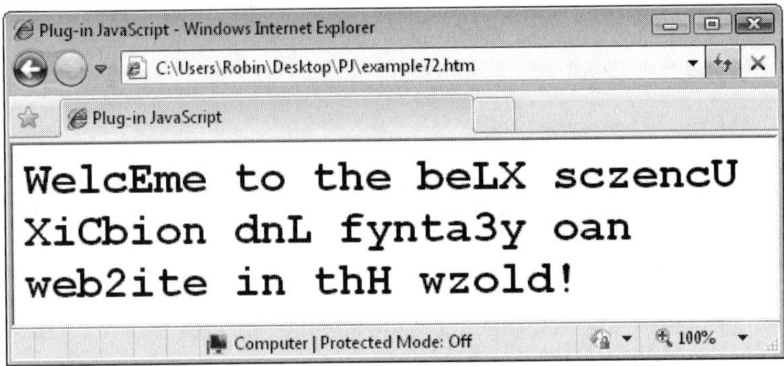

FIGURE 9-3 This plug-in creates an interesting text reveal effect.

About the Plug-in

This plug-in takes an object containing some text and replaces it with random characters, then slowly changes them to reveal the original text. It requires the following arguments:

- `id` An object, object ID, or array of objects and/or object IDs
- `msecs` The number of milliseconds it should take to reveal the text

Variables, Arrays, and Functions

`j`	Local variable that iterates through `id` if it is an array
`html`	Local variable containing the HTML content of `id`
`len`	Local variable containing the length of `html`
`freq`	Local variable containing the period in milliseconds between each call to `DoMatrixTotext()`
`matrix`	Local string variable originally containing scrambled text
`count`	Local variable for counting the steps of the transformation
`chars`	Local string variable containing all the upper- and lowercase letters and the digits 0 to 9
`iid`	Local variable returned form the call to `setInterval()`, to be used when calling `clearInterval()`
`innerText`	Property of `id` in non-Firefox browsers containing the object's text
`textContent`	Property of `id` in Firefox browsers containing the object's text
`innerHTML`	Property of `id` containing its HTML
`INTERVAL`	Global variable with the value 30
`MT_Flag`	Property of `id` that is `true` when a call to `MatrixToText()` is already in progress on it

`substr()`	Function to return a substring
`Math.round()`	Function to turn a floating point number into an integer, rounding the number up or down, whichever is closest
`Math.floor()`	Function to turn a floating point number into an integer, always rounding the number down
`Math.random()`	Function to return a random number between 0 and 1
`SetInterval()`	Function to start repeating interrupts
`clearInterval()`	Function to stop repeating interrupts
`Html()`	Plug-in to return the HTML of an object
`DoMatrixToText()`	Function to reveal the original text

How It Works

This plug-in begins by iterating through `id` if it is an array, recursively calling itself to individually process each element, like this:

```
if (id instanceof Array)
{
   for (var j = 0 ; j < id.length ; ++j)
      MatrixToText(id[j], msecs)
   return
}
```

The `MT_Flag` property of `id` is then tested. If it's true, a call to this plug-in is already operating on the object, so it returns. Otherwise, the property is set to `true` to indicate that a call is in progress on the `id`, as follows:

```
if (O(id).MT_Flag) return
else O(id).MT_Flag = true
```

Next, `html` is given the HTML contents of `id`, `len` its length, and `freq` the frequency with which the `DoMatrixToText()` subfunction needs to be called in order for the transition to take `msecs` milliseconds. In addition, the string variable `matrix` is created, which will hold the random text as it is slowly revealed; `count`, the counter for each step, is initialized to 0; and `chars`, the string containing all possible characters for scrambling the text, is populated with the characters a–z, A–Z and 0–9, as follows:

```
var html   = Html(id)
var len    = html.length
var freq   = Math.round(msecs / INTERVAL)
var matrix = ''
var count  = 0
var chars  = 'ABCDEFGHIHJKLMOPQRSTUVWXYZ' +
             'abcdefghijklmnopqrstuvwxyz' +
             '0123456789'
```

Next, a `for()` loop iterates through each character in `html`, replacing it with a random character from `chars` (if it is not a newline or space), like this:

```
for (var j = 0 ; j < len ; ++j)
{
   if (html[j] == '\n' || html[j] == ' ') matrix += html[j]
   else matrix += chars[Math.floor(Math.random() * chars.length)]
}
```

The value in `matrix` is then assigned to either the `innerText` or `textContent` property of `id`, according to which one is supported by the current browser, and the regular interrupts to the subfunction that will perform the reveal are set up, like this:

```
if (O(id).innerText) O(id).innerText   = matrix
else                 O(id).textContent = matrix
var iid = setInterval(DoMatrixToText, freq)
```

The DoMatrixToText() Subfunction

This function does the revealing by using a `for()` loop each time it is called up to replace `len / 20` characters in the string matrix with the correct values. This is sufficient to change only enough for each step, so that the transition will take `msecs` milliseconds, as follows:

```
for (j = 0 ; j < len / 20 ; ++j)
{
   var k   = Math.floor(Math.random() * len)
   matrix = matrix.substr(0, k) + html[k] + matrix.substr(k + 1)
}
```

The value of 20 was determined by performing several tests with strings of different sizes and timing them. It's not an exact value, so you might find you want to tweak it. The new value in `matrix` is then assigned to the correct property of `id` in order to display it:

```
if (O(id).innerText) O(id).innerText   = matrix
else                 O(id).textContent = matrix
```

Finally, the `count` variable is incremented within an `if()` statement. If the new value is the same as `INTERVAL`, the transition has completed, so the `MT_Flag` property of `id` is set to `false` to indicate that the transition is over. Its `innerHTML` property is then restored to its original value, and the repeating interrupts are cancelled, like this:

```
if (++count == INTERVAL)
{
   O(id).MT_Flag = false
   O(id).innerHTML = html
   clearInterval(iid)
}
```

The function then returns and, if there are still characters to be revealed, it is called up again in `freq` milliseconds time, and so forth, until the transition has finished.

How To Use It

To use this plug-in, pass it an object, such as a div or span that contains some text, and tell it how long the reveal transition should take, as with this example:

```
<font face='Courier New' size='6'><b>
<div id='text'>Welcome to the best science fiction and fantasy fan
website in the world!</div>
</b></font>

<script>
window.onload = function()
{
   MatrixToText('text', 3000)
}
</script>
```

The Plug-in

```
function MatrixToText(id, msecs)
{
    if (id instanceof Array)
   {
      for (var j = 0 ; j < id.length ; ++j)
         MatrixToText(id[j], msecs)
      return
   }

   if (O(id).MT_Flag) return
   else O(id).MT_Flag = true

   var html   = Html(id)
   var len    = html.length
   var freq   = Math.round(msecs / INTERVAL)
   var matrix = ''
   var count  = 0
   var chars  = 'ABCDEFGHIHJKLMOPQRSTUVWXYZ' +
                'abcdefghijklmnopqrstuvwxyz' +
                '0123456789'

   for (var j = 0 ; j < len ; ++j)
   {
      if (html[j] == '\n' || html[j] == ' ') matrix += html[j]
      else matrix += chars[Math.floor(Math.random() * chars.length)]
   }

   if (O(id).innerText) O(id).innerText   = matrix
   else                 O(id).textContent = matrix

   var iid = setInterval(DoMatrixToText, freq)

   function DoMatrixToText()
```

```
        {
            for (j = 0 ; j < len / 20 ; ++j)
            {
                var k  = Math.floor(Math.random() * len)
                matrix = matrix.substr(0, k) + html[k] + matrix.substr(k + 1)
            }

            if (O(id).innerText) O(id).innerText   = matrix
            else                 O(id).textContent = matrix


            if (++count == INTERVAL)
            {
                O(id).MT_Flag = false
                O(id).innerHTML = html
                clearInterval(iid)
            }
        }
    }
```

PLUG-IN 73 TextToMatrix()

This plug-in provides the inverse functionality to the `MatrixToText()` plug-in. It takes some text and slowly scrambles it over a period of time specified by you. Figure 9-4 shows some text that has been fully scrambled with this plug-in.

About the Plug-in

This plug-in takes an object containing some text and replaces it with random characters over a time period you specify. It requires the following arguments:

- **`id`** An object, object ID, or array of objects and/or object IDs
- **`msecs`** The number of milliseconds it should take to scramble the text

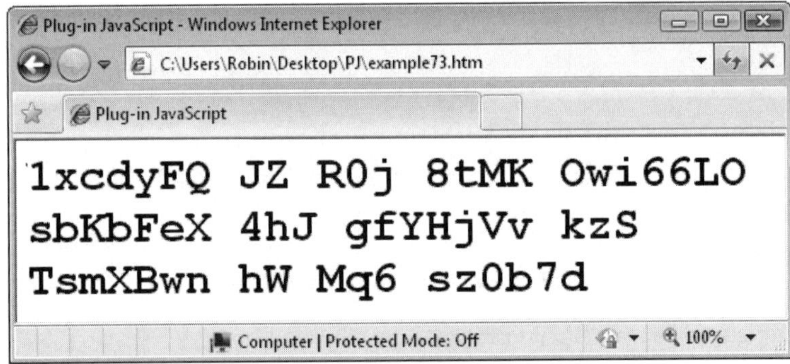

FIGURE 9-4 This plug-in slowly scrambles text over a specified length of time.

Variables, Arrays, and Functions

j	Local variable that iterates through id if it is an array
text	Local variable containing the HTML content of id
len	Local variable containing the length of html
freq	Local variable containing the period in milliseconds between each call to DoMatrixTotext()
count	Local variable for counting the steps of the transformation
chars	Local string variable containing all the upper- and lowercase letters and the digits 0 to 9
iid	Local variable returned from the call to setInterval(), to be used when calling clearInterval()
innerText	Property of id in non-Firefox browsers containing the object's text
textContent	Property of id in Firefox browsers containing the object's text
INTERVAL	Global variable with the value 30
TM_Flag	Property of id that is true when a call to TextToMatrix() is already in progress on it
substr()	Function to return a substring
Math.floor()	Function to turn a floating point number into an integer, always rounding the number down
Math.random()	Function to return a random number between 0 and 1
SetInterval()	Function to start repeating interrupts
clearInterval()	Function to stop repeating interrupts
Html()	Plug-in to return the HTML of an object
DoTextToMatrix()	Function to scramble the original text

How It Works

This plug-in works in almost the same fashion as the MatrixToText() plug-in except that the string text is slowly scrambled over time and assigned to the id object to display it—a full explanation can be found in the notes in the section "Plug-in 72: MatrixToText()."

How To Use It

To use this plug-in, pass it an object, such as a div or span that contains some text, and tell it how long the scramble transition should take, as with this example:

```
<font face='Courier New' size='6'><b>
<div id='text'>Welcome to the best science fiction and fantasy fan
website in the world!</div>
</b></font>

<script>
window.onload = function()
```

```
{
   TextToMatrix('text', 3000)
   FadeOut('text', 3000)
}
</script>
```

Note that I snuck in a call to the `FadeOut()` plug-in in this example as it makes for an interesting combined effect of the scrambling text slowly fading away—this is just one example of how you can combine these plug-in to produce even more complex and interesting results.

You may also notice that I omitted the `interruptible` argument to `FadeOut()`. Therefore, this passes a value of 'undefined' for that argument to the function, which will be treated as if it was the value `false` and so it saves on typing.

The Plug-in

```
function TextToMatrix(id, msecs)
{
    if (id instanceof Array)
   {
      for (var j = 0 ; j < id.length ; ++j)
         TextToMatrix(id[j], msecs)
      return
   }

   if (O(id).TM_Flag) return
   else O(id).TM_Flag = true

   var text  = Html(id)
   var len   = text.length
   var freq  = Math.round(msecs / INTERVAL)
   var count = 0
   var chars = 'ABCDEFGHIHJKLMOPQRSTUVWXYZ' +
               'abcdefghijklmnopqrstuvwxyz' +
               '0123456789'
   var iid   = setInterval(DoTextToMatrix, freq)

   function DoTextToMatrix()
   {
      for (var j = 0 ; j < len / 20 ; ++j)
      {
         var k = Math.floor(Math.random() * len)
         var l = Math.floor(Math.random() * chars.length)

         if (text[k] != '\n' && text[k] != '\r' && text[k] != ' ')
            text = text.substr(0, k) + chars[l] + text.substr(k + 1)
      }

      if (O(id).innerText) O(id).innerText   = text
      else                 O(id).textContent = text
```

```
            if (++count == INTERVAL)
            {
               O(id).TM_Flag = false
               clearInterval(iid)
            }
         }
      }
```

PLUG-IN 74 ColorFade()

This plug-in provides a very smooth transition effect between two different colors, and you can use it with either an object's text or its background colors. Figure 9-5 shows two elements that have been set to fade colors. The first continuously alternates between yellow and blue text and background colors, while the second fades from black to light blue when the mouse is passed over it.

About the Plug-in

This plug-in changes the text or background color of the contents of an object over a specified period of time. It requires the following arguments:

- `id` An object or object ID or an array of objects and/or object IDs
- `color1` The start color expressed as a six-digit hexadecimal number
- `color2` The end color expressed as a six-digit hexadecimal number
- `what` The property to change, either 'text' for the text color, or 'back' (or anything other than 'text') for the background color
- `msecs` The number of milliseconds the transition should take
- `number` The number of times the transition should repeat, with 0 meaning infinite repeats

Figure 9-5 This plug-in is great for banners and mouseover highlights.

Variables, Arrays, and Functions

j	Local variable that indexes into id if it is an array, and for splitting the colors into triplets
step	Local variable containing the amount of change between each transition frame
index	Local variable used as a multipliers fort generating color values
count	Local variable containing a counter for counting the repeats
direc	Local variable containing the direction of color change, either 1 or –1
cols[]	Local array containing the 'from' color triplets
steps[]	Local array containing the step between each color triplet
prop	Local variable containing the property to change either color or backgroundColor
iid	Local variable containing the value returned by setInterval(), to be used later by clearInterval()
temp	Local variable used for building up each transition color
CF_Flagtext	Property of id that is true if a color change transition is in effect on it
CF_Flagback	Property of id that is true if a background color change transition is in effect on it
INTERVAL	Global variable with the value 30
DoColorFade()	Subfunction to perform the color changes
ZeroToFF()	Sub-subfunction to ensure values are integers between 0 and 255 (equal to 00 to FF hexadecimal)
DecHex()	Plug-in to convert a decimal value to hexadecimal
setInterval()	Function to set up repeating interrupts
clearInterval()	Function to stop repeating interrupts
Math.round()	Function to turn a floating point number into an integer
Math.max()	Function to return the maximum of two values
Math.min()	Function to return the minimum of two values

How It Works

This function starts by iterating through id if it is an array, recursively calling itself to process each element individually, like this:

```
if (id instanceof Array)
{
   for (var j = 0 ; j < id.length ; ++j)
      ColorFade(id[j], color1, color2, what, msecs, number)
   return
}
```

Next, a pair of flags are checked to see whether a fade is already in process on `id`. If the argument `what` has the value 'text', then the `CF_Flagtext` property of `id` is tested or set. Otherwise, if it is 'back', its `CF_Flagback` property is tested or set, like this:

```
if (O(id)['CF_Flag' + what])
{
   if (!O(id)['CF_Int' + what]) return
   else clearInterval(O(id)['CF_IID' + what])
}
else O(id)['CF_Flag' + what] = true
```

If a fade is running and the plug-in is not set to interruptible, the plug-in returns; otherwise, any current repeating interrupts are halted, ready for new ones to be set up. If the flag is not set, it is assigned the value `true` to indicate that a fade is in progress.

After this, if either of the colors was passed without the preceding required # character, it is added:

```
if (color1[0] == '#') color1 = color1.substr(1)
if (color2[0] == '#') color2 = color2.substr(1)
```

Next, various local variables are assigned values that will be used later:

```
var step  = Math.round(msecs / INTERVAL)
var index = 0
var count = 0
var direc = 1
var cols  = []
var steps = []
```

The last five are simple initializations, while the first one gives `step` a value that will calculate the difference between transition frames so that the whole effect will take `msecs` milliseconds.

After this, the `cols[]` array is populated with the triplet color values, and the `steps[]` array with the step values for each triplet between each frame, like this:

```
for (var j = 0 ; j < 3 ; ++j)
{
      var tmp  = HexDec(color2.substr(j * 2, 2))
      cols[j]  = HexDec(color1.substr(j * 2, 2))
      steps[j] = (tmp - cols[j]) / step
}
```

The local variable `prop` is then assigned a property name, either `color` or `backgroundColor`, depending on the value in the argument `what`:

```
if (what == 'text') var prop = 'color'
else        var prop = 'backgroundColor'
```

This is what makes the plug-in dual functional: either the foreground or background color will be changed.

Finally, in the setup section of code, the value in `interruptible` is saved, and the `setInterval()` function is called to set up repeating interrupts to the `DoColorFade()` subfunction every `INTERVAL` milliseconds. The value returned by the function is then stored in `CF_IID` to be used later when `clearInterval()` is called:

```
O(id)['CF_Int' + what] = interruptible
O(id)['CF_IID' + what] = setInterval(DoColorFade, INTERVAL)
```

The DoColorFade Subfunction

This function starts off by preparing the variable `temp` with an initial # character to start a color string. A `for()` loop then iterates through the `cols[]` array, calculating the current frame's color values, converting them to hexadecimal, and then appending them to `temp`. After that, the value in `temp` is assigned to the property of `id` stored in `prop`:

```
var temp ='#'

for (var j = 0 ; j < 3 ; ++j)
   temp += DecHex(ZeroToFF(cols[j] + index * steps[j]))

S(id)[prop] = temp
```

After this, the `index` variable is incremented by the value in `direc`. If `direc` is 1, `index` increases by 1; if it is –1, it decreases by 1, like this:

```
if ((index += direc) > step || index < 0)
```

If the new value of `index` is either greater than `step` or less than 0, the transition is complete, so the following code is executed to reverse the direction of fade by negating `direc`. Then, if all repeats are finished, it cancels the repeating interrupts:

```
direc = -direc

if (++count == number)
{
   O(id)['CF_Flag' + what] = false
   clearInterval(iid)
}
```

The ZeroToFF() Sub-subfunction

This function takes the value passed to it in `num` and uses the `Math.max()` function to ensure it is not less than 0, the `Math.min()` function to ensure it isn't greater than 255, and the `Math.round()` function to turn it into an integer, like this:

```
return Math.round(Math.min(255, Math.max(0, num)))
```

How To Use It

To use this plug-in, pass it an object, such as a div or span that contains some text; provide starting and ending values in strings such as '#123456'; decide whether to change the text or background color by setting an argument for `what` of 'text' or 'back'; choose a length of time in milliseconds for the transition; and finally, decide how many times you want the transition to repeat.

Here's an example that uses the plug-in in two different ways. One highlights some text by constantly transitioning it between the two colors supplied, and the other reacts to `onmouseover` and `onmouseout` events to fade between the two colors:

```
<center>
   <b>
      <font face='Verdana' size='6'>
         <span id='t'>New - See our latest offers!</span><br />
         <span id='m'>Mouseover Me</span>
      </font>
   </b>
</center>

<script>
window.onload = function()
{
   ColorFade('t', '#ffffff', '#0000ff', 'text', 2000, 0)
   ColorFade('t', '#ff0000', '#ffff00', 'back', 2000, 0)

   O('m').onmouseover = function() { fade('#000000', '#0088ff') }
   O('m').onmouseout  = function() { fade('#0088ff', '#000000') }

   function fade(a, b)
   {
      ColorFade('m', a, b, 'text', 200, 1)
   }
}
</script>
```

The text section creates two spans with the IDs 't' and 'm'. In the `<script>` section, the first two commands set both the background and text colors of 't' to transition between yellow ('#ffff00') and blue ('#0000ff'). Because a `number` argument of 0 is passed, the transitions continue infinitely.

Below this, the 'm' span has its `onmouseover` and `onmouseout` events attached to a small function called `fade()` that calls `ColorFade()` with a `number` argument of 1, so that each transition happens only once. This means that when the mouse passes over, the color fades to light blue ('#0000ff'), and when the mouse moves away it fades back to black ('#000000').

Pass your mouse over the second span to see the smooth fading mouseover effect you can achieve for links and other elements.

NOTE *Odd transitions change the color of an object from the first to the second color, while even ones change it back again. This means that* `number` *argument values of 1, 3, 5, and so on will leave the second color on display, while 2, 4, 6, and so on will restore the first color after all transitions are over.*

The Plug-in

```
function ColorFade(id, color1, color2, what, msecs, number, interruptible)
{
    if (id instanceof Array)
   {
      for (var j = 0 ; j < id.length ; ++j)
         ColorFade(id[j], color1, color2, what, msecs, number)
      return
   }

   if (O(id)['CF_Flag' + what])
   {
      if (!O(id)['CF_Int' + what]) return
      else clearInterval(O(id)['CF_IID' + what])
   }
   else O(id)['CF_Flag' + what] = true

   if (color1[0] == '#') color1 = color1.substr(1)
   if (color2[0] == '#') color2 = color2.substr(1)

   var step  = Math.round(msecs / INTERVAL)
   var index = 0
   var count = 0
   var direc = 1
   var cols  = []
   var steps = []

   for (var j = 0 ; j < 3 ; ++j)
   {
      var tmp   = HexDec(color2.substr(j * 2, 2))
      cols[j]   = HexDec(color1.substr(j * 2, 2))
      steps[j] = (tmp - cols[j]) / step
   }

   if (what == 'text') var prop = 'color'
   else      var prop = 'backgroundColor'

   O(id)['CF_Int' + what] = interruptible
   O(id)['CF_IID' + what] = setInterval(DoColorFade, INTERVAL)

   function DoColorFade()
   {
      var temp ='#'

      for (var j = 0 ; j < 3 ; ++j)

         temp += DecHex(ZeroToFF(cols[j] + index * steps[j]))

      S(id)[prop] = temp

      if ((index += direc) > step || index < 0)
      {
         direc = -direc
```

```
            if (++count == number)
            {
               O(id)['CF_Flag' + what] = false
               clearInterval(O(id)['CF_IID' + what])
            }
         }

         function ZeroToFF(num)
         {
            return Math.round(Math.min(255, Math.max(0, num)))
         }
      }
   }
```

PLUG-IN 75 FlyIn()

With this plug-in, you can make text (or any object) fly into its position in a document from any location you choose and at whatever speed you wish. Figure 9-6 shows a list of five items set to fly in from the bottom of the browser, one per second over the course of five seconds.

About the Plug-in

This plug-in flies an object into its final location over a time you specify. It requires these arguments:

- **id** An object or object ID or an array of objects and/or object IDs
- **x** If specified, the relative horizontal offset at which the animation should start—it may be a positive or negative value
- **y** If specified, the relative vertical offset at which the animation should start—it may be a positive or negative value
- **msecs** The number of milliseconds the animation should take

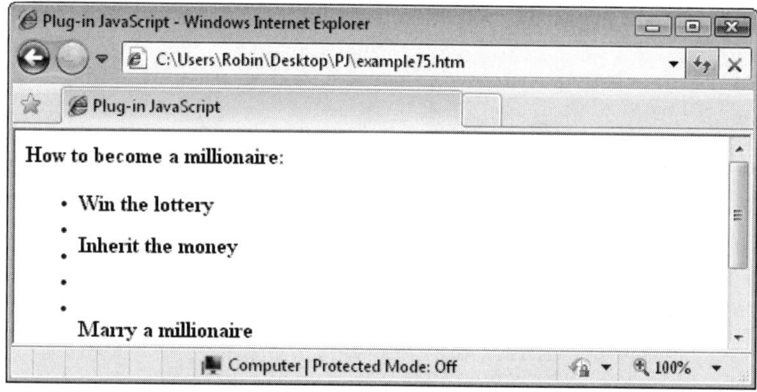

FIGURE 9-6 Instead of having static objects, why not fly them in at the start?

Variables, Arrays, and Functions

j	Local variable to iterate through id if it is an array
tox, toy	Local variables containing the original (and final) location of id
fromx, fromy	Local variables containing the start location of id for the animation
xstep, ystep	Local variables containing the amount by which to move id in each frame
count	Local variable to count the animation frames
ABS	Global variable with the value 'absolute'
FI_Flag	Property of id that is true if a fly-in is already in progress on it
setInterval()	Function to start repeating interrupts
clearInterval()	Function to end repeating interrupts
DoFlyIn()	Subfunction to perform the animation
Position()	Plug-in to set the style position property of an object
GoTo	Plug-in to move an object to a new location

How It Works

This plug-in starts by using j to iterate through id if it is an array and recursively calling itself to individually process each element:

```
if (id instanceof Array)
{
   for (var j = 0 ; j < id.length ; ++j)
      FlyIn(id[j], x, y, msecs)
   return
}
```

Next, the FI_Flag property of id is checked. If it is true, a fly-in is already in progress on the object so it returns. Otherwise, the property is given the value true to indicate that a fly-in is running on id, like this:

```
if (O(id).FI_Flag) return
else O(id).FI_Flag = true
```

After that, the various local variables that will be used by the DoFlyIn() subfunction are set up, as follows:

```
var tox   = X(id)
var toy   = Y(id)
var fromx = tox + x
var fromy = toy + y
var xstep = x / (msecs / INTERVAL)
var ystep = y / (msecs / INTERVAL)
var count = 0
```

The variables `tox` and `toy` save the current location of the object as a record of where to fly it into. The start location for the animation is then placed in `fromx` and `fromy`, the step value for each dimension of each frame is stored in `xstep` and `ystep`, and the counter `count` is initialized.

Finally, in the setup section, the `id` object is released from the HTML and given a style position property of 'absolute', using the global variable `ABS`. This allows it to be moved anywhere within the document. Next, the `setInterval()` function is called to start repeating interrupts to the `DoFlyIn()` subfunction every `INTERVAL` milliseconds. The result of calling the function is saved in `iid` to be used later when `clearInterval()` is called:

```
Position(id, ABS)
var iid = setInterval(DoFlyIn, INTERVAL)
```

The DoFlyIn() Subfunction

This function simply uses the `GoTo()` plug-in to move `id` to each location in the animation, like this:

```
GoTo(id, fromx - xstep * count, fromy - ystep * count)
```

An `if()` statement then checks `count` to see whether it has a value greater than or equal to `msecs / INTERVAL`. If it does, the fly-in has completed and the following code is executed, but whether it does or doesn't equal that value, `count` is incremented after the test is made, like this:

```
if (count++ >= msecs / INTERVAL)
{
```

If the fly-in has finished, the `FI_Flag` property of `id` is set to `false` to indicate this, `GoTo()` is called to ensure that `id` is placed at exactly the correct location (because `xstep` and `ystep` will usually be floating point values and the final values calculated using them could be off by a pixel or two). Then the repeating interrupts are stopped with a call to `clearInterval()`, like this:

```
O(id).FI_Flag = false
GoTo(id, tox, toy)
clearInterval(iid)
```

The function then returns and, if the fly-in hasn't yet finished, it will be called again in `INTERVAL` milliseconds, and so on until the animation has completed.

How To Use It

To use this plug-in, pass it an object and specify where you wish the object to fly in from by providing relative horizontal and vertical coordinates in the next two arguments. You also have to tell the plug-in how long the animation should take in milliseconds.

Here's an example that flies some list elements up from the browser bottom, with each arriving at its destination one second after the one above it:

```
<b>How to become a millionaire:<ul>
   <li><span id='a'>Win the lottery</span></li>
   <li><span id='b'>Inherit the money</span></li>
   <li><span id='c'>Marry a millionaire</span></li>
   <li><span id='d'>Become a movie or pop star</span></li>
   <li><span id='e'>Invest $130/month in stocks for 40 years!</span></li>
</ul></b>

<script>
window.onload = function()
{
   h = GetWindowHeight()

   FlyIn('a', 0, h, 1000)
   FlyIn('b', 0, h, 2000)
   FlyIn('c', 0, h, 3000)
   FlyIn('d', 0, h, 4000)
   FlyIn('e', 0, h, 5000)
}
</script>
```

In case you were wondering, statistically the stock market has returned 11 percent on average per year over the last several decades. And, according to any compound interest calculator, $130 invested every month over 40 years, and at an average of 11% interest per year, will return a gross amount of $1,007,490.02, before taxes and fees.

Of course inflation will eat away at that amount, approximately halving its actual value each decade, so the final amount in today's money would probably be closer to $250,000, pre tax and fees. Still, it's not bad for having invested only $62,400 in total. By the way, I am not an investment advisor and this doesn't constitute advice for you to make any investments.

But I digress, so back to the HTML part of the example. This HTML section creates a simple list and places its element within spans. The `<script>` section then places the height of the browser into the variable `h` and issues five calls to `FlyIn()` with the different object IDs, a start location just under the bottom of the screen, and animation periods from 1 to 5 seconds.

You can just as easily fly the elements in from the browser top by specifying a `y` value of –20 or so, or from the left or right edges by using values of `-W('object')-50` for the `x` argument when flying form the left, or `GetWindowWidth()` for the `x` argument if flying in from the right. In fact, you can specify any relative `x` and `y` coordinates you like so objects can fly in at any angle.

TIP *Because objects have to be given a style position property of 'absolute' in order to move them about, if you have not enclosed the object (or a set of objects) in a suitable container with set dimensions such as a div or span, other elements of the HTML could move themselves to fill in the space previously occupied by the object (or objects). Tables are also good place holders for objects that you will be flying in.*

The Plug-in

```
function FlyIn(id, x, y, msecs)
{
   if (id instanceof Array)
   {
      for (var j = 0 ; j < id.length ; ++j)
         FlyIn(id[j], x, y, msecs)
      return
   }

   if (O(id).FI_Flag) return
   else O(id).FI_Flag = true

   var tox   = X(id)
   var toy   = Y(id)
   var fromx = tox + x
   var fromy = toy + y
   var xstep = x / (msecs / INTERVAL)
   var ystep = y / (msecs / INTERVAL)
   var count = 0

   Position(id, ABS)
   var iid = setInterval(DoFlyIn, INTERVAL)

   function DoFlyIn()
   {
      GoTo(id, fromx - xstep * count, fromy - ystep * count)

      if (count++ >= msecs / INTERVAL)
      {
         O(id).FI_Flag = false
         GoTo(id, tox, toy)
         clearInterval(iid)
      }
   }
}
```

PLUG-IN 76

TextRipple()

This plug-in gives an interesting ripple effect to text, changing the size of characters next to each other to provide a wave that runs from the start to the end of the string. Figure 9-7 shows the list elements from the previous plug-in, `FlyIn()`, but here they have their `onmouseover` events attached to this plug-in.

About the Plug-in

This plug-in performs a wave or ripple effect from the start to end of text contained within an object. It requires the following arguments:

- **`id`** An object, object ID, or an array of objects and/or object IDs
- **`number`** The number of times to repeat the ripple—infinite, if `number` is 0
- **`msecs`** The number of milliseconds the ripple should take

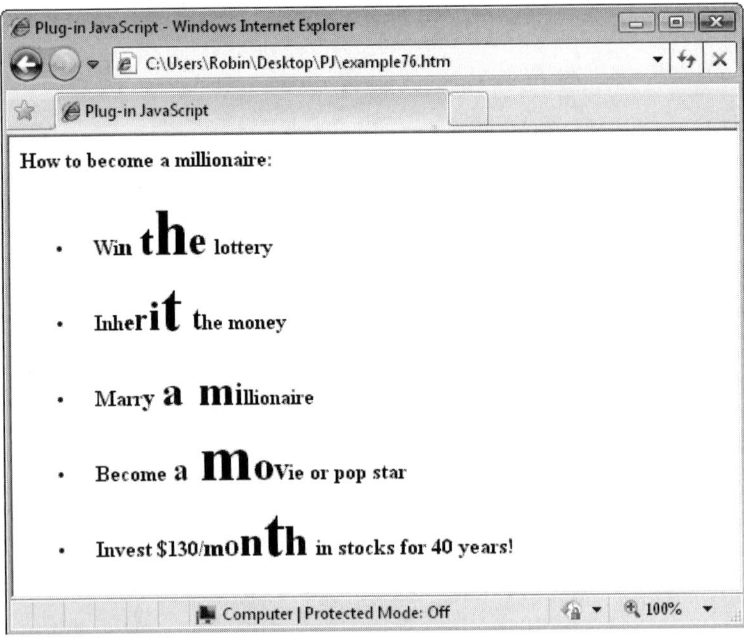

FIGURE 9-7 This plug-in provides a great effect for drawing people's attention.

Variables, Arrays, and Functions

`j`	Local variable used for iterating through `id` if it is an array
`html`	Local variable containing the HTML content of `id`
`len`	Local variable containing the length of `html`
`freq`	Local variable containing the time between each call to `DoTextRipple()` in milliseconds, such that the ripple will take `msecs` milliseconds to complete
`ctr1`, `ctr2`	Local variables for counting each character in a ripple, and each repeat of the animation respectively
`iid`	Local variable containing the result of calling `setInterval()` to be used later when calling `clearInterval()`
`temp`	Local variable that holds the HTML for each step of the animation
`innerHTML`	Property of `id` containing its HTML
`innerText`	Property of `id` in non-Firefox browsers containing its text content
`textContent`	Property of `id` in Firefox browsers containing its text content
`TR_Flag`	Property of `id` which is `true` when a ripple is in process on it

`Html()`	Plug-in to return the HTML content of an object
`InsVars()`	Plug-in to insert values into a string
`DoTextRipple()`	Subfunction to perform the animation
`setInterval()`	Function to set up repeating interrupts
`clearInterval()`	Function to stop repeating interrupts
`substr()`	Function to return a substring

How It Works

This plug-in starts by using `j` to iterate through `id` if it is an array and recursively calling itself to individually process each element:

```
if (id instanceof Array)
{
   for (var j = 0 ; j < id.length ; ++j)
      TextRipple(id[j], number, msecs)
   return
}
```

Next, the `TR_Flag` property of `id` is checked. If it is true, a ripple is already in progress on the object and it returns. Otherwise, the property is given the value `true` to indicate that a ripple is running on `id`, like this:

```
if (O(id).TR_Flag) return
else O(id).TR_Flag = true
```

After that, the local variable `html` is given a copy of the HTML content of `id`; `len` is set to its length; `freq` is assigned the time in milliseconds between each call to `DoTextRipple()` such that the ripple will take `msecs` milliseconds; two counters, `ctr1` and `ctr2`, are initialized; and `setInterval()` is called to set up repeating interrupts to the `DoTextRipple()` subfunction every `freq` milliseconds, like this:

```
var html = Html(id)
var len  = html.length
var freq = msecs / len
var ctr1 = 0
var ctr2 = 0
var iid  = setInterval(DoTextRipple, freq)
```

The variable `iid` is given the value returned by `setInterval()`, which will be used later when `clearInterval()` is called.

The DoTextRipple() Subfunction

This function starts off by assigning `temp` the left hand part of `html`, prior to any font size changes, with `ctr1` indexing the point at which the fonts will be manipulated:

```
var temp = html.substr(0, ctr1)
```

Next, each character in `html` that will have its font size changed is processed within a `for()` loop such that the outside characters of the group are the smallest, the ones just in from them are larger, and the largest one is in the center, as follows:

```
for (var j = 0 ; j < 7 ; ++j)
   temp += InsVars("<font size='+#1'>#2</font>",
      4 - Math.abs(j - 3), html.substr(ctr1 + j, 1))
```

The part that determines this is `4 - Math.abs(j - 3)`, which, for the values 0 through 6 of `j`, gives the following font size values (because the `Math.abs()` function makes all negative numbers positive): 1, 2, 3, 4, 3, 2, 1.

Once all the font sizes have been calculated and stored in `temp` using the `InsVars()` plug-in to insert the values into a string containing `<font size= ...>` statements, the `innerHTML` property of `id` is assigned this string to display it, along with the remaining, unchanged portion of `html`:

```
Html(id, temp + html.substr(ctr1 + j))
```

An `if()` statement then increments `ctr1` and checks whether it equals the value in `len`. If so, the animation has finished and the code following is executed:

```
if (++ctr1 == len)
{
```

If the ripple is finished, then `ctr1` is reset and another `if()` statement checks whether there are any more repeats of the interrupt remaining, like this:

```
ctr1 = 0

if (++ctr2 == number)
{
   if (O(id).innerText) O(id).innerText = html
   else                 O(id).textContent = html

   O(id).TR_Flag = false
   clearInterval(iid)
}
```

If the repeats have finished, the value in `html` is saved back into `id` as text, not HTML (Otherwise, unwanted extra HTML tags would be added by the browser—the time for saving HTML to the property is only when the font sizes are being changed).

Next, the `TR_Flag` property of `id` is set to `false` to indicate that all ripples have completed, and the `clearInterval()` function is called to stop any future calls to the subfunction, passing it the value previously stored in `iid`.

The function then returns but will be called up again in `freq` milliseconds if there are still outstanding animation frames to display.

How To Use It

To use this animation, pass it an object, such as a div or span containing only text with no HTML markup or other tags; tell it the number of times to repeat the ripple; and give it the length of time in milliseconds that the animation should take.

Here's an example that takes the list from the `FlyIn()` plug-in and attaches each entry to an `onmouseover` event to trigger the ripple:

```
<b>How to become a millionaire:<ul>
   <li><font size='+4'> </font>
      <span id='a'>Win the lottery</span></li>
   <li><font size='+4'> </font>
      <span id='b'>Inherit the money</span></li>
   <li><font size='+4'> </font>
      <span id='c'>Marry a millionaire</span></li>
   <li><font size='+4'> </font>
      <span id='d'>Become a movie or pop star</span></li>
   <li><font size='+4'> </font>
      <span id='e'>Invest $130/month in stocks for 40 years!</span></li>
</ul></b>

<script>
window.onload = function()
{
   O(Array('a', 'b', 'c', 'd', 'e'), 'onmouseover', ripple)

   function ripple()
   {
      TextRipple(this, 1, 500)
   }
}
</script>
```

To prevent the text from moving down on the page as the larger characters in a ripple increase its height, each line on which a ripple can be triggered has the html `<font size='+4'> </font>` immediately preceding it. This ensures that the height of the line is always set to the maximum +4 size of font used by the plug-in. You can also use CSS styling, tables, and other methods to enclose lines that will be rippled and prevent them moving themselves or other elements about.

The `<script>` section passes an array of the objects to the `O()` plug-in, along with the 'onmouseover' event name as a string, and the name of the function `ripple` below it. The `ripple` function then uses the `this` keyword, which acts as a pseudo object representing the object that triggered the event. This saves having to pass arguments to the function, keeping the code short and simple.

The Plug-in

```
function TextRipple(id, number, msecs)
{
   if (id instanceof Array)
   {
      for (var j = 0 ; j < id.length ; ++j)
         TextRipple(id[j], number, msecs)
      return
   }
```

```
   if (O(id).TR_Flag) return
   else O(id).TR_Flag = true

   var html = Html(id)
   var len  = html.length
   var freq = msecs / len
   var ctr1 = 0
   var ctr2 = 0
   var iid  = setInterval(DoTextRipple, freq)

   function DoTextRipple()
   {
      var temp = html.substr(0, ctr1)

      for (var j = 0 ; j < 7 ; ++j)
         temp += InsVars("<font size='+#1'>#2</font>",
            4 - Math.abs(j - 3), html.substr(ctr1 + j, 1))

      O(id).innerHTML = temp + html.substr(ctr1 + j)


      if (++ctr1 == len)
      {
         ctr1 = 0

         if (++ctr2 == number)
         {
            if (O(id).innerText) O(id).innerText = html
            else                 O(id).textContent = html

            O(id).TR_Flag = false
            clearInterval(iid)
         }
      }
   }
}
```

CHAPTER 10

Audio and Visual Effects

In this chapter, there are a number of handy plug-ins you can use for creating light boxes and slide shows (or combining the two), making rotating billboards for placing advertising or news updates, or making objects pulsate as you pass the mouse over them.

There are also plug-ins to help you create professional looking charts with the help of Google Charts, present YouTube videos in a variety of ways with a single function call, and play sounds in response to events or for any other reason.

Lightbox()

With this plug-in you can display an image or any object in the center of the browser with the outside darkened and made transparent by amounts you can specify. Your users can then view these objects with minimum distraction and simply click them to dismiss the light box. Figure 10-1 shows a photograph being displayed using this plug-in.

About the Plug-in

This plug-in displays a photo (or other object) centered in the browser, with a darkened frame over the web page behind it. It requires the following arguments:

- `id` An object or object ID—this may not be an array
- `col1` A starting color for the frame
- `col2` An ending color for the frame
- `opacity` The final opacity of the frame
- `msecs` The time in milliseconds the transition should take

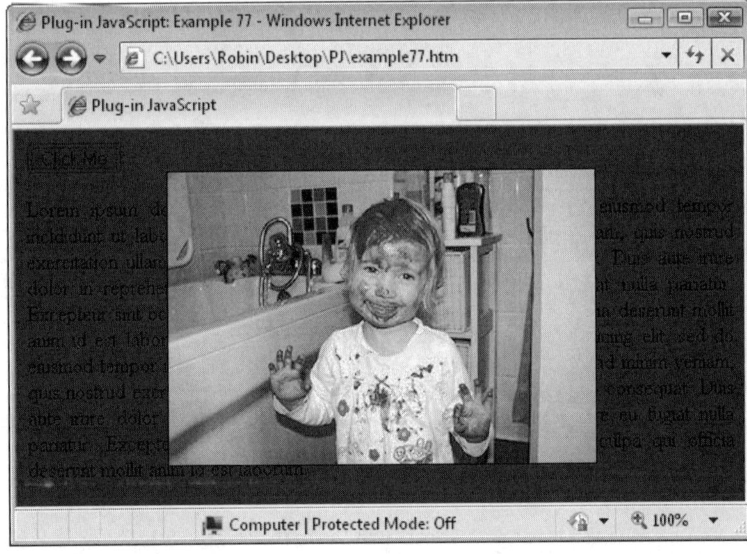

FIGURE 10-1 Show off your favorite photographs with this light box plug-in.

Variables, Arrays, and Functions

newdiv	New div object created to use for the frame
LB_DIV	Object ID of the new div
cursor	Style property of id that sets the mouse cursor to a pointer when it is over id, indicating that it is clickable
overflow	Style property of document.body set to 'hidden' during the display of id to prevent scrolling
zIndex	Style properties of both the frame and id, set to bring them to the forefront of the browser
onclick	Event of id set to dismiss the light box if clicked
HID	Global variable with the value 'hidden'
ABS	Global variable with the value 'absolute'
ZINDEX	Global variable containing the highest zIndex property used so far
DismissLB()	Subfunction to dismiss the light box
Hide()	Plug-in to hide an object
Show()	Plug-in to show a previously hidden object
Position()	Plug-in to set an object's style position property
Locate()	Plug-in to set an object's style position property and move it to a new location
Resize()	Plug-in to resize an object
Opacity()	Plug-in to set an object's opacity
Center()	Plug-in to center an object in the browser
GetWindowWidth()	Plug-in to return the width of the browser
GetWindowHeight()	Plug-in to return the height of the browser
Fade()	Plug-in to fade the opacity of an object to a new level
FadeIn()	Plug-in to fade the opacity of an object to 100
FadeOut()	Plug-in to fade the opacity of an object to 0
ColorFade()	Plug-in to fade the color of an object between two colors
Chain	Plug-in to chain two or more plug-ins in a sequence
InsVars()	Plug-in to insert values into a string
createElement()	Function to create a new HTML element
setAttribute()	Function to set an attribute of an HTML element
appendChild()	Function to append a child HTML element

How It Works

This plug-in starts off by setting the mouse cursor when over id into a pointer, to indicate that it is clickable (doing so dismisses the light box), like this:

```
S(id).cursor = 'pointer'
```

Then, if this is the first time the plug-in has been called, a new div object with the ID of 'LB_DIV' is created and appended to the HTML for use as the darkened frame around id—otherwise, the div has previously been created so this code is skipped:

```
if (!O('LB_DIV'))
{
   var newdiv = document.createElement('div')
   newdiv.setAttribute('id', 'LB_DIV')
   document.body.appendChild(newdiv)
}
```

Next, the overflow property of the document.body is set to 'hidden' to disable scrolling the web page, then both the frame and id are hidden with a call to Hide(). This is so that they can both be moved about and otherwise modified without these actions being seen by the user.

After that, the frame is moved to the top left of the browser and resized to fill the entire window, and its zIndex property is set to the highest value used so far (held in ZINDEX), like this:

```
S(document.body).overflow = HID
Hide(Array(id, 'LB_DIV'))
Locate('LB_DIV', ABS, 0, 0)
Resize('LB_DIV', GetWindowWidth(), GetWindowHeight())
S('LB_DIV').zIndex = ZINDEX
```

Having set up the frame, id is processed next by setting its opacity to 0, which releases it from the HTML by calling Position() to set its style position attribute to 'absolute'. Next, its zIndex is set to a value that is 1 higher than the frame's, and the ZINDEX global variable is also incremented to contain this higher value:

```
Opacity(id, 0)
Position(id, ABS)
S(id).zIndex = ++ZINDEX
```

With both objects now prepared, the Show() plug-in is called to re-enable the objects in the browser, and id is centered. Next, the new div (with the ID 'LB_DIV') is faded to the value in opacity over msecs milliseconds, id is faded in to an opacity of 100, and the background color of the frame is faded between col1 and col2 over the same time period, like this (remembering that FadeIn() fades an object from 0 percent to 100 percent opacity):

```
Show(Array(id, 'LB_DIV'))
Center(id)
Fade('LB_DIV', 0, opacity, msecs)
FadeIn(id, msecs, 0)
ColorFade('LB_DIV', col1, col2, 'back', msecs, 1)
```

Finally, in the display section of code, the onclick event of id is set to call up the DismissLB() subfunction when clicked, as follows:

```
O(id).onclick = DismissLB
```

The DismissLB() Subfunction

This function is called whenever id is clicked. The first thing it does is fade the frame's opacity back down to 0 and its background color from col2 back to col1, like this:

```
Fade('LB_DIV', opacity, 0, msecs)
ColorFade('LB_DIV', col2, col1, 'back', msecs, 1)
```

At the same time, a chain is created to perform three actions in sequence: first, fade out id; second, hide id; and third, restore any scrollbars to document.body, as follows:

```
Chain(Array(
   InsVars("FadeOut(Array('#1', 'LB_DIV'), #2, 0)", id, msecs),
   InsVars("Hide(Array('#1', 'LB_DIV'))", id),
   "S(document.body, 'overflow', 'auto')"
```

How To Use It

To use this plug-in, you need to have an image (or any other object) already prepared. Most likely you will also have set its style.display attribute to 'none' so that it is not visible in the web page, like this:

```
<img id='photo' src='photo6.jpg' border='1' style='display:none'>
```

Next you can attach the plug-in to an event such as an onclick or onmouseover to pop the object up in a light box. Here's an example that uses an onclick event:

```
<button id='link' type='button'>Click Me</button>
<img id='photo' src='photo6.jpg' border='1' style='display:none'>

<script>
window.onload = function()
{
   O('link').onclick = function()
   {
      Lightbox('photo', '#888888', '000000', 80, 500, 1)
   }
}
</script>
```

The HTML section of this example creates a button with a link to the anonymous inline function, along with an image object with the ID 'photo'. The <script> section simply contains the function that calls up the Lightbox() plug-in.

When a light box is in use, none of the elements underneath it that are usually clickable (or have onmouseover events attached) will work until the light box is removed. This is because the div object it creates covers the entire browser window and has a higher zIndex value than everything except the light box contents, which makes it especially useful when you wish to force the user to focus only on one thing, such as entering log-in details or accepting notification of an error, and so on.

TIP *The reason for requiring the two color arguments of* `col1` *and* `col2` *is to allow for web pages of any color background, which can then be faded to any other color of your choice for the light box frame. If your website has standard black text on a white background, I recommend you try fading the light box between the color values #888888 (midgray) and #000000 (black). Or, you can be creative and fade between contrasting colors for an even more eye-catching effect. The value you choose for the* `opacity` *argument will also greatly change the transition effect.*

The Plug-in

```
function Lightbox(id, col1, col2, opacity, msecs)
{
   S(id).cursor = 'pointer'

   if (!O('LB_DIV'))
   {
      var newdiv = document.createElement('div')
      newdiv.setAttribute('id', 'LB_DIV')
      document.body.appendChild(newdiv)
   }

   S(document.body).overflow = HID
   Hide(Array(id, 'LB_DIV'))
   Locate('LB_DIV', ABS, 0, 0)
   Resize('LB_DIV', GetWindowWidth(), GetWindowHeight())
   S('LB_DIV').zIndex = ZINDEX

   Opacity(id, 0)
   Position(id, ABS)
   S(id).zIndex = ++ZINDEX

   Show(Array(id, 'LB_DIV'))
   Center(id)
   Fade('LB_DIV', 0, opacity, msecs)
   FadeIn(id, msecs, 0)
   ColorFade('LB_DIV', col1, col2, 'back', msecs, 1)

   O(id).onclick = DismissLB

   function DismissLB()
   {
      Fade('LB_DIV', opacity, 0, msecs)
      ColorFade('LB_DIV', col2, col1, 'back', msecs, 1)
      Chain(Array(
         InsVars("FadeOut(Array('#1', 'LB_DIV'), #2, 0)", id, msecs),
         InsVars("Hide(Array('#1', 'LB_DIV'))", id),
         "S(document.body, 'overflow', 'auto')"
      ))
   }
}
```

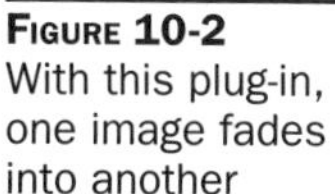

FIGURE 10-2 With this plug-in, one image fades into another

PLUG-IN 78 Slideshow()

With this plug-in, you can display a sequence of images in a slide show. Figure 10-2 shows this plug-in being used in conjunction with the previous plug-in, `Lightbox()`, to create a slide show on a darkened background.

About the Plug-in

This plug-in takes an empty container such as a div or span and displays a continuously rotating sequence of images that fade into each other. It requires the following arguments:

- **`id`** An object or object ID—this may not be an array
- **`images`** An array of images (preferably of the same dimensions)
- **`msecs`** The time each fade transition should take in milliseconds
- **`wait`** The time in milliseconds to wait between each transition—if this value is set to the string 'stop', it tells the plug-in to stop any current slide show and exit

Variables, Arrays, and Functions

`index`	Local variable used for indexing the array of images
`newimg`	Local variable containing a new image object
`SS_Stop`	Property of `id` which, if `true`, stops the slide show
`SS_IMG1`, `SS_IMG2`	Object IDs of the two new image objects
`src`	Property of each image object containing its source file

ABS	Global variable with the value 'absolute'
setTimeout()	Function to set up an interrupt to a function after a specified period
DoSlideshow()	Subfunction to perform the fade transitions
Locate()	Plug-in to set an object's style position property and move it to a new location
Opacity()	Plug-in to set an object's opacity
FadeIn()	Plug-in to center an object in the browser
FadeBetween()	Plug-in to fade between two objects
createElement()	Function to create a new HTML element
setAttribute()	Function to set an attribute of an HTML element
appendChild()	Function to append a child HTML element

How It Works

This plug-in begins by setting `len` to the number of items in `images` and setting the `SS_Stop` attribute of `id` to either `true` or `false`, depending on whether the `wait` argument contains the string 'stop'. If it does, the value `true` is assigned so the subfunction will know to stop the fade transitions. The line of code looks like this:

```
var len        = images.length
O(id).SS_Stop = (wait == 'stop') ? true : false
```

As well as checking the `wait` arguments to see if it has the value 'stop', the `SS_Flag` property of `id` is tested; if it is `true`, a slide show is already in operation on this `id`, so the following code is not executed:

```
if (!O(id).SS_Stop && !O(id).SS_Flag)
```

Otherwise, as long as the `wait` argument contains a number, the previous code is then entered.

Here, if there is no object with the ID 'SS_IMG1', this is the first time the plug-in has been called, so it populates the `id` container object with two new image objects having the IDs 'SS_IMG1' and 'SS_IMG2'. It then overlays these objects over each other by locating the second one in the same position as the first, like this:

```
var newimg = document.createElement('img')
newimg.setAttribute('id', 'SS_IMG1')
O(id).appendChild(newimg)

newimg = document.createElement('img')
newimg.setAttribute('id', 'SS_IMG2')
O(id).appendChild(newimg)

Locate('SS_IMG2', ABS, 0, 0)
```

These lines illustrate how you can add new elements to a DOM tree at any point. First, use `document.createElement()` to create a new element object, then set any attributes using `setAttribute()`, and finally, use `appendChild()` to append the new element to the DOM.

Next, the variable `index` is initialized to 0; this will be used later to index the next image in a slide show. The first image object is then assigned the contents of the first element in the `images` array, which will be the location of a photo or other image:

```
var index         = 0
O('SS_IMG1').src = images[0]
O(id).SS_Flag     = true
```

The `SS_Flag` property is also set to `true` to indicate that a slide show is in progress. After that, the second image has its opacity is set to 0 to make it invisible, and the first image is faded in over a period of `msecs` milliseconds:

```
Opacity('SS_IMG2', 0)
FadeIn('SS_IMG1', msecs, 0)
```

Finally, in the setup section of code, the `setTimeout()` function is called to set up an interrupt to call the `DoSlideshow()` subfunction after a period of `msecs + wait` milliseconds. This accounts for the time it will take the first image to fade in, plus the time required for the wait:

```
setTimeout(DoSlideshow, msecs + wait)
```

The DoSlideshow() Subfunction

The job of this function is to transition a fade between two images and then initiate an interrupt to call itself again when the next transition is due (unless it is cancelled).

The first thing this function does is load the first image with the current value in the `images` array, as indexed by `index`. The first time it calls this, nothing happens since the same image has already been loaded. However, on all future transitions it has the effect of taking the picture that is being displayed in the second image and duplicating it in the first, so that they both are showing the same picture:

```
O('SS_IMG1').src = images[index]
```

Since both images are showing the same picture, it is safe to set the first one to be fully visible and the second one to invisible, like this:

```
Opacity('SS_IMG1', 100)
Opacity('SS_IMG2', 0)
```

Having made this swap, the `index` variable is incremented to point to the next picture in the slide show and, if it becomes larger than the number of images in the `images` array, it is reset to 0 (using the `%` operator) to start again at the beginning, as follows:

```
index = ++index % len
```

Next, it's time to load in the next picture listed in the `images` array into the second image, because the first image is the one currently being displayed, and the second has been made invisible ready to do this:

```
O('SS_IMG2').src = images[index]
```

I will explain the following statement shortly, but here it is for reference:

```
var next = InsVars("O('SS_IMG1').src = '#1'",
   images[(index + 1) % len])
```

Now that each image holds a different picture, it's a simple matter to call the `FadeBetween()` plug-in to fade between the two, like this:

```
FadeBetween('SS_IMG1', 'SS_IMG2', msecs, next)
```

This makes the second image the visible one and the first one invisible. At this point, the image states are the same as at the start of the subfunction.

The value of the `next` argument in the `FadeBetween()` call is a string containing a callback function, which is mostly used by chains to link them together. However, in this case it is just passing a statement to be executed once the plug-in completes its work.

The contents of `next`, which I previously glossed over, creates a statement that will load the next picture in the slide show into the first image once the fade between the two images is finished and the first image is now invisible (and available for use in this way).

This is done to preload the picture so that it is cached in the browser and, next time round the loop, when the picture is loaded into image 2, it will be fetched from the cache without any delays while it is downloaded from the server.

This means program execution is ready to go round the loop again. However, the next interrupt call to the subfunction is only set up if the `SS_Stop` property of `id` is `false`, because if it is `true` then a call has been made requesting the slide show to stop:

```
if (!O(id).SS_Stop) setTimeout(DoSlideshow, msecs + wait)
```

Otherwise, if the slide show is stopped, the `SS_Flag` property of `id` is set to `false` to indicate this:

```
else O(id).SS_Flag = false
```

How To Use It

To use this plug-in, prepare an empty div or span and pass it to the plug-in along with an array containing the URLs of the images for the show and two timers: the first for how long each fade transition should take and the second for the length of pause between changing images, both in milliseconds.

Here's an example that combines this plug-in with the previous one, `Lightbox()`, to create a slide show in a light box:

```
<button id='link' type='button'>Click Me</button>
<div id='show'></div>

<script>
window.onload = function()
{
   Resize('show', 320, 240)
   Hide('show')
   photos = Array('photo1.jpg', 'photo2.jpg',
      'photo3.jpg', 'photo4.jpg', 'photo5.jpg')
```

```
    O('link').onclick = function()
    {
       Slideshow('show', photos, 500, 2000)
       Lightbox('show', '#888888', '000000', 80, 500, 1)
    }
}
</script>
```

In the HTML section, a button is created that will call the anonymous, inline function when clicked, while underneath it there's an empty div. In the `<script>` section, the div is resized (with a call to `Resize()`) to the dimensions required so that the `Slideshow()` function can center it correctly—without these dimensions, if the contents of the div is not ready when the `Center()` call is made, the object might appear off center.

The div is also hidden with a call to `Hide()` because now that it has dimensions it will push any content below it out of the way. Then the array `photos` is populated with the URLs of five photos, and the function calls both `Slideshow()` and `Lightbox()` to merge the two plug-ins together.

Because the `Lightbox()` plug-in dismisses its contents when you click it, the slide show will not stop, even though it isn't visible. If you click the button again, the `Slideshow()` plug-in will realize that it is still running and simply continue the slide show.

If you want to turn the slide show off, you need to set the `SS_Stop` property of 'show' to 1 or `true`, and the next time a slide change is due it will stop:

```
O('show').SS_Stop = true
```

TIP *This plug-in is designed so that you can place the containing object anywhere you like and the slide show will occur at that position; you don't have to use it in a light box if you don't want to.*

The Plug-in

```
function Slideshow(id, images, msecs, wait)
{
   var len        = images.length
   O(id).SS_Stop = (wait == 'stop') ? true : false

   if (!O(id).SS_Stop && !O(id).SS_Flag)
   {
      if (!O('SS_IMG1'))
      {
         var newimg = document.createElement('img')
         newimg.setAttribute('id', 'SS_IMG1')
         O(id).appendChild(newimg)

         newimg = document.createElement('img')
         newimg.setAttribute('id', 'SS_IMG2')
         O(id).appendChild(newimg)

         Locate('SS_IMG2', ABS, 0, 0)
      }
```

```
      var index        = 0
      O('SS_IMG1').src = images[0]
      Opacity('SS_IMG2', 0)
      FadeIn('SS_IMG1', msecs, 0)
      setTimeout(DoSlideshow, msecs + wait)
   }

   function DoSlideshow()
   {
      O('SS_IMG1').src = images[index]
      Opacity('SS_IMG1', 100)
      Opacity('SS_IMG2', 0)

      index = ++index % images.length
      O('SS_IMG2').src = images[index]
      var next = InsVars("O('SS_IMG1').src = '#1'",
         images[(index + 1) % len])
      FadeBetween('SS_IMG1', 'SS_IMG2', msecs, 0, next)

      if (!O(id).SS_Stop) setTimeout(DoSlideshow, msecs + wait)
      else O(id).SS_Flag = false
   }
}
```

PLUG-IN 79 Billboard()

This plug-in is similar to the `Slideshow()` plug-in in that it fades between objects in a sequence. The difference is that the `Billboard()` plug-in allows you to put any objects in a show, and they must already exist in the document (whereas the `Slideshow()` plug-in pulls images in by their URLs only when needed).

A great use for this plug-in is to rotate banners or other advertisements, which can be images, divs, spans, or other objects. Figure 10-3 shows one image in a sequence being displayed using this plug-in.

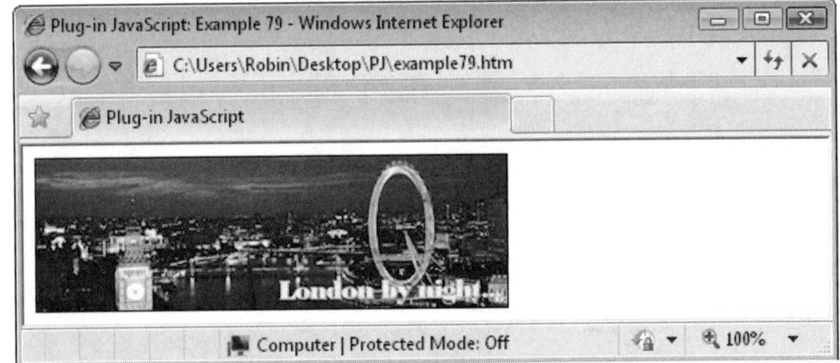

Figure 10-3 This plug-in creates a billboard of rotating objects and/or images.

About the Plug-in

This plug-in takes a containing object such as a div or span and an array of objects held within it, which it then rotates like an automated billboard. It requires the following arguments:

- **`id`** An object or object ID—this cannot be an array
- **`objects`** An array of objects or object IDs
- **`random`** If `true`, the objects will be displayed in random order
- **`msecs`** The time in milliseconds that each fade between objects should take
- **`wait`** The time in milliseconds to wait before fading to the next object

Variables, Arrays, and Functions

`j`	Local variable used as an index to iterate through the `objects` array
`len`	Local variable containing the number of items in the `objects` array
`index`	Local variable used to reference each object to be displayed
`h`	Local variable containing the cumulative height of each object for locating them in their required locations
`rand`	Local variable containing a random number between 0 and `len` – `1`
`BB_Ready`	Property of `id` that is `true` if the objects have already been positioned in their places
`BB_Stop`	Property of `id` that is `true` if the billboard rotation is disabled
`REL`	Global variable with the value 'relative'
`FadeOut()`	Plug-in to fade out an object
`FadeIn()`	Plug-in to fade in an object
`Locate()`	Plug-in to apply a style position and location to an object
`H()`	Plug-in to return an object's height
`DoBillboard()`	Subfunction to rotate the contents of the billboard
`setTimeout()`	Function to set up an interrupt to a function in the future
`clearTimeout()`	Function to stop any timeout that has been set
`slice()`	Function to return a portion of an array
`Math.floor()`	Function to turn a floating point number into a rounded down integer
`Math.random()`	Function to return a random number

How It Works

This plug-in begins by setting the local variable `len` to the number of items in the `objects` array:

```
var len = objects.length
```

Next, it checks whether it has already been called by examining the BB_Ready property of id. If it is not true, then the objects have not yet been moved to their required locations, so the following code is executed, which begins with setting up some variables.

First len is assigned the number of items in objects, and then the O(id).BB_Index property of id and the local variable h are initialized to 0, like this:

```
var h            = 0
O(id).BB_Index = 0
```

After setting up the local variables, the BB_Ready property of id is set to true so that future calls to the plug-in will know that the objects have been properly located. Then all items in objects other than the first are faded out by passing them through the slice() function to split them off, and a value of 1 millisecond is used for the transition to make it virtually instantaneous. This has the effect of leaving only the first item visible:

```
O(id).BB_Ready = true
FadeOut(objects.slice(1), 1, 0)
```

After that, a for() loop iterates through all but the first item in objects, subtracting the height of each previous object from the local variable h. Each object is then released from its position in the web page and given a style position attribute of 'relative' (using the global variable REL).

Each object's x coordinate is set to 0 to line it up with the left-hand side of the first one, and its y coordinate is set to h, which is a negative number containing the sum of all the heights of the objects above the current one, thus moving the object up the browser and placing it directly on top of the first one:

```
for (j = 1 ; j < len ; ++j)
{
   h -= H(O(objects[j-1]))
   Locate(O(objects[j]), REL, 0, h)
}
```

Next, if the wait argument has the value 'stop', the BB_Stop property of id is set to true, indicating that the billboard transitions should stop; otherwise, it is assigned the value false:

```
O(id).BB_Stop = (wait == 'stop') ? true : false
```

After that, as long as BB_Stop is not true and as long as the billboard is not already running (the BB_Flag property of id will be true if it is), an interrupt is set to call the DoBillboard() subfunction in msecs + wait milliseconds:

```
if (!O(id).BB_Stop && !O(id).BB_Flag)
   O(id).BB_IID = setTimeout(DoBillboard, msecs + wait)
```

The result returned by the call is placed in the BB_IID property of id for used when calling clearTimeout().

The DoBillboard() Subfunction

This function starts by setting the `BB_Flag` property of `id` to `true` to indicate that the billboard is running:

```
O(id).BB_Flag = true
```

It then checks the `BB_Stop` property of `id` to see whether it can continue or should stop:

```
if (O(id).BB_Stop)
{
   O(id).BB_Flag = false
   clearTimeout(O(id).BB_IID)
   return
}
```

If `BB_Stop` is `true`, then a request has been made to stop the transition, so the function will reset `BB_Flag` to `false`, stop any timeout that is due, and return. No more interrupts will occur on it, unless the plug-in is called again—at which time the transitions pick up from where they left off. This allows you to, for example, pause the transitions if the mouse passes over an object and resume them again when it leaves.

Otherwise, the function continues running and the next thing to happen is the currently displayed object gets faded out:

```
else FadeOut(objects[O(id).BB_Index], msecs, 0)
```

Then, if the argument `random` is `true` (or 1), the subsequent object to display should be selected at random, which is done by this code:

```
var rand = O(id).BB_Index
while (rand == O(id).BB_Index )
   rand = Math.floor(Math.random() * len)
O(id).BB_Index = rand
```

Here `rand` is assigned the value of the `O(id).BB_Index` property, which points to the currently displayed object. Then a `while()` statement repeatedly selects random numbers, placing them in the variable `rand`, until it is *not* the same as `O(id).BB_Index`. This ensures that the next object displayed in the billboard won't be the same as the current one.

Once a value is found, it is placed in `O(id).BB_Index`. Otherwise, if `random` is not true, the objects are displayed in sequential order and `O(id).BB_Index` is incremented. If it becomes greater than the number of items in the `objects` array, it is reset to 0 (using the `%` operator):

```
else O(id).BB_Index = ++O(id).BB_Index  % len
```

At this point, `O(id).BB_Index` represents the next object to be displayed, so a call is made to the `FadeIn()` plug-in to fade it in:

```
FadeIn(objects[O(id).BB_Index ], msecs, 0)
```

Finally, any currently pending interrupt is cancelled and another interrupt is set up to call the subfunction again in `msecs + wait` milliseconds, giving enough time for both the fade transition and the wait period to pass:

```
clearTimeout(O(id).BB_IID)
O(id).BB_IID = setTimeout(DoBillboard, msecs + wait)
```

How To Use It

To use this plug-in, you need to first prepare a containing object to hold all the items that will be rotated in the billboard. Then place the subobjects within it, and you're ready to call the plug-in from JavaScript.

Here's an example that combines the divs used in Plug-in 67, `RollOver()`, with a new image of the same dimensions:

```
<div id='billb' style='display:none'>

   <div id='b1'><img id='p1' src='palace.png' align='left' style=
   'padding-right:10px'>For sale: 600 room, 300 year old central London
   house, located close to all the amenities, right in the heart of
   Westminster city.</div>

   <div id='b2'><img id='p2' src='plan.png' align='right' style=
   'padding-left:10px'>829,818 sq ft: Historical setting, famous
   residents, exquisitely decorated throughout. Phone 555 1234 for more
   details.</div>

   <img id='b3' src='london.png' />

</div>

<script>
window.onload = function()
{
   S('billb').border = 'solid 1px'
   Resize('billb', 320, 100)
   objects = Array('b1', 'b2', 'b3')
   Resize(objects, 320, 100)
   S(objects, 'background.Color', '#ffffff')
   Show('billb')
   Billboard('billb', objects, 1, 500, 3000)

   O('billb').onmouseover = pause
   O('billb').onmouseout  = resume

   function pause()
   {
      Billboard('billb', '', '', '', 'stop')
   }

   function resume()
   {
```

```
      Billboard('billb', objects, 1, 500, 3000)
   }
}
</script>
```

I laid out the HTML so that you can clearly see the three subobjects within the main containing object (with the ID 'billb'), which has its style display attribute set to 'hidden' so as not to show the subobjects.

In the `<script>` section, the containing object is given a solid 1-pixel border (which is not necessary but improves the look) and resized it to 320 by 100 pixels. The subobjects are then also resized to those dimensions so that all elements are the same, then `Show()` is called to re-enable the displaying of the container div, and then the `Billboard()` plug-in is called to start things.

Next, the `onmouseover` and `onmouseout` events of 'billb' are attached to the functions `pause()` and `resume()`. The `pause()` function needs only to pass the argument names of 'billb' to reference the container object and the value 'stop' in the `wait` argument. In this instance, all other arguments will be ignored, so they have been set to the empty string. The `resume()` function, however, should be identical to the initial call made to start the billboard in the first place.

As you pass your mouse over the billboard it will stop rotating, but it will resume once you move it away. Of course, the objects in this example are not linked to anything, but you will probably use this plug-in for advertising and make them clickable; you can even include forms within the objects.

NOTE *To place all the subobjects in the same location, they must start off lined up underneath each other in the browser. In the case of divs, this will already be the case, but spans and images may require a* `<br />` *tag placed after them to ensure the correct positioning. The* `Billboard()` *plug-in then subtracts the height of all previous objects to place each consecutive one over the first. Should you forget to line them all up this way, some of the objects will not display correctly, if at all.*

The Plug-in

```
function Billboard(id, objects, random, msecs, wait)
{
   var len = objects.length

   if (!O(id).BB_Ready)
   {
      var h          = 0
      O(id).BB_Index = 0

      O(id).BB_Ready = true
      FadeOut(objects.slice(1), 1, 0)

      for (j = 1 ; j < len ; ++j)
      {
         h -= H(O(objects[j-1]))
```

```
            Locate(O(objects[j]), REL, 0, h)
        }
    }

    O(id).BB_Stop = (wait == 'stop') ? true : false

    if (!O(id).BB_Stop && !O(id).BB_Flag)
        O(id).BB_IID = setTimeout(DoBillboard, msecs + wait)

    function DoBillboard()
    {
        O(id).BB_Flag = true

        if (O(id).BB_Stop)
        {
            O(id).BB_Flag = false
            clearTimeout(O(id).BB_IID)
            return

        }
        else FadeOut(objects[O(id).BB_Index ], msecs, 0)

        if (random)
        {
            var rand = O(id).BB_Index
            while (rand == O(id).BB_Index )
                rand = Math.floor(Math.random() * len)
            O(id).BB_Index = rand
        }
        else O(id).BB_Index = ++O(id).BB_Index  % len

        FadeIn(objects[O(id).BB_Index ], msecs, 0)
        O(id).BB_IID = setTimeout(DoBillboard, msecs + wait)
    }
}
```

PLUG-IN 80

GoogleChart()

Among many other products, Google offers a great program for creating and displaying charts. However, to make the best use of it there are many options you need to set up and a lot of documentation to be read. This plug-in distills the main features of the service into a set of basic arguments you can pass to it, making the service extra easy to use. Figure 10-4 shows the plug-in being used to display a 3-D pie chart.

About the Plug-in

This plug-in takes a container such as a div or span and inserts an image into it, which it fetches from the Google Charts service. It requires the following arguments:

- `id` An object or object ID—this cannot be an array
- `title` The chart title
- `tcolor` The title color

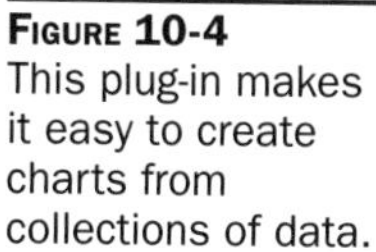

Figure 10-4 This plug-in makes it easy to create charts from collections of data.

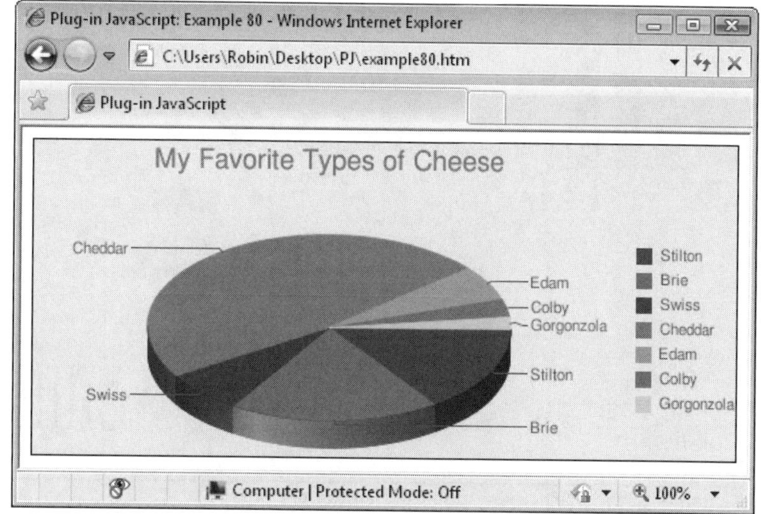

- **tsize** The title font size
- **type** The type of chart, any of 'line', 'vbar', 'hbar', 'gometer', 'pie', 'pie3d', 'venn', or 'radar'—see Table 10-1 for more details (and see Figure 10-5 for some example chart types)
- **bwidth** The bar width if the chart is a bar chart
- **labels** A string of data labels, separated by | characters
- **legends** A string of data legends, separated by | characters
- **colors** A string of colors, one for each item of data, in six digit hex values, separated by commas
- **bgfill** The background fill color as a six-digit hex string
- **data** The data, as a string of numeric values, separated by commas

Table 10-1 The Supported Values for the `type` Argument and the Charts They Create

Type value	Chart type
'line'	Standard line chart
'vbar'	Vertical bar chart
'hbar'	Horizontal bar chart
'gometer'	Google Go Meter
'pie'	Standard pie chart
'pie3d'	3D pie chart
'venn'	Venn diagram
'radar'	Radar chart

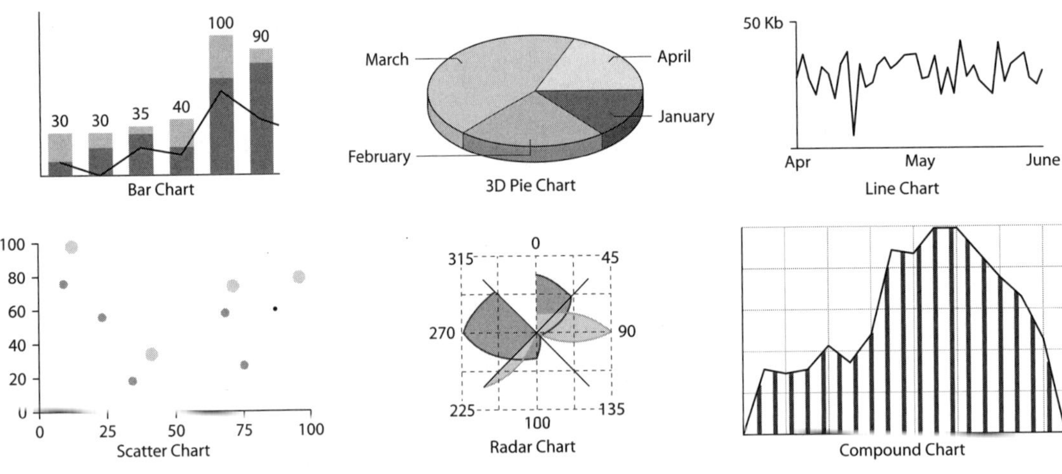

FIGURE 10-5 Some of the chart types supported by Google Charts

Variables, Arrays, and Functions

`types`	Local associative array used to turn values in the `type` argument into the keywords required by Google Charts
`t1`	Local variable containing the escaped `title`
`t2`	Local variable containing the `type` of chart as a Google Charts keyword
`tail`	Local variable containing the query string for sending to Google
`innerHTML`	Property of `id` containing its HTML
`UNDEF`	Global variable containing the string 'undefined'
`escape()`	Function to escape a string, making it suitable for use in a query string

How It Works

This plug-in begins by populating the associative array `types` with the eight types of chart names as used by the plug-in and their corresponding keywords, as passed on to Google Charts, like this:

```
var types =
{
   'line'    : 'lc',
   'vbar'    : 'bvg',
   'hbar'    : 'bhg',
   'gometer' : 'gom',
   'pie'     : 'p',
   'pie3d'   : 'p3',
   'venn'    : 'v',
   'radar'   : 'r'
}
```

Next, the `type` argument is tested to see if it has a value. If not, it is given the value 'pie', which, therefore, becomes the default for when no type is given:

```
if (typeof type == UNDEF) type = 'pie'
```

Then `title` is passed through the `escape()` function to make it suitable for passing in a query string URL tail, and `title` is then placed in the variable `t1`. Meanwhile, the keyword for the chart type to send to Google is looked up by referencing the `type` argument in the `types` array, as follows (such that if, for example, `type` has the value 'hbar', `t2` will be assigned the value 'bhg', and so on):

```
var t1 = escape(title)
var t2 = types[type]
```

After this, a selection of arguments that are required for most charts (such as the chart's title, width, height, and so on) are assembled into the variable `tail`, each separated by an `&` entity, like this:

```
var tail = 'chtt='           + t1
         + '&amp;cht='       + t2
         + '&amp;chs='       + width + 'x' + height
         + '&amp;chbh='      + bwidth
         + '&amp;chxt=x,y'
         + '&amp;chd=t:'     + data
```

Then, if values for them have been passed to the plug-in, a set of five `if()` statements adds other arguments to `tail`:

```
if (tcolor && tsize) tail += '&amp;chts='      + tcolor + ',' + tsize
if (labels)          tail += '&amp;chl='       + labels
if (legends)         tail += '&amp;chdl='      + legends
if (colors)          tail += '&amp;chco='      + colors
if (bgfill)          tail += '&amp;chf=bg,s,' + bgfill
```

With `tail` now containing the completed query string, it is appended to the Google Charts URL and then placed in an `<img ... >` tag, which is then assigned to the HTML of `id`:

```
Html(id, "<img src='http://chart.apis.google.com/chart?" +
   tail + "' />")
```

This results in the chart displaying within the `id` container object.

How To Use It

To use this plug-in, start with an empty div, span, or other container that has an `innerHTML` property, and then pass this object along with all the required parameters to the plug-in, as in this example:

```
<div id='chart'></div>

<script>
window.onload = function()
```

```
{
   title   = 'My Favorite Types of Cheese'
   tcolor  = 'FF0000'
   tsize   = '20'
   type    = 'pie3d'
   width   = '530'
   height  = '230'
   bwidth  = ''
   labels  = 'Stilton|Brie|Swiss|Cheddar|Edam|Colby|Gorgonzola'
   legends = labels
   colors  = 'BD0000,DE6B00,284B89,008951,9D9D9D,A5AB4B,8C70A4,FFD200'
   bgfill  = 'EEEEFF'
   data    = '14.9,18.7,7.1,47.3,6.0,3.1,2.1'

   GoogleChart('chart', title, tcolor, tsize, type, bwidth, labels,
      legends, colors, bgfill, width, height, data)

   Resize('chart', width, height)
   S('chart').border = 'solid 1px'
}
</script>
```

To simplify this example, all the arguments have been separately assigned to variables, which are then passed to the plug-in. Also, the containing div is resized to the width and height of the chart and is given a 1-pixel, solid border. This results in a fully self-contained div, displaying the chart as returned by Google. You can get more information about Google Charts at *code.google.com/apis/chart/*.

TIP *The Google Charts API has a limit of 50,000 calls per day from each website, so if your site is making that many calls or more, you should run the plug-in once in your browser, right-click, save the image, and upload it to your web server. That way, you can display it as often as you like using* `<img>` *tags.*

The Plug-in

```
function GoogleChart(id, title, tcolor, tsize, type, bwidth,
   labels, legends, colors, bgfill, width, height, data)
{
   var types =
   {
      'line'    : 'lc',
      'vbar'    : 'bvg',
      'hbar'    : 'bhg',
      'gometer' : 'gom',
      'pie'     : 'p',
      'pie3d'   : 'p3',
      'venn'    : 'v',
      'radar'   : 'r'
   }
```

```
   if (typeof type == UNDEF) type = 'pie'

   var t1                    = escape(title)
   var t2                    = types[type]
   var tail                  = 'chtt='            + t1
                             + '&amp;cht='        + t2
                             + '&amp;chs='        + width  + 'x' + height
                             + '&amp;chbh='       + bwidth
                             + '&amp;chxt=x,y'
                             + '&amp;chd=t:'      + data

   if (tcolor && tsize) tail += '&amp;chts='      + tcolor + ',' + tsize
   if (labels)          tail += '&amp;chl='       + labels
   if (legends)         tail += '&amp;chdl='      + legends
   if (colors)          tail += '&amp;chco='      + colors
   if (bgfill)          tail += '&amp;chf=bg,s,' + bgfill

   Html(id, "<img src='http://chart.apis.google.com/chart?" +
      tail + "' />")
}
```

PLUG-IN 81

PlaySound()

This plug-in lets you play a sound as a result of a mouse move or button event, a keyboard event, or any other reason. Figure 10-6 reintroduces the avatars used in previous chapters, but this time their `onmouseover` events are attached to this plug-in.

About the Plug-in

This plug-in takes an empty container such as a div or span and embeds an audio player in it to play a sound. It requires the following arguments:

- **`id`** An object or object ID—this cannot be an array
- **`file`** The URL of an audio file, generally a WAV or similar file
- **`loop`** If 'true', the sound will loop continuously; if 'stop', it will stop a previously playing sound; any other value will play the sound once

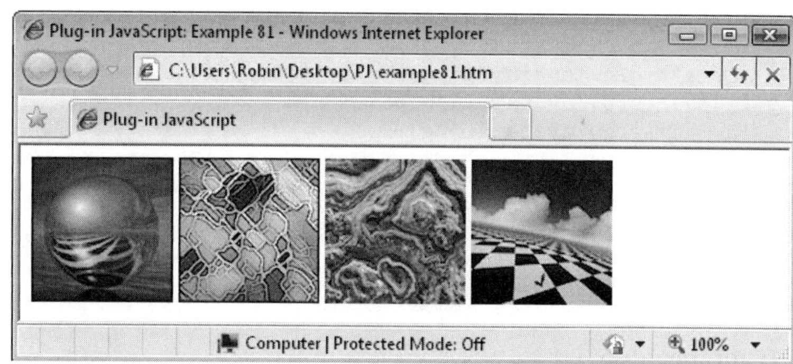

FIGURE 10-6 When you pass the mouse over these images, a sound will play.

Variables, Arrays, and Functions

innerHTML	Property of id containing its HTML
Resize()	Plug-in to resize an object
Locate()	Plug-in to set an object's style position and location
InsVars()	Plug-in to insert values into a string

How It Works

This plug-in first resizes id so that it has no width or height and then gives it an 'absolute' style position so that it cannot affect any other objects in the web page, like this:

```
Resize(id, 0, 0)
Locate(id, ABS, 0, 0)
```

Next, if the argument loop contains the string value 'stop', then any currently playing sound is stopped by setting the innerHTML property of id to the empty string, thus removing any previously embedded sound player:

```
if (loop == 'stop') O(id).innerHTML = ''
```

Otherwise, the innerHTML property of id is assigned the correct HTML to embed a sound player and auto start the sound playing, looping it if loop contains the string value 'true', like this:

```
else O(id).innerHTML =
   InsVars("<embed src='#1' hidden='true' " +
      "autostart='true' loop='#2' />", file, loop)
```

How To Use It

Playing a sound is as easy as passing an empty container such as a div or span to the plug-in, along with the URL of the sound to play and, if required, the value 'true' in the argument loop. Here's an example that attaches the plug-in to the onmouseover events of four images:

```
<span id='sound'></span>

<img id='a1' src='avatar1.jpg'>
<img id='a2' src='avatar2.jpg'>
<img id='a3' src='avatar3.jpg'>
<img id='a4' src='avatar4.jpg'>

<script>
window.onload = function()
{
   ids = Array('a1', 'a2', 'a3', 'a4')
   O(ids, 'onmouseover', bloop)

   function bloop()
```

```
   {
      PlaySound('sound', 'bloop.wav', 0)
   }
}
</script>
```

NOTE *This plug-in relies on the browser having a plug-in of its own already installed to play sounds, which is true in the majority of cases. Browsers without a sound plug-in will simply ignore this code. Also, there may be a slight delay before some sounds begin playing, so this plug-in works best when immediate playback is not essential. If you do need instant sounds, the most robust way to accomplish this is probably to write a Flash script, or obtain a Flash sound player and embed it. Also, small files will play quicker than large ones.*

The Plug-in

```
function PlaySound(id, file, loop)
{
   Resize(id, 0, 0)
   Locate(id, ABS, 0, 0)

   if (loop == 'stop') O(id).innerHTML = ''
   else O(id).innerHTML =
      InsVars("<embed src='#1' hidden='true' " +
         "autostart='true' loop='#2' />", file, loop)
}
```

PLUG-IN 82 EmbedYouTube()

With this plug-in, you can forget about all the HTML and other code needed to display a YouTube video because it's all handled for you with a single function call. Figure 10-7 shows the Emmy Award winning movie *Dr Horrible's Sing-Along Blog* being played using this plug-in.

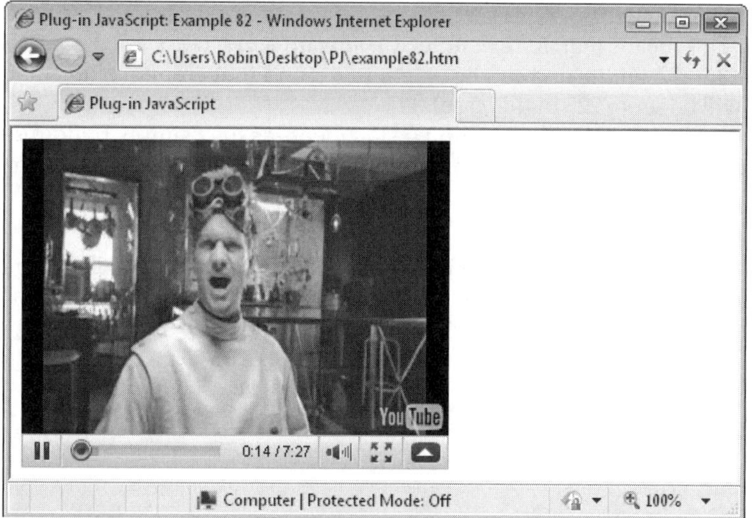

FIGURE 10-7 Displaying YouTube videos is easy with this plug-in.

About the Plug-in

This plug-in returns the HTML code required to embed a YouTube video. It requires the following arguments:

- **video** A YouTube video identifier such as 'apEZpYnN_1g'
- **width, height** The width and height at which to display the video
- **hq** If 'true' (and it is available), the video is played in high quality
- **full** If 'true', the video is allowed to be viewed in full screen mode
- **auto** If 1, the video starts playing automatically

Variables, Arrays, and Functions

temp	Local variable containing the HTML to display the video
InsVars()	Plug-in to insert values into a string

How It Works

This plug-in begins by assigning to hq the query string to use to display a video in high quality (if the argument hq is 1 or true); otherwise, it is assigned the empty string:

```
if (hq) hq = '&amp;ap=%2526fmt%3D18'
else    hq = ''
```

The next four lines of code account for when one or both of the width or height arguments are omitted, assigning sensible default values to them that will display a video in a 4:3 aspect ratio, if required:

```
if (width && !height) height = width  * 0.7500
if (!width && height) width  = height * 1.3333
if (!width)           width  = 425
if (!height)          height = 324
```

This means that, for example, if you want a video to be 300 pixels wide you can enter that for the width, and set the height to '', and that empty value will be calculated for you (it will be set to 225 in this case).

I will gloss over the remaining statements as they simply build the string variable temp using the various HTML parameters required and then return the string.

How To Use It

To use this plug-in, you need to have prepared a container object such as a div or span and then pass this, along with the result of calling the plug-in, to the Html() plug-in to insert the HTML code into the object. The following example shows how:

```
<span id='movie'></span>

<script>
window.onload = function()
```

```
{
   Html('movie', EmbedYouTube('apEZpYnN_1g', 320, 240,
      'true', 'true', 1))
}
</script>
```

All you have to decide is the width and height for the video and whether to allow high quality, full screen, and auto starting. At the most basic, you can issue a simple call such as the following to place the video in a web page, ready for the user to click its Play button:

```
Html('movie', EmbedYouTube('apEZpYnN_1g'))
```

The Plug-in

```
function EmbedYouTube(video, width, height, hq, full, auto)
{
   if (hq) hq = '&amp;ap=%2526fmt%3D18'
   else    hq = ''

   if (width && !height) height = width  * 0.7500
   if (!width && height) width  = height * 1.3333
   if (!width)           width  = 425
   if (!height)          height = 324

   var temp = InsVars("<object width='#1' height='#2'>"       +
      "<param name='movie' value='http://www.youtube.com/v/" +
      "#3&amp;fs=1&amp;autoplay=#4#5'>", width, height, video,
      auto, hq)

   temp += InsVars("</param><param name='allowFullScreen' "  +
      "value='#1'></param><param name='allowscriptaccess' "  +
      "value='always'></param>", full)

   temp += InsVars("<embed src='http://www.youtube.com"      +
      "/v/#1&amp;fs=1&amp;autoplay=#2#3' type='application/" +
      "x-shockwave-flash' allowscriptaccess='always' "       +

      "allowfullscreen='true'", video, auto, hq)

   temp += InsVars("width='#1' height='#2'></embed></object>",
      width, height)

   return temp
}
```

PLUG-IN 83 PulsateOnMouseover()

With this plug-in, you can create an onmouseover hover effect for an object that slowly fades it in and out again, over a time and by an amount you specify. Figure 10-8 shows the same image attached to this plug-in using three different levels of fading and transition times.

FIGURE 10-8 Attach this plug-in to an object and it will pulsate when the mouse passes over it.

About the Plug-in

This plug-in takes an object and attaches to its `onmouseover` and `onmouseout` events to create a pulsating effect. It requires the following arguments:

- **`id`** An object or object ID or an array of objects and/or object IDs
- **`op1`** The default opacity for the object, between 0 and 100
- **`op1`** The opacity to which the object should be faded, between 0 and 100
- **`msecs`** The number of milliseconds each full cycle should take

Variables, Arrays, and Functions

`j`	Local variable used to index into `id` if it is an array
`finish`	Local variable set to `true` if the pulsating stops
`faded`	Local variable set to `true` when the object is faded (or fading), otherwise `false`
`iid`	Local variable assigned the result of calling `setInterval()` to be used later when `clearInterval()` is called
`FA_Level`	Property of `id` used by the `Fade()` plug-in to set its opacity
`FA_Flag`	Property of `id` used by the `Fade()` plug-in and set to `true` to indicate that a fade transition is in progress, otherwise it is `false` or 'undefined'
`onmouseover`	Event attached to `id` triggered when the mouse passes over
`onmouseout`	Event attached to `id` triggered when the mouse passes out
`PulseateOn()`	Subfunction that sets up the main variables
`DoPulsate()`	Sub-subfunction that performs the transitions
`Fade()`	Plug-in to fade an object from one opacity level to another
`setInterval()`	Function to set up repeating interrupts to another function
`clearInterval()`	Function to stop the repeating interrupts

How It Works

This plug-in begins by checking whether `id` is an array. If it is, it iterates through it and recursively calls itself, separately passing each element of the array to be processed individually, like this:

```
if (id instanceof Array)
{
   for (var j = 0 ; j < id.length ; ++j)
         PulsateOnMouseover(id[j], op1, op2, msecs)
   return
}
```

Next, the variable `finish` is set to `false`—it will later be set to `true` whenever the mouse passes out of an object and the pulsating has to stop. The `iid` variable is also declared, which will be used to store the value returned by the `setInterval()` function:

```
var finish = false
var iid
```

After this, the opacity of `id` is set to the level in the argument `op1`, to which the `FA_Level` property of `id` is also set. This property is used by the `Fade()` plug-in, but this plug-in needs to access it in order to know when an object has faded in or out by the correct amount:

```
Opacity(id, op1)
O(id).FA_Level = op1
```

Finally, in the setup section, the mouse events of `id` are attached to the `PulsateOn()` subfunction for starting the pulsations, and to an inline, anonymous function that sets the variable `finish` to `true` when the mouse moves away from an object, like this:

```
O(id).onmouseover = PulsateOn
O(id).onmouseout  = function() { finish = true }
```

The PulsateOn() Subfunction

This function's job is to set up the variables required prior to calling the `DoPulsate()` sub-subfunction. It first declares the variable `faded` and assigns it the value of `false`, indicating that the object is faded in—it will be `true` when it is faded out. The `finish` variable is also set to `false` in case the plug-in has been restarted after having been previously stopped:

```
var faded = false
finish    = false
```

If the variable `iid` has a value, a previous call has been made to the plug-in, so it is passed to the `clearInterval()` function to stop any repeating interrupts that may currently be in place. After that, `setInterval()` is called to set up repeating interrupts to the `DoPulsate()` plug-in every `INTERVAL` milliseconds, like this:

```
if (iid) clearInterval(iid)
iid = setInterval(DoPulsate, INTERVAL)
```

The DoPulsate() Sub-subfunction

This function is where the pulsating is made to occur. and it is in two parts: one for fading out and the other for fading in. The first part checks the `faded` variable and, if it is not `true`, the object is not faded out. Next it checks the `FA_Level` property of `id` and, if it is the same as the value in `op1`, then `id` is at its default opacity and is ready to be faded out. Here is the line of code that performs these two tests:

```
if (!faded && O(id).FA_Level == op1)
```

Inside the `if()` statement, a further check is made to see whether the `finish` variable has been set to `true`. If it has, rather than fade the object out, it's necessary to stop the repeating interrupts, like this:

```
if (finish) clearInterval(iid)
```

When the function next returns, it will not be called up again unless a new set of repeating interrupts is triggered by another `onmouseover` event.

However, if `finish` is not `true`, then it's business as usual for the function, which instigates a fade out by calling the `Fade()` plug-in with a final opacity value of `op2`. The variable `faded` is also set to `true` to indicate that the object is faded or is in the process of doing so, like this:

```
Fade(id, op1, op2, msecs / 2, 0)
faded = true
```

The transition duration of `msecs / 2` is used because there are two transitions in each full cycle, so each transition must take only half the value in `msecs` to complete.

In the second part of this function, if the variable `faded` is `true`, the `FA_Flag` property of `id` is tested. This property is set to `true` by the `Fade()` plug-in whenever a fade transition is in progress and is set to `false` once a transition has completed. If `FA_Flag` is `true`, the function will return because a fade is in progress, and it must not be interrupted:

```
else if (!O(id).FA_Flag)
```

Otherwise, the code within the `if()` statement will be executed, as follows:

```
Fade(id, op2, op1, msecs / 2, 0)
faded = false
```

Here a call to `Fade()` is made with a final opacity value of `op1` to fade the object back to its default opacity level, and the variable `faded` is set to `false` to indicate that the object is faded in or is in the process of doing so.

How To Use It

The plug-in is written so that it will always fade back to the default opacity for an object when the mouse is moved away. To use it, attach it to any objects that you would like to pulsate when the mouse passes over them. These can be images, divs, spans, or anything that has an opacity property that can be changed.

Here's an example that uses the same image three times, with each attached to the plug-in using different arguments:

```
<img id='a' src='ghost.png' />
<img id='b' src='ghost.png' />
<img id='c' src='ghost.png' />

<script>
window.onload = function()
{
   PulsateOnMouseover('a', 100, 66,  500)
   PulsateOnMouseover('b', 66, 100,  750)
   PulsateOnMouseover('c', 100,  0, 1000)
}
</script>
```

The first image is set to pulsate between opacity levels of 100 and 66, so it will lighten by a third and back again on each pulsation, over a duration of 500 milliseconds. The second one starts with a default opacity level of 66 and a fade value of 100 so, rather than fade out, it will in fact darken by about a third and lighten back again during each pulsation, which will take three quarters of a second to complete. The final image simply fades between full and zero opacity and back again over the course of a second.

The Plug-in

```
function PulsateOnMouseover(id, op1, op2, msecs)
{
   if (id instanceof Array)
   {
      for (var j = 0 ; j < id.length ; ++j)
         PulsateOnMouseover(id[j], op1, op2, msecs)
      return
   }

   var finish = false
   var iid

   Opacity(id, op1)
   O(id).FA_Level     = op1
   O(id).onmouseover  = PulsateOn
   O(id).onmouseout   = function() { finish = true }

   function PulsateOn()
   {
      var faded = false
      finish    = false

      if (iid) clearInterval(iid)
      iid = setInterval(DoPulsate, INTERVAL)

      function DoPulsate()
      {
```

```
            if (!faded && O(id).FA_Level == op1)
            {
               if (finish) clearInterval(iid)

               else
               {
                  Fade(id, op1, op2, msecs / 2, 0)
                  faded = true
               }
            }
            else if (!O(id).FA_Flag)
            {
               Fade(id, op2, op1, msecs / 2, 0)
               faded = false
            }
         }
      }
   }
```

CHAPTER 11

Cookies, Ajax, and Security

When developing with JavaScript, you often need ways to store and retrieve data from both the user's web browser and the web server. This chapter provides you with the plug-ins you need to manage the transfer of cookies between the web document and browser and to handle Ajax calls between the browser and web server.

There are also a couple of plug-ins you can use to bust a web page out of frames if it has been loaded inside one and to allow you to put your e-mail address in a web document in such a way that it is easily clickable or copyable by a surfer, but not by web bots that harvest e-mail addresses for spamming.

ProcessCookie()

With this plug-in, you can save cookies to a user's computer and read them back again later. This lets you keep track user names, shopping carts, or any data you need to keep current as a user browses your site and changes pages. Figure 11-1 shows the cookie 'username' being read back and its value displayed using an `alert()` message.

About the Plug-in

This plug-in can save a cookie, read it in from the computer, or delete it. It requires the following arguments:

- `action` The action to take with the cookie, out of 'save', 'read', or 'erase'
- `name` The cookie's name
- `value` The value to be stored in the cookie
- `seconds` The number of seconds after which the cookie should expire
- `path` The domain and path to which the cookie applies
- `domain` The domain name of the website, such as *mydomain.com*
- `secure` If this has the value 1, the browser should use SSL when sending the cookie

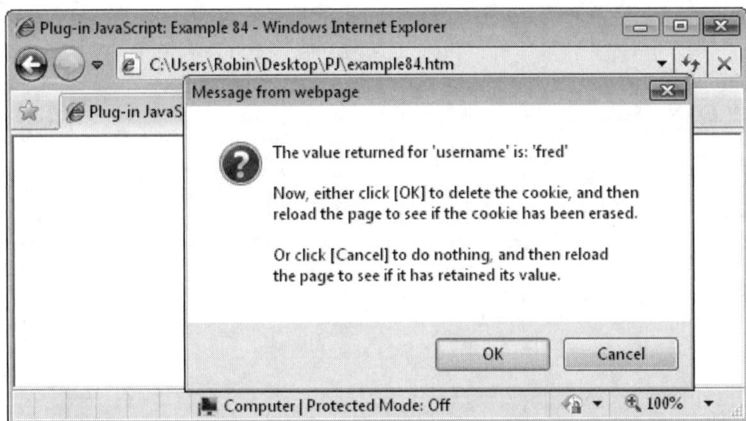

Figure 11-1 Setting and reading cookie values with this plug-in

Variables, Arrays, and Functions

`date`	Local variable containing a new date object
`expires`	Local variable containing the expiry time and date
`start`	Local variable set to point to the start of cookie data
`end`	Local variable set to point to the end of cookie data
`document.cookie`	The `cookie` property of the `document` use for accessing the cookie
`toGMTString()`	Function to convert a date to Greenwich Mean Time
`Date()`	Function to return a new date object
`setTime()`	Function to set a time
`getTime()`	Function to return a time
`indexOf()`	Function to return the location of one string within another
`substring()`	Function to return a portion of a string
`escape()`	Function to encode a string to a form suitable for transferring over the internet
`unescape()`	Function to decode an escaped string

How It Works

This program is in three parts. The first is executed when the `action` argument contains the value 'save'. It creates a new `date` object and sets it to the current time and date, like this:

```
var date = new Date()
date.setTime(date.getTime() + seconds * 1000)
```

Saving a Cookie

Next, the `expires` variable is given the correct value to make the cookie expire in `seconds` seconds, the `path` variable is assigned the path on the server to which the cookie applies, the `domain` and `secure` arguments are added (if they have values), and the cookie is set by assigning these values to `document.cookie`, as follows:

```
var expires     = seconds ? '; expires=' + date.toGMTString() : ''
path            = path    ? '; path='    + path               : ''
domain          = domain  ? '; domain='  + domain             : ''
secure          = secure  ? '; secure='  + secure             : ''
document.cookie = name + '=' + escape(value) + expires + path
```

Reading a Cookie

In the next section, a cookie is read back from the computer, starting by checking whether or not there are any existing cookies on the computer; if there are not, the value `false` is returned:

```
if (!document.cookie.length) return false
```

Otherwise, the cookie is looked up by setting the variable `start` to point to the string containing the value in `name` followed by the = sign, by using a call to `indexOf()`. If it is not found, a value of –1 is returned, so the value `false` is returned by the plug-in:

```
var start = document.cookie.indexOf(name + '=')
if (start == -1) return false
```

If both these tests pass, then the cookie has been found, so `start` is set to point to the portion of the cookie string directly after the `name` and = sign:

```
start += name.length + 1
```

The variable `end` is then set to the end of the string by finding the character `;` that terminates all cookie strings bar the last one:

```
var end = document.cookie.indexOf(';', start)
```

If it is not found, it means this was the last cookie and it is the end of the string. Therefore, the following line of code returns either the location of the following `;`, or the end of the string and places it back in `end`:

```
end = (end == -1) ? document.cookie.length : end
```

Finally, the cookie value is returned:

```
return unescape(document.cookie.substring(start, end))
```

Erasing a Cookie

The code to erase a cookie makes use of a recursive call by passing the cookie name and a value of the empty string, along with a time one minute in the past, back to itself with an `action` argument of 'save':

```
ProcessCookie('save', name, '', -60)
```

How To Use It

To use this plug-in, put the action in the `action` argument, which should be a value of 'save', 'read', or 'erase', and then pass the cookie's name and any other values needed.

For example, to set the cookie 'password' to the value 'mypass' with an expiry date of one hour from now, you would use the following:

```
ProcessCookie('save', 'password', 'mypass', 60 * 60, '/')
```

Once a cookie has been set, you can read it back like this:

```
value = ProcessCookie('read', 'password', '', '', '/')
```

Or, you can delete a cookie like this:

```
ProcessCookie('erase', 'password', '', '', '/')
```

The final path argument specifies which part of the server the cookie applies to. The value of '/' means that everywhere, from the document root upward, can access the cookie. However, you can restrict the scope by, for example, changing the path to a subfolder such as '/chat'. Or you can simply omit the argument to give the same scope as if it had the value '/'. If you do so, you can also shorten the calls used to read and erase the cookie, like this:

```
value = ProcessCookie('read', 'password')
ProcessCookie('erase', 'password')
```

Remember that the path (or no path) you use must be the same for all accesses to the same cookie, otherwise you will not be able to reliably read and write it. Also, you will probably not need to use the domain and secure arguments, which is why I omitted them from the preceding examples, but if you do they are available.

Here's an example that lets you test that cookies are being reliably transferred:

```
<script>
window.onload = function()
{
   value = ProcessCookie('read', 'username')
   if (value != false)
      alert("The value returned for 'username' is: '" + value + "'")
   else alert("The cookie 'username' has no value.")

   alert("Click OK to store cookie 'username' with the value 'fred'")
   ProcessCookie('save', 'username', 'fred', 60 * 60 * 24)

   alert("Click OK to retrieve the cookie")
   value = ProcessCookie('read', 'username')

   if (confirm("The value returned for 'username' is: '" + value     +
      "'\n\nNow, either click [OK] to delete the cookie, and then\n" +
      "reload the page to see if the cookie has been erased.\n\nOr " +
      "click [Cancel] to do nothing, and then reload\nthe page to "  +

      "see if it has retained its value.\n"))
      ProcessCookie('erase', 'username')
}
</script>
```

This JavaScript first fetches the cookie 'username' and, if it has a value, it is displayed. The first time you load this page, that cookie won't exist so you'll see an alert pop up and tell you so.

Next, the cookie is created and assigned the value 'fred', with alert messages before and after so you can see the result of each action.

Finally, a confirm dialog is called up in which you can click either the OK button to erase the cookie or the Cancel button to leave it alone. I suggest you click OK and then reload the page to see that the cookie has been erased. Then follow through the alerts again, but this time click the Cancel button and reload the page, and you'll see that the cookie's value has been retained.

The Plug-in

```
function ProcessCookie(action, name, value, seconds, path,
   domain, secure)
{
   if (action == 'save')
   {
      var date = new Date()
      date.setTime(date.getTime() + seconds * 1000)

      var expires     = seconds ? '; expires=' + date.toGMTString() : ''
      path            = path    ? '; path='    + path               : ''
      domain          = domain  ? '; domain='  + domain             : ''
      secure          = secure  ? '; secure='  + secure             : ''
      document.cookie = name + '=' + escape(value) + expires + path
   }
   else if (action == 'read')
   {
      if (!document.cookie.length) return false
      else
      {
         var start = document.cookie.indexOf(name + '=')

         if (start == -1) return false
         else
         {
            start   += name.length + 1
            var end = document.cookie.indexOf(';', start)
            end     = (end == -1) ? document.cookie.length : end

            return unescape(document.cookie.substring(start, end))
         }
      }
   }
   else if (action == 'erase')
      ProcessCookie('save', name, '', -60)
}
```

PLUG-IN 85 CreateAjaxObject()

Ajax is the power behind the vastly improved user interaction of Web 2.0. It stands for Asynchronous JavaScript and XML, which is really a contrived acronym for a background call made to a web server. Using this plug-in, you can easily create a new Ajax object that can be used to send and request information to and from a web server in the background, without the user being aware of it.

Unlike in the past, when a `POST` or `GET` stopped action in the browser until it completed, with Ajax the browser handles the request without disrupting the web application.

Figure 11-2 shows a simple HTML file that has been fetched from the web server and inserted into a div, using this plug-in in conjunction with the next one, `GetAjaxRequest()`.

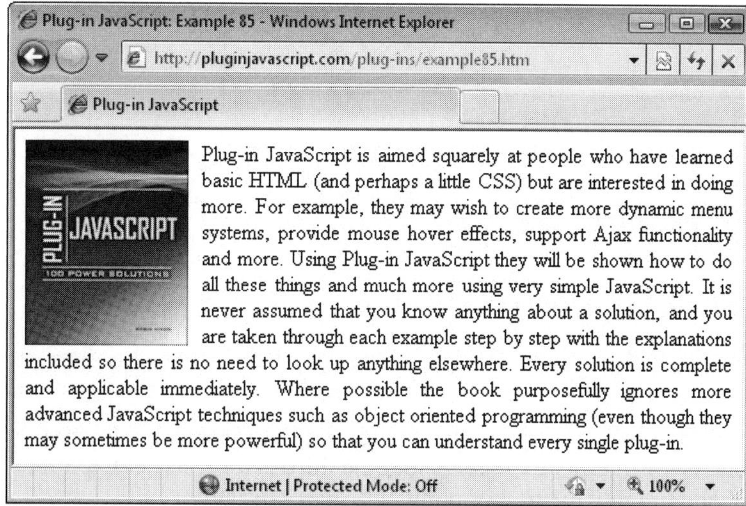

FIGURE 11-2 The contents of a web page has been inserted into a div.

About the Plug-in

This plug-in creates an Ajax object ready for making background calls to the web server. It requires the following arguments:

- **`id`** An object or object ID—this may not be an array
- **`callback`** The function to pass the returned data to once it has been retrieved

Variables, Arrays, and Functions

`ajax`	Local Ajax object
`readyState`	Property of `ajax` containing its state
`status`	Property of `ajax` containing its status
`responseText`	Property of `ajax` containing the text returned by the Ajax call
`XMLHttpRequest()`	Function used by non-Microsoft browsers to create an Ajax object
`ActiveXObject()`	Function used by Microsoft browsers to create an Ajax object

How It Works

Since the Ajax request object has to be created in different ways for different browsers, this plug-in uses pairs of `try{} ... catch{}` statements to try each method in turn until one works or until all have been tried and `false` is returned, like this:

```
try
{
   var ajax = new XMLHttpRequest()
}
catch(e1)
{
   try
```

```
    {
       ajax = new ActiveXObject("Msxml2.XMLHTTP")
    }
    catch(e2)
    {
       try
       {
          ajax = new ActiveXObject("Microsoft.XMLHTTP")
       }
       catch(e3)
       {
          ajax = false
       }
    }
}
```

The first `try()` works with any browser but Internet Explorer version 6 or lower, the second is for Internet Explorer 6, and the third is for Internet Explorer 5. Therefore, the tests are made roughly in order of popular browser usage.

Assuming one of the `try()` functions succeeds, `ajax` is a new Ajax object; otherwise, it contains the value `false`. If it isn't an object, then the plug-in will return `false`; otherwise the following code attaches an inline, anonymous function to the `onreadystatechange` event of `ajax`, as follows:

```
if (ajax) ajax.onreadystatechange = function()
{
   if (this.readyState   == 4   &&
       this.status       == 200 &&
       this.responseText != null)

   callback.call(this.responseText)
}
```

This subfunction is called every time the `readyState` property of `ajax` changes and checks whether it has a value of 4, the `status` property has a value of 200, and the `responseText` property is not `null`. If all these tests are satisfied, it means an Ajax request was successful, so the function passed in the `callback` argument is called, passing it the data returned in `this.responseText`.

The actual Ajax call is not made by this plug-in. It merely catches the event ready to populate `id` with the value that is returned by an Ajax call. The Ajax call itself is made in the next two plug-ins, `GetAjaxRequest()` and `PostAjaxRequest()`.

How To Use It

Generally, you will not use this function directly if you call either `GetAjaxRequest()` or `PostAjaxRequest()` to handle your Ajax calls, because they will call it for you; as in the following code, which loads some data into a div:

```
<div id='a'></div>

<script>
window.onload = function()
```

```
{
   url = 'ajaxtest.htm'
   GetAjaxRequest('a', todiv, url)

   function todiv()
   {
      Html('a', this)
   }
}
</script>
```

The function `todiv()` is passed to the plug-in (note that parentheses have been omitted from the function, otherwise only the value returned by it would be passed) and is later called back by it when the returned data is ready. At that point, it retrieves the data using the `this` keyword and assigns it to the `innerHTML` property of the div using the `Html()` plug-in.

You need to know that Ajax is a tightly controlled process to prevent hackers using it to inject malevolent code from other servers. Therefore, only files or programs on the same server as the one containing the Ajax can be accessed. For example, if you wanted to pull a copy of the Google home page into a div on your website, it would not be possible and the Ajax call would fail.

Therefore, the preceding example will not work if you test it on another server unless you also copy the *ajaxtest.htm* file to it. However, you can verify that it works by calling the script up from the *Plug-in JavaScript* website, using this URL:

http://pluginjavascript.com/plug-ins/example85.htm

The Plug-in

```
function CreateAjaxObject(id, callback)
{
   try
   {
      var ajax = new XMLHttpRequest()
   }
   catch(e1)
   {
      try
      {
         ajax = new ActiveXObject("Msxml2.XMLHTTP")
      }
      catch(e2)
      {
         try
         {
            ajax = new ActiveXObject("Microsoft.XMLHTTP")
         }
         catch(e3)
         {
            ajax = false
         }
      }
   }
```

```
   if (ajax) ajax.onreadystatechange = function()
   {
      if (this.readyState   == 4   &&
          this.status       == 200 &&
          this.responseText != null)

      callback.call(this.responseText)
   }

   return ajax
}
```

PLUG-IN 86 GetAjaxRequest()

This plug-in uses the previous one, `CreateAjaxObject()`, to load the Wikipedia home page into a div. Of course, Ajax can be used for much more than grabbing web pages, such as checking whether a username is taken when signing up to a website or updating news feeds, reader comments, or chat, and so on. However, I decided to pull in a web page for the sake of simplicity, so that you can quickly verify that these plug-ins are working for you, as shown in Figure 11-3.

About the Plug-in

This plug-in fetches data from a website in the background. It requires the following arguments:

- **`id`** An object or object ID—this cannot be an array
- **`callback`** The function to pass the returned data to once it has been retrieved
- **`url`** The URL with which to communicate
- **`args`** Any arguments to pass to the URL

FIGURE 11-3 The Wikipedia home page has been inserted into a div.

Variables, Arrays, and Functions

nocache	Local variable assigned a random string to prevent caching
ajax	Local variable assigned an Ajax object
CreateAjaxObject()	Plug-in to return a new Ajax object
open()	Method of ajax for opening a request
send()	Method of ajax for sending a request
Math.random()	Function to return a random number

How It Works

This plug-in uses the GET method to communicate with a server, which passes data in the tail of the URL called a query string. However, browser caching will often interfere with repeated requests of this type, serving up only the cached data from previous requests. Therefore, the variable nocache is created and assigned a random string to ensure that no two GET calls will be the same and therefore will not be cached:

```
var nocache = '&nocache=' + Math.random() * 1000000
```

Next, the variable ajax is assigned the new Ajax object returned by calling CreateAjaxObject(), and if the result is not true (meaning the call was unsuccessful) a value of false is returned:

```
var ajax = new CreateAjaxObject(id)

if (!ajax) return false
```

If execution reaches this point, the Ajax object was successfully created, so the open method of ajax is called, passing it the string 'GET' for the type of request. This is followed by a string comprising the URL to be called that was passed in url, the arguments supplied in args, the nocache string just created, and the value true to tell the browser to make an asynchronous call (a value of false would tell it to make a synchronous call):

```
ajax.open('GET', url + '?' + args + nocache, true)
```

Finally, the call is made and the value true is returned to indicate success:

```
ajax.send(null)
return true
```

How To Use It

To use this plug-in, decide what data you wish to load and from where, then call the plug-in, passing it a function to call back when the data has been retrieved and any arguments that require passing.

The following example is somewhat interesting in that it gets around the problem of being unable to access websites other than the one the Ajax web page came from by calling a PHP script on the server, which then fetches the requested data without a hitch:

```
<div id='a'></div>

<script>
window.onload = function()
```

```
{
   url  = 'http://pluginjavascript.com/plug-ins/ajaxget.php'
   args = 'url=http://wikipedia.org/'
   GetAjaxRequest('a', todiv, url, args)

   function todiv()
   {
      Html('a', this)
   }
}
</script>
```

The *ajaxget.php* program is a very simple, one-liner that looks like this:

```
<?php if (isset($_GET['url'])) echo file_get_contents($_GET['url']); ?>
```

If your server supports PHP (and most do), you can use the same script on it to check whether the server has been sent a query string looking something like *url=http://website.com?args=vals*. (In the case of the preceding example, the *args=vals* section is specified in the line that assigns the string *url=http://wikipedia.org* to the `args` variable).

The *ajaxget.php* script then uses the `file_get_contents()` PHP function to fetch the requested data (in this case the Wikipedia home page), which is then returned using the PHP `echo` command, which outputs the data it just fetched.

The `todiv()` callback function, which was passed to `GetAjaxRequest()`, is then called back and passed the retrieved data, which it then promptly inserts into the `innerHTML` property of the div.

As with the previous Ajax example, the restrictions put in place by browsers require that the example and PHP files reside on the same server, so here's a link you can try it out with:

http://www.pluginjavascript.com/plug-ins/example86.htm

The Plug-in

```
function GetAjaxRequest(id, type, url, args)
{
   var nocache = '&nocache=' + Math.random() * 1000000
   var ajax    = new CreateAjaxObject(id, type)
   if (!ajax) return false

   ajax.open('GET', url + '?' + args + nocache, true)
   ajax.send(null)
   return true
}
```

PLUG-IN 87 PostAjaxRequest()

This plug-in is very similar to `GetAjaxRequest()` except that it uses a `POST` request to interact with the web server. In Figure 11-4, the weather at the airport in Anchorage, Alaska, has been extracted from the *weather.gov* RSS feed. Here it is displayed in raw form, but you can easily write some JavaScript to use only the items of data you want and format them to your requirements.

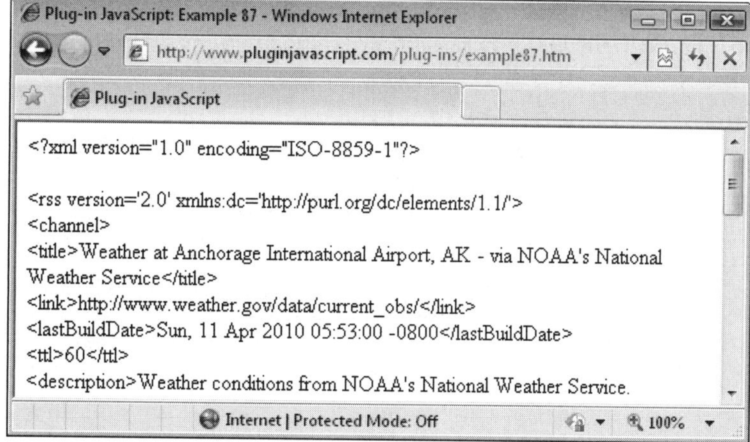

FIGURE 11-4 With this plug-in you can extract data from an RSS feed into a code tag.

About the Plug-in

This plug-in fetches data from a website in the background. It requires the following arguments:

- `id` An object or object ID—this cannot be an array
- `callback` The function to pass the returned data to once it has been retrieved
- `url` The URL with which to communicate
- `args` Any arguments to pass to the URL

Variables, Arrays, and Functions

`contenttype`	Local variable containing the content type used for URL-encoded forms
`ajax`	Local variable assigned an Ajax object
`CreateAjaxObject()`	Plug-in to return a new Ajax object
`open()`	Method of `ajax` for opening a request
`setRequestHeader()`	Method of `ajax` for setting various headers
`send()`	Method of `ajax` for sending a request
`Math.random()`	Function to return a random number

How It Works

This plug-in is as simple as `GetAjaxRequest()`. It starts by setting the content type of the date in the request being sent to that of a URL-encoded form. It then creates the Ajax object with a call to `CreateAjaxObject()`, and if the result is not `true`, returns the value `false` as it cannot proceed any further:

```
var contenttype = 'application/x-www-form-urlencoded'
var ajax        = new CreateAjaxObject(id, callback)
if (!ajax) return false
```

If the object creation was successful, it goes on to open up the request, passing a type of 'POST' in `POST`, the URL in `URL`, and the value `true`, for an asynchronous request:

```
ajax.open('POST', url, true)
```

Next, the content type, content length, and connection headers are sent:

```
ajax.setRequestHeader('Content-type',   contenttype)
ajax.setRequestHeader('Content-length', args.length)
ajax.setRequestHeader('Connection',     'close')
```

Finally, the request is sent and the value `true` is returned to indicate success:

```
ajax.send(args)
return true
```

How To Use It

You call this plug-in in exactly the same way as `GetAjaxRequest()`—it's just that the process used by the plug-in to perform the Ajax is a `POST`, not a `GET` request. Therefore, the target of the request also needs to respond to the `POST` request, as is the case with the following example, which fetches the weather details at Anchorage, Alaska airport:

```
<div id='a'></div>

<script>
window.onload = function()
{
   url  = 'ajaxpost.php'
   args = 'url=http://www.weather.gov/xml/current_obs/PANC.rss'
   PostAjaxRequest('a', todiv, url, args)

   function todiv()
   {
      var rss = this.replace(/\</g, '&lt;')
      rss     =  rss.replace(/\>/g, '&gt;')
      rss     =  rss.replace(/\n/g, '<br />')
      Html('a', rss)
   }
}
</script>
```

The URL supplied to the plug-in is the PHP script *ajaxpost.php*, which is in the same folder as the example file. It's another simple one-line PHP script, which looks like this:

```
<?php if (isset($_POST['url'])) echo file_get_contents($_POST['url']); ?>
```

This is almost the same as the *ajaxget.php* script except that it processes `POST` requests. You can copy it to your own server, where it should work fine if it supports PHP.

This example is a little more interesting than the previous two in that an RSS feed is fetched. It's no different than a web page as far as Ajax is concerned, but displaying it after it has been retrieved poses a problem, in that it contains several XML tags that won't show up under HTML.

To correct this, the callback function `todiv()` has been modified to exchange all occurrences of the < and > symbols with their HTML entity equivalents `<` and `>` and all linefeed characters are changed to `<br />` tags.

For reasons previously stated, the PHP and example should be in the same folder of the same server, so here's a URL you can use to test the example:

http://www.pluginjavascript.com/plug-ins/example87.htm

NOTE *With XML, you would probably want to parse the tree to extract just the elements you want, but if you are fetching only text or HTML, you have all the tools you need to easily make all types of Ajax calls and act appropriately on the data they return.*

The Plug-in

```
function PostAjaxRequest(id, callback, url, args)
{
   var contenttype = 'application/x-www-form-urlencoded'
   var ajax        = new CreateAjaxObject(id, callback)
   if (!ajax) return false

   ajax.open('POST', url, true)
   ajax.setRequestHeader('Content-type',   contenttype)
   ajax.setRequestHeader('Content-length', args.length)
   ajax.setRequestHeader('Connection',     'close')
   ajax.send(args)
   return true
}
```

PLUG-IN 88 FrameBust()

This is a simple but always useful plug-in that checks whether it is running inside a frame and, if it is, busts out of it, placing the current page in its own parent page. This can be useful when you find that other sites link to your pages, but bury them inside iframes so that they do not display at their best. Figure 11-5 shows one web page embedded within another and displaying an optional confirm dialog, offering to bust out of the frame.

About the Plug-in

This plug-in can close any embedding frame, making a web page the parent web page for the current tab or window. It supports the following optional argument:

- **`message`** If this has a value, it will be displayed in a confirm dialog window offering the user the option to click OK to close the surrounding frame. If it doesn't have a value, the plug-in will automatically and silently close the embedding frame.

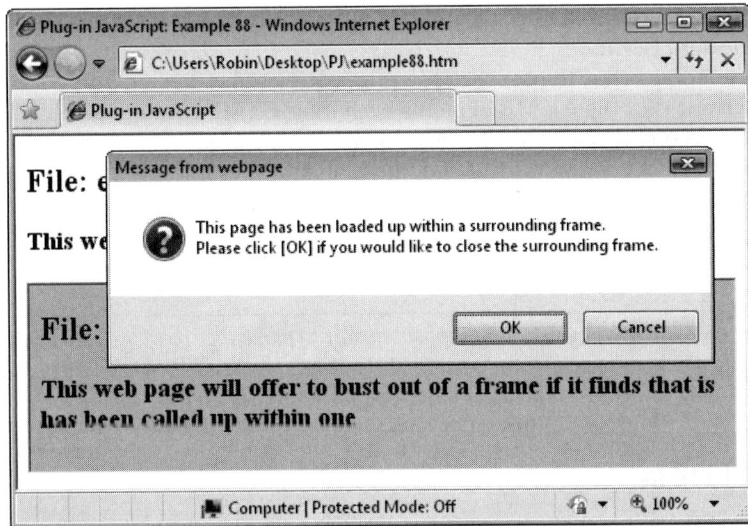

FIGURE 11-5 With this plug-in you can bust your web pages out of embedding frames.

Variables, Arrays, and Functions

`top`	Object representing the outermost of any frame set
`self`	Object representing the current document
`top.location`	Property of `top` containing URL of its document
`self.location.href`	Property of `self.location` containing its URL
`confirm()`	Function to offer a yes/no confirm dialog

How It Works

This plug-in either makes the current document the top one by setting its URL to that of the top object's, or it displays a message (if the message argument has a value) that offers the user the choice of breaking out of frames or leaving them as they are.

How To Use It

To use this plug-in, either call it without an argument if you never want your pages to be embedded in frames, or pass a message for a confirm dialog, to which the response is to click OK to bust out of frames or Cancel to keep the pages as they are. Here's an example of passing a message:

```
<script>
FrameBust("This page has been loaded up within a surrounding frame.\n" +
   "Please click [OK] if you would like to close the surrounding frame.")
</script>
```

You can use `\n` or other escaped characters in the message to control the way it displays.

If you don't wish to provide a message and want all pages to bust out of frames, just leave the message string out of the call to `FrameBust()`.

The Plug-in

```
function FrameBust(message)
{
   if (top != self)
   {
      if (message)
      {
         if (confirm(message))
            top.location.replace(self.location.href)
      }
      else top.location.replace(self.location.href)
   }
}
```

PLUG-IN 89

ProtectEmail()

Spamming these days is worse than ever now that the spammers have access to huge botnets of hacked computers and use automated programs to continuously trawl the web looking for e-mail addresses to harvest. However, e-mail is still extremely important and you usually need to display your e-mail address prominently on your site.

Thankfully, with this plug-in you can display your e-mail address in such a way that your users can click or copy it, yet it will be obfuscated from automatic e-mail harvesters, as shown in Figure 11-6, where the e-mail address is both copyable and clickable but doesn't actually appear as a whole in the web page.

About the Plug-in

This plug-in obfuscates an e-mail address in such a way that spam harvesting programs should not be able to find it. It requires as many arguments as you like because you break your e-mail address into multiple strings and then pass them all as parameters.

Variables, Arrays, and Functions

`j`	Local variable used to iterate through the `arguments` array
`a`	Local variable containing the e-mail address to display
`arguments`	Array containing all the arguments passed to a function

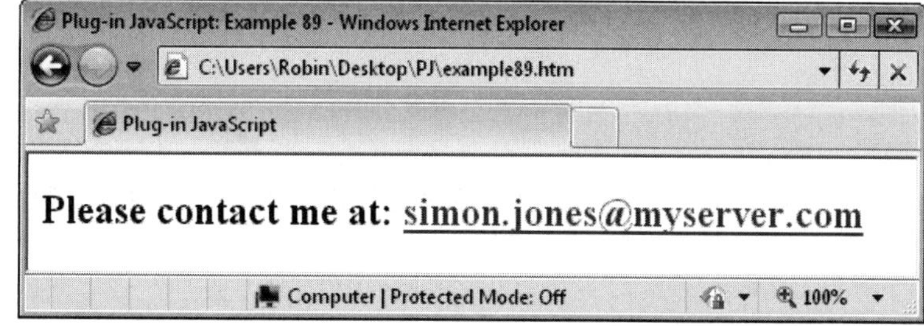

FIGURE 11-6 Use this plug-in to keep your e-mail address visible but unharvestable.

How It Works

This is a simple function that relies on the fact that all arguments sent to a function can be accessed via the `arguments` array. What it does is piece all the arguments it is sent back together to reconstruct an e-mail address using a `for()` loop, like this:

```
var a = ''
for (var j=0 ; j < arguments.length ; ++j)
   a += arguments[j]
```

The variable a is then used to create a hyperlink to the e-mail address, with the code itself using segmented strings to further obfuscate matters. The result is then returned, like this:

```
return "<a hr" + "ef" + "='mai" + "lt" + "o:" + a + "'>" + a + "</a>"
```

How To Use It

To use this plug-in, break your e-mail address up into multiple strings and then pass them all to the plug-in. Here's an example showing how to do this for the e-mail address *simon.jones@myserver.com.*

```
<h2>Please contact me at: <span id='email'></span>.</h2>

<script>
window.onload = function()
{
   Html('email', ProtectEmail('sim', 'on.j', 'ones',
      '@myserv', 'er.c', 'om'))
}
</script>
```

Where you wish the e-mail address to be shown, just place an empty span and give it an ID. You can then insert the e-mail address into the `innerHTML` property of the span from within a section of JavaScript. If you ensure that the e-mail address is completely broken into parts, it is doubtful that any known automatic harvester will be able to extract it for spamming purposes.

The Plug-in

```
function ProtectEmail()
{
   var a = ''

   for (var j=0 ; j < arguments.length ; ++j)
      a += arguments[j]

   return "<a hr" + "ef" + "='mai" + "lt" + "o:" + a + "'>" + a + "</a>"
}
```

CHAPTER 12

Forms and Validation

Form validation is something you must do on your web server to ensure that you receive the data that is required and remove any attempts at hacking or compromising your server or the data on it. However, it is very helpful to your users if you also provide validation directly in the browser.

For example, it can be particularly helpful to provide extra assistance when a user is filling in a form to save it from having to be represented to them if it fails validation at the server. It also cuts down on your bandwidth usage and keeps the optimum number of concurrent users on the server.

This chapter includes plug-ins to provide extra hints for blank form fields that must be filled out, to provide the ability to resize text area inputs if a user types more than the expected amount of text, to check that e-mail addresses and passwords are valid, to clean up user input strings, and to check that credit card number checksums validate.

PLUG-IN 90 FieldPrompt()

When a form field hasn't been entered, there's a large blank area of white space that isn't being used. With this plug-in you can display a prompt in the field that disappears as soon as the user starts typing into it. Figure 12-1 shows two empty input fields containing prompts that were created using this plug-in, in a similar way to the new HTML5 *placeholder* feature.

About the Plug-in

This plug-in takes a form input object and, if it is blank, displays a prompt of your choosing. It requires the following arguments:

- `id` An object or object ID—this cannot be an array
- `prompt` The prompt string to display
- `inputcolor` The color to use for displaying user input
- `promptcolor` The color in which to display the font
- `promptstyle` The font style to use for the prompt, such as 'italic'

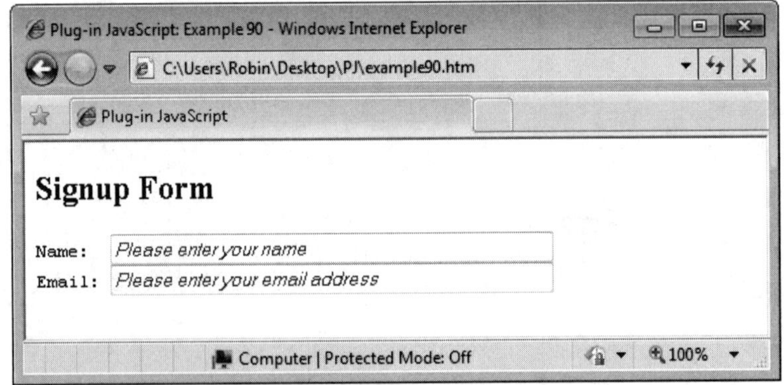

FIGURE 12-1 This plug-in provides additional information to your users.

Variables, Arrays, and Functions

FP_Empty	Property of id that is true when the input field doesn't contain any input, otherwise false
value	Property of id containing its contents
fontStyle	Style property of id containing the font style of the field
color	Style property of id containing the color of the field text
FP_Off()	Subfunction called when the user moves the cursor into the field
FP_On()	Subfunction called when the user moves out of a field

How It Works

This plug-in starts by giving the input and prompt colors and styles default values if none have been passed to it, like this:

```
inputcolor  = inputcolor  ? inputcolor  : '#000000'
promptcolor = promptcolor ? promptcolor : '#888888'
promptstyle = promptstyle ? promptstyle : 'italic'
```

Next, the `FP_On()` subfunction is called to display the supplied prompt if the field is empty, and the `onfocus` and `onblur` events of `id` are attached to the `FP_Off()` and `FP_On()` subfunctions so that the prompt can be switched in and out according to whether the user has clicked within the field or outside of it:

```
FP_On()
O(id).onfocus = FP_Off
O(id).onblur  = FP_On
```

The FP_Off() Subfunction

This function is called when the field gains focus. It first checks the `value` property of `id` to see whether it contains the prompt string. If it does, then the prompt needs to be removed ready for the user to type in some input, like this:

```
O(id).FP_Empty  = true
O(id).value     = ''
S(id).fontStyle = ''
S(id).color     = inputcolor
```

Here, the `FP_Empty` property of `id` is set to `true` to indicate that the field is empty, the field's `value` is set to the empty string, any font style is turned off, and the field text `color` is set to the value in the `inputcolor` argument:

If the field doesn't contain the value in `prompt`, then the `FP_Empty` property is set to `false`.

The FP_On() Subfunction

This function displays the value in `prompt` as long as the field doesn't already have a value entered by the user, which it checks by examining the `value` property of `id`. It also allows the code within to be executed if the field contains the prompt string. The reason for this is that if the user reloads the page while a prompt is displayed, the `value` property will already be set to the prompt before this function runs. This is the code that inserts the prompt:

```
O(id).FP_Empty   = true
O(id).value      = prompt
S(id).fontStyle = promptstyle
S(id).color      = promptcolor
```

Here the `FP_Empty` property is first set to `true` to indicate that there isn't any user entered text in the field, `value` is assigned the string in `prompt`, and the `fontStyle` and `color` properties of the prompt are set.

However, if the `value` property does contain text entered by the user, the `FP_Empty` property of `id` is set to `false` to indicate this.

How To Use It

To use this plug-in, pass it a form field object, a prompt string, and optional color and style arguments. Here's an example that creates two fields, both displaying different prompts:

```
<h2>Signup Form</h2>
<pre>
Name:  <input id='name'  type='text' size='50'/>
Email: <input id='email' type='text' size='50'/>
</pre>

<script>
window.onload = function()
{
   FieldPrompt('name', "Please enter your name",
      '#000000', '#444444', 'italic')
   FieldPrompt('email', "Please enter your email address",
      '#000000', '#444444', 'italic')
}
</script>
```

The two calls to `FieldPrompt()` can also use the plug-in's default values, like this:

```
FieldPrompt('name', "Please enter your name")
FieldPrompt('email', "Please enter your email address")
```

The Plug-in

```
function FieldPrompt(id, prompt, inputcolor, promptcolor, promptstyle)
{
   inputcolor  = inputcolor  ? inputcolor  : '#000000'
   promptcolor = promptcolor ? promptcolor : '#888888'
   promptstyle = promptstyle ? promptstyle : 'italic'

   FP_On()

   O(id).onfocus = FP_Off
   O(id).onblur  = FP_On
```

```
   function FP_Off()
   {
      if (O(id).value == prompt)
      {
         O(id).FP_Empty  = true
         O(id).value     = ''
         S(id).fontStyle = ''
         S(id).color     = inputcolor
      }
      else O(id).FP_Empty = false
   }

   function FP_On()
   {
      if (O(id).value == '' || O(id).value == prompt)
      {
         O(id).FP_Empty  = true
         O(id).value     = prompt
         S(id).fontStyle = promptstyle
         S(id).color     = promptcolor
      }
      else O(id).FP_Empty = false
   }
}
```

PLUG-IN 91

ResizeTextarea()

When you offer a textarea field in a form in which users can enter more than a single line of input, it can be difficult to decide how large to make it. If it is too small, users will have to scroll back and forth through it when making revisions. On the other hand, if it is too large, it wastes space and can look intimidating, implying that a large amount of text is expected to be input.

This plug-in provides the solution by allowing you to specify minimum and maximum vertical heights within which the textarea is allowed to expand or contract, according to the amount of text entered. In Figure 12-2, a 64 by 3 column textarea is displayed, in which some text is being entered.

Then, in Figure 12-3, a total of 8 lines of text have been input, and the textarea has expanded accordingly.

About the Plug-in

This plug-in adjusts the height of a textarea field according to the amount of text it contains, within bounds that you specify. It requires the following arguments:

- **id** An object or object ID or an array of objects and/or object IDs
- **min** Optional argument specifying the minimum height that `id` can be reduced to
- **max** Optional argument specifying the maximum height that `id` can be enlarged to

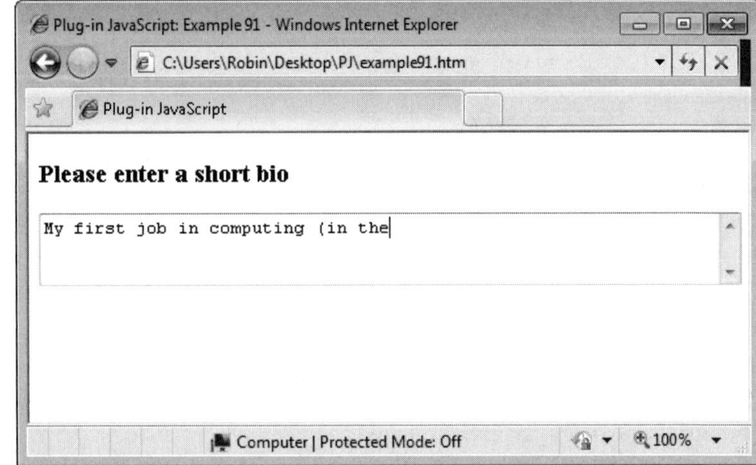

Figure 12-2 Some text is being entered into a textarea form field.

Variables, Arrays, and Functions

`j`	Local variable for iterating through `id` if it is an array
`onmouseup`	Event of `id` that calls the subfunction after a mouse click
`onkeyup`	Event of `id` that calls the subfunction after a key press
`scrollHeight`	Property of `id` containing its total height in pixels
`clientHeight`	Property of `id` containing its visible height pixels
`rows`	Property of `id` containing its number of rows
`DoResizeTextarea()`	Subfunction to resize the height of `id`

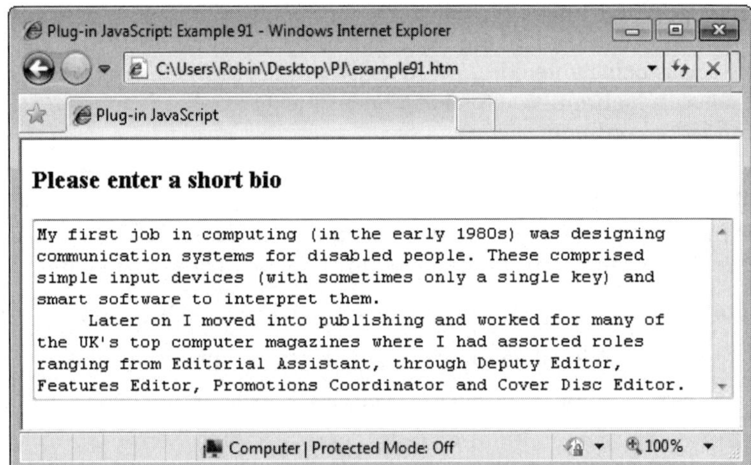

Figure 12-3 After several more lines are entered, the textarea expands accordingly.

How It Works

This plug-in starts by calling itself recursively if `id` is an array, passing each element to be processed individually, like this:

```
if (id instanceof Array)
{
   for (var j = 0 ; j < id.length ; ++j)
      ResizeTextarea(id[j], min, max)
   return
}
```

Next, if `min` or `max` have not been passed values, they are assigned defaults of 0 and 100 lines, respectively:

```
min = min ? min : 0
max = max ? max : 100
```

Finally, in the setup section, the `onmouseup` and `onkeyup` events of `id` are assigned to the `DoResizeTextarea()` subfunction:

```
O(id).onmouseup = DoResizeTextarea
O(id).onkeyup   = DoResizeTextarea
```

The DoResizeTextarea() Subfunction

This function contains just two `while()` loops. The first one continuously increases the number of rows that `id` has until either the text in the textarea is fully visible, or the maximum number of rows in the argument `max` is reached:

```
while (O(id).scrollHeight > O(id).clientHeight && O(id).rows < max)
   ++O(id).rows
```

The second `while()` loop performs the inverse, reducing the height of the textarea so that it is only as large as the text it contains or until it reaches the minimum height supplied in the argument `min`:

```
while (O(id).scrollHeight < O(id).clientHeight && O(id).rows > min)
   --O(id).rows
```

NOTE *While automatically expanding and reducing the textarea seems to work fine on most major browsers, once the `clientHeight` property in Firefox has been increased it doesn't seem to reduce it back down again if text is deleted, so the textarea will net shrink. If you can think of a way to get Firefox to reduce as well as increase a textarea according to the text within it, please let me know via the website.*

How To Use It

To use this plug-in, prepare the textarea by setting it to the width and height you need, then pass it to the plug-in, along with an optional minimum and maximum height. This example shows how:

```
<h3>Please enter a short bio</h3>
<textarea id='ta' rows='3' cols=64'></textarea>

<script>
window.onload = function()
{
   ResizeTextarea('ta', 3, 8)
}
</script>
```

In this example, a minimum height of 3 and a maximum height of 8 rows have been passed. However, you can omit one or both of these arguments, in which case minimum and maximum values of 0 and 10 will be used.

The Plug-in

```
function ResizeTextarea(id, min, max)
{
   if (id instanceof Array)
   {
      for (var j = 0 ; j < id.length ; ++j)
         ResizeTextarea(id[j], min, max)
      return
   }

   min = min ? min : 0
   max = max ? max : 10

   O(id).onmouseup = DoResizeTextarea
   O(id).onkeyup   = DoResizeTextarea

   function DoResizeTextarea()
   {
      while (O(id).scrollHeight > O(id).clientHeight && O(id).rows < max)
         ++O(id).rows

      while (O(id).scrollHeight < O(id).clientHeight && O(id).rows > min)
         --O(id).rows
   }
}
```

PLUG-IN 92 ValidateEmail()

With this plug-in, you can make a quick test on a supplied e-mail address to determine whether it is legally structured. This lets you filter out typos, as well as people simply entering nonsense to see what will happen. Figure 12-4 shows the result of testing the fictitious e-mail address *bill@gates.com*, which validates since it is correctly formed.

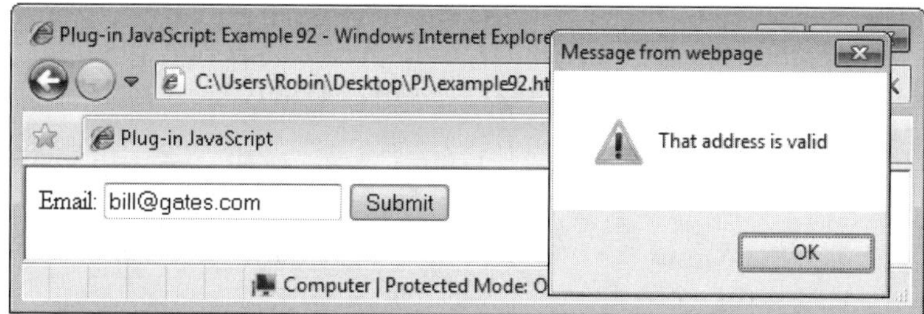

FIGURE 12-4 This plug-in tests whether an e-mail address validates.

About the Plug-in

This plug-in checks whether an e-mail address is correctly structured and in a valid format. It requires the following argument:

- **`email`** A string containing the e-mail address to validate

Variables, Arrays, and Functions

`at`	Local variable containing the position of the `@` sign in `email`
`left`	Local variable containing the part of `email` before the `@`
`right`	Local variable containing the part of `email` after the `@`
`llen`	Local variable containing the length of `left`
`rlen`	Local variable containing the length of `right`
`test()`	Function to test for a match in a string
`indexOf()`	Function to locate the first occurrence of one string in another

How It Works

This function tests various aspects of a supplied string to check whether it conforms to the correct standards for an e-mail address. It starts off by seeing if there is an `@` symbol in the string, using a call to `indexOf()`:

```
var at = email.indexOf('@')
```

Then, if there is no `@` or the argument contains characters that are not word characters (a–z, A–Z, or 0–9), hyphens, periods, or the `@`, underline, or plus symbols, the plug-in returns `false`, as it has already been determined that the e-mail address is invalid, as follows:

```
if (at == -1 || /[^\w\-\.\@\_\+]/.test(email)) return false
```

Next, the variables `left` and `right` are assigned the string on either side of the `@` symbol, and the variables `llen` and `rlen` are then set to the lengths of each, like this:

```
var left  = email.substr(0, at)
var right = email.substr(at + 1)
var llen  = left.length
var rlen  = right.length
```

Using these values, if `left` is less than 1 or greater than 64 characters, or `right` is less than 4 or greater than 254 characters, or if there is no period after the @ symbol, then e-mail address is invalid, and so the plug-in returns `false`:

```
if (llen < 1 || llen > 64 || rlen < 4 || rlen > 254 ||
   right.indexOf('.') == -1) return false
```

After all these tests, the format of the e-mail address appears to be valid, so the value `true` is returned:

```
   return true
```

NOTE *A valid e-mail address should be of the form* 1–64 characters@1–254 characters. *It can contain the letters a–z or A–Z, the digits 0–9, and the hyphen, period, underline and plus characters. No other characters are recommended, even though some may seem to be supported, as they could conflict with shell scripts or other programs used to process emails. If you need to support other characters place them into the regular expression passed to the* `test()` *function in the second line of the plug-in. Also there should always be a period after the @ symbol to divide the domain name from the top level domain extension.*

How To Use It

To use this plug-in, pass it a string containing an e-mail address, and it will return either `true` or `false`, depending on whether the e-mail address is valid. Here's an example that will let you test the plug-in by entering different e-mail addresses:

```
Email: <input id='email' type='text' name='email' />
<button id='button'>Submit</button>

<script>
window.onload = function()
{
   O('button').onclick = function()
   {
      if (ValidateEmail(O('email').value)) alert("That address is valid")
      else alert("That email address is invalid")
   }
}
</script>
```

The HTML section creates an input field and then places a button after it. The `<script>` section then attaches an anonymous, inline function to the button via its `onclick` event, which validates the e-mail address each time it is clicked.

The Plug-in

```
function ValidateEmail(email)
{
   var at = email.indexOf('@')
```

```
    if (at == -1 || /[^\w\-\.\@\_\+]/.test(email)) return false

    var left  = email.substr(0, at)
    var right = email.substr(at + 1)
    var llen  = left.length
    var rlen  = right.length

    if (llen < 1 || llen > 64 || rlen < 4 || rlen > 254 ||
       right.indexOf('.') == -1) return false

    return true
}
```

PLUG-IN 93

ValidatePassword()

To help your users pick more secure passwords, you may wish to require them to be of a certain format, such as including both upper- and lowercase characters, as well as digits and punctuation. With this plug-in, you can choose any or all of these and the plug-in will return `true` or `false`, depending on whether the user has satisfied your requirements. In Figure 12-5 the password that has been entered has not verified.

About the Plug-in

This plug-in takes a password string and then returns either `true` or `false`, depending on whether it satisfies the conditions also passed as arguments. It requires the following arguments:

- **`pass`** The password to validate
- **`min`** The minimum password length
- **`max`** The maximum password length
- **`upper`** If `true` or 1, at least one uppercase character must be in `pass`
- **`lower`** If `true` or 1, at least one lowercase character must be in `pass`
- **`dig`** If `true` or 1, at least one digit must be in `pass`
- **`punct`** If `true` or 1, at least one nonalphanumeric character must be in `pass`

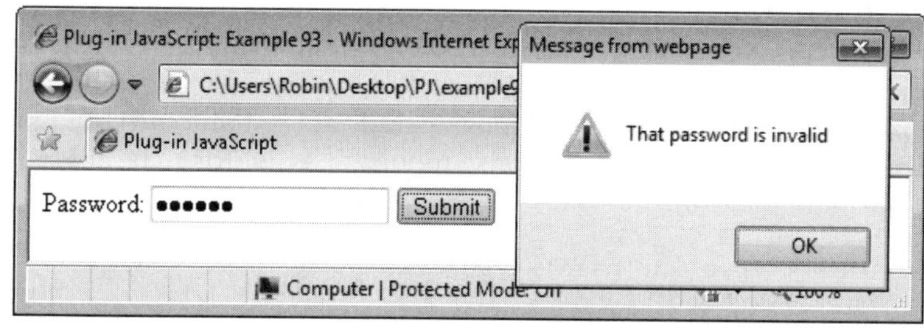

FIGURE 12-5 Ensure your users enter strong passwords with this plug-in.

Variables, Arrays, and Functions

`len`	Local variable containing the length of `pass`
`valid`	local variable that is `true` if `pass` validates, otherwise `false`
`test()`	Function to test for a match in a string

How It Works

This plug-in first assigns the length of the password to `len` and initializes `valid` with the value `true`, which it will retain if it passes the tests to determine its validity:

```
var len   = pass.length
var valid = true
```

Next, `pass` is checked to ensure it is within the lengths required by the `min` and `max` arguments, and `valid` is assigned the value `false` if not:

```
if (len < min || len > max) valid = false
```

The following four tests are made only if the argument they work from is `true` or has the value 1. For example, the following statement returns `false` if the argument `upper` is `true` or 1 *and* there is not at least one uppercase letter in `pass`:

```
else if (upper && !/[A-Z]/.test(pass)) valid = false
```

The following three statements do the same for lowercase letters, digits, and punctuation (nonalphanumeric) characters:

```
else if (lower  && !/[a-z]/.test(pass))        valid = false
else if (dig    && !/[0-9]/.test(pass))        valid = false
else if (punct  && !/[^a-zA-Z0-9]/.test(pass)) valid = false
```

If `pass` meets all these tests, then `valid` will retain its initial value of `true`, which is then returned; otherwise, one of the tests will set `valid` to `false`, and that value will be returned:

```
return valid
```

How To Use It

To use this plug-in, pass it a password string and the arguments you want for the password to meet your security requirements. The following example uses the strictest policy the plug-in supports, in which the password must include at least one each of upper- and lowercase letters, digits, and punctuation. It also requires passwords to be at least 8 characters long (but no more than 16):

```
Password: <input id='pass' type='password' name='pass' />
<button id='button'>Submit</button>

<script>
```

```
window.onload = function()
{
   O('button').onclick = function()
   {
      if (ValidatePassword(O('pass').value, 8, 16, 1, 1, 1, 1))
         alert("That password is valid")
      else alert("That password is invalid")
   }
}
</script>
```

The Plug-in

```
function ValidatePassword(pass, min, max, upper, lower, dig, punct)
{
   var len   = pass.length
   var valid = true

   if      (len < min || len > max)             valid = false
   else if (upper  && !/[A-Z]/.test(pass))        valid = false
   else if (lower  && !/[a-z]/.test(pass))        valid = false
   else if (dig    && !/[0-9]/.test(pass))        valid = false
   else if (punct  && !/[^a-zA-Z0-9]/.test(pass)) valid = false

   return valid
}
```

PLUG-IN 94

CleanupString()

This plug-in provides a number of string manipulation functions that often come in handy. For example, don't you hate it when you enter a credit card or phone number into a web form, only to be told you aren't allowed to use spaces and must enter it again? If your content management system doesn't like spaces either, this plug-in can remove them before they arrive at your server. It can also remove all digits, text, or punctuation, convert from lower- to uppercase text (and vice versa), and even change all groups of multiple spaces into just a single space. Figure 12-6 shows a credit card number being entered into a web form including spaces.

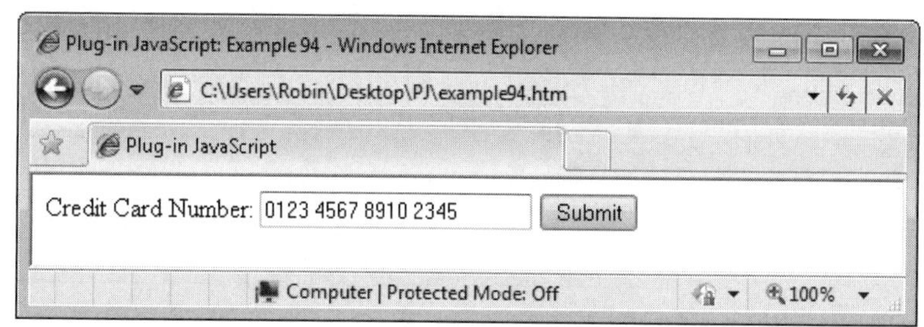

FIGURE 12-6 A user has entered a sequence of credit card numbers with spaces.

Figure 12-7 shows the input after the user has clicked the Submit button—all the spaces are now removed, leaving only the card number behind.

About the Plug-in

This plug-in takes a string and can perform one or more of several actions on it. It requires the following arguments:

- **`string`** The string to clean up
- **`allspaces`** If `true` or 1, all spaces in `string` are removed
- **`alldigs`** If `true` or 1, all digits in `string` are removed
- **`alltext`** If `true` or 1, all text in `string` is removed
- **`allpunct`** If `true` or 1, all punctuation in `string` is removed
- **`uptolow`** If `true` or 1, all uppercase characters in `string` are converted to lowercase
- **`lowtoup`** If `true` or 1, all lowercase characters in `string` are converted to uppercase
- **`spacestosingle`** If `true` or 1, all groups of multiple spaces in `string` are reduced to a single space

Variables, Arrays, and Functions

`replace()`	Function to replace one value with another in a string

How It Works

This plug-in goes through each of the arguments it is supplied in turn. If the argument has the value `true` or 1, then the matching `replace()` function is performed on the string. For example, the following statement removes all spaces from `string` when the `allspaces` argument is 1 or `true`:

```
if (allspaces) string = string.replace(/[\s]/g, '')
```

All the remaining statements are very similar, differing only by the regular expressions used for testing.

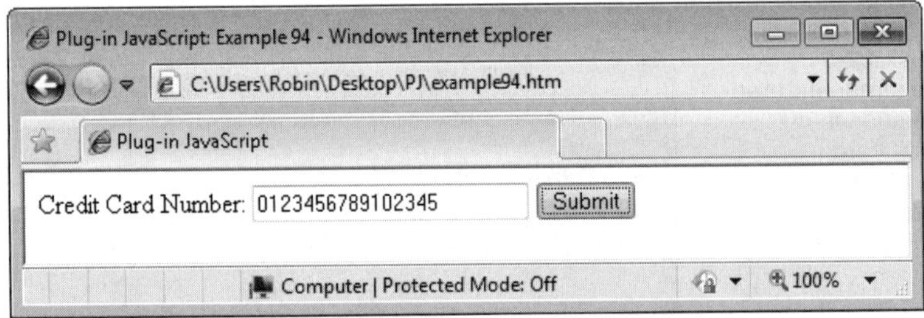

FIGURE 12-7 This plug-in has automatically stripped out the spaces.

How To Use It

To use this plug-in, pass it a string along with the arguments needed to perform the changes required on the string. The modified string will then be returned. Here's an example that cleans up a credit card number by removing all spaces, text, and punctuation from it:

```
Credit Card Number:
<input id='ccnum' type='text' name='ccnum' size='24' />
<button id='button'>Submit</button>

<script>
window.onload = function()
{
   O('button').onclick = function()
   {
      O('ccnum').value =
         CleanupString(O('ccnum').value , 1 ,0 ,1, 1, 0, 0, 0)
   }
}
</script>
```

To use this in a web form, you could change the `onclick` event used in this example to the `onsubmit` event of your form. If you do, make sure that when the plug-in has finished execution, the function you point the event to returns `true`, because any other value will likely cancel the form submission, and a return value of `false` certainly will cancel it.

The Plug-in

```
function CleanupString(string, allspaces, alldigs, alltext, allpunct,
   uptolow, lowtoup, spacestosingle)
{
   if (allspaces)      string = string.replace(/[\s]/g, '')
   if (alldigs)        string = string.replace(/[\d]/g, '')
   if (alltext)        string = string.replace(/[a-zA-Z]/g, '')
   if (allpunct)       string = string.replace(/[^\sa-zA-Z0-9]/g, '')
   if (uptolow)        string = string.toLowerCase()
   if (lowtoup)        string = string.toUpperCase()
   if (spacestosingle) string = string.replace(/[\s]/g, ' ')

   return string
}
```

PLUG-IN 95

ValidateCreditCard()

With this plug-in, you can check that a credit card number you are given by a user is at least of the correct format and has the right checksum before submitting it to a card processing company. Figure 12-8 shows a set of made up credit card details that did not pass the validation.

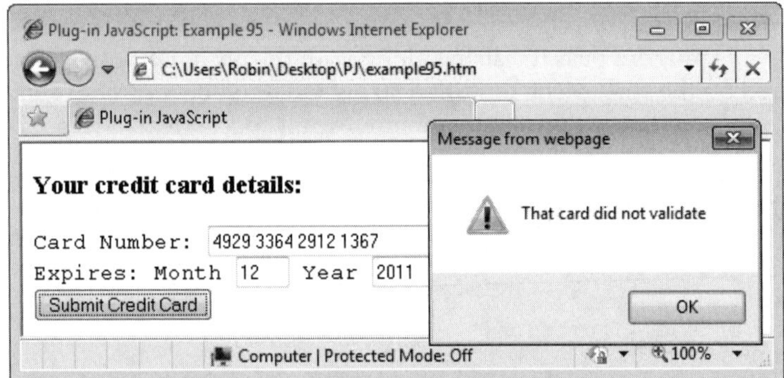

FIGURE 12-8 Checking whether credit card details match basic requirements

About the Plug-in

This plug-in takes details about a credit card and returns `true` or `false` depending whether the card passes checksum and date verification. It requires the following arguments:

- **`number`** A credit card number
- **`month`** The card's expiry month
- **`year`** The card's expiry year

Variables, Arrays, and Functions

`left`	Local variable containing the first 4 digits of `number`
`cclen`	Local variable containing the number of digits in `number`
`chksum`	Local variable containing the card's checksum
`date`	Local date object
`substr()`	Function to return a portion of a string
`getTime()`	Function to get the current time and date
`getFullYear()`	Function to get the year as a 4-digit number
`getMonth()`	Function to get the month

How It Works

This function first ensures that all three parameters passed to it are strings by adding the empty string to them, like this:

```
number += ''
month  += ''
year   += ''
```

Next, each argument is processed through the `CleanupString()` plug-in to ensure that they are in the formats required:

```
number = CleanupString(number, true, false, true, true)
month  = CleanupString(month,  true, false, true, true)
year   = CleanupString(year,   true, false, true, true)
```

After this, the variable `left` is assigned the first 4 digits of `number`, `cclen` is set to the card number's length, and `chksum` is initialized to 0:

```
var left    = number.substr(0, 4)
var cclen   = number.length
var chksum  = 0
```

Next, several `if() ... else if()` statements check that `left` contains a valid sequence that matches a known brand of credit card and, if it does, that the card number length in `cclen` is correct for the card type. If `left` doesn't match a known card, or it matches one but `cclen` is the wrong length, then the plug-in returns `false` to indicate that the card didn't verify.

If these initial tests are passed, the card's checksum is then calculated using an algorithm invented by IBM scientist Hans Peter Luhn (for further details see *en.wikipedia.org/wiki/Luhn_algorithm*), like this:

```
for (var j = 1 - (cclen % 2) ; j < cclen ; j += 2)
   if (j < cclen) chksum += number[j] * 1

for (j = cclen % 2 ; j < cclen ; j += 2)
{
   if (j < cclen)
   {
      d = number[j] * 2
      chksum += d < 10 ? d : d - 9
   }
}

if (chksum % 10 != 0) return false
```

Finally, the date is looked up and compared to the values supplied to the plug-in, so that even if the card has validated this far, the plug-in will still return `false` if the card has expired:

```
var date = new Date()
date.setTime(date.getTime())
if (year.length == 4) year = year.substr(2, 2)

   if (year > 50)                              return false
   else if (year  < (date.getFullYear() - 2000)) return false
   else if ((date.getMonth() + 1) > month       return false
   else                                        return true
```

How To Use It

To use this plug-in, pass it a card number, expiry date, and month and it will return `true` or `false`. Of course, this algorithm tests only whether the card meets certain requirements and not whether the user has entered a genuine card or whether the card has been revoked or is over the user's credit limit, and so on. The purpose of the plug-in is mainly to catch typing errors and people entering random data to see what happens.

This example shows how you might use the plug-in:

```
<h3>Your credit card details:</h3>
<font face='Courier New'>
Card Number: <input id='ccnum' type='text' name='n' size='24' /><br />
Expires: Month <input id='ccmonth' type='text' name='m' size='2' />
Year <input id='ccyear' type='text' name='y' size='4'  /><br />
<button id='button'>Submit Credit Card</button>

<script>
window.onload = function()
{
   O('button').onclick = function()
   {
      if (ValidateCreditCard(O('ccnum').value,
         O('ccmonth').value, O('ccyear').value))
            alert("That card validated successfully")
      else alert("That card did not validate")
   }
}
</script>
```

When incorporating the plug-in with your own code you will probably want to replace the `onclick` event attachment used in the example with a function attached to the `onsubmit` event of your form. Also, make sure that when you do this your function returns `true` if the card verifies to allow the form submission to complete, and `false` (along with probably displaying an error message) if the card doesn't validate, to stop the form submission going through.

NOTE *Only years up to 2050 are currently supported in order to base card dates around the years 1950 to 2050. If you are reading a well thumbed copy of this book and it's coming up to mid century, and JavaScript is still being used, well, you may wish to increase the value 50 in the 4th to last line to a higher value a few years ahead of the current year.*

The Plug-in

```
function ValidateCreditCard(number, month, year)
{
   number     += ''
   month      += ''
   year       += ''
   number      = CleanupString(number, true, false, true, true)
   month       = CleanupString(month,  true, false, true, true)
```

```
year        = CleanupString(year,   true, false, true, true)
var left    = number.substr(0, 4)
var cclen   = number.length
var chksum  = 0

if (left >= 3000 && left <= 3059 ||
    left >= 3600 && left <= 3699 ||
    left >= 3800 && left <= 3889)
{ // Diners Club
   if (cclen != 14) return false
}
else if (left >= 3088 && left <= 3094 ||
    left >= 3096 && left <= 3102 ||
    left >= 3112 && left <= 3120 ||
    left >= 3158 && left <= 3159 ||
    left >= 3337 && left <= 3349 ||
    left >= 3528 && left <= 3589)
{ // JCB
   if (cclen != 16) return false
}
else if (left >= 3400 && left <= 3499 ||
    left >= 3700 && left <= 3799)
{ // American Express
   if (cclen != 15) return false
}
else if (left >= 3890 && left <= 3899)
{ // Carte Blanche
   if (cclen != 14) return false
}
else if (left >= 4000 && left <= 4999)
{ // Visa
   if (cclen != 13 && cclen != 16) return false
}
else if (left >= 5100 && left <= 5599)
{ // MasterCard

   if (cclen != 16) return false
}
else if (left == 5610)
{ // Australian BankCard
   if (cclen != 16) return false
}
else if (left == 6011)
{ // Discover
   if (cclen != 16) return false
}
else return false // Unrecognized Card

for (var j = 1 - (cclen % 2) ; j < cclen ; j += 2)
   if (j < cclen) chksum += number[j] * 1

for (j = cclen % 2 ; j < cclen ; j += 2)
{
```

```
      if (j < cclen)
      {
         d = number[j] * 2
         chksum += d < 10 ? d : d - 9
      }
   }

   if (chksum % 10 != 0) return false

   var date = new Date()
   date.setTime(date.getTime())

   if (year.length == 4) year = year.substr(2, 2)

   if (year > 50)                                return false
   else if (year  < (date.getFullYear() - 2000)) return false
   else if ((date.getMonth() + 1) > month        return false
   else                                          return true
}
```

CHAPTER 13

Solutions to Common Problems

There are a number of plug-ins that didn't fit clearly within any of the previous chapters, so I've included them here. They offer features such as keeping your copyright notices current each new year; a less intrusive, in-browser alert window that doesn't prevent you from accessing the rest of the current document; a function to provide tooltips for any object; the facility to add cursor trails to the mouse pointer; and a way to make a web page touch enabled for use with tablet computers and other touch devices.

PLUG-IN 96 RollingCopyright()

This simple plug-in is worth using on any pages where a copyright notice is included, because no matter how many years ago you last updated the page, it will always show the current year, as shown by the screen grab in Figure 13-1.

About the Plug-in

This plug-in takes a start year for when the copyright began and returns a copyright string using that and the current year. It requires the following argument:

- **start** The start year as a four-digit number

Variables, Arrays, and Functions

date	Local date object
Date()	Function to return a new date object
getFullYear()	Function to return a four digit year

How It Works

This plug-in creates a new date object and assigns it the current year as a four-digit number, like this:

```
var date = new Date()
date     = date.getFullYear()
```

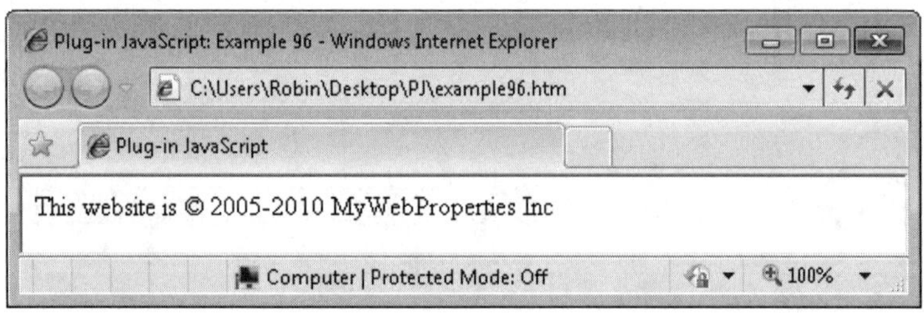

FIGURE 13-1 Keep your copyright notices up-to-date with this plug-in.

Then the two dates are returned preceded by a copyright symbol:

```
return '&copy; ' + start + "-" + date
```

How To Use It

To use this plug-in, pass it the starting year for the copyright and then assign the string it returns to an element in your document, as in the following example:

```
<span id='copy'></span>

<script>
window.onload = function()
{
   Html('copy', InsVars("This website is #1 MyWebProperties Inc",
      RollingCopyright(2005)))
}
</script>
```

The HTML section creates a span that will be used to display the copyright message, and then the `<script>` section uses the `InsVars()` plug-in to insert the result of calling `RollingCopyright()` into a sentence, which is then assigned to the `innerHTML` property of the span.

The Plug-in

```
function RollingCopyright(start)
{
   var date = new Date()
   date     = date.getFullYear()

   return '&copy; ' + start + "-" + date
}
```

Alert()

The built-in JavaScript `alert()` function is great for help with debugging or for alerting users about something important. However, the function is a *modal* dialog, which means that it takes over the browser, preventing access to anything within it other than the alert window. What's worse, if a web page calls `alert()` in a loop it will effectively lock you out of the browser, even preventing you from closing it.

This plug-in provides a handy replacement for the function that is much more user friendly in that it is not modal, and all other parts of the browser remain accessible while it

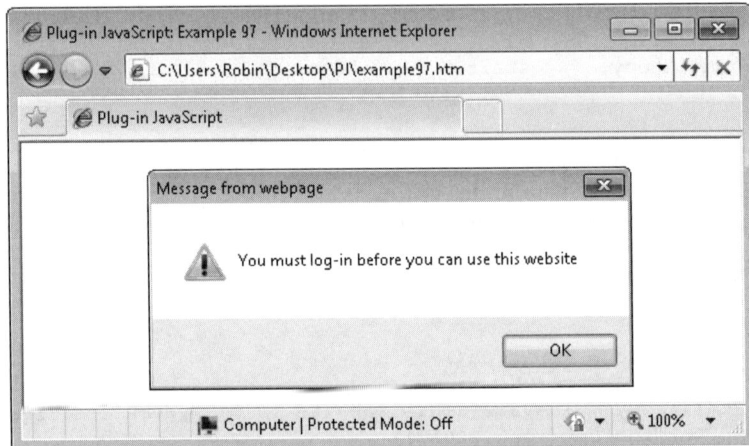

FIGURE 13-2 A standard Internet Explorer alert message

is displayed. It also features smart scrolling; unlike the regular `alert()` window that just gets bigger and bigger depending on the size of message, this plug-in will provide scrollbars instead, so that it always remains the same size. Figure 13-2 shows a standard `alert()` dialog.

Figure 13-3 shows this plug-in used to display the same message as Figure 13-2. It is fairly similar to the Internet Explorer alert window, but it also uses some styling similar to that used by Firefox and other web browsers, so it should look good on all major browsers.

About the Plug-in

This plug-in takes a message and displays it in an in-browser alert dialog. It requires the following argument:

- **`value`** A string, value, or expression to display

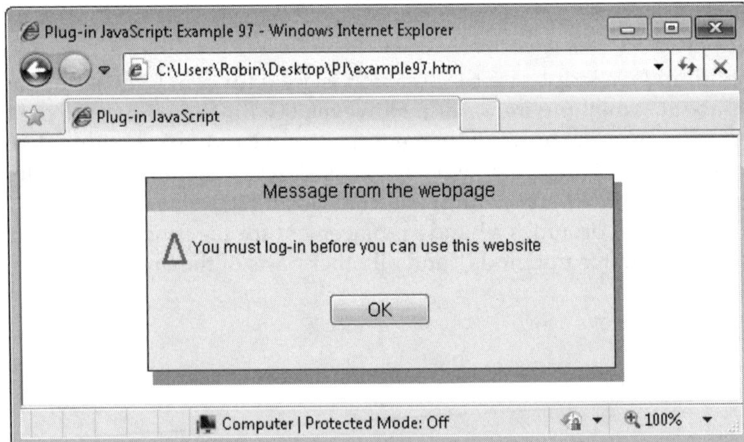

FIGURE 13-3 A message displayed by the Alert() plug-in

Variables, Arrays, and Functions

divs	Local array containing the IDs of the two main divs
newdiv	Local object used for creating new divs
warn	Local variable containing the HTML for the warning triangle
ok	Local variable containing the HTML for the OK button
mess	Local variable containing the HTML of the message
html	Local variable containing the HTML for the alert contents
ALERT_DIV & SHADOW_DIV & ALERT_TITLE & ALERT_MESSAGE & ALERT_OK	IDs of the various elements created by this plug-in
innerHTML	Property of various objects containing their HTML
backgroundColor	Property of various objects containing their background colors
fontFamily	Property of various objects containing their fonts
fontSize	Property of various objects containing their font sizes
padding	Property of the message area containing its padding
paddingTop	Property of the title area containing its top padding
textAlign	Property of the title containing its text alignment
overflow	Property of the message area containing its overflow setting
border	Property of the main div containing its border setting
onclick	Event of the OK button attached to AlertHide()
AlertHide()	Subfunction to hide the alert
Position()	Plug-in to set an object's style position property
Resize()	Plug-in to resize and object
Center()	Plug-in to center an object both vertically and horizontally
GoTo()	Plug-in to move an object to a new position
Opacity()	Plug-in to set the opacity of an object
visible()	Plug-in to make an object visible
Invisible()	Plug-in to make an object invisible
createElement()	Function to create a new HTML element
setAttribute()	Function to set an attribute of an HTML element
appendChild()	Function to append a child object to an element

How It Works

This plug-in starts by creating an array of the main two divs it uses, then four strings are created to hold the warning triangle HTML, the OK button, the alert message itself, and two new subdivs that will contain the alert's title and message HTML:

```
var divs = Array('ALERT_DIV', 'SHADOW_DIV')
var warn = "<font color=red size=6 style='vertical-align:middle;'>" +
           "&#916;</font> "
var ok   = "<center><input id='ALERT_OK' type='submit' /></center>"
```

```
var mess = warn + value + '<br /><br />' + ok
var html = "<div id='ALERT_TITLE'></div>" +
           "<div id='ALERT_MESSAGE'></div>"
```

Next, if the object with the ID 'ALERT_DIV' doesn't exist, it means this is the first time the plug-in has been called, so the two main divs are created, like this:

```
var newdiv = document.createElement('div')
newdiv.setAttribute('id', 'SHADOW_DIV')
document.body.appendChild(newdiv)
newdiv = document.createElement('div')
newdiv.setAttribute('id', 'ALERT_DIV')
document.body.appendChild(newdiv)
```

These statements create new divs with the IDs 'ALERT_DIV' and 'SHADOW_DIV', attaching them to the document body. The divs are then released from their location in the HTML, resized, and centered, and the shadow div has its opacity set to 50 percent, as follows:

```
Position(divs, ABS)
Resize('ALERT_DIV',  350, 140)
Resize('SHADOW_DIV', 354, 146)
Center('ALERT_DIV')
GoTo('SHADOW_DIV', X('ALERT_DIV') + 4, Y('ALERT_DIV') + 6)
Opacity('SHADOW_DIV', 50)
```

Next, the divs are hidden with a call to the subfunction `AlertHide()`, and the main div's `innerHTML` property is assigned the value of `html`, which contains the HTML with which to create the two subdivs, both of which are then resized:

```
AlertHide()
Html('ALERT_DIV', html)
Resize('ALERT_TITLE',   350, 22)
Resize('ALERT_MESSAGE', 330, 98)
```

After this, a number of style elements are set up, and the `innerHTML` of the title and message divs is assigned, like this:

```
Html('ALERT_TITLE', 'Message from the webpage')
Html('ALERT_MESSAGE', mess)

S('ALERT_TITLE').backgroundColor = '#acc5e0'
S('ALERT_TITLE').fontFamily      = 'Arial'
S('ALERT_TITLE').paddingTop      = '2px'
S('ALERT_TITLE').textAlign       = 'center'
S('ALERT_TITLE').fontSize        = '14px'
O('ALERT_MESSAGE').innerHTML     = mess
S('ALERT_MESSAGE').fontFamily    = 'Arial'
S('ALERT_MESSAGE').fontSize      = '12px'
S('ALERT_MESSAGE').padding       = '10px'
S('ALERT_MESSAGE').overflow      = 'auto'
S('ALERT_DIV').backgroundColor   = '#f0f0f0'
```

```
S('ALERT_DIV').border           = 'solid #444444 1px'
S('SHADOW_DIV').backgroundColor = '#444444'
O('ALERT_OK').value             = '       OK       '
```

These statements set the correct colors, fonts, alignments, padding, and borders for the elements, and the message alert has its overflow property set to 'auto', so that larger messages will have scrollbars added if necessary to scroll through the content.

Finally, the `onclick` event of the OK button is attached to the `AlertHide()` subfunction, and the divs are made visible, like this:

```
O('ALERT_OK').onclick = AlertHide
Visible(divs)
```

The plug-in ends with the `AlertHide()` subfunction, which is called when the OK button is clicked:

```
function AlertHide()
{
   Invisible(divs)
}
```

How To Use It

You use this plug-in in the same manner as the built-in `alert()` function: by simply passing a value or expression to display, like this:

```
Alert("You must log-in before you can use this website")
```

Or, here's an example that combines a string and an expression:

```
Alert("The product of 6 and 7 is " + 6 * 7)
```

One of the best things about this plug-in is that you can use it to watch values changing in real time without having to click OK after each alert message as you would with the standard `alert()` function. Here's an example you can try that creates repeating interrupts to call the plug-in and display the current mouse coordinates, which change as you move the mouse about:

```
window.onload = function()
{
   setInterval(mousecoords, INTERVAL)

   function mousecoords()
   {
      Alert("Mouse X = " + MOUSE_X + " | Mouse Y = " + MOUSE_Y)
   }
}
```

In this particular example, because the calls to `Alert()` repeat continuously, nothing will happen if you click the OK button to dismiss the message, as another `Alert()` call is made INTERVAL milliseconds later. If you want to test the plug-in with a single call just try a command such as this:

```
Alert("This is a test alert message")
```

NOTE *Don't confuse the two functions because they use the same letters. The original JavaScript function starts with a lowercase letter 'a', and is called* `alert()`*, while the new plug-in begins with an upper case letter 'A' and is called* `Alert()`.

The Plug-in

```
function Alert(value)
{
   var divs = Array('ALERT_DIV', 'SHADOW_DIV')
   var warn = "<font color=red size=6 style='vertical-align:middle;'>" +
              "&#916;</font> "
   var ok   = "<center><input id='ALERT_OK' type='submit' /></center>"
   var mess = warn + value + '<br /><br />' + ok
   var html = "<div id='ALERT_TITLE'></div>" +
              "<div id='ALERT_MESSAGE'></div>"

   if (!O('ALERT_DIV'))
   {
      var newdiv = document.createElement('div')
      newdiv.setAttribute('id', 'SHADOW_DIV')
      document.body.appendChild(newdiv)
      newdiv = document.createElement('div')
      newdiv.setAttribute('id', 'ALERT_DIV')
      document.body.appendChild(newdiv)
      Position(divs, ABS)
      Resize('ALERT_DIV',  350, 140)
      Resize('SHADOW_DIV', 354, 146)
      Center('ALERT_DIV')
      GoTo('SHADOW_DIV', X('ALERT_DIV') + 4, Y('ALERT_DIV') + 6)
      Opacity('SHADOW_DIV', 50)
   }

   AlertHide()
   Html('ALERT_DIV', html)
   Resize('ALERT_TITLE',   350, 22)
   Resize('ALERT_MESSAGE', 330, 98)
   Html('ALERT_TITLE', 'Message from the webpage')
   Html('ALERT_MESSAGE', mess)

   S('ALERT_TITLE').backgroundColor = '#acc5e0'
   S('ALERT_TITLE').fontFamily      = 'Arial'
   S('ALERT_TITLE').paddingTop      = '2px'
   S('ALERT_TITLE').textAlign       = 'center'
   S('ALERT_TITLE').fontSize        = '14px'
```

```
    S('ALERT_MESSAGE').fontFamily     = 'Arial'
    S('ALERT_MESSAGE').fontSize       = '12px'
    S('ALERT_MESSAGE').padding        = '10px'
    S('ALERT_MESSAGE').overflow       = 'auto'
    S('ALERT_DIV').backgroundColor    = '#f0f0f0'
    S('ALERT_DIV').border             = 'solid #444444 1px'
    S('SHADOW_DIV').backgroundColor   = '#444444'
    O('ALERT_OK').value               = '      OK      '
    O('ALERT_OK').onclick             = AlertHide

    Visible(divs)

    function AlertHide()
    {
       Invisible(divs)
    }
}
```

PLUG-IN 98 ReplaceAlert()

If you like the Alert() plug-in, you can use this one to replace the default JavaScript alert() with it and use it all the time. Figure 13-4 shows the alert() function being called to display the mouse's current coordinates but in fact, the Alert() plug-in is handling the message display, as it has now replaced the default function.

About the Plug-in

This is probably the shortest plug-in in the book, and it requires no arguments to change the default action of alert() to use the new Alert() plug-in.

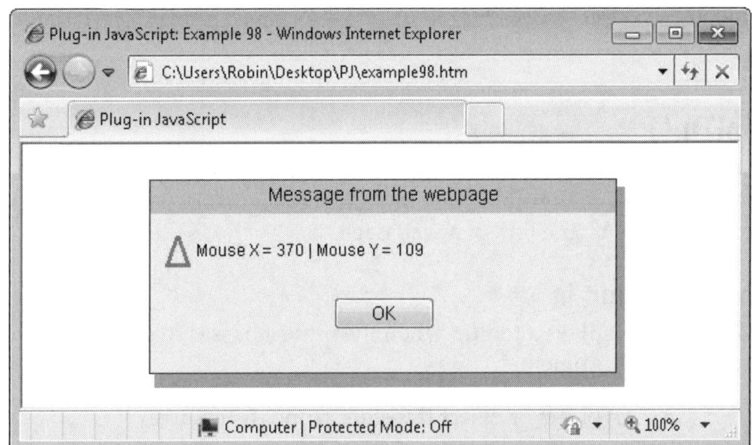

FIGURE 13-4 With this plug-in, all calls to alert() will use the new Alert() plug-in.

Variables, Arrays, and Functions

alert	Property of the window object specifying which code to use for handling alerts

How It Works

This plug-in simply attaches the `Alert()` plug-in to the `alert` event of the `window` object, like this:

```
window.alert = Alert
```

How To Use It

To replace the default JavaScript `alert()` function with the new `Alert()` plug-in, just call `ReplaceAlert()`. The following example is modified from the one used in the previous plug-in, `Alert()` to call the default `alert()` function, which has been diverted to use the new `Alert()` plug-in:

```
window.onload = function()
{
   ReplaceAlert()
   setInterval(mousecoords, INTERVAL)

   function mousecoords()
   {
      alert("Mouse X = " + MOUSE_X + " | Mouse Y = " + MOUSE_Y)
   }
}
```

The Plug-in

```
function ReplaceAlert()
{
   window.alert = Alert
}
```

PLUG-IN 99 ToolTip()

With this plug-in, you can add tooltips that fade in and out over a period to any object, with a range of fully configurable display options. Figure 13-5 shows a tooltip that has been attached to the Home link of a web page.

About the Plug-in

This plug-in displays a tooltip when the mouse passes over an attached object. It requires the following arguments:

- **`id`** An object or object ID—this cannot be an array
- **`tip`** The tip message to display, which may contain HTML
- **`font`** The font to use

FIGURE 13-5 Use this plug-in to attach smoothly fading tooltips to objects.

- **`size`** The font size to use
- **`textc`** The text color to use
- **`backc`** The background color to use
- **`bordc`** The border color to use
- **`bstyle`** The border style to use
- **`bwidth`** The border width to use, in pixels
- **`msecs`** The time each fade out or in should take in milliseconds
- **`timeout`** The time after which the tooltip will automatically fade out in milliseconds; if 0 or not passed, the tooltip will not automatically fade out

Variables, Arrays, and Functions

`tt`	Local variable containing the string 'TT_' concatenated with the ID name of `id`
`newdiv`	Local variable containing the new div object
`MOUSE_X`	Global variable containing the current horizontal location of the mouse cursor
`MOUSE_Y`	Global variable containing the current vertical location of the mouse cursor
`ZINDEX`	Global variable containing the highest `zIndex` value so far used
`Hidden`	Property of the new div: `true` when the tooltip is hidden, otherwise `false`
`IID`	Property of the new div used to cancel any pending interrupt that may have been set using `setTimeoout()`
`zIndex`	Property of the new div set to bring it to the front of all objects
`fontFamily`	Property of the new div containing its font family
`fontSize`	Property of the new div containing its font size
`padding`	Property of the new div containing its padding

color	Property of the new div containing its text color
backgroundColor	Property of the new div containing its background color
bordercolor	Property of the new div containing its border color
borderStyle	Property of the new div containing its border style
borderWidth	Property of the new div containing its border width
innerHTML	Property of the new div containing its HTML
onmouseover	Event of `id` attached to `DoToolTip()`
onmouseout	Event of `id` attached to `ToolTipHide()`
DoToolTip()	Subfunction to display a tooltip
ToolTipHide()	Subfunction to hide a tooltip
FadeIn()	Plug-in to fade an object in
FadeOut()	Plug-in to fade out an object
Px()	Plug-in to add the suffix 'px' to a number
setTimeout()	Function to set up an interrupt to a function at a future time
clearTimeout()	Function to cancel an interrupt set by `setTimeout()`

How It Works

This plug-in first creates a new div for each different tooltip, with an ID comprising the string 'TT_' and the ID name of `id`, and then creates a local variable to hold this ID, like this:

```
var tt = 'TT_' + O(id).id
```

Next, if the div for the tooltip for `id` hasn't yet been created, this is done using the following code:

```
var newdiv = document.createElement('div')
newdiv.setAttribute('id', tt)
document.body.appendChild(newdiv)
```

The opacity of the new div is then set to 0 to hide it, and it is released from the HTML by giving it a style position attribute of 'absolute', using the global variable `ABS`:

```
Opacity(tt, 0)
Position(tt, ABS)
```

Next, all the arguments are given default values for any that have not been given a value:

```
font   = font   ? font   : 'Arial'
size   = size   ? size   : 'small'
textc  = textc  ? textc  : '#884444'
backc  = backc  ? backc  : '#ffff88'
bordc  = bordc  ? bordc  : '#aaaaaa'
bstyle = bstyle ? bstyle : 'dotted'
bwidth = bwidth ? bwidth : 1
msecs  = msecs  ? msecs  : 250
```

After that, various style settings based on these values are applied to the new div, and the contents of the tip argument are placed in its innerHTML property, as follows:

```
S(tt).fontFamily      = font
S(tt).fontSize        = size
S(tt).padding         = '3px 5px 3px 5px'
S(tt).color           = textc
S(tt).backgroundColor = backc
S(tt).borderColor     = bordc
S(tt).borderStyle     = bstyle
S(tt).borderWidth     = Px(bwidth)

Html(tt, tip)
```

Finally, in the setup section, the DoToolTip() and ToolTipHide() subfunctions are attached to the onmouseover and onmouseout events of id, and the Hidden property of id is set to false to indicate that the tooltip is not currently visible:

```
O(id).onmouseover = DoToolTip
O(id).onmouseout  = ToolTipHide
O(tt).Hidden      = false
```

The DoToolTip() Subfunction

This function moves the tooltip div referred to by tt to a location 15 pixels to the right and 15 down from the mouse position, sets its zIndex property to the highest value used so far plus 1 (to ensure it displays above all other elements), fades the tooltip in, and sets the tooltip's Hidden attribute to false to indicate that it is now visible:

```
GoTo(tt, MOUSE_X + 15, MOUSE_Y + 15)
O(tt).zIndex = ZINDEX + 1
FadeIn(tt, msecs)
O(tt).Hidden = false
```

With the tooltip now displayed, if a timeout has been specified then setTimeout() is called to create an interrupt call to the ToolTipHide() subfunction in timeout milliseconds, to fade it away again (after first cancelling any timeout that may currently be in place), like this:

```
if (O(tt).IID) clearTimeout(O(tt).IID)
O(tt).IID = setTimeout(ToolTipHide, timeout)
```

The ToolTipHide() Subfunction

This function simply checks whether the tooltip is currently hidden. If it is, it has nothing to do and returns; otherwise, it fades out the tooltip and sets its Hidden attribute to true to indicate the new setting:

```
FadeOut(tt, msecs)
O(tt).Hidden = true
```

How To Use It

To use this plug-in, all you need to do is pass it an object and the tip message to display, like this:

```
ToolTip('home', 'Visit the Home page')
```

You can also pass any or all of the other supported arguments to tailor the output. The following example illustrates attaching a tooltip to a link using all the available options:

```
<h2>
<a id='home'  href='/'      >Home</a> |
<a id='news'  href='/news' >News</a> |
<a id='blog'  href='/blog' >Blog</a> |
<a id='links' href='/links'>Links</a>
</h2>

<script>
window.onload = function()
{
   tip = 'Click this link to return<br />to the main home page'
   ToolTip('home', tip, 'Verdana', '12px', '#444444', '#eeeeff',
      '#008888', 'solid', '1', 500, 5000)
   O('links').title = tip
}
</script>
```

The HTML section sets up four links and gives them IDs. Then the `<script>` section attaches a tooltip to the first link. As you can see by the `<br />` included in the string assigned to tip, HTML is supported, enabling you to configure the tooltip any way you like.

There is also a standard title tag attached to the final link so that you can compare the way it displays with this plug-in by passing the mouse over that link too.

The Plug-in

```
function ToolTip(id, tip, font, size, textc, backc, bordc,
   bstyle, bwidth, msecs, timeout)
{
   var tt = 'TT_' + O(id).id

   if (!O(tt))
   {
      var newdiv = document.createElement('div')
      newdiv.setAttribute('id', tt)
      document.body.appendChild(newdiv)
      Opacity(tt, 0)
      Position(tt, ABS)

      font   = font   ? font   : 'Arial'
      size   = size   ? size   : 'small'
      textc  = textc  ? textc  : '#884444'
      backc  = backc  ? backc  : '#ffff88'
      bordc  = bordc  ? bordc  : '#aaaaaa'
```

```
            bstyle = bstyle ? bstyle : 'dotted'
            bwidth = bwidth ? bwidth : 1
            msecs  = msecs  ? msecs  : 250

            S(tt).fontFamily      = font
            S(tt).fontSize        = size
            S(tt).padding         = '3px 5px 3px 5px'
            S(tt).color           = textc
            S(tt).backgroundColor = backc
            S(tt).borderColor     = bordc
            S(tt).borderStyle     = bstyle
            S(tt).borderWidth     = Px(bwidth)
            O(tt).innerHTML       = tip
         }

         O(id).onmouseover = DoToolTip
         O(id).onmouseout  = ToolTipHide
         O(tt).Hidden      = false

         function DoToolTip()
         {
            GoTo(tt, MOUSE_X + 15, MOUSE_Y + 15)
            O(tt).zIndex = ZINDEX + 1
            FadeIn(tt, msecs)
            O(tt).Hidden = false

            if (timeout)
            {
               if (O(tt).IID) clearTimeout(O(tt).IID)
               O(tt).IID = setTimeout(ToolTipHide, timeout)
            }
         }

         function ToolTipHide()
         {
      if (!O(tt).Hidden)
      {
         FadeOut(tt, msecs)
         O(tt).Hidden = true
      }
   }
}
```

PLUG-IN 100 CursorTrail()

This plug-in can provide a great visual aid for your users, or you can use it as a special effect. It leaves a trail of ten images behind the mouse cursor, with each image a little more faded out than the one in front of it, so that it gives a smoother flowing appearance than, for

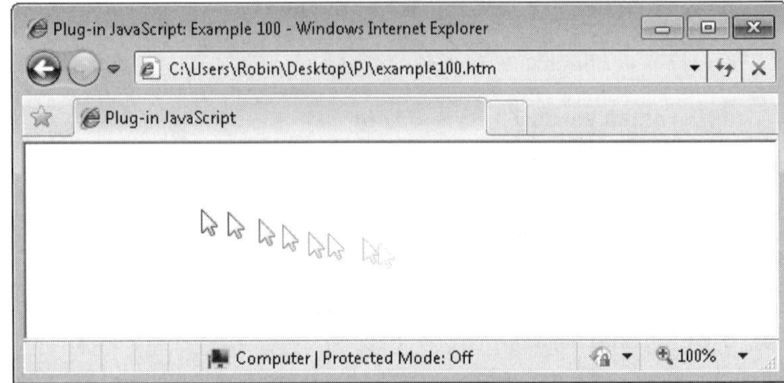

FIGURE 13-6 Add cursor trails to the mouse pointer by calling this plug-in.

example, the built-in Windows cursor trail utility. It also allows you to select your own images for the trail. Figure 13-6 shows a cursor trail created using the mouse pointer image supplied with this plug-in on the *pluginjavascript.com* website.

About the Plug-in

This plug-in creates a trail of images that follow the mouse pointer. It requires the following arguments:

- **`image`** The URL of an image to use for the trail
- **`length`** The length of the trail, with smaller numbers being shorter
- **`state`** If 1 or `true` the trails are turned on; a value of 0 or `false` turns them off

Variables, Arrays, and Functions

`j`	Local variable for iterating through the ten images
`w`	Local variable containing the width of the browser
`h`	Local variable containing the height of the browser
`c`	Local variable containing the string 'CT_'
`newimg`	Local variable containing each new image as it is created
`zIndex`	Property of each image set to bring them in front of all other elements
`ABS`	Global variable with the value 'absolute'
`MOUSE_X` & `MOUSE_Y`	Global variables containing the horizontal and vertical mouse coordinates
`ZINDEX`	Global variable containing the highest `zIndex` property so far used
`GoTo()`	Plug-in to move an object to a new location
`Hide()`	Plug-in to hide an object
`Show()`	Plug-in to show an object that has been hidden

Position()	Plug-in to set the style position property of an object
Opacity()	Plug-in to set the opacity of an object
GetWindowWidth()	Plug-in to return the width of the browser
GetWindowHeight()	Plug-in to return the height of the browser
createElement()	Function to create a new HTML element
setAttribute()	Function to set an attribute of an object
appendChild()	Function to attach a child object to an object
setInterval()	Function to start repeating interrupts to another function
clearInterval()	Function to stop repeating interrupts

How It Works

To start with, this plug-in saves the width and height of the browser in w and h and sets c to the string 'CT_', a prefix that will be used when assigning IDs to the image objects that will be created:

```
var w = GetWindowWidth()
var h = GetWindowHeight()
var c = 'CT_'
```

Next, if state is not 1 or true, any repeating interrupts are cancelled, and the plug-in returns, which turns off the mouse trails:

```
if (!state) return clearInterval(CT_IID)
```

At the next line of code, if no object has the ID 'TT_0', it means this is the first time the plug-in has been called, so all the image objects are created and set to style positions of 'absolute' (so that they can be moved about). In addition, their opacity is set to different levels so that the ones furthest away from the mouse cursor are the most faded, the images are loaded from the URL supplied in image, and the X and Y properties of each image are assigned starting values of –9999 to place them well off screen, as follows:

```
if (!O('TT_0'))
{
   for (var j = 0 ; j < 10 ; ++j)
   {
      var newimg = document.createElement('img')
      newimg.setAttribute('id', c + j)
      document.body.appendChild(newimg)
      Position(newimg, ABS)
      Opacity(newimg, (j + 1) * 9)
      newimg.src = image
      O(c + j).X = -9999
      O(c + j).Y = -9999
   }
}
```

With everything prepared, the final command in the setup section starts the repeating interrupts to the DoCurTrail() subfunction:

```
CT_IID = setInterval(DoCurTrail, length)
```

The DoCurTrail() Subfunction

This function performs the moving of all the trail images, which it manages with a for() loop, within which the first command moves the image for the current iteration to its new position:

```
for (var j = 0 ; j < 10 ; ++j)
{
   GoTo(c + j, O(c + j).X + 2, O(c + j).Y + 2)
```

For example, when j has the value 5, the image with the ID calculated with the expression c + j is manipulated, which is 'CT_5'. The number 2 in the code places the images down and to the right by two pixels.

Next, the zIndex property of the image is set to the maximum zIndex so far used plus 1, to ensure that it will display on top of all other elements:

```
S(c + j).zIndex = ZINDEX + 1
```

Then, if the image is set to display directly under the mouse pointer, the image is hidden. If it wasn't hidden, the user could never click a link because a trail image would be between the mouse pointer and the clickable object underneath it:

```
if (O(c + j).X == MOUSE_X && O(c + j).Y == MOUSE_Y) Hide(c + j)
```

Otherwise, if the image is away from the mouse pointer, it is shown:

```
else Show(c + j)
```

Next, as long as j has a value greater than 0 (and therefore is indexing the nine trail images above the first), the image location of the image one behind the current one is set to that of the current image:

```
if (j > 0)
{
   O(c + (j - 1)).X = O(c + j).X
   O(c + (j - 1)).Y = O(c + j).Y
}
```

Finally, the highest numbered image (with the ID 'CT_9') is set either to the current mouse location or, if the mouse is off screen, to a position well off the start of the screen (with the values 12 and 20 representing the width and height of the mouse pointer):

```
O(c + 9).X = MOUSE_X < (w - 12) ? MOUSE_X : -9999
O(c + 9).Y = MOUSE_Y < (h - 20) ? MOUSE_Y : -9999
```

Only this highest numbered image needs to be given the mouse coordinates, because each time around the loop the coordinates of each item are copied down to the one behind it. For example, the next time around the image with the ID 'CT_8' will be passed the values in the image with the ID 'CT_9', and so on.

How To Use It

To use this plug-in, pass it the URL of an image to display as the trail, a value for how long the trail should be (with 1 being the smallest), and a value of `true` or 1 for the `state` argument, like this:

```
CursorTrail('mousepointer.gif', 20, 1)
```

To turn the effect off, just change the `state` argument to 0 or `false`, like this:

```
CursorTrail('mousepointer.gif', 20, 0)
```

For example, Figure 13-7 shows the file *snowflake.gif* being used in place of *mousepointer.gif*, with the following code:

```
<script>
window.onload = function()
{
   CursorTrail('snowflake.gif', 20, 1)
}
</script>
```

TIP *For an even more interesting effect, try displaying animated GIFs in the cursor trail instead of static ones.*

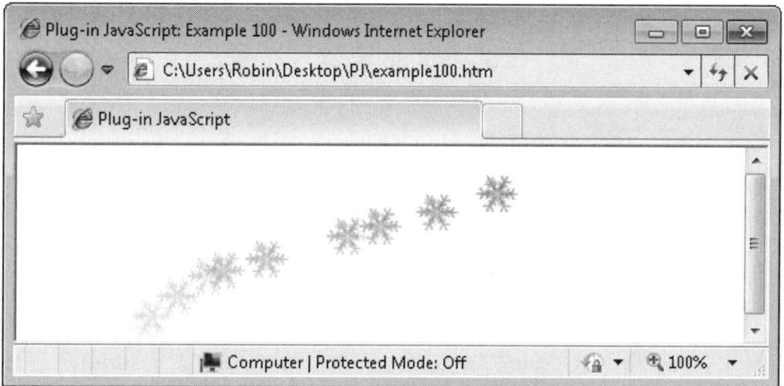

FIGURE 13-7 You can use this plug-in to provide seasonal or festive cursor trails.

The Plug-in

```
function CursorTrail(image, length, state)
{
   var w = GetWindowWidth()
   var h = GetWindowHeight()
   var c = 'CT_'

   if (!state) return clearInterval(CT_IID)

   if (!O('TT_0'))
   {
      for (var j = 0 ; j < 10 ; ++j)
      {
         var newimg = document.createElement('img')
         newimg.setAttribute('id', c + j)
         document.body.appendChild(newimg)
         Position(newimg, ABS)
         Opacity(newimg, (j + 1) * 9)
         newimg.src = image
         O(c + j).X = -9999
         O(c + j).Y = -9999
      }
   }

   CT_IID = setInterval(DoCurTrail, length)

   function DoCurTrail()
   {
      for (var j = 0 ; j < 10 ; ++j)
      {
         GoTo(c + j, O(c + j).X + 2, O(c + j).Y + 2)
         S(c + j).zIndex = ZINDEX + 1

         if (O(c + j).X == MOUSE_X && O(c + j).Y == MOUSE_Y) Hide(c + j)
         else Show(c + j)

         if (j > 0)
         {
            O(c + (j - 1)).X = O(c + j).X
            O(c + (j - 1)).Y = O(c + j).Y
         }
      }

      O(c + 9).X = MOUSE_X < (w - 12) ? MOUSE_X : -9999
      O(c + 9).Y = MOUSE_Y < (h - 20) ? MOUSE_Y : -9999
   }
}
```

TouchEnable()

Interest in touch screen devices really picked up momentum with Apple's release of the iPad in the spring of 2010, so I couldn't resist adding a bonus 101st plug-in to this collection. Here's the final plug-in, which allows you to touch-enable a web page. Figure 13-8 shows a copy of the web page for *Plug-in PHP*, a companion book to this one, in which a small frame has been attached to the top of the browser window with links to turn touch-enabling on and off.

About the Plug-in

This plug-in changes the mouse click action so that a click and drag operation becomes a scroll operation, allowing users of touch-enabled screens to scroll a document up, down, left, and right simply by touching the screen and moving their finger (or a stylus) about, in the same manner they would using an iPhone, iPad, Android phone, or other touch device. It requires the following argument:

- **`state`** If 1 or `true`, touch enabling is turned on; otherwise, it is turned off

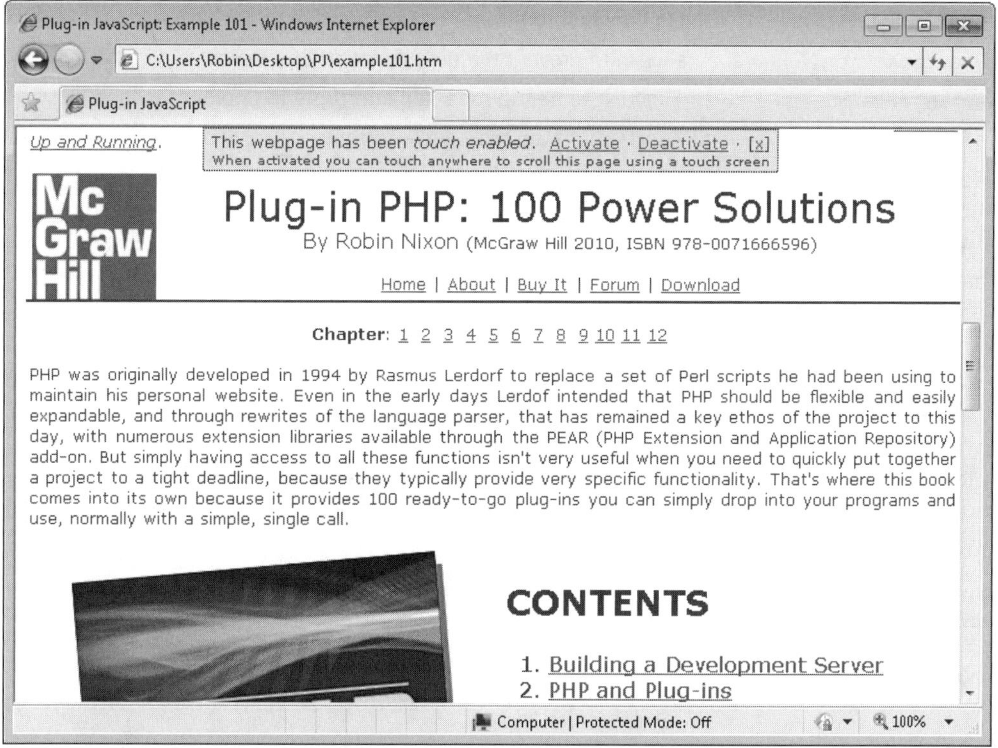

FIGURE 13-8 With this plug-in you can touch-enable your web pages.

Variables, Arrays, and Functions

db	Local variable used as shorthand for document.body
iid	Local variable containing the result of calling setInterval() to be used later when calling clearInterval()
flag	Local variable set to true when touch enabling is on
oldmousex & oldmousey	Temporary copies of MOUSE_X and MOUSE_Y to save the mouse position when StartTE() is called
tempmousex & tempmousey	Temporary copies of MOUSE_X and MOUSE_Y used in DoTE() to see if the mouse has moved
MOUSE_X & MOUSE_Y	Global variables containing the location of the mouse cursor
MOUSE_IN	Global variable set to true if the mouse is within the bounds of the browser, otherwise false
onmousedown & onmouseup	Events of the document body that trigger when the mouse is clicked and released
StartTE()	Subfunction to begin touch enabling
DoTE()	Sub-subfunction to scroll the document as required
StopTE()	Subfunction to turn off touch enabling
PreventAction()	Plug-in to prevent the default action of an event
setInterval()	Function to set up repeated interrupts to another function
clearInterval()	Function to stop repeated interrupts
scrollBy()	Function to scroll the document body by a specified amount

How It Works

This plug-in starts by making a copy of document.body in the local variable db, thus creating a shorthand reference to shorten the code:

```
var db = document.body
```

The state argument is then tested and, if it is 1 or true, touch enabling is being turned on, so the variables iid and flag are initialized, PreventAction() is called to disable the default actions for drag and select operations on the document body, and the onmousedown and onmouseup events of the document body are attached to the StartTE() and StopTE() subfunctions, as follows:

```
var iid  = null
var flag = false
PreventAction(db, 'both', true)
db.onmousedown = StartTE
db.onmouseup   = StopTE
```

If state is 0 or false, then touch enabling is to be turned off, so PreventAction() is called to restore the default actions for drag and select operations on the document body, its onmousedown and onmouseup event hooks are removed, and the plug-in returns:

```
PreventAction(db, 'both', false)
db.onmousedown = ''
db.onmouseup   = ''
return
```

The StartTE() Subfunction

This function first checks the `flag` variable to see whether touch control has already been enabled. If it has, `false` is returned; otherwise, copies of the mouse cursor position are placed in temporary variables to compare later to see if the document body should be scrolled, like this:

```
var oldmousex  = MOUSE_X
var oldmousey  = MOUSE_Y
var tempmousex = MOUSE_X
var tempmousey = MOUSE_Y
```

Next, `flag` is set to `true` to indicate that touch control has been enabled, and `setInterval()` is called to set up repeating interrupts to `DoTE()`:

```
flag = true
iid  = setInterval(DoTE, 10)
```

The DoTE() Sub-subfunction

This function first checks whether the mouse button is currently held down and is within the bounds of the browser, like this:

```
if (MOUSE_DOWN && MOUSE_IN)
```

If the mouse button is either not down or not within the browser's bounds, the `StopTE()` subfunction is called to release the current scroll. Otherwise, a test is made to see whether the mouse has moved from the position that was stored in the variables `tempmousex` and `tempmousey` when `StartTE()` was first called:

```
if (MOUSE_X != tempmousex || MOUSE_Y != tempmousey)
```

If the mouse has moved, `tempmousex` and `tempmousey` are updated to the new mouse location, like this:

```
tempmousex = MOUSE_X
tempmousey = MOUSE_Y
```

Next, the window is scrolled by the difference between the current mouse location and the one that was stored in `oldmousex` and `oldmousey` when `StartTE()` was first called, like this:

```
window.scrollBy(oldmousex - MOUSE_X, oldmousey - MOUSE_Y)
```

This causes oldmousex and oldmousey to retain the location of the mouse at the point when the mouse button was clicked, and this location is compared to the current mouse location to determine the amount by which the document body should be scrolled.

However, the variables tempmousex and tempmousey are used only to see whether the mouse has moved since the last interrupt to the DoTE() sub-subfunction and to decide whether a scroll is required. The scrolling is always relative to the values stored in oldmousex and oldmousey, not those in tempmousex and tempmousey.

The StopTE() Subfunction

This function simply sets the flag variable to false to indicate that a scroll is not currently in operation and clears the repeating intervals. The document will not scroll again until the mouse button is held down once more—the same action as touching a touch screen.

How To Use It

To use this plug-in, call it up with a value of 1 or true, like this:

```
TouchEnable(1)
```

To turn it off again, call it with a value of 0 or false, like this:

```
TouchEnable(0)
```

The following example shows how you can embed on and off controls for this feature in a web page, in a similar way to the one shown in Figure 13-8:

```
<div id='enabled'><font size='2' face='Verdana'>
This webpage has been <i>touch enabled</i>.  
<a href="javascript:TouchEnable(1)"
title="Turn on touchscreen control">Activate</a> &#183;
<a href="javascript:TouchEnable(0)"
title="Turn off touchscreen control">Deactivate</a> &#183;
[<a href="javascript:ZoomDown('enabled', 1, 1, 1000);
FadeOut('enabled', 1000)"title="Remove this panel">x</a>]</font>
<br /><font size='1' face='Verdana'>
When activated you can touch anywhere to scroll this page
using a touch screen</font></div>

<script>
Locate('enabled', 'fixed', 0, -100)
S('enabled').backgroundColor = '#eeeeaa'
S('enabled').padding         = '2px 5px 2px 5px'
S('enabled').border          = 'dotted black 1px'
Opacity('enabled', 0)
GoToEdge('enabled', 'top', 50)
FadeIn('enabled', 1000)
</script>
```

Just add this code to any existing web page that is long enough to require scrolling.

NOTE *Thanks for reading this book, and I hope you decide to use many of these plug-ins on your own websites. Don't forget that all the plug-ins and example files are available for download on the companion website at* pluginjavascript.com, *where you can also go to obtain more information, leave comments or suggestions, or ask questions in the book's online forum. I visit the forum regularly and I am always pleased to hear from readers. I will do my best to try and help you solve any problems you may have with your current coding projects.*

The Plug-in

```
function TouchEnable(state)
{
   var db = document.body

   if (state)
   {
      var iid  = null
      var flag = false

      PreventAction(db, 'both', true)

      db.onmousedown = StartTE
      db.onmouseup   = StopTE
   }
   else
   {
      PreventAction(db, 'both', false)

      db.onmousedown = ''
      db.onmouseup   = ''

      return
   }

   function StartTE(e)
   {
      if (!flag)
      {
         var oldmousex  = MOUSE_X
         var oldmousey  = MOUSE_Y
         var tempmousex = MOUSE_X
         var tempmousey = MOUSE_Y

         flag = true

         iid  = setInterval(DoTE, 10)
      }

      return false

      function DoTE()
      {
```

```
            if (MOUSE_DOWN && MOUSE_IN)
            {
               if (MOUSE_X != tempmousex || MOUSE_Y != tempmousey)
               {
                  tempmousex = MOUSE_X
                  tempmousey = MOUSE_Y
                  window.scrollBy(oldmousex - MOUSE_X, oldmousey - MOUSE_Y)
               }
            }
            else StopTE()
         }
      }

      function StopTE()
      {
         flag = false
         clearInterval(iid)
      }
   }
```

Index

B

C

D

E

F

I

N